For Reference

Not to be taken from this room

Dictionary of literary
PSEUDONYMS

Dictionary of literary
PSEUDONYMS

*a selection of popular modern writers in English
fourth edition*

FRANK ATKINSON

A BINGLEY BOOK

LIBRARY ASSOCIATION  AMERICAN LIBRARY
PUBLISHING, LONDON ASSOCIATION, CHICAGO

Published by Library Association Publishing Ltd, 7 Ridgmount Street, London, WC1E 7AE. Simultaneously published in the USA by The American Library Association, 50 East Huron Street, Chicago, Illinois 60611. Typeset by Library Association Publishing Ltd in 9/11 pt Times. Printed and bound in Great Britain by Redwood Burn Ltd, Trowbridge, Wiltshire

First published 1975
Second edition 1977
Third edition 1982
Fourth, enlarged edition 1987

In Memory, as always, of W C Fields

British Library Cataloguing in Publication Data

Atkinson, Frank, *1922–*
   Dictionary of literary pseudonyms : a
   selection of popular modern writers in
   English.—4th ed.
   1. Anonyms and pseudonyms—Dictionaries
   I. Title
   808   Z1041

   ISBN 0–85157–401–7

Library of Congress Cataloging-in-Publication Data

Atkinson, Frank, 1922–
   Dictionary of literary pseudonyms.

   1. Anonyms and pseudonyms, English—Dictionaries.
   2. Anonyms and pseudonyms, American—Dictionaries.
   I. Title.
   Z1065.A83   1986   808'.03'21   86–28775

   ISBN 0–8389–2045–4

CONTENTS

INTRODUCTION TO THE FIRST EDITION

We had a bottle of port for dinner, and drank dear Willie's health. He said, 'Oh, by the by, did I tell you I've cut my first name William, and taken the second name Lupin? In fact, I'm only known at Oldham as Lupin Pooter. If you were to 'Willie' me there, they wouldn't know what you meant.'

The names wished on us by our parents don't always please, and lots of people fiddle about varying the order of the components to suit themselves better; or they manage to get themselves nicknamed. The Grossmiths, in the piece quoted above from *The diary of a nobody*, satirised this harmless foible – but quite gently. And they did allow young W L Pooter, who could not come to terms with life as a Willie, to prosper as Lupin. His champagne flows at the end of the book.

Choosing a pen-name

Authors are great name-fiddlers, and many have performed quite drastic nomenectomies in order to achieve a satisfactory pseudonym. Arthur Elliott Elliott-Cannon lopped off Arthur and the spare Elliott; Reginald David Stanley Courtney-Browne excised his three forenames, and most understandably, Richard Nathaniel Twisleton-Wykeham-Fiennes writes as Richard Fiennes.

Many people would like to adopt an entirely new name, but most of them are inhibited by family and friends, business and other encumbrances. In the separate world of books, however, writers please themselves. They choose the name, it is solemnised on the title-page and perpetuated in lists, catalogues and the less-probing bibliographies.

Generally speaking, there is no deep thought, and little ingenuity, in the devising of pseudonyms. Obvious punning and word association provide one popular method: for example, Cecil John Street became John Rhode; Morris West about-faced to Michael East and Owen Seaman thought up Nauticus. Very basic anagrams or part anagrams, such as Melusa Moolson for Samuel Solomon, John Gannold for John Langdon and Walter De La Mare's Walter Ramal, come a close second.

Producing a more profound pseudonym takes a little longer. *Life* magazine carried a letter from Edward Stratemeyer, author of the Rover

Boys stories in the 1920s, explaining how he got his pseudonym of Arthur M Winfield:

One evening when writing, with my mother sitting near sewing, I remarked that I wanted an unusual name – that I wasn't going to use my own name on the manuscript. She thought a moment and suggested Winfield. 'For then', she said, 'you may win in that field.' I thought that good. She then supplied the first name saying, 'You are going to be an author, so why not make it Arthur?'

Stratemeyer added the M himself, reasoning that as M stood for thousand, it might help to sell thousands of books.

Corey Ford, in his *Time of laughter*, quotes this Stratemeyer letter, and also gives a highly dubious version of how he selected a pseudonym for himself. 'Unfortunately,' he writes, 'I did not have Mr Stratemeyer's mother to help me out. So I shut my eyes, opened the New York telephone directory at random and put my finger on a name. The name turned out to be Runkelschmelz, so I threw the phone book away and thought up John Riddell.'

Part of a package

It is not always personal preference alone that motivates an author's name change. Often it is done to match a particular type of book, on the grounds that any product sells better under a familiar label. Westerns, for example, should appear to be the work of lean and saddle-sore cowpokes, a six-shooter in either hand – with which, presumably, after bacon and beans round the ole campfire, they whack their typewriter keys.

So, when offering their readers *Rustlers and powder-smoke, Hopalong Cassidy, The big corral*, or similar horsesweat, the respective authors Charles Horace Snow, Louis L'Amour and Archibald Lynn Joscelyn, become Charles Ballew, Tex Burns and Al Cody.

Romantic fiction, on the other hand, is not expected to be penned by the Bucks and Hanks of this world. That *genre* requires authors' names suggestive of crisp, clean blouses and commonsense, yet with a hint of madcap moments; names like Elaine Carr, Phyllis Marlow and Caroline Holmes – all three of which are pseudonyms of one Charles Mason.

Tandem names

When two writers work together and decide to share a pseudonym, they rarely come up with an Ellery Queen. (And even Dannay and Lee took some time to drop Barnaby Ross in favour of the peerless Ellery.) Usually, like married couples naming their house Marjalf or Gladern, they make one name from bits of the two. Kelley Roos is made up from two surnames (Audrey Kelley and William Roos), as is Manning Coles (Adelaide Manning and Cyril Coles).

The two first names of Constance and Gwenyth Little, lopped fore and aft, form this couple's pseudonym of Conyth Little; while David Eliades and Robert Forrest Webb decided on David Forrest for their joint works.

Hilary Aidan St George Saunders and John Leslie Palmer, on the other hand, settled firstly for Francis Beeding as a joint pseudonym and later for David Pilgrim, simply because they liked these names.

The game of the name
All this suggests that the pseudonym business is a bit of a lark. For the most part, as far as British and American writers are concerned, it is. Although some of them are compelled (or find it politic) for professional or contractual reasons not to publish under their real names, very few can be in fear of serious prosecution or persecution.

It is often said that some writers adopt pseudonyms in order to deceive the taxman. At best, this could be only playing for time. Death and taxes are still the two certainties of life.

So it really is a game – a mixture of fantasising crossword puzzling and riddle-me-ree. When the game gets a good grip on a writer he may soon, like John Creasey, Michael Angelo Avallone Jr, or a number of others, clock up a double-figure pseudonym total. Some real fanatics for false names have acquired bumper collections. François Marie Arouet is usually cited as the top man in this field. In addition to the pseudonym Voltaire, he is credited with some 136 others; but most of them he used only for signing letters. Within the scope of this work, however, Lauran Paine leads the field with sixty-five discovered pen-names.

What a tangled web
The real name-pseudonym area of research is more full of snags than most. In the first place there is the writers' intention to deceive. This may be an ephemeral and relatively light-hearted intention – as witnessed by the number of authors who freely declare their pen-names in the various biographical reference works. Or it may be a serious and long-standing determination such as that of the former librarian Eric Leyland, of whom Lofts and Adley, in their *Men behind boys' fiction*, say: 'Written nearly 150 books for young people...and another 100 books under various pen-names which are strictly private.'

Shifts do occur, from the second group to the first, as circumstances change – usually for business reasons. The commercial success of a writer often leads to her, or his, pseudonyms being blazoned on dust jackets and in advertisements.

Secondly, there are the publishers. With few exceptions, those contacted in the course of compiling this work may be divided into two groups. One group considers authors' pseudonyms to be such close and vital secrets that any enquiry after them is treated, at best, as an impertinence but, more often, as attempted subversion. The other group consists of firms carrying on business in cheerful ignorance of the true identity of many of those whose work they publish. Enquiries there caused amused surprise that anybody should be interested. As to practical help, well that's not possible because no-one really knows and then, you see, royalties are mostly paid to authors' agents and no-one, apparently, cares.

Call me Sappho, call me Chloris

Of the writers who kindly replied to our enquiries, a number were vague about the various names under which they had written. Of those who were certain, two gave spellings of their pseudonyms which differed from those on the title-pages of their books. It is not surprising then, that the great catalogues of the British Museum and the Library of Congress, and the *British national bibliography* and the *Cumulative book index*, are sometimes at odds with one another as to whether a name is real or assumed. For the period 1900-1950, volume eight of Halkett and Laing's *Dictionary of anonymous and pseudonymous English literature* is a further contender except, of course, when it quotes the British Museum catalogue as its authority. Since 1968, the cumulations and indexes of the *British national bibliography* have not distinguished between real names and pseudonyms.

A few threads teased out

This dictionary is limited to writers in English and the selection has been made from those writing in the years 1900 to date. It is hoped that it will help librarians and booksellers to answer some of the many questions which are asked about authors – particularly contemporary authors – who write under more than one name. It may also assist in solving some of the queries about pseudonymous contributors to newspapers and magazines during the early decades of this century.

On a less practical, but equally justifiable level, there is the intention to satisfy people's curiosity. W P Courtney called his book on British anonymous and pseudonymous writings, which was published in 1908, *The secrets of our national literature*. In the first paragraph he wrote: 'The pleasure of finding out the secrets of our neighbours appeals to most minds.'

Many readers are even more curious about their favourite authors than they are about their neighbours. This book may give them some small pleasure.

F A

April 1975

INTRODUCTION TO THE FOURTH EDITION

There are many and various reasons given by people in the book world for authors adopting pseudonyms, and some of these have been mentioned in the introductions to previous editions of this dictionary. The silliest theory, propounded by David Pryce-Jones with all the certainty of divine revelation, appeared in 1978 in the *Telegraph Sunday magazine*: 'It is librarians', he wrote, 'who encourage pseudonyms, because they are unwilling to buy more than two or three books a year by the same author.'

The most interesting and surprising pseudonym-disclosure of recent years was made on 23 September 1984. In an article in the *Sunday Times* it was stated that the publishers Jonathan Cape had rejected, in 1982, a novel by Doris Lessing which had been submitted to them under the pseudonym of Jane Somers. Subsequently, it was published (*The diary of a good neighbour*) by Michael Joseph.

Doris Lessing gave as her reasons for using a pseudonym the fact that it not only allowed her 'to escape from the cage of my reputation', but also to prove the incompetence of publishers' readers.

During the period of research for this edition it was good to discover that Edward Gorey was still producing his obvious and unlovely anagrammatic pseudonyms: Ogred Weary and Dreary Wodge are now joined by Regera Dowdy. We also learned from Peggy Anne Bechko that she was formerly an artists' model and gift wrapper and that, as P A Bechko and as Bill Haller, she writes such works as *Night of the flaming guns*, *Sidewinder's trail* and *Dead man's feud*.

This edition contains over 2,000 names and pseudonyms more than did the previous one – due, in part, to the helpfulness of many authors, literary agents, publishers, librarians and readers. I am grateful to all who have written to me offering useful suggestions.

Littlehampton   Frank Atkinson
Sussex
January 1986

Real names

§ §

Name: the particular combination
of sounds employed as the
individual designation of a single
person – Oxford English dictionary

§ §

AARONS, Edward Sidney
  Ayres, Paul
  Ronns, Edward
ABBOTT, Harold Daniel
  Deborah, Leonard
ABRAHALL, Clare Hoskyns
  Drury, C M
  Drury, Clare
ABRAHAM, James Johnston
  Harpole, James
ABRAHAM, Peter L
  Graham, Peter
ABRAHAMS, Doris Caroline
  Brahms, Caryl
ABRAHAMS, Henry B
  Henry, B A
ABRAHAMSON, Maurice Noel
  Chub, Sergeant
ACLAND, Alice
  Marreco, Anne
ACWORTH, Marion W
  Neon
ADAM, C G M
  Stewart, C R

ADAM, Robin
  MacTyre, Paul
ADAM, Ronald
  Blake
ADAM SMITH, Janet Buchanan
  Carleton, Janet
ADAMS, Agnes
  Logan, Agnes
ADAMS, Arthur Henry
  James, James
ADAMS, Charles William Dunlop
  Montrose
ADAMS, Cleve Franklin
  Charles, Franklin
  Spain, John
ADAMS, Clifton
  Gant, Jonathan
  Kinkaid, Matt
  Randall, Clay
ADAMS, Franklin Pierce
  F P A
ADAMS, Harriet S
  Keene, Carolyn (*after*
  Edward Stratemeyer)
ADAMS, Henry
  Compton, Frances Snow
ADAMS, Herbert
  Gray, Jonathan
ADAMS, Peter Robert Charles
  Adams, Perseus
ADAMS, Robert Martin
  Krapp, Robert Martin
ADAMS, Samuel Hopkins
  Fabian, Warner

1

ADCOCK, A St John
Cobber, *Lance Corporal*
ADDIS, E E
Drax, Peter
ADDIS, Hazel Iris
Adair, Hazel
Heritage, A J
Mao
ADDLESHAW, Percy
Hemingway, Percy
ADLER, Bill
David, Jay
ADLER, Irving
Irving, Robert
AGATE, James
Prentis, Richard
Sir Topaz
Warrington, George
AGELASTO, Charlotte Priestley
Watson, C P
AHERN, Margaret McCrohan
O'Connell, Peg
AIKEN, John
Paget, John
AINSWORTH, Mary Dinsmore
Salter, Mary D
Salter Ainsworth, Mary D
AITKEN, Andrew
Arnold, Wilcox
AITKEN, E H
E H A
AKERMAN, Anthony Charles
Anthony, Charles
ALBANESI, Effie Maria
Rowlands, Effie Adelaide
ALBERT, Harold A
Priestly, Mark
ALBERT, Marvin H
Quarry, Nick
Rome, Anthony
Rome, Tony
ALBRITTON, Carol *and*
 MAXWELL, Patricia Anne
Trehearne, Elizabeth

ALDEN, Isabella Macdonald
Pansy
ALDRED, Margaret
Saunders, Anne
ALDRICH, Rhoda Truax
Truax, Rhoda
ALEXANDER, Colin James
Jay, Simon
ALEXANDER, Janet
McNeill, Janet
ALEXANDER, Joan
Pepper, Joan
ALEXANDER, John McKnight
Linter, Lavender
ALEXANDER, Robert William
Butler, Joan
Temple, Ruth
ALGER, Leclaire Gowans
Leodhas, Sorche Nic
Macleodhas, Sorche
ALGIE, James
Lloyd, Wallace
ALINGTON, Argentine Francis
Talbot, Hugh
ALINGTON, Cyril Argentine
Westerham, S C
ALLAN, Frederick William
Leo, Alan
ALLAN, Mabel Esther
Estoril, Jean
Hagon, Priscilla
Pilgrim, Anne
ALLAN, Philip Bertram Murray
Cabochon, Francis
Phillip, Alban M
ALLAN, Ted
Maxwell, William
ALLASON, Rupert
West, Nigel
ALLBEURY, Theo Edward le Bouthillier
Allbeury, Ted
Butler, Richard
Kelly, Patrick

ALLDRIDGE, John Stratten
Stratton, John
ALLEGRO, John Marco
McGill, Ian
ALLEN, Elizabeth Chase
Percy, Florence
ALLEN, Grant
Power, Cecil
Rayner, Olive Pratt
ALLEN, Henry
Fisher, Clay
Henry, Will
ALLEN, Hubert Raymond
Guthrie, David
Helley, Denis
Jones, Llewellyn
ALLEN, John E
Aquarius
Bisonius
Danforth, Paul M
ALLEN, Kenneth Sydney
Carter, Avis Murton
Scott, Alastair
ALLEN, Samuel Washington
Vesey, Paul
ALLEN, Stephen Valentine
Allen, Steve
Stevens, William Christopher
ALLEN-BALLARD, Eric
Allen, Eric
ALLFREE, P S
Blackburn, Martin
ALLISON, William
Blinkhoalie
ALMEDINGEN, Martha Edith von
Almedingen, E M
ALMOND, Brian
Vaughan, Julian
ALPERS, Mary Rose
Campion, Sarah
AMBLER, Eric *and* RODDA, Charles
Reed, Eliot

AMES, Francis
Watson, Frank
AMES, Jennifer
Greig, Maysie
AMES, R F
Black, Jack
AMES, Sarah Rachel
Gainham, Sarah
AMIS, Kingsley
Markham, Robert
AMY, William Lacey
Allan, Luke
ANDERS, Edith Mary
England, Edith M
ANDERSON, Alexander
Surfaceman
ANDERSON, Betty
Canyon, Claudia
ANDERSON, *Lady* Flavia
Portobello, Petronella
ANDERSON, Martin
Cynicus
'**ANDERSON, Poul**
Craig, A A
Karageorge, Michael
Sanders, Winston P
ANDREWS, Claire *and*
ANDREWS, Keith
Claire, Keith
ANDREWS, John Arthur
Bach, Sebastian
ANDREWS, Lucilla
Gordon, Diana
Marcus, Joanna
ANDREWS, Naomi Cornelia
Madgett, Naomi Long
ANGUS, Sylvia
Lazlo, Kate
ANSELL, Edward Clarence Trelawney
Crad, Joseph

3

ANSLE, Dorothy Phoebe
  Conway, Laura
  Elsna, Hebe
  Lancaster, Vicky
  Snow, Lyndon
ANTHONY, Barbara
  Barber, Antonia
ANTHONY, E
  Parr, *Dr* John Anthony
ANTHONY, Edward
  Cleo et Anthony
  Gate, A G
APPIGNANESI, Lisa
  Ayre, Jessica
APPLEBY, Carol McAfee
  Morgan, Carol McAfee
APPLEMAN, John Alan
  Daley, Bill
  Montrose, James St David
APPLIN, Arthur
  Swift, Julian
APPS, Edwin *and*
 DEVANEY, Pauline
  Wraith, John
ARCHIBALD, Edith Jessie
  Eye Witness
ARD, William
  Kerr, Ben
  Wills, Thomas
ARDEN, Adrian
  Ariel
ARMITAGE, John
  Hin Me Geong
ARMITAGE, Reginald
  Gay, Noel
ARMSTRONG, Charlotte
  Valentine, Jo
ARMSTRONG, Douglas
  Douglas, Albert
  Windsor, Rex
ARMSTRONG, Paul
  Right Cross
ARMSTRONG, Richard
  Renton, Cam

ARMSTRONG, T I F *see*
 FYTTON ARMSTRONG, T I
ARMSTRONG, William
 Alexander
  Hazelton, Alexander
ARSHAVSKY, Abraham Isaac
  Shaw, Artie
ARTER, Wallace E
  Kay, Wallace
ARTHUR, Chester Alan
  Arthur, Gavin
ARTHUR, Frances Browne
  Cunningham, Ray
ARTHUR, Herbert
  Arthur, Burt
ARTHUR, Ruth M
  Huggins, Ruth Mabel
ASH, Brian
  Dorland, Henry
ASHBROOK, Hariette Cora
  Shane, Susannah
ASHBY, Rubie Constance
  Freugon, Ruby
ASHFORD, F C
  Charles, Frederick
ASHLEY, Arthur Ernest
  Vivian, Francis
ASHMORE, Basil
  Marlin, Roy
ASHTON, *Lady*
  Garland, Madge
ASHTON, Winifred
  Dane, Clemence
ASHTON-WARNER, Sylvia
  Henderson, Sylvia
  Sylvia
ASHWORTH, Edward Montague
  Abbott, Johnston
ASIMOV, Isaac
  Dr A
  French, Paul
ASTON, *Sir* George
  Amphibian
  Southcote, George

ATKEY, Philip
Merriman, Pat
Perowne, Barry
ATKINS, Frank A
Ash, Fenton
Ashley, Fred
Aubrey, Frank
St Mars, F
ATKINS, Meg Elizabeth
Moore, Elizabeth
ATKINSON, Frank
Curnow, Frank
Shallow, Robert
ATKINSON, John
Aye, John
ATKINSON, Nancy
Benko, Nancy
ATTENBOROUGH, Bernard George
Rand, James S
ATTHILL, Robert Anthony
Atthill, Robin
AUBREY-FLETCHER, Sir Henry Lancelot
Wade, Henry
AUCHINCLOSS, Louis
Lee, Andrew
AUDEMARS, Pierre
Hodemart, Peter
AUSTIN, Benjamin Fish
Nitsua, Benjamin
AUSTIN, John and AUSTIN, Richard
Gun Buster
AVALLONE, Michael Angelo Jr
Blaine, James
Carter, Nick
Conway, Troy
Dalton, Priscilla
Dane, Mark
De Pre, Jean-Anne
Highland, Dora
Michaels, Steve
Nile, Dorothea

Noon, Ed
Noone, Edwina
Patrick, John
Stanton, Vance
Stuart, Sidney
AVENELL, Donne
King, Charles
AVERY, Harold
Westridge, Harold
AVEY, Ruby D
Page, Vicky
AWDRY, Richard Charles
Charles, Richard
AYCKBOURNE, Alan
Allen, Ronald

BABCOCK, Frederick
Mark, Matthew
BABCOCK, Maurice P
Bea, Empy
BABER, Douglas
Ritson, John
BACK, Karl John
Australianus
BACKUS, Jean L
Montross, David
BACON, Elizabeth
Morrow, Betty
BACON, Josephine Dodge
Lovell, Ingraham
BADENI, June
Wilson, Jane
BAILEY, Francis Evans
Wilson, Ann
BAILEY, Gordon
Gordon, Keith
BAILEY, Irene Temple
Bailey, Temple
BAIN, Kenneth Bruce Findlater
Findlater, Richard
BAIR, Patrick
Gurney, David
BAKER, Anne
Cross, Nancy

BAKER, Betty
Renier, Elizabeth
BAKER, C
Circuit Breaker
BAKER, Kate
K B
BAKER, Laura
Minier, Nelson
BAKER, Louise Alice
Alien
BAKER, Marcell Genée
Miller, Marc
BAKER, Marjorie
McMaster, Alison
BAKER, Mary Gladys Steel
Stuart, Sheila
BAKER, Ray Stannard
Grayson, David
BAKER, Sarah S T
Aunt Friendly
BAKER, William Howard
Arthur, William
Ballinger, W A
Reid, Desmond
Saxon, Peter
BAKER, William Howard *and*
 MCNEILLY, Wilfred
Ballinger, W A
BALCHIN, Nigel
Spade, Mark
BALDWIN, Dorothy
Jones, Clara
BALDWIN, Gordon C
Baldwin, Gordo
Gordon, Lew
BALDWIN, Michael
Jesse, Michael
BALDWIN, Oliver
Hussingtree, Martin
BALFOUR, Eve *and*
 HERNDEN, Beryl
Hearnden, Balfour
BALFOUR, William
Russell, Raymond

BALINE, Israel
Berlin, Irving
BALL, Brian N
Kinsey-Jones, Brian
BALL, Doris Bell Collier
Bell, Josephine
BALLARD, Willis Todhunter
Agar, Brian
Ballard, P D
Ballard, Todhunter
Bonner, Parker
Bowie, Sam
Carter, Nick
D'Allard, Hunter
Hunt, Harrison
Hunter, George
Hunter, John
MacNeil, Neil
Shepherd, John
BALLINGER, William Sanborn
Freyer, Frederic
Sanborn, B X
BALOGH, Penelope
Fox, Petronella
BALY, Elaine
Browning, Vivienne
BAMBERGER, Helen R
Berger, Helen
BAMBERGER, Helen R *and*
 BAMBERGER, Raymond S
Aresbys, The
BAMFIELD, Veronica
Wood, Mary
BANBURY, Olive Lethbridge
Lethbridge, Olive
BANCROFT, Marie Constant
O'Connor, Philip
BANDER, Peter
Jones, Melville
BANDY, Eugene Franklin Jr
Franklin, Eugene
BANGS, Robert Babbitt
Babbitt, Robert

BANNISTER, Patricia
Veryan, Patricia
BAR-ZOHAR, Michael
Barak, Michael
BARACH, Alvan Leroy
Coignard, John
BARBA, Harry
Baron Mikan
Ohan
BARBER, Dulan Friar
Fletcher, David
BARBER, Margaret Fairless
Fairless, Michael
BARBER-STARKEY, Roger
Shropshire Lad
BARCLAY, George
Kinnoch, R G B
BARCLAY, Oliver Rainsford
Triton, A N
BARCLAY, Vera C
Beech, Margaret
BARCZA, Alicja
Orme, Alexandra
BARDIN, John Franklin
Ashe, Douglas
Tree, Gregory
BARFIELD, Arthur Owen
Burgeon, G A L
BARFORD, John Leslie
Philebus
BARKER, Albert H
King, Reefe
Macrae, Hawk
BARKER, Clarence Hedley
Hedley, Frank
Seafarer
BARKER, Dudley
Black, Lionel
Matthews, Anthony
BARKER, E M
Jordan, Nell
BARKER, Ilse Eva L
Talbot, Kathrine

BARKER, Leonard Noel
Noel, L
BARKER, Michael
Barker, Jack
BARKER, Ronald Ernest
Ronald, E B
BARKER, Ronnie
Wiley, Gerald
BARKER, S Omar
Canusi, Jose
Squires, Phil
BARKER, Will
Demarest, Doug
BARLING, Muriel Vere
Barling, Charles
Barrington, P V
Barrington, Pamela
BARLOW, James
Forden, James
BARLTROP, Mabel
Octavia
BARNARD, Marjorie Faith *and*
ELDERSHAW, Flora Sydney
Eldershaw, M Barnard
BARNES, Arthur *and*
KUTTNER, Henry
Kent, Kelvin
BARNES, Julian
Kavanagh, Dan
Seal, Basil
BARNES, Patricia
Abercrombie, Patricia Barnes
BARNITT, Nedda Lemmon
Lamont, N B
BARNSLEY, Alan G
Fielding, Gabriel
BARONAS, Aloyzas
Aliunas, S
BARR, Patricia
Hazard, Laurence
BARR, Robert
Sharp, Luke

BARRADELL-SMITH, Walter
Bird, Lilian
Bird, Richard
BARRAUD, E M
Johns, Hilary
BARRE, Jean
Lindsay, Lee
BARRETT, Alfred Walter
Andom, R
BARRETT, Geoffrey John
Anders, Rex
Blaine, Jeff
Cole, Richard
Kilbourn, Matt
Macey, Carn
Rickard, Cole
Royal, Dan
Sanders, Brett
Summers, D B
Wade, Bill
BARRETT, Hugh Gilchrist
Bellman, Walter
BARRETT, Romana
Lane, Carla
BARRIE, Susan
Charles, Anita
Kent, Pamela
BARRINGTON, Howard
Stone, Simon
BARROW, Albert Stewart
Sabretache
BARROWS, Marjorie
Alden, Jack
Dixon, Ruth
BARRY, John Arthur
L L
BARTHOLOMEW, John Eric
Morecambe, Eric
BARTLETT, Marie
Lee, Rowena
Rift, Valerie
BARTLETT, Stephen
Slade, Gurney

BARTLETT, Vernon
Oldfield, Peter
BARTON, Emily Mary
E M B
BARTON, Eustace Robert
Eustace, Robert
BARTROP, Edgar James
Portrab
BASCH, Ernst
Ashton, A B
Ashton, E B
Ashton, E E
BASHAM, Daisy
Aunt Daisy
BASHFORD, *Sir* Henry Howarth
Carp, Augustus
BASS, Clara May
Overy, Claire May
BASSETT, Ronald
Clive, William
BASSLER, Thomas J
Bass, T J
BASTIN, John
Sturgus, J B
BATEMAN, Robert Moyes
Moyes, Robin
BATES, Herbert Ernest
Flying Officer X
BATT, Malcolm John
Malcolm, John
BATTYE, Gladys
Lynn, Margaret
BAUM, Lyman Frank
Akens, Floyd
Bartlett, Laura
Cook, John Estes
Fitzgerald, *Captain* Hugh
Metcalf, Suzanne
Stanton, Schuyler
Van Dyne, Edith
BAUMANN, Arthur A
A A B
BAUMANN, Margaret
Lees, Marguerite

BAX, *Sir* Arnold
  O'Byrne, Dermot
BAXTER, Elizabeth
  Holland, Elizabeth
BAXTER, John
  Loran, Martin
BAYBARS, Taner
  Bayliss, Timothy
BAYER, Eleanor *and*
 BAYER, Leo
  Bayer, Oliver Weld
BAYER, William
  St John, Leonie
BAYLEY, Barrington John
  Aumbry, Alan
  Woods, P F
BAYLISS, John Clifford
  Clifford, John
BAYLY, Ada Ellen
  Lyall, Edna
BAYNES, Dorothy Julia
  Creston, Dormer
BAYS, J W
  Roadster
BEADLE, Gwyneth Gordon
  Gordon, Glenda
BEAMISH, Annie O'Meara de Vic
  Beamish, Noel de Vic
BEAR, Joan E
  Mayhew, Elizabeth
BEARDMORE, George
  Stokes, Cedric
  Wolfenden, George
BEATTY, Patricia
  Bartholomew, Jean
BEATY, Betty
  Campbell, Karen
  Ross, Catherine
BEATY, David
  Stanton, Paul
BEAUCHAMP, Kathleen
 Mansfield
  Berry, Matilda
  Mansfield, Katherine

BEAUMONT, *Dr* Edgar
  Halifax, Clifford
BECHKO, Peggy Anne
  Haller, Bill
BECHOFFER ROBERTS, C E
  Ephesian
BECK, Lily Adams
  Barrington, E
  Moresby, Louis
BECK, Roland Stanley
  St Anbeck, Roland
BECKER, Peter
  Vul' Indlela
BECKER, Stephen David
  Dodge, Steve
BECKET, Ronald Brymer
  Anthony, John
BECKWITH, Burnham Putnam
  Putnam, John
BEDFORD-JONES, Henry
  Keyes, Gordon
  Wycliffe, John
BEDFORD-JONES, Henry;
 FRIEDE, Donald *and*
 FEARING, Kenneth
  Bedford, Donald F
BEEBE, Elswyth Thane
  Thane, Elswyth
BEER, Eloise
  Beer, Lisl
  Drake, Lisl
BEESTON, L J
  Camden, Richard
  Davies, Lucian
BEETON, D R
  Barratt, Robert
BEGBIE, Harold
  Gentleman with a Duster
BEHAN, Brendan
  Street, Emmett
BEHANNA, Gertrude Florence
  Burns, Elizabeth
BEILES, Sinclair
  Wu Wu Meng

BEITH, John Hay
  Hay, Ian
  Junior Sub
BELANEY, Archie
  Grey Owl
BELCHEM, Ronald Frederick
King
  Belchem, David
BELL, Alexander
  Young, Filson
BELL, Alison Clare Harvey
  Bell, Leigh
BELL, Eric Temple
  Taine, John
BELL, Gerard
  Landis, John
BELL, John Keble
  Howard, Keble
  Methuen, John
BELL, Joyce
  Colin, Jean
BELL, Martin
  Oates, Titus
BELLASIS, Margaret Rosa
  Marton, Francesca
BENARY, Margot
  Benary-Isbert, Margot
BENCHLEY, Robert
  Fawkes, Guy
BENDER, Arnold
  Philippi, Mark
BENDIT, Gladys
  Presland, John
BENJAMIN, Lewis S
  Melville, Lewis
BENNETT, Arnold
  King, Sampson
  Tonson, Jacob
BENNETT, Dorothy
  Kingsley, Laura
BENNETT, Geoffrey Martin
  Sea-Lion
BENNETT, J J
  Jackstaff

BENNETT, Laura; HARVEY,
Jean *and* MACKENZIE, Tina
  Harlowe, Justine
BENNETT, William E
  Armstrong, Warren
BENNETTS, Pamela
  James, Margaret
BENSON, Arthur Christopher
  Carr, Christopher
BENSON, Michael
  Thomas, Michael
BENTLEY, Edmund Clerihew
  Clerihew, E
BENTLEY, Frederick Horace
  Wilson, D M
BENTLEY, James W B
  Claughton-James, James
  Nostalgia
BENTLEY, Margaret
  Ellis, Kathy
  Stephens, Frances
BENTLEY, Phyllis
  Bachelor of Arts, A
BENTLEY, Verna Bessie
  Harden, Verna Loveday
BENTON, Peggie
  Burke, Shifty
BERESFORD, Claude R De La
Poer
  Seebee
BERESFORD, Leslie
  Pan
BERGER, Evelyn Miller
  Brown, Evelyn Berger
BERGER, Josef
  Digges, Jeremiah
BERMANGE, Maurine J L
  Ross, Maggie
BERNSTEIN, Alec
  Baron, Alexander
BEST, Allena
  Berry, Erick
  Maxton, Anne

BEST, Carol Anne
Ashe, Susan
Darlington, Con
Martin, Ann
Wayne, Marcia
BEST, Rayleigh Breton Amis
Amis, Breton
Bentinck, Ray
Haddow, Leigh
Hughes, Terence
Roberts, Desmond
Wilde, Leslie
BETHELL, Leonard Arthur
Cailloux, Pousse
Severn, Forepoint
BETHELL, Mary
Hayes, Evelyn
BETTANY, F G
N O B
BEUTTLER, Edward I O
Butler, Ivan
BEVAN, Aneurin
Celticus
BEVAN, Tom
Bamfylde, Walter
BEVANS, Florence Edith
Remington, Jemima
BEYNON, Jane
Lewis, Lange
BHATIA, Jamunadevi
Bhatia, June
Edwards, June
Forrester, Helen
Rana, J
BHATTACHARYA, Basudeb
Acharya, Pundit
Basudeb, Sree
BICKERSTAFFE-DREW,
Alexander Francis
Ayscough, John
BICKHAM, Jack Miles
Clinton, Jeff
Miles, John

BICKLE, Judith
Tweedale, J
BIDWELL, Marjory Elizabeth
Sarah
Gibbs, Mary Ann
BIERCE, Ambrose
Bowers, *Mrs* J Milton
Grile, Dod
Herman, William
Sloluck, J Milton
BIERMANN, June *and*
TOOHEY, Barbara
Bennett, Margaret
BIGG, Patricia Nina
Ainsworth, Patricia
BILSKY, Eva
Aunt Eva
BINDER, Otto
Binder, Eando
Coleridge, John
Giles, Gordon A
O'Brien, Dean D
BINGHAM, E A *and*
LA COSTE, Guy R
Berton, Guy
BINGHAM, Madeleine
Mannering, Julia
BINGLEY, David Ernest
Adams, Bart
Benson, Adam
Bridger, Adam
Canuck, Abe
Carver, Dave
Chatham, Larry
Chesham, Henry
Coltman, Will
Coniston, Ed
Dorman, Luke
Fallon, George
Horsley, David
Jefford, Bat
Kingston, Syd
Lynch, Eric
Martell, James

BINGLEY, David Ernest (cont'd)
North, Colin
Plummer, Ben
Prescott, Caleb
Remington, Mark
Roberts, John
Romney, Steve
Silvester, Frank
Starr, Henry
Tucker, Link
Wigan, Christopher
Yorke, Roger
BINNS, Ottwell
Bolt, Ben
BIOY-CASARES, Adolfo *and*
BORGES, Jorge Luis
Bustos Domecq, Honorio
Suárez Lynch, B
BIRCH, Jack Ernest Lionel *and*
MURRAY, Venetia Pauline
Flight, Frances
BIRD, Cyril Kenneth
Fougasse
BIRD, Dennis Leslie
Noel, John
BIRD, William Henry Fleming
Fleming, Harry
BIRKENHEAD, *Earl of see*
Smith, Frederick William Robin
BIRKENHEAD, Elijah
Birkenhead, Edward
BIRKIN, Charles
Lloyd, Charles
BIRNEY, Hoffman
Kent, David
BIRO, Balint Stephen
Biro, Val
BIRREN, Faber
Lang, Gregor
Lang, Martin
BIRT, Francis Bradley
Bradley, Shelland
BISHOP, Curtis Kent
Brandon, Curt

BISHOP, Morchard
Stoner, Oliver
BISHOP, Morris Gilbert
Johnson, W Bolingbroke
BISHOP, Stanley
Edgar, Icarus Walter
BISSET-SMITH, G T
Bizet, George
BLACK, Dorothy
Black, Kitty
BLACK, Hazleton
Graham, Scott
BLACK, Ladbroke Lionel Day
Day, Lionel
Urquhart, Paul
BLACK, Oliver
Black, Jett
BLACKBURN, Barbara
Grant, Jane
BLACKBURN, James Garford
Garford, James
BLACKBURN, Victoria Grace
Fan-Fan
BLACKETT, Veronica
Heath, Veronica
BLACKMORE, Anauta
Anauta
BLAGBROUGH, Harriet
Eastertide
BLAIKLOCK, Edward
Grammaticus
BLAIR, Dorothy
Bolitho, Ray D
BLAIR, Dorothy *and*
PAGE, Evelyn
Scarlett, Roger
BLAIR, Eric
Orwell, George
BLAIR, Kathryn
Brett, Rosalind
Conway, Celine
BLAIR, Norma Hunter
Hunter, Alison

BLAIR, Pauline Hunter
Clare, Helen
Clarke, Pauline
BLAIR, Walter
Post, Mortimer
BLAIR-FISH, Wallace Wilfred
Blair
BLAKE, George
Vagabond
BLAKE, Leslie James
Tabard, Peter
BLAKE, Sally Mirliss
Sara
BLAKE, Wilfrid Theodore
Wing Adjutant
BLAKESTON, Oswell *and*
BURFORD, Roger d'Este
Simon
BLAND, *Mrs* Edith (Nesbit)
Bland, E
Bland, *Mrs* Hubert
Nesbit, E
BLAND, *Mrs* Edith (Nesbit)
and BLAND, Hubert
Bland, Fabian
BLAND, Hubert
Hubert
BLASER, Robin
Avalon
BLATCHFORD, Robert
Nunquam
BLAUSTEIN, Albert P
De Graeff, Allen
BLAUTH-MUSZKOWSKI, Peter
Blauth, Christopher
BLECH, William James
Blake, William
Blake, William James
BLEWITT, Dorothy
Praize, Ann
BLISH, James
Atheling, William *Jr*

BLIXEN-FINECKE, Karen
Christence, *Baroness*
Andrézel, Pierre
Blixen, Karen
Dinesen, Isak
BLOCH, Robert
Fiske, Tarleton
Folke, Will
Hindin, Nathan
Kane, Wilson
Sheldon, John
BLOCK, Lawrence
Harrison, Chip
Kavanagh, Paul
BLOFELD, John
Chu Feng
BLOOD, Marje
McKenzie, Paige
BLOOM, Jack Don
Donne, Jack
BLOOM, Ursula
Burns, Sheila
Essex, Mary
Harvey, Rachel
Mann, Deborah
Prole, Lozania
Sloane, Sara
BLOOMER, Arnold
More, Euston
BLOOMFIELD, Anthony John
Westgate
Westgate, John
BLOOR, W A
Scott, A
BLOSSOM, D Bradford
Bradford, De Witt
BLOXAM, John Francis
Lawrence, Bertram
X
BLUNDELL, Harold
Bellairs, George
BLUNDELL, V R
Nixon, Kathleen

BLYTH, Harry
  Meredith, Hal
BLYTON, Enid
  Pollock, Mary
BOATFIELD, Jeffrey
  Jeffries, Jeff
BOBIN, John W
  Ascott, Adelie
  Greenhalgh, Katherine
  Nelson, Gertrude
BODENHAM, Hilda
  Boden, Hilda
BODINGTON, Nancy Hermione
  Smith, Shelley
BOEHM, David Alfred
  Masters, Robert V
BOGGIS, David
  Vaughan, Gary
BOGGS, Helen
  Gwynne, Nell
  Bernard
BOGGS, Winifred
  Burke, Edmund
BOHANNAN, Laura M Smith
  Bowen, Elenore Sith
BOLES, Harold Wilson
  Boles, Hal
BOLSTER, *Sister* M Angela
  Bolster, Evelyn
BOLTON, Miriam
  Davis, Stratford
  Sharman, Miriam
BOND, Florence D F
  Demarest, Anne
BOND, Gladys Baker
  Mendel, Jo
  Walker, Holly Beth
BOND, Grace
  Todhunter, Philippa
BONHAM, Barbara
  North, Sara
BONSALL, Crosby Newell
  Newell, Crosby

BOON, Violet Mary
  Williams, Violet M
BOONE, Charles Eugene
  Boone, Pat
BOORSTIN, Daniel Joseph
  Professor X
BOOTH, Edwin
  Blunt, Don
  Hazard, Jack
BOOTH, John Bennion
  Costs
BOOTH, Philip Arthur
  Werner, Peter
BOOTH, Rosemary
  Murray, Frances
BORBOLLA, Barbara
  Martyn, Don
BORCHARD, Ruth
  Medley, Anne
BORDEN, Deal
  Borden, Leo
BOREMAN, Linda
  Lovelace, Linda
BORG, Philip Anthony John
  Bexar, Phil
  Borg, Jack
  Pickard, John Q
BORGES, Jorge Luis *and*
BIOY-CASARES, Adolfo
  Bustos Domecq, Honorio
  Suárez Lynch, B
BORLAND, Harold Glen
  Borland, Hal
  West, Ward
BORLAND, Kathryn K *and*
SPEICHER, Helen Ross
  Abbott, Alice
  Land, Jane and Ross
BORNEMAN, Ernest
  McCabe, Cameron
BORNEMANN, Eva
  Geisel, Eva
BOSHELL, Gordon
  Bee

BOSTICCO, Mary
  Bey, Isabelle
BOSWORTH, Allan R
  Boyd, Alamo
BOSWORTH, Willan George
  Borth, Willan G
  Leonid
  Worth, Maurice
BOTTOMLEY, Kate Madeline
  Vera
BOULTON, A Harding
  Harding, Richard
BOUMA, J L
  Shannon, Steve
BOUNDS, Sydney J
  Marshal, James
  Saunders, Wes
BOURQUIN, Paul
  Amberley, Richard
BOWDEN, Jean
  Barry, Jocelyn
  Bland, Jennifer
  Curry, Avon
  Dell, Belinda
BOWEN, John *and*
 BULLMORE, Jeremy
  Blake, Justin
BOWEN, Reuben
  Kajar
BOWEN-JUDD, Sara Hutton
  Woods, Sara
BOWER, John Graham
  Klaxon
BOWERING, George
  Panavision Kid, The
BOWMAN, Gerald
  Magnus, Gerald
BOYD, Elizabeth Orr
  MacCall, Isabel
BOYD, Martin à Beckett
  Mills, Martin
BOYES, W Watson
  Oyster, An

BOYLE, John Howard Jackson
  Dawson, Michael
BOYLES, Clarence Scott
  Brown, Will C
BRACKMAN, Arnold C
  Bunker, *Capt* Moss
BRADBURY, Parnell
  Dermott, Stephen
  Lynn, Stephen
BRADBURY, Ray
  Spaulding, Leonard
BRADBY, Rachel
  Anderson, Rachel
BRADLEY, Ian *and*
 HOLLOWS, Norman F
  Duplex
BRADLEY, Katherine H *and*
 COOPER, Edith E
  Field, Michael
BRADLEY, Marion Z
  Chapman, Lee
  Dexter, John
  Gardner, Miriam
  Graves, Valerie
  Ives, Morgan
BRADLEY, Marion Z *and*
 COULSON, Juanita
  Wells, John J
BRADSHAW-JONES, Malcolm
 Henry
  Jones, Bradshaw
BRADY, Jane Frances
  White, Jane
BRAEME, Charlotte Monica
  Clay, Bertha M
BRAHAM, Hal
  Colton, Mel
  Trask, Merrill
BRAINERD, Edith *and*
 BRAINERD, J Chauncey
  Rath, E J
BRAITHWAITE, Althea
  Althea

BRAMBLEBY, Ailsa
Craig, Jennifer
BRAMWELL, James Guy
Byrom, James
BRAND, Charles Neville
Lorne, Charles
BRANDENBERG, Alyce
Christina
Aliki
BRAUN, Wilbur
Albert, Ned
Brandon, Bruce
Fernway, Peggy
Ring, Basil
Warren, Wayne
BRAYBROOKE, Patrick
P B
BRECKENFELD, Vivian Gurney
Breck, Vivian
BREETVELD, James Patrick
Mann, Avery
BRENAN, Edward Fitzgerald
Beaton, George
Brenan, Gerald
BRENNAN, John
Welcome, John
BRENT, Peter Ludwig
Peters, Ludovic
BRERETON, John Le Gay
Garstang, Basil
BRESLIN, Howard
Niall, Michael
BRETHERTON, C H
Algol
BRETNOR, Reginald
Briarton, Grendel
BRETON-SMITH, Clare
Boon, August
Caldwell, Elinor
Vernon, Claire
Wilde, Hilary
BRETT, Leslie Frederick
Brett, Michael

BRETT, Mary Elizabeth
Brett, Molly
BRIDGES, Thomas Charles
Beck, Christopher
Bridges, Tom
BRIGGS, Phyllis
Briggs, Philip
BRIGHOUSE, Harold *and*
WALTON, John
Conway, Olive
BRIGHT, Mary C
Egerton, George
BRIGHT, Robert
Douglas, Michael
BRINSMEAD, Hesba
Brinsmead, H F
Hurgerford, Pixie
BRINTON, Henry
Fraser, Alex
BRISTER, Richard
Grove, Will O
Lewin, C L
Richmond, George
BROCK, Alan St Hill
Dewdney, Peter
BROCKIES, Enid Florence
Magriska, Hélène, *Countess*
BRODEY, Jim
Femora
Taylor, Ann
BRODIE, John
Guthrie, John
BRODIE, Julian Paul *and*
GREEN, Alan Baer
Denbie, Roger
BROGAN, Colm
Candidus
BROGAN, Denis
Barrington, Maurice
BROOKE, Peter
Carson, Anthony
BROOKER, Bertram
Herne, Huxley

BROOKES, Ewart Stanley
Tyler, Clarke
BROOKMAN, Laura L
Wilson, Edwina H
BROOKS, Anne
Carter, Ann
Carter, Anne
Milburn, Cynthia
Millburn, Cynthia
BROOKS, Collin
Brook, Barnaby
BROOKS, Edwy Searles
Comrade, Robert W
Gray, Berkeley
Gunn, Victor
BROOKS, Ern
Orion
BROOKS, Jeremy
Meikle, Clive
BROOKS, Raymond
Rivers, Gayle
BROOKS, Vivian Collin
Mills, Osmington
BROSIA, D M
D'Ambrosio, Raymond
BROSSARD, Chandler
Harper, Daniel
BROWN, E
Cavendish
BROWN, George Douglas
Douglas, George
King, Kennedy
BROWN, Ivor
I B
BROWN, John
Browning, John
BROWN, John J
Sherashevski, Boris
BROWN, John Ridley
Castle, Douglas
BROWN, Kay
Back-Back
BROWN, L Rowland
Grey, Rowland

BROWN, Laurence Oliver
Oliver, Laurence
BROWN, Margaret Elizabeth Snow
Brown, Marel
BROWN, May
Blake, Vanessa
Brown, Mandy
BROWN, Morna D
Ferrars, E X
Ferrars, Elizabeth
BROWN, Robert McAfee
St Hereticus
BROWN, Rosalie
Moore, Rosalie
BROWN, Tina
Boot, Rosie
BROWN, Zenith
Conrad, Brenda
Ford, Leslie
Frome, David
BROWNE, Charles Farrar
Ward, Artemus
BROWNE, Harry T
John o' the North
BROWNE, Howard
Evans, John
BROWNE, Thomas Alexander
Boldrewood, Rolf
BROWNJOHN, Alan
Berrington, John
BROWNLEE, Frances
Dickinson, Frankie
BROXON, Mildred Downey
Skaldaspillir, Sigfriour
BRUFF, Nancy
Gardner, Nancy Bruff
BRUNDAGE, John Herbert
Herbert, John
BRUNDLE, John
John, A Suffolk Herd Boy
BRUNNER, John
Loxmith, John
Staines, Trevor
Woodcott, Keith

BRUSTLEIN, Daniel
Alain
BRUSTLEIN, Janice
Janice
BRUTUS, Dennis
Bruin, John
BRYANT, Baird
Baron, Willie
BRYANT, Denny
Drake, Winifred
BRYANT, Edward
Talbot, Lawrence
BRYSON, Charles
Barry, Charles
BUCHAN, Anna
Douglas, O
BUCHAN, John Stuart
Erskine, Douglas
BUCHANAN, B J
Shepherd, Joan
BUCHANAN, Marie
Curzon, Clare
Petrie, Rhona
BUCK, Pearl S
Sedges, John
BUCK, William Ray
Buchanan, William
BUCKBY, Samuel
Blair, Frank
BUCKHAM, Bernard
B B B
BUCKLAND-WRIGHT, Mary
Hume, Frances
BUCKLEY, Fergus Reid
Crumpet, Peter
BUDD, John
Prescot, Julian
BUDD, William John
Budd, Jackson
Jackson, Wallace
BUDDEE, Paul
Richards, Paul
BUGAEV, Boris Nikolaevich
Biely, Andrey

BUGGIE, Olive M
Bugy, Oly
BUITENKANT, Nathan
Mark, David
BULLARD, Arthur
Edwards, Albert
BULLEID, H A V
Collins, D
BULLETT, Gerald
Fox, Sebastian
BULLMORE, Jeremy *and*
BOWEN, John
Blake, Justin
BULLOCK, Michael Hale
Hale, Michael
BULMER, Henry Kenneth
Akers, Alan Burt
Blake, Ken
Bulmer, Kenneth
Corley, Ernest
Frazier, Arthur
Johns, Kenneth
Kent, Philip
Krauss, Bruno
Langholm, Neil
Maras, Karl
Pike, Charles R
Quiller, Andrew
Silver, Richard
Zetford, Tully
BULMER, Henry Kenneth *and*
NEWMAN, John
Johns, Kenneth
BULMER-THOMAS, Ivor
Thomas, Ivor
BUMPUS, Doris Marjorie
Alan, Marjorie
BUNCE, Oliver Bell
Censor
BUNCH, David R
Groupe, Darryl R
BUNDEY, Ellen Milne
Dunne, Lyell

BUNTING, D G
George, Daniel
BURBRIDGE, Edith Joan
Cockin, Joan
BURDEN, Jean
Ames, Felicia
BURFORD, Roger d'Este
East, Roger
BURFORD, Roger d'Este *and*
BLAKESTON, Oswell
Simon
BURG, David
Dolberg, Alexander
BURGE, Milward Rodon Kennedy
Kennedy, Milward
BURGESS, Mary
Burgess, Sally
BURGESS, Thornton W
Thornton, W B
BURGIN, G B
Smee, Wentworth
BURKE, John
Burke, Owen
BURKE, John Frederick
Burke, Jonathan
Esmond, Harriet
George, Jonathan
Jones, Joanna
Miall, Robert
Morris, Sara
Sands, Martin
BURKHARDT, Eve *and*
BURKHARDT, Robert
Ferdinand
Bliss, Adam
Eden, Rob
Jardin, Rex
BURKS, Arthur J
Critchie, Estil
Whitney, Spencer
BURNE, Clendennin Talbot
Hawkes, John
BURNETT, Hallie
Hutchinson, Anne

BURNETT, Hugh
Phelix
BURNETT, W R
Monahan, John
Updyke, James
BURNETT-SMITH, Annie S
Swan, Annie S
BURNS, Bernard
Auld, Philip
BURNS, Vincent
Burns, Bobby
BURRAGE, Alfred M
Ex-Private X
BURROUGHS, William
Lee, William
BURROWS, Hermann
Rag Man
BURTON, Alice Elizabeth
Kerby, Susan Alice
BUSCHLEN, John Preston
Preston, Jack
BUSH, Christopher
Home, Michael
BUSH-FEKETE, Marie Ilona
Fagyas, Maria
BUSSY, Dorothy
Olivia
BUTLER, Arthur Ronald
Butler, Richard
BUTLER, Bill
Sabbah, Hassan i
BUTLER, Gwendolyn
Melville, Jennie
BUTLER, Samuel
Owen, John Pickard
BUTLER, Teresa Mary
Hooley, Teresa
BUTLER, William Vivian
('writing as')
Marric, J J
BUTTERS, Dorothy Gilman
Gilman, Dorothy
BUTTERS, Paul
Williamson, Paul

BUTTERWORTH, Frank Nestle
Blundell, Peter
BUTTERWORTH, Michael
Kemp, Sarah
Salisbury, Carola
BUTTERWORTH, William Edmund
Beech, Webb
Blake, Walker E
Scholefield, Edmund O
BUTTON, Margaret
Leona
BUXTON, Anne
Maybury, Anne
Troy, Katherine
BYERS, Amy
Barry, Ann
BYFORD-JONES, Wilfred
Quaestor
BYHNER, Witter
Morgan, Emanuel
BYRNE, John Keyes
Leonard, Hugh

§ §

Oh Amos Cottle! —
Phoebus what a name
To fill the speaking trump
of future fame.
— Lord Byron. English bards and
Scotch reviewers

§ §

CABLE, James
Hugo, Grant
CADELL, Elizabeth
Ainsworth, Harriet
CAESAR, Gene
Laredo, Johnny
Sterling, Anthony

CAESAR, Richard Dynely *and* **MAYNE, William J C**
James, Dynely
· **CAFFYN, Kathleen M**
Iota
CAIN, Arthur Homer
King, Arthur
CAIN, Paul
Ruric, Peter
CALDWELL, Janet Taylor *and* **REBACK, Marcus**
Caldwell, Taylor
Reiner, Max
CALLAHAN, Claire Wallis
Hartwell, Nancy
CALLARD, Thomas H
Ross, Sutherland
CAMERON, Elizabeth Jane
Duncan, Jane
CAMERON, Lou
Adams, Justin
Arnold, L J
Cameron, Julie
Cartier, Steve
Marvin, W R
CAMERON, William Ernest
Allerton, Mark
CAMM, Frederick James
N I
Waysider
CAMPBELL, Alice Ormond
Ingram, Martin
CAMPBELL, Barbara Mary
Cam
CAMPBELL, Gabrielle Margaret Vere
Bowen, Marjorie
Paye, Robert
Preedy, George
Preedy, George R
Shearing, Joseph
Winch, John
CAMPBELL, John Lorne
Chanaidh, Fear

20

CAMPBELL, John Wood *Jr*
  Stuart, Don A
CAMPBELL, Judith
  Grant, Anthony
CAMPBELL, Margaret *and*
JANSEN, Johanna
  Bayard, Fred
CAMPBELL, R O
  Staveley, Robert
CAMPBELL, Ramsay
  Comfort, Montgomery
  Undercliffe, Errol
CAMPBELL, Sydney George
  Campbell, Stuart
CAMPBELL, Walter Stanley
  Vestal, Stanley
CAMPBELL, William Edward
March
  March, William
CAMPION, Sidney
  Swayne, Geoffrey
CANADAY, John
  Head, Matthew
CANAWAY, W H
  Canaway, Bill
  Hamilton, William
  Hermes
CANNING, Victor
  Gould, Alan
CAPLIN, Alfred Gerald
  Capp, Al
CAPRIANI, Vincent
  Massey, Charlotte
CAPSTICK, Elizabeth
  Scott, Elizabeth
CARAS, Roger
  Sarac, Roger
CARDENA, Clement
  De Laube
CARDIF, Maurice
  Lincoln, John
CARDOZO, Lois S
  Duncan, Lois
  Kerry, Lois

CARDUS, *Sir* Neville
  Cricketer
CAREW, John Mohun
  Carew, Tim
CAREW-SLATER, Harold James
  Carey, James
CAREY, Joyce
  Mallory, Jay
CARGILL, Morris *and*
HEARNE, John
  Morris, John
CARLE, C E *and* DORN,
Dean M
  Morgan, Michael
CARLISLE, R H
  Hawkeye
CARLTON, Effie Crockett
  Canning, Effie
CARLTON, Grace
  Garth, Cecil
CARMAN, Bliss
  Norman, Louis
CARNEGIE, Raymond Alexander
  Carnegie, Sacha
CARNEY, Jack
  Eff, B
CARNWATH, *Lady see*
WETHERELL-PEPPER, Joan
Gertrude
CARR, Barbara Irene Veronica
Comyns
  Comyns, Barbara
CARR, John Dickson
  Dickson, Carr
  Dickson, Carter
CARR, Margaret
  Carroll, Martin
  Kerr, Carole
CARR, Terry
  Edwards, Norman
CARRIER, Robert *and*
DICK, Oliver Lawson
  Oliver, Robert

CARRINGTON, Charles Edmund
Edmonds, Charles
CARRINGTON, Hereward
Lavington, Hubert
CARTER, Bryan
Carter, Nick
CARTER, Compton Irving
Carter, John L
CARTER, Ernest
Giffin, Frank
CARTER, Felicity Winifred
Bonett, Emery
CARTER, Frances Monet
Evans, Frances
CARTER, John Franklin
Diplomat
Franklin, J
Unofficial Observer
CARTER, Thomas
Wood, J Claverdon
CARTWRIGHT, Justin
Crispin, Suzy
Sutton, Penny
CARUSO, Joseph
Barnwell, J O
CARY, Joyce
Cary, Arthur
Joyce, Thomas
CASEMENT, Christina
Maclean, Christina
CASEY, Michael T *and*
CASEY, Rosemary
Casey, Mart
CASMAN, Frances White
Keene, Frances W
CASSELEYR, Camille
Danvers, Jack
CASSIDAY, Bruce
Bingham, Carson
Day, Max
CASSIDY, Robert John
Gilrooney

CASSILL, Ronald Verlin
Aherne, Owen
Webster, Jesse
CASSITY, June
Mo, Manager
CASSON, Frederick
Beatty, Baden
CASTLE, Brenda
Ferrand, Georgina
CASTLE, Frances Mundy
Whitehouse, Peggy
CASTLE, Frank
Thurman, Steve
CASTLE SMITH, *Mrs* G
Brenda
CATALANI, Victoria
Haas, Carola
CATHER, Willa
Micklemann, Henry
CATHERALL, Arthur
Channel, A R
Corby, Dan
Hallard, Peter
CATTO, Maxwell Jeffrey
Catto, Max
Finkell, Max
Kent, Simon
CAULFIELD, Max
McCoy, Malachy
CAUTE, David
Salisbury, John
CAVE, Hugh Barnett
Beck, Allen
Case, Justin
Vace, Geoffrey
CAVE, Peter
Maxwell, Peter
CAVERHILL, William Melville
Melville, Alan
CEBULASH, Mel
Farrell, Ben
Harlan, Glen
Jansen, Jared

CEDER, Georgiana Dorcas
  Dor, Ana
CHADWICK, Joseph
  Barton, Jack
  Callahan, John
  Conroy, Jim
CHADWICK, Paul
  House, Brant
CHALKE, Herbert
  Blacker, Hereth
CHALLANS, Mary
  Renault, Mary
CHALMERS, Patrick
  P C
CHALONER, John Seymour
  Chalon, Jon
CHAMBERS, Aidan
  Blacklin, Malcolm
CHANCE, John Newton
  Chance, Jonathan
  Drummond, John
  Lymington, John
  Newton, David C
CHANDLER, Arthur
  Whitley, George
CHAPMAN, Mary I *and*
 CHAPMAN, John Stanton
  Chapman, Mariston
  Selkirk, Jane
CHAPMAN, Raymond
  Nash, Simon
CHAPMAN-MORTIMER,
 William Charles
  Mortimer, Chapman
  Mortimer, Charles
CHAPPELL, George S
  Traprock, Walter E
CHARBONNEAU, Louis
  Young, Carter Travis
CHARLES, Richard
  Awdry, R C
CHARLIER, Roger Henri
  Rochard, Henry

CHARLTON, Joan *and others*
  Heptagon
CHARNOCK, Joan
  Thomson, Joan
CHASE, Virginia
  Perkins, Virginia Chase
CHAUNDLER, Christine
  Martin, Peter
CHEETHAM, James
  Cheetham, Hal
CHERRY, Carolyn Janice
  Cherryh, C J
CHESHIRE, David Frederick
  Chester, Tom
  Dale, Laura
  Johns, Frederick
CHESHIRE, Gifford Paul
  Cheshire, Giff
  Merriman, Chad
  Pendleton, Ford
CHESTER, Charlie
  Noone, Carl
CHESTERMAN, Jean
  Kenward, Jean
CHESTERTON, G K
  Arion
  G K C
CHETHAM-STRODE, Warren
  Douglas, Noel
  Hamilton, Michael
CHEVALIER, Paul Eugene
 George
  George, Eugene
CHEYNE, *Sir* Joseph
  Munroe, R
CHIBNALL, Marjorie McCallum
  Morgan, Marjorie
CHILD, Philip A G
  Wentworth, John
CHIPPERFIELD, Joseph E
  Craig, John Eland
CHISHOLM, Lilian
  Alan, Jane
  Lorraine, Anne

CHITTY, Margaret Hazel
Whitton, Barbara
CHITTY, *Sir* Thomas Willes
Hinde, Thomas
CHOSACK, Cyril
Maclean, Barry
CHOVIL, Alfred Harold
Brook, Peter
CHRISTIE, *Dame* Agatha
Mallowen, Agatha Christie
Westmacott, Mary
CHRISTIE, Annie Rothwell
Rothwell, Annie
CHRISTIE, Douglas
Campbell, Colin
Durie, Lynn
CHRISTOPHER, Matt F
Martin, Fredric
CHURCH, Elsie
Parrish, Jean J
CITOVITCH, Enid
Baldry, Enid
CLAIR, Colin
Nicolai, C L R
CLAMP, Helen M E
Leigh, Olivia
CLARK, Alfred Alexander
Gordon
Hare, Cyril
CLARK, Charles Heber
Adeler, Max
CLARK, Dorothy *and*
McMEEKIN, Isabel
McMeekin, Clark
CLARK, Douglas
Ditton, James
CLARK, Frederick Stephen
Dalton, Clive
CLARK, Mabel Margaret
Storm, Lesley
CLARK, Maria
Clark, Mary Lou
CLARK, Marie Catherine Audrey
Curling, Audrey

CLARK, Marjorie
Rivers, Georgia
CLARK, Mary Elizabeth *and*
QUIGLEY, M C
Clark, Margery
CLARK, Patricia D R
Lorrimer, Claire
Robins, Patricia
CLARK, Winifred
Finley, Scott
CLARKE, Brenda
Honeyman, Brenda
CLARKE, David
Waldo, Dave
CLARKE, Dorothy Josephine
Shaw, Josephine
CLARKE, Henry Charles
Clarke, Hockley
CLARKE, J Calvitt
Addison, Carol
Grant, Richard
CLARKE, *Lady*
Fitzgerald, Errol
CLARKE, Percy A
Frazer, Martin
Lander, Dane
Lytton, Jane
Nielson, Vernon
CLARKE, Rebecca Sophia
May, Sophie
CLARKE, Sylvestre
Buffalo Child Long Lance
CLAY, Michael John
Griffin, John
CLAYTON, *Reverend* F H
Irishman, An
CLAYTON, Richard H M
Haggard, William
CLEARY, C V H
Day, Harvey
Duncan, A H
Norris, P E
CLEAVER, Hylton Reginald
Crunden, Reginald

CLEGG, Paul
  Vale, Keith
CLEMENS, Brian
  O'Grady, Tony
CLEMENS, Paul
  Cadwallader
CLEMENS, Samuel Langhorne
  Twain, Mark
CLEMO, Reginald John
  Clemo, Jack
CLEVELY, Hugh Desmond
  Claymore
  Claymore, Tod
CLINE, Norma
  Klose, Norma Cline
CLOPET, Liliane M C
  Bethune, Mary
CLUNE, Anne
  Clissmann, Anne
CLUTTERBUCK, Richard
  Jocelyn, Richard
CLYDE, Leonard Worswick
  Baron, Peter
CLYMER, Eleanor
  Kinsey, Elizabeth
CLYNE, Douglas
  Sinclair, Alasdair
COAD, Frederick R
  Sosthenes
  Sutton, I M
COATES, Anthony
  Mandeville, D E
COBB, Clayton W
  Patten, J
COBB, Ivo Geikie
  Weymouth, Anthony
COCKBURN, Claud Francis
  Cork, Patrick
  Drew, Kenneth
  Helvick, James
  Pitcairn, Frank
COERR, Eleanor Beatrice
  Hicks, Eleanor
  Page, Eleanor

COFFEY, Edward Hope
  Hope, Edward
COFFMAN, Virginia
  Cross, Victor
  Du Vaul, Virginia
  Du Vaul, Virginia C
  Duval, Jeanne
  Stanfield, Anne
COHEN, Morton N
  Moreton, John
COHEN, Victor
  Caldecott, Veronica
COKE, Desmond
  Blinders, Belinda
COLE, G(eorge) D(ouglas) H(oward)
  Cole, Douglas
  Populus
COLE, Lois Dwight
  Avery, Lynn
  Dudley, Nancy
  Dwight, Allan
  Eliot, Anne
COLE, Margaret A
  Renton, Julia
  Saunders, Ione
COLEMAN, William Lawrence
  Coleman, Lonnie
COLEMAN-COOKE, John C
  Ford, Langridge
COLES, Albert John
  Stewer, Jan
COLES, Cyril Henry *and*
  MANNING, Adelaide Frances Oke
  Coles, Manning
  Gaite, Francis
COLES, Phoebe Catherine
  Fraser, Peter
COLEY, Rex
  Ragged Staff
COLFER, Rebecca B
  R

COLLIE, Ruth
Stitch, Wilhelmina
COLLIN SMITH, Rodney
Collin, Rodney
COLLINGS, Edwin
Blackwell, John
COLLINGS, I J
Collings, Jillie
George, Vicky
COLLINGS, Joan
Sutherland, Joan
COLLINS, Dale
Fennimore, Stephen
COLLINS, Mildred
Collins, Joan
COLLINS, Vere Henry
Tellar, Mark
COLLINSON OWEN, H
C O
COLLOMS, Brenda
Cross, Brenda
Hughes, Brenda
**COLTMAN-ALLEN, Ernest
Vivian**
Dudley, Ernest
Lydecker, J J
COMBER, Elizabeth
Han Suyin
COMBER, Lillian
Beckwith, Lillian
COMBER, Rose
Star, Elison
COMFORT, Alex
Hornbrooke, Obadiah
COMPTON, D G
Compton, Guy
Lynch, Frances
CONARAIN, Alice Nina
Bowyer, Nina
Conarain, Nina
Hoy, Elizabeth
CONDON, Madeline B
Haefer, Hanna

CONE, Molly
More, Caroline
CONE, P C L
Clapp, Patricia
CONLY, Robert Carroll
O'Brien, Richard C
CONNER, Reardon
Connor, Patrick Reardon
Malin, Peter
CONNOLLY, Cyril
Palinurus
CONNOR, Joyce Mary
Marlow, Joyce
CONNOR, Tony
Anthony, John
CONNOR, *Sir* William
Cassandra
CONQUEST, Robert
Arden, J E M
CONRAD, Isaac
Conrad, Jack
COOK, Dorothy Mary
Cameron, D Y
Carlisle, D M
Clare, Elizabeth
COOK, Ida
Burchell, Mary
COOK, Marjorie Grant
Grant, Marjorie
Seaford, Caroline
COOK, Ramona Graham
Graham, Ramona
COOK, Robert W A
Cook, Robin
COOK, William Everett
Cook, Will
Everett, Wade
Keene, James
Peace, Frank
Riordan, Dan
COOKE, C H
Bickerdyke, John
COOKE, Diana
Witherby, Diana

COOKSON, Catherine
  Fawcett, Catherine
  Marchant, Catherine
COOLBEAR, Marian H
  Colbere, Hope
COOMBS, Joyce
  Hales, Joyce
  Scobey, Marion
COOPER, Colin Symons
  Benson, Daniel
COOPER, Edith E *and*
BRADLEY, Katherine H
  Field, Michael
COOPER, Edmund
  Avery, Richard
COOPER, Gordon
  Colam, Lance
COOPER, John
  Finch, John
  Lloyd, John
COOPER, John Dean
  Cooper, Jeff
COOPER, John Murray
  Sutherland, William
COOPER, Mae Klein *and*
KLEIN, Grace
  Farewell, Nina
COPE, *Sir* **Zachary**
  Zeta
COPELAND, Lewis
  Henry, Lewis C
COPPAGE, George Herman
  Jubilate
COPPEL, Alfred
  Gilman, Robert Cham
  Marin, A C
  Marin, Alfred
COPPER, Dorothy
  Carter, Diana
  Dickens, Irene
  Grant, Carol
  Green, Linda

CORBY, Jane
  Carew, Jean
  Holden, Joanne
CORCORAN, Barbara
  Dixon, Paige
CORDES, Theodore K
  Casey, T
  Daedalus
  Erskine-Gray
CORK, Barry
  Causeway, Jane
CORLEY, Edwin *and*
MURPHY, John
  Buchanan, Patrick
CORNISH, Doris Mary
  Lisle, Mary
CORNWELL, David John Moore
  Le Carré, John
CORRALL, Alice Enid
  Glass, Justine
CORTEZ-COLUMBUS, Robert
Cimabue
  Kennedy, R C
CORY, Charles Barney
  Nox, Owen
COSENS, Abner
  Wayfarer
COSTA, Gabriel
  Callisthenes
COTLER, Gordon
  Gordon, Alex
COULSON, John
  Bonett, John
COULSON, Juanita *and*
BRADLEY, Marion Z
  Wells, John J
COULSON, Robert Stratton *and*
DE WEESE, T Eugene
  Stratton, Thomas
COULTER, Stephen
  Mayo, James
COURAGE, John
  Goyne, Richard

COURNOS, Helen
  Norton, Sybil
COURNOS, John
  Courtney, John
  Gault, Mark
COURSE, Pamela
  Becket, Lavinia
  Mansbridge, Pamela
COURTIER, Sidney Hobson
  Chestor, Rui
COURTNEY-BROWNE, Reginald
  D S
  Browne, Courtney
COUSINS, Margaret
  Johns, Avery
  Masters, William
  Parrish, Mary
COVE, Joseph Walter
  Gibbs, Lewis
COVERT, Alice Lent
  Dale, Maxine
  Lowell, Elaine
COWARD, Noël
  Whittlebot, Hernia
COWLISHAW, Ranson
  Wash, R
  Woodrook, R A
COWPER, Francis
  Roe, Richard
COX, A B
  Berkeley, Anthony
  Iles, Francis
COX, Edith Muriel
  Goaman, Muriel
COX, Euphrasia Emeline
  Cox, Lewis
  Parsons, Bridget
COX, John
  Cox, Jack
  Roberts, David
COX, Julia
  Julia

COX, William Robert
  Frederic, Mike
  Reeve, Joel
  Spellman, Roger G
  Ward, Jonas
COX, William Trevor
  Trevor, William
COXALL, Jack Arthur
  Dawson, Oliver
COYNE, Joseph E
  Berch, William O
CRADOCK, Phyllis Nan Sortain
  Cradock, Fanny
  Dale, Frances
CRADOCK, Phyllis Nan Sortain
  and CRADOCK, John
  Bon Viveur
CRAIG, Edward Anthony
  Carrick, Edward
CRAIG, Mary
  Craig, M S
  Hill, Alexis
  Shura, Mary Francis
CRAIGIE, Dorothy M
  Craigie, David
CRAIGIE, Pearl Mary Teresa
  Hobbes, John Oliver
CRAINE, John Henry
  Jason
CRAWFORD, John Richard
  Walker, J
CRAWFORD, Phyllis
  Turner, Josie
CRAWFORD, Sallie
  Trotter, Sallie
CREASEY, Clarence Hamilton
  Cressy, Edward
CREASEY, John
  Ashe, Gordon
  Cooke, M E
  Cooke, Margaret
  Cooper, Henry St John
  Deane, Norman
  Fecamps, Elise

Frazer, Robert Caine
Gill, Patrick
Halliday, Michael
Hogarth, Charles
Hope, Brian
Hughes, Colin
Hunt, Kyle
Mann, Abel
Manton, Peter
Marric, J J
Marsden, James
Martin, Richard
Mattheson, Rodney
Morton, Anthony
Ranger, Ken
Reilly, William K
Riley, Tex
York, Jeremy
CREBBIN, Edward Horace
Sea-wrack
CRICHTON, Eleanor
McGavin, Moyra
CRICHTON, Kyle
Forsythe, Robert
CRICHTON, Lucilla Matthew
Andrews, Lucilla
CRICHTON, Michael
Hudson, Jeffrey
Lange, John
CRICHTON, Michael *and*
CRICHTON, Douglas
Douglas, Michael
CRISP, Anthony Thomas
Crisp, Tony
Western, Mark
CRISP, S E
Crispie
CRITCHETT, Richard Claude
Carton, Richard Claude
CRITCHLOW, Dorothy
Dawson, Jane
CROCCHIOLA, Stanley Francis Louis
Stanley, F

CROFT-COOKE, Rupert
Bruce, Leo
Croft, Taylor
CROLY, Jane Cunningham
June, Jenny
CROMPTON, Margaret Norah
Mair, Margaret
CRONIN, Bernard
Adair, Dennis
North, Eric
CRONIN, Brendan Leo
Cronin, Michael
Miles, David
CROOK, Compton Newby
Tall, Stephen
CROSBIE, Hugh Provan
Carrick, John
Crosbie, Provan
CROSBY, Harry C
Anvil, Christopher
CROSHER, Geoffrey Robins
Kesteven, G R
CROSLAND, Susan (Watson)
Barnes, Susan
CROSS, John Keir
MacFarlane, Stephen
CROSSEN, Kendell Foster
Barlay, Bennett
Chaber, M E
Crossen, Ken
Foster, Richard
Monig, Christopher
Richards, Clay
CROUDACE, Glyn
Monnow, Peter
CROUNSE, Helen Louise
Jackson, Joyce
CROWE, *Lady* (Bettina)
Lum, Peter
CROWLEY, Aleister *see*
CROWLEY, Edward Alexander
CROWLEY, Edward Alexander
Abhavananda
Carr, H D

CROWLEY, Edward Alexander
(cont'd)
  Crowley, Aleister
  Fénix, *Comte de*
  Frater, Perdurabo
  Gentleman of the University
    of Cambridge
  Khan, Khaled
  St E A of M and S
  Shivaji, Mahatma Guru Sri
    Paramahansa
  Svareff, *Count* Vladimir
  Therion, The Master
CRUICKSHANK, Charles Greig
  Greig, Charles
CRUTTENDEN, Nellie
  Jenny Wren
CRYER, Neville
  Fern, Edwin
CUMBERLAND, Marten
  O'Hara, Kevin
CUMMING, Robert Dalziel
  Skookum Chuck
CUMMINGS, Bruce Frederick
  Barbellion, W N P
CUMMINS, Mary Warmington
  Mackie, Alice
  Melville, Jean
CUNNINGHAM, Chet
  Cunningham, Cathy
CUNNINGHAM, Virginia Myra
Mundy
  Mundy, V M
CURNOW, Allen
  Whim Wham
CURRIE, *Lady*
  Fane, Violet
CURRY, Colin Thomas
  Douglas, Colin
CURRY, Thomas Albert
  Jefferis, Jeff
CURRY, Winifred J P
  Primrose, Jane

CURTIS, Sharon *and*
CURTIS, Thomas Dale
  London, Laura
CUST, Barbara Kate
  Fanshawe, Caroline
  Ward, Kate
CUTHBERTSON, James Lister
  C
CUTHRELL, Faith Baldwin
  Baldwin, Faith

§ §

*A man that should call everything
by its right name would hardly
pass the streets without being
knocked down as a common
enemy.*
– Marquis of Halifax. Works

§ §

DA CRUZ, Daniel
  Ballentine, John
  Cross, T T
DACHS, David
  Stanley, Dave
DAINTON, William
  Dainton, Courtney
DAKERS, Elaine
  Lane, Jane
DALE, Margaret
  Miller, Margaret J
DALE, R J
  Vinton, V V
DALLY, Ann
  Mullins, Ann
DALRYMPLE-HAY, Barbara *and*
DALRYMPLE-HAY, John
  Hay, John
DALTON, Gilbert
  Carstairs, Rod
  Norton, Victor

DALZEL-JOB, Patrick
Dalzel, Peter
DANBY, Mary
Calvert, Mary
Reed, Simon
Stevens, Andy
DANEFF, Stephen Constantine
Constant, Stephen
DANIEL, Glyn Edmund
Rees, Dilwyn
DANIELL, Albert Scott
Bowood, Richard
Daniell, David Scott
DANIELS, Dorothy
Dorsett, Danielle
Gray, Angela
Kavanaugh, Cynthia
Ross, Helaine
Somers, Suzanne
Thayer, Geraldine
Weston, Helen Gray
DANNAY, Frederic
Nathan, Daniel
**DANNAY, Frederic *and*
LEE, Manfred B**
Queen, Ellery
Ross, Barnaby
DANSON, Frank Corse
Dickson, Frank C
DARBY, Edith M
Greenfield, Bernadette
DAREFF, Hal
Foley, Scott
DARGAN, Olive
Burke, Fielding
D'ARLEY, Catherine
Arley, Catherine
DAS, Kamala
Madhavikutty
DAUGHTREY, Olive Lydia
Earle, Olive L
DAUKES, Sidney Herbert
Fairway, Sidney

DAVENTRY, Leonard John
Alexander, Martin
DAVID, Julia
Draco, F
DAVIDSON, Edith May
May, Roberta E
DAVIDSON, Margaret
Compere, Mickie
Davidson, Mickie
DAVIDSON, Simon
Gray, Simon
Holliday, James
Reade, Hamish
DAVIES, Betty Evelyn
Warwick, Pauline
DAVIES, D Jacob
Jacob, Herbert Mathias
DAVIES, David Margerison
Margerison, David
DAVIES, Edith
Jay, Joan
DAVIES, Hilda A
Tanis
DAVIES, Ivor Novello
Novello, Ivor
DAVIES, Joan Howard
Drake, Joan
DAVIES, John
Whitaker, Ray
DAVIES, John Christopher Hughes
Davies, Christie
DAVIES, John Evan Weston
Mather, Berkely
DAVIES, Leslie Purnell
Berne, Leo
Blake, Robert
Bridgeman, Richard
Evans, Morgan
Jefferson, Ian
Peters, Lawrence
Philips, Thomas
Thomas, G K
Vardre, Leslie
Welch, Rowland

DAVIES, Robertson
Marchbanks, Samuel
DAVIS, Arthur Hoey
Rudd, Steele
DAVIS, Burton *and*
DAVIS, Clare Ogden
Saunders, Lawrence
DAVIS, Frances
Alda, Frances
DAVIS, Frederick Clyde
Coombs, Murdo
Ransome, Stephen
DAVIS, Frederick William
Campbell, Scott
DAVIS, Gwen
Fink, Brat
DAVIS, Hope Hale
Hale, Hope
DAVIS, Julia
Draco, F
DAVIS, Lavinia
Farmer, Wendell
DAVIS, Lily May *and*
DAVIS, Rosemary
Davis, Rosemary L
DAVIS, Lois Carlile
Lamplaugh, Lois
DAVIS, Martha Wirt
Arsdale, Wirt Van
DAVIS, Robert Prunier
Brandon, Joe
DAVIS, Rosemary *and*
DAVIS, Lily May
Davis, Rosemary L
DAVIS, Will R
Wallace, John
DAVISON, Frank Cyril Shaw
Coalfleet, Pierre
DAVISON, Geoffrey
Duncan, George
DAWES, Edna
Dane, Eva

DAWSON, William Henry
Hawthorne, Ernest H
Lowndes, George
DAY, George Harold
Quince, Peter
DAY LEWIS, Cecil
Blake, Nicholas
DE BANZIE, Eric *and*
RESSICH, John S M
Baxter, Gregory
DE BELLET, Liane
De Facci, Liane
DE CAIRE, Edwin
Moodie, Edwin
DE CAMP, L Sprague
Lyon, Lyman R
Wells, J Wellington
DE CHAIR, Somerset
Hon Member for X
DE CRISTOFORO, R J
Cristy, R J
DE FREES, Madeline
Gilbert, *Sister* Mary
DE FREITAS, Michael
Michael X
DE FREYNE, George
Bridges, Victor
DE JONG, David Cornel
Breola, Tjalmar
**DE KIRILINE LAWRENCE,
Louise**
De Kiriline, Louise
DE LA MARE, Walter
Ramal, Walter
DE LA PASTURE, Edmée E M
Delafield, E M
DE LAUNAY, André Joseph
Launay, André
Launay, Droo
DE LEEUW, Cateau W
Hamilton, Kay
Lyon, Jessica
DE MENDELSSOHN, Hilde
Spiel, Hilde

DE REGNIERS, Beatrice Schenk
Kitt, Tamara
DE ROSA, Peter
Boyd, Neil
DE SCHANSCHIEFF, Juliet
Dymoke
Dymoke, Juliet
DE VOTO, Bernard Augustine
August, John
Hewes, Cady
DE WEESE, T Eugene *and*
COULSON, Robert Stratton
Stratton, Thomas
DEAL, Borden
Borden, Lee
Borden, Leigh
DEAN, Mary
Mee, Mary
DEAN, Robert George
Griswold, George
DEE, Stephanie
Plowman, Stephanie
DEGHY, Guy *and*
WATERHOUSE, Keith
Froy, Herald
Gibb, Lee
DEGRAS, Henry Ernest
Benney, Mark
DEINDORFER, Robert G
Bender, Jay
Dender, Jay
Greene, Robert
DEL REY, Lester
McCann, Edson
Van Lhin, Erik
Wright, Kenneth
St John, Philip
DEL REY, Lester *and*
POHL, Frederik
McCann, Edson
DELAFOSSE, Frederick Montague
Vardon, Roger
DELANEY, Mary Murray
Lane, Mary D

DELANY, Joseph Francis
Dane, Joel Y
DELOUGHERY, Grace L
Wiest, Grace L
DELVES-BROUGHTON,
Josephine
Bryan, John
DEMING, Richard
Franklin, Max
Moor, Emily
Moreno, Nick
DEMPEWOLFF, Richard F
Day, Michael
Frederick, Dick
Wolf, Frederick
DENHAM, Mary Orr
Caswell, Anne
Orr, Mary
DENHOLM, David
Forrest, David
DENNEY, Diana
Ross, Diana
DENNIS, Geoffrey Pomeroy
Browne, Barum
DENNIS-JONES, Harold
Hamilton, Paul
Hessing, Dennis
DENNISON, Enid
Lloyd, Willson
DENNISTON, Elinore
Allan, Dennis
Foley, Rae
DENNY, Norman George
Dale, Norman
DENNYS, Elisabeth
Onslow, Katherine
DENT, Anthony
Amplegirth, Anthony
Lampton, Austen
DENTON, John
Longley, John
DENVIL, Jane Gaskell
Gaskell, Jane

33

D'ERLANGER, *Baron* Frederic A
  Regnal, F
DERLETH, August William
  Grendon, Stephen
  Heath, Eldon
  Holmes, Kenyon
  Mason, Tally
  West, Michael
DERN, Erolie Pearl
  Courtland, Roberta
  Craig, Georgia
  Dern, Peggy
  Gaddis, Peggy
  Jordan, Gail
  Lee, Carolina
  Lindsay, Perry
  Sherman, Joan
DESMARAIS, Ovide E
  Demaris, Ovid
DEVANEY, Pauline *and*
  APPS, Edwin
  Wraith, John
DEVINE, David McDonald
  Devine, D M
  Devine, Dominic
DEWAR, Hubert Stephen Lowry
  Wessex Redivivus
DEWEY, Thomas Blanchard
  Brandt, Tom
  Wainer, Cord
DI PRIMA, Diane
  Darrich, Sybah
DICK, Kay
  Lane, Edward
DICK, Oliver Lawson *and*
  CARRIER, Robert
  Oliver, Robert
DICK-ERIKSON, Cicely Sibyl
  Alexandra
  Dick, Alexandra
  Ericson, Sybil
  Erikson, Charlotte
  Hay, Frances

DICK-HUNTER, Noel
  N D H
DICK-LAUDER, George Andrew
  Lauder, George
DICKINSON, Anne Hepple
  Hepple, Anne
DICKSON, Emma Wells
  Eveleth, Stanford
DIENES, Zoltan
  Zed
DIETRICH, Robert S
  Davis, Gordon
DIETZ, Howard
  Freckles
DILCOCK, Noreen
  Christian, Jill
  Ford, Norrey
  Walford, Christian
DILLARD, Polly Hargis
  Hargis, Pauline
  Hargis, Polly
DILLON, E J
  Lanin, E B
DILNOT, George
  Froest, Frank
DINGLE, Aylward Edward
  Cotterell, Brian
  Sinbad
DINNER, William *and*
  MORUM, William
  Smith, Surrey
DISCH, Thomas
  Hargrave, Leonie
  Thorpe, Dobbin
DISCH, Thomas M *and*
  SLADEK, John Thomas
  Demijohn, Thom
  Knye, Cassandra
DIVINE, Arthur Durham
  Divine, David
  Rame, David
DIXON, Arthur
  Whye, Felix

DIXON, Ella Hepworth
  Wynman, Margaret
DIXON, Roger
  Christian, John
  Lewis, Charles
DOANE, Pelagie
  Hoffner, Dorothy
DOBER, Conrad K
  Conrad, Con
DOBSON, Julia Lissant
  Tugendhat, Julia
DODD, Wayne D
  Wayne, Donald
DODGE, Josephine Daskam
  Bacon, J D
DOERFFLER, Alfred
  Dunn, Harris
  Ford, Fred
  Thomas, Carl H
DOHERTY, Ivy Ruby
  Hardwick, Sylvia
DOLBEY, Ethel M
  Hawthorne, E M D
DONALDSON, Stephen R
  Stephens, Reed
DONALDSON, William
  Legris, Jean-Luc
  Root, Henry
DONN-BYRNE, Brian Oswald
  Byrne, Donn
DONNELLY, Augustine
  Bullen Bear
DONOVAN, John
  Hennessey, Hugh
DONOVAN, Peter
  P O'D
DONSON, Cyril
  Hartford, Via
  Kidd, Russell
  Mackin, Anita
  Pinder, Chuck
DOOLITTLE, Hilda
  H D

DORGAN, Thomas Aloysius
  Tad
DORLING, Henry Taprell
  Taffrail
DORN, Dean M *and*
  CARLE, C E
  Morgan, Michael
DORR, Julia Caroline
  Thomas, Caroline
DOUBLEDAY, Neltje
  Blanchan, Neltje
DOUGLAS, Archibald C
  Nemo
DOUGLAS, Keith
  Hatred, Peter
DOUGLAS, Mary
  Tew, Mary
DOUGLAS, Norman *and*
  FITZGIBBON, Elsa
  Normyx
DOUGLASS, Percival Ian
  Bear, I D
  Crane, Henry
DOWNEY, Edmund
  Allen, F M
DOYLE, Charles
  Doyle, Mike
DRACKETT, Phil
  King, Paul
DRAGO, Harry Sinclair
  Ermine, Will
  Lomax, Bliss
DRESSER, Davis
  Baker, Asa
  Blood, Matthew
  Carson, Sylvia
  Culver, Kathryn
  Davis, Don
  Halliday, Brett
  Shelley, Peter
  Wayne, Anderson
DRESSER, Davis *and*
  ROLLINS, Kathleen
  Debrett, Hal

35

DREW, Jane B
Fry, Jane
DREXLER, Rosalyn
Sorel, Julia
DRIVER, Christopher
Archestratus
DRUMMOND, Alison
Schaw, Ruth
DRUMMOND, Cherry
Evans, Cherry
DRUMMOND, Edith
Carman, Dulce
DRUMMOND, Edith Victoria
Chichester
Stirling, Veda
DRUMMOND, Humphrey
Ap Evans, Humphrey
DRURY, Maxine Cole
Creighton, Don
DRYHURST, Michael John
Darling, V H
DU BOIS, Theodora
McCormick, Theodora
DUBACHEK, Ivo D
Duka, Ivo
DUDDINGTON, Charles Lionel
Campbell, Berkeley
Nightingale, Charles
DUDLEY-SMITH, Trevor
Black, Mansell
Burgess, Trevor
Fitzalan, Roger
Hall, Adam
North, Howard
Rattray, Simon
Scott, Warwick
Smith, Caesar
Trevor, Elleston
DUFF, Charles
Chernichewski, Vladimir

DUFF, Douglas Valder
Mainsail
Savage, Leslie
Stanhope, Douglas
Wickloe, Peter
DUFFIELD, Dorothy Dean
Duffield, Anne
DUFFY, Agnes Mary
Vox, Agnes Mary
DUGGAN, Denise Valerie
Egerton, Denise
DUGGLEBY, Jean Colbeck
Kennedy, Diana
DUGHMAN, John Karl *and*
DUGHMAN, Frieda Mae
Churchill, Luanna
DUKE, Anita
Hewett, Anita
DUKE, Madelaine
Donne, Maxim
Duncan, Alex
DUKENFIELD, William Claude
Bogle, Charles
Criblecoblis, Otis
Fields, W C
Jeeves, Mahatma Kane
DUNCAN, Actea
Thomas, Carolyn
DUNCAN, Kathleen
Simmons, Catherine
Simmons, Kim
DUNCAN, Robert Lipscomb
Roberts, James Hall
DUNCAN, Sara Jeanette
Grafton, Garth
DUNCAN, William Murdoch
Cassells, John
Dallas, John
Graham, Neill
Locke, Martin
Malloch, Peter
Marshall, Lovat
DUNK, Margaret
Duke, Margaret

DUNKERLEY, Elsie Jeanette
  Oxenham, Elsie Jeanette
DUNKERLEY, William Arthur
  Oxenham, John
DUNLOP, Agnes M R
  Kyle, Elisabeth
  Ralston, Jan
DUNN, Mary
  Faid, Mary
DUNNE, Finlay Peter
  Dooley, Martin
DUNNETT, Dorothy
  Halliday, Dorothy
DUNSING, Dee
  Mowery, Dorothy
DUPUY-MAZUEL, Henri
  Catalan, Henri
DURBRIDGE, Francis *and*
  MCCONNELL, James Douglas
  Rutherford
  Temple, Paul
DURGNAT, Raymond
  Green, O O
DURRELL, Lawrence
  Norden, Charles
DURST, Paul
  Bannon, Peter
  Chelton, John
  Cochran, Jeff
  Shane, John

§ §

Who gave you this name?
My godfathers and godmothers.
— Church of England Catechism

§ §

EAGAN, Frances W
  Seeker, A
EAGLESTONE, Arthur Archibald
  Dataller, Roger

EAMES, Helen Mary
  Mercury
EARNSHAW, Patricia
  Mann, Patricia
EASTWOOD, Helen B
  Baxter, Olive
  Ramsay, Fay
EBBETT, Eve
  Burfield, Eva
EBBS, Robert
  Pitchford, Harry Ronald
  Severn, Richard
EBEL, Suzanne
  Goodwin, Suzanne
  Shelbourne, Cecily
EBERLE, Irmengarde
  Allen, Allyn
  Carter, Phyllis Ann
EBERT, Arthur Frank
  Arthur, Frank
ECCLESHARE, Colin
  O P
EDELSTEIN, Hyman
  Synge, Don
EDEN, Dorothy
  Paradise, Mary
EDGAR, Alfred
  Lyndon, Barrie
EDGLEY, Leslie
  Bloomfield, Robert
EDGLEY, Leslie *and*
  EDGLEY, Mary
  Hastings, Brook
EDMISTON, Helen J M
  Robertson, Helen
EDMONDS, Helen
  Ferguson, Helen
  Kavan, Anna
EDMONDS, Ivy Gordon
  Gordon, Gary
  Gross, Gene
EDMONDSON, Sybil
  Armstrong, Sybil

EDMONDSON Y COTTON,
 José Mario Garry Ordonez
  Edmondson, G C
  Gast, Kelly P
EDMUNDSON, Joseph
  Burton, Conrad
  Jody, J M
EDWARD, Ann Elizabeth
  West, Anna
EDWARD, Irene
  Barr, Elisabeth
EDWARDES, Michael
  Cassilis, Robert
EDWARDS, Florence
  Edwards, Laurence
  Jolly, Susan
EDWARDS, Frederick Anthony
  Edwards, Charman
  Van Dyke, J
EDWARDS, George Graveley
  Graveley, George
EGLETON, Clive
  Blake, Patrick
  Tarrant, John
EHRENBERG, Golda
  Scott, Katherine
EHRENBORG, *Mrs* C G
  Trew, Cecil G
EHRLICH, Bettina
  Bettina
EIDEN, Paul *and*
 SABRE, Mel R
  Stagge, Delano
EIKER, Mathilde
  Evermay, March
EISENSTADT-JELEZNOV,
 Mikhail
  Argus, M K
EISENSTAT, Jane Sperry
  Sperry, J E
ELDERSHAW, Flora Sydney *and*
 BARNARD, Marjorie Faith
  Eldershaw, M Barnard

ELGIN, Betty
  Kirby, Kate
ELIADES, David *and*
 WEBB, Robert Forrest
  Forrest, David
ELLERBECK, Rosemary
  L'Estrange, Anna
  Thorne, Nicola
  Yorke, Katherine
ELLERMAN, Annie Winifred
  Bryher
  Bryher, Winifred
ELLETT, Harold Pincton
  Burnaby, Nigel
ELLIOT, Andrew George
  MacAndrew, Rennie
ELLIOT, Christopher
  Marriot, John
ELLIOTT-CANNON, Arthur
 Elliott
  Cannon, Elliott
  Forde, Nicholas
  Martyn, Miles
ELLIS, Oliver
  Briony, Henry
ELLISON, James
  Brother Flavius
ELLISON, Joan
  Robertson, Elspeth
ELLISON, Virginia Howell
  Howell, Virginia Tier
  Leong, Gor Yun
  Mapes, Mary A
  Mussey, Virginia T H
  Soskin, V H
ELTING, Mary
  Brewster, Benjamin
  Cole, Davis
  Tatham, Campbell
ELWART, Joan Frances
  Elwart, Joan Potter
  Trawle, Mary Elizabeth

ELY, George Herbert *and*
L'ESTRANGE, C James
  Strang, Herbert
EMANUEL, Victor Rousseau
  Egbert, H M
  Rousseau, Victor
EMERSON, Ernest
  Milky White
EMMS, Dorothy
  Charques, Dorothy
ENGEL, Lyle Kenyon
  Kenyon, Larry
  Kenyon, Paul
ENGLISH, Jean Ellen
  French, Ellen Jean
EPSTEIN, Beryl
  Williams, Beryl
EPSTEIN, Beryl *and*
EPSTEIN, Samuel
  Allen, Adam
  Coe, Douglas
EPSTEIN, Samuel
  Campbell, Bruce
ERNST, Paul F
  Edson, George Alden
  Stern, Paul F
ESCHERLICH, Elsa Antonie
  Falk, Elsa
ESCOTT, Jack Leonard
  Scott, Jack S
ESTRIDGE, Robin
  Loraine, Philip
EVANS, Constance May
  Gray, Jane
  O'Nair, Mairi
EVANS, George
  Geraint, George
EVANS, George *and*
EVANS, Kay
  Bird, Brandon
  Evans, Harris
EVANS, Glyn
  Ifans, Glyn

EVANS, Gwynfil Arthur
  Gwynne, Arthur
  Western, Barry
EVANS, Hilary Agard
  Agard, H E
EVANS, Hugh Austin
  Austin, Hugh
EVANS, Jean
  Shaw, Jane
EVANS, Julia
  Hobson, Polly
EVANS, Kathleen
  Kaye, Evelyn
EVANS, Kay *and* EVANS,
George
  Bird, Brandon
  Evans, Harris
EVANS, Kay *and* EVANS, Stuart
  Tracey, Hugh
EVANS, Marguerite Florence
  Barcynska, Hélène, *Countess*
  Sandys, Oliver
EVANS, Stuart *and* EVANS, Kay
  Tracey, Hugh
EVELYN, John Michael
  Underwood, Michael
EVENS, George Bramwell
  Romany
EVERETT, *Mrs* H D
  Douglas, Theo
EVERSLEY, David E C
  Small, William
EVERSON, William Oliver
  Brother Antoninus
EWART, Ernest Andrew
  Cable, Boyd
EWART-BIGGS, Christopher
  Elliott, Charles
EWENS, Gwendoline Wilson
  Ashley, Gladys
  Wilson, Gwendoline
EWER, Monica
  Crosbie, Elizabeth

EYERLY, Jeanette *and*
GRIFFITH, Valeria W
 Griffith, Jeannette
EYLES, Kathleen Muriel
 Tennant, Catherine
EYSSELINCK, Janet Gay
 Burroway, Janet

§ §

What are names but air?
— S.T. Coleridge — Names

§ §

FABRY, Joseph B
 Fabrizius, Peter
FADIMAN, Edwin J
 Mark, Edwina
FAIRBAIRN, R H
 R H F
FAIRBURN, Eleanor
 Carfax, Catherine
 Gayle, Emma
 Lyons, Elena
FAIRCHILD, John
 Esterhazy, Louise J
FAIRCHILD, William
 Cranston, Edward
FAIRFIELD, Cecily Isabel
 West, Rebecca
FAIRLIE, Gerard
 Sapper
FALK, Katherine *and others*
 Heptagon
FALK, Millicent *and others*
 Heptagon
FALL, William E
 Erimus
FALLA, Frank
 Sarnian
FANTHORPE, Robert Lionel
 Barton, Lee
 Fane, Bron

 Roberts, Lionel
 Thanet, Neil
 Thorpe, Trebor
 Torro, Pel
FANTONI, Barry
 Addio, E I
 Flannel, J C
 Gasket, Bamber
 Krin, Sylvie
 Slagg, Glenda
FANTONI, Barry *and*
INGRAMS, Richard
 Thribb, E J
FARGUS, Fredrick John
 Conway, Hugh
FARJEON, Eve
 Jefferson, Sarah
FARJEON, Joseph Jefferson
 Swift, Anthony
FARMER, Philip José
 Trout, Kilgore
FARMERS, Eileen Elizabeth
 Lane, Elizabeth
FARNDALE, W A J
 Farndale, James
FARNILL, Barrie
 Wellington, John
FARQUHAR, Jesse Carlton *Jr*
 Scott, John-Paul
FARRELL, Anne Elisabeth
 Allaben, Anne E
FARRELL, Michael
 Burke, Michael
 Gulliver, Lemuel
FARRIS, John Lee
 Bracken, Steve
FARROW, R
 Vincent, John
FARSON, Daniel
 Excellent, Matilda
FAST, Howard
 Cunningham, E V
 Ericson, Walter

FAST, Julius
  Barnett, Adam
FAULKNER, Anne Irvin
  Faulkner, Nancy
FAUST, Frederick
  Austin, Frank
  Baxter, George Owen
  Bolt, Lee
  Brand, Max
  Butler, Walter C
  Challis, George
  Dawson, Peter
  Dexter, Martin
  Evan, Evin
  Evans, Evan
  Frederick, John
  Frost, Frederick
  Lawton, Dennis
  M B
  Manning, David
  Morland, Peter Henry
  Owen, Hugh
  Silver, Nicholas
  Uriel, Henry
FAY, E F
  Bounder, The
FAY, Judith
  Nicholson, Kate
FEAGLES, Anita MacRae
  Macrae, Travis
FEAR, William H
  Reynolds, John
FEARING, Kenneth;
  BEDFORD-JONES, Henry *and*
  FRIEDE, Donald
  Bedford, Donald F
FEARN, John Russell
  Statten, Vargo
  Winiki, Ephraim
FEARON, Percy
  Poy
FEEHAN, *Sister* Mary Edward
  Clementia

FEHRENBACH, T R
  Freeman, Thomas
FEILDING, Dorothy
  Fielding, A E
FEINBERG, Bea
  Freeman, Cynthia
FEIWEL, Raphael Joseph
  Fyvel, T R
FELDMAN, Eugene P R
  Burroughs, Margaret
FELL, Barry
  Barraclough, Howard
FELL, Frederick Victor
  Fredericks, Vic
FELL, William Richmond
  Richmond, William
FELLOWES-GORDON, Ian
  Collier, Douglas
  Gordon, Ian
FELLOWS, Dorothy Alice
  Collyer, Doric
  Hunt, Dorothy
FELSEN, Henry Gregor
  Vicker, Angus
FELSTEIN, Ivor
  Steen, Frank
FELTON, Ronald Oliver
  Welch, Ronald
FENN, Caroline K *and*
  MCGREW, Julia
  McGrew, Fenn
FENN, George Manville
  Manville, George
FENWICK-OWEN, Roderic
  Owen, Roderic
FERGUSON, Charles W
  Gregory, Hilton
FERGUSON, Evelyn
  Nevin, Evelyn C
FERGUSON, Ida May
  Fergus, Dyjan
FERGUSON, Marilyn
  Renzelman, Marilyn

41

FERGUSON, Rachel
Columbine
Rachel
FERGUSON, William Blair
Morton
Morton, William
FERGUSSON HANNAY, *Lady*
Leslie, Doris
FERNEYHOUGH, Roger
Edmund
Hart, R W
FETHERSTONHAUGH, Patrick
William Edward
Fetherston, Patrick
FETTER, Elizabeth
Lees, Hannah
FEW, Eunice Beatty
Few, Betty
FICHTER, George S
Kensinger, George
Warner, Matt
Ziliox, Marc
FICKLING, Forrest E *and*
FICKLING, Gloria
Fickling, G G
FIELD, M J
Freshfield, Mark
FIELDING, Alexander
Fielding, Xan
FIELDING, Archibald
Fielding, Dorothy
FIELDING, Molly Hill
Field, Hill
FIGGIS, Darrell
Ireland, Michael
FINDLATER, Richard
Bain, Bruce
FINK, Merton
Finch, Matthew
Finch, Merton
FINKEL, George
Pennage, E M
FINLAY, Ian
Philaticus

FINLEY, Martha Farquharson
Farquharson, Martha
FINN, *Sister* **Mary Paulina**
Pine, M S
FINNEY, Jack
Braden, Walter
FINNIN, Mary
Hogarth, John
FIRTH, Violet Mary
Fortune, Dion
FISCHER, Bruno
Gray, Russell
FISCHER, Matthias Joseph
Laurence, Robert
FISH, Robert Lloyd
Lamprey, A C
Pike, Robert
Pike, Robert L
FISHER, A Stanley T
Scarrott, Michael
FISHER, Dorothea F C
Canfield, Dorothy
FISHER, Douglas George
Douglas, George
FISHER, Edward
Fisher, A E
FISHER, John
Piper, Roger
FISHER, Stephen Gould
Fisher, Steve
Gould, Stephen
Lane, Grant
FISHER, Veronica Suzanne
Veronique
FISHMAN, Jack *and*
ORGILL, Douglas
Gilman, J D
FITCHETT, W H
Vedette
FITZGERALD, Beryl
Hoffman, Louise
FITZGERALD, Desmond
Gerald, Daryl

FITZGERALD, Lawrence P
Lawrence, Jack
FITZ-GERALD, S J A
Hannaford, Justin
FITZGERALD, Seymour Vesey
S V F G
FITZGIBBON, Elsa *and*
DOUGLAS, Norman
Normyx
FITZHARDINGE, Joan
Margaret
Phipson, Joan
FITZMAURICE-KELLY, James
J F-K
FLACK, Isaac Harvey
Graham, Harvey
FLAGG, John
Gearon, John
FLANAGAN, Ellen
Raskin, Ellen
FLANAGAN, James
Long, Myles
FLANNER, Janet
Genêt
FLEET, William Henry
Thistleton, *Hon* Francis
FLEISCHER, Anthony
Hofmeyer, Hans
FLEISHMANN, Helle
Kuthumi
FLEMING, Ronald
Fleming, Rhoda
Frazer, Renee
Langley, Peter
FLETCHER, Constance
Fleming, George
FLETCHER, Harry L Verne
Fletcher, John
Garden, John
Hereford, John
FLETCHER, J S
Son of the Soil

FLEUR, Anne Elizabeth
Elizabeth, Anne
Lancaster, A F
Sari
FLEXNER, Stuart
Fletcher, Adam
FLOREN, Lee
Austin, Brett
Franchon, Lisa
Hall, Claudia
Hamilton, Wade
Harding, Matt
Harding, Matthew Whitman
Horton, Felix Lee
Jason, Stuart
Lang, Grace
Nelson, Marguerite
Smith, Lew
Sterling, Maria Sandra
Thomas, Lee
Turner, Len
Watson, Will
Wilson, Dave
FLUCK, Diana
Dors, Diana
FLUHARTY, Vernon L
Carder, Michael
O'Mara, Jim
FLYNN, *Sir* J A
Oliver, Owen
FLYNN, Mary
Livingstone, Margaret
FOCKE, E P W
Ernest, Paul
FOLSOM, Franklin Brewster
Brewster, Benjamin
Brewster, Franklin
Gorham, Michael
Hopkins, Lyman
Nesbit, Troy
FOOT, Michael
Cassius

FOOT, Michael;
 HOWARD, Peter *and*
 OWEN, Frank
　Cato
FOOTE, Carol
　Odell, Carol
FOOTE, Carol *and* **GILL, Travis**
　Odell, Gill
FORBES, Deloris Stanton
　Forbes, Stanton
　Wells, Tobias
FORBES, Deloris Stanton *and*
 RYDELL, Helen
　Rydell, Forbes
FORBES, Marcelle Azra
　Morphy, *Countess*
FORD, Corey
　Riddell, John
FORD, T Murray
　Le Breton, Thomas
FORD, T W
　Clay, Weston
　Shott, Abel
FORDE, Claude Marie
　Claude
FORSTER, Reginald Kenneth
　Kendal, Robert
FORSYTHE, Robin
　Dingwall, Peter
FORTE, Christine
　Forster, Christine
FORTIER, Cora B
　Maxine
FOSDICK, Charles Austin
　Castlemon, Harry
FOSTER, Don
　Saint-Eden, Dennis
FOSTER, George Cecil
　Seaforth
FOSTER, Jess Mary Mardon
　White, Heather
FOSTER, Marian Curtis
　Mariana

FOULDS, Elfrida Vipont
　Vipont, Charles
　Vipont, Elfrida
FOUTS, Edward Lee
　Lee, Edward
FOWKES, Aubrey
　Boy
FOWLER, Eric
　Mardle, Jonathan
FOWLER, Gene
　Long, Peter
FOWLER, Helen
　Foley, Helen
FOWLER, Henry Watson
　Egomet
　Quilibet
　Quillet
FOWLER, Kenneth A
　Brooker, Clark
FOX, Charles
　Jeremy, Richard
FOX, Frank
　Renar, Frank
FOX, Gardner F
　Cooper, Jefferson
　Cooper, Lynna
　Gardner, Jeffrey
　Kendricks, James
　Malors, Simon
　Matthews, Kevin
　Somers, Bart
FOX, James
　Holmes, Grant
FOX, Mona Alexis
　Brand, Mona
FOX, Norman Arnold
　Sabin, Mark
FOX, Winifred *and others*
　Heptagon
FOXALL, P A
　Vincent, Jim
FOXE, Arthur Norman
　Foda, Aun

FRAENKEL, Heinrich
  Assiac
FRANCE, Ruth
  Henderson, Paul
FRANCE-HAYHURST,
  Evangeline
  France, Evangeline
FRANCES, Stephen Daniel
  Janson, Hank
FRANCIS, Anne
  Ellis, Olivia
FRANCIS, Arthur Bruce Charles
  Bruce, Charles
FRANCIS, Dorothy Brenner
  Alden, Sue
  Goforth, Ellen
  Louis, Pat
FRANCIS, Stephen D
  Williams, Richard
FRANCK, Frederick S
  Fredericks, Frank
FRANK, *Mrs* M J
  A L O M
  Lady of Manitoba, A
FRANK, Waldo David
  Search-Light
FRANKAU, Julia Davis
  Danby, Frank
FRANKAU, Pamela
  Naylor, Eliot
FRANKEN, Rose *and*
  MELONEY, W B
  Grant, Margaret
  Meloney, Franken
FRANKLIN, Cynthia
  Neville, C J
FRANKLIN, Stella Maria
  Sarah Miles
  Brent, *of Bin Bin*
FRASER, Anthea
  Cameron, Lorna
  Graham, Vanessa
FRASER-HARRIS, D
  Grange, Ellerton

FRAZEE, Steve
  Jennings, D
FRAZER, James Ian Arbuthnot
  Frazer, Shamus
FREDE, Richard
  Frederics, Jocko
  Macdowell, Frederics
FREEDGOOD, Morton
  Godey, John
FREELING, Nicolas
  Nicolas, F R E
FREEMAN, Gillian
  Elizabeth, von S
  S, Elizabeth von
FREEMAN, Graydon La Verne
  Freeman, Larry
  Thompson, James H
  Wood, Jerry
FREEMAN, John Crosby
  Guthrie, Hugh
  McDowell, Crosby
FREEMAN, Kathleen
  Cory, Caroline
  Fitt, Mary
  Wick, Stuart Mary
FREEMAN, R Austin
  Ashdown, Clifford
FREEMAN, R Austin *and*
  PITCAIRN, John James
  Ashdown, Clifford
FREEMANTLE, Brian
  Evans, Jonathan
  Gant, Richard
  Maxwell, John
  Winchester, Jack
FRENCH, Alice
  Thanet, Octave
FREWER, Glyn
  Lewis, Mervyn
FREWIN, Leslie Ronald
  Dupont, Paul
FREY, Charles Weiser
  Findley, Ferguson

FRIEDBERG, Gertrude
  Tonkongy, Gertrude
FRIEDE, Donald;
 FEARING, Kenneth *and*
 BEDFORD-JONES, Henry
  Bedford, Donald F
FRIEDLANDER, Peter
  French, Fergus
FRIEDMAN, Eve Rosemary
  Friedman, Rosemary
  Tibber, Robert
  Tibber, Rosemary
FRIEDMAN, Jacob Horace
  Friedman, Elias
  Friedman, John
  Pater, Elias
FRIEND, Oscar Jerome
  Jerone, Owen Fox
FROST, C Vernon
  Child, Charles B
FROST, J W
  Glenelg
FROST, Kathleen Margaret
  Merivale, Margaret
FRY, Christopher
  Harris, Christopher
FRY, Clodagh Micaela Gibson
  Gavin, Amanda
FRYEFIELD, Maurice P
  Brooks, W A
  Brooks, William Allan
  Holmes, Arnold W
FTYARAS, Louis George
  Alexander, L G
FULLBROOK, Gladys
  Hutchinson, Patricia
FULLER, Edmund
  Amicus Curiae
FULLER, Harold Edgar
  Fuller, Ed
  Fulman, Al
FULLER, Henry Blake
  Page, Stanton

FULLER, James Franklin
  Ignotus
FULLERTON, Alexander
  Fox, Anthony
FULLERTON, Gail
  Putney, Gail J
FURLONG, Vivienne
  Welburn, Vivienne
FURPHY, Joseph
  Collins, Tom
FYTTON ARMSTRONG, T I
  Gawsworth, John

§ §

James Gatz – that was really, or at least legally, his name.
– F Scott Fitzgerald. The Great Gatsby

§ §

GAINES, Robert
  Summerscales, Rowland
GALBRAITH, J K
  Epernay, Mark
GALL, Michel
  Richardson, Humphrey
GALLAGHER, Frank
  Hogan, David
GALLUN, Raymond Z
  Callahan, William
GALSWORTHY, John
  Sinjohn, John
GANDLEY, Kenneth Royce
  Jacks, Oliver
  Royce, Kenneth
GANTNER, Neilma B
  Sidney, Neilma
GARBER, Nellia B
  Berg, Ila
GARD, Joyce
  Reeves, Joyce

GARDINER, Alfred George
  Alpha of the Plough
GARDINER, Dorothea Frances
  Frank, Theodore
GARDNER, Erle Stanley
  Corning, Kyle
  Fair, A A
  Green, Charles M
  Kendrake, Carleton
  Kenny, Charles J
  Parr, Robert
  Tillray, Les
GARDNER, Jerome
  Gilchrist, John
GARDNER, Richard
  Cummings, Richard
GARFIELD, Brian
  Garland, Bennett
  Hawk, Alex
  Ives, John
  Mallory, Drew
  O'Brian, Frank
  Ward, Jonas
  Wynne, Brian
  Wynne, Frank
GARNER, Hugh
  Warwick, Jarvis
GARNETT, David
  Burke, Leda
GARRATT, Alfred
  Garratt, Teddie
GARRETT, Edward Peter
  Garrett, Garet
GARRETT, Randall
  Bupp, Walter
  Gordon, David
  Langart, Darrel T
GARRETT, Randall *and*
JANIFER, Laurence M
  Phillips, Mark
GARRETT, Randall *and*
SILVERBERG, Robert
  Randall, Robert

GARRETT, Winifred Selina
  Dean, Lyn
GARRISON, Webb Black
  Webster, Gary
GARRITY, David James
  Garrity
GARROD, John Williams *and*
PAYNE, Ronald Charles
  Castle, John
GARVEY, Eric William
  Herne, Eric
GARVIN, Amelia Beers
(Warnock)
  Hale, Katherine
GARVIN, J L
  Calehas
GARWOOD, Godfrey Thomas
  Thomas, Gough
GASE, Richard
  Gale, John
GASPAROTTI, Elizabeth
  Seifert, Elizabeth
GASTON, William J
  Bannatyne, Jack
  Gaston, Bill
GAULDEN, Ray
  Ray, Wesley
GAULT, William Campbell
  Duke, Will
GAUNT, Arthur N
  Nettleton, Arthur
GAUTIER-SMITH, Peter
Claudius
  Conway, Peter
GAZE, Richard
  Gale, John
GEACH, Christine
  Dawson, Elizabeth
  Lowing, Anne
  Neil, Frances
  Wilson, Christine
GEEN, Clifford
  Berkley, Tom

GEHMAN, Richard Boyd
  Christian, Frederick
  Scott, Martin
GEIS, Bernard *and*
 GEIS, Darlene Stern
  Stevens, Peter
GEIS, Darlene Stern
  Kelly, Ralph
  London, Jane
GEISEL, Theodor Seuss
  Dr Seuss
  Lesieg, Theo
GELB, Norman
  Mallery, Amos
GELLIS, Roberta
  Daniels, Max
  Hamilton, Priscilla
  Jacobs, Leah
GEORGE, Peter
  Peters, Bryan
GEORGE, Robert Esmonde
 Gordon
  Sencourt, Robert
GERAHTY, Digby George
  Standish, Robert
GERARD, Edwin
  Trooper Gerardy
GERMANO, Peter
  Bertin, Jack
  Cord, Barry
  Kane, Jim
GERRITY, David James
  Garrity, Calli Goran
  Hardin, Mitch
GERSHON, Karen
  Tripp, Karen
GERSON, Noel Bertram
  Edwards, Samuel
  Lewis, Paul
  Phillips, Leon
  Vail, Philip
  Vaughan, Carter A
GESSNER, Lynne
  Clarke, Merle

GIBBS, Norah
  Boyd, Prudence
  Garland, Lisette
  Ireland, Noelle
  Merrill, Lynne
  Ritchie, Claire
  Shayne, Nina
  Wayne, Heather
  Whittington, Sara
GIBSON, G H
  Ironbark
GIBSON, Walter Brown
  Brown, Douglas
  Grant, Maxwell
  Kineji, Maborushi
GIBSON, William
  Mass, William
GIFFORD, James Noble
  Noble, Emily
  Saxon, John
GIGGAL, Kenneth
  Ross, Angus
GILBERT, Ruth Gallard
  Ainsworth, Ruth
GILBERT, William Schwenck
  Bab
  Tomline, F Latour
GILBERTSON, Mildred
  Gilbert, Nan
  Mendel, Jo
GILCHRIST, Alan
  Cowan, Alan
GILDEN, Katya *and*
 GILDEN, Bert
  Gilden, K B
GILDERDALE, Michael
  Flemming, Sarah
GILL, T M
  Sabattis
GILL, Travis *and*
 FOOTE, Carol
  Odell, Gill
GILL, Winifred *and others*
  Heptagon

GILLES, Daniel
Johnson, Marigold
GILLESSE, John Patrick
O'Hara, Dale
Starr, John A
GILLHAM, Elizabeth Wright Enright
Enright, Elizabeth
GILMAN, Dorothy
Butters, Dorothy Gilman
GILMER, Elizabeth Meriwether
Dix, Dorothy
GILMORE, James Robert
Kirke, Edmund
GILZEAN, Elizabeth Houghton
Houghton, Elizabeth
Hunton, Mary
GINZBERG, Asher
Achad Haan
GIRDLESTON, A H
A H G
GIRLING, Zoë
Hare, Martin
GITTINGS, Jo
Manton, Jo
GLADDEN, Edgar Norman
Mansfield, N
GLASER, Eleanor Dorothy
Zonik, Eleanor Dorothy
GLASER, Kurt
Glaser, Comstock
GLASKIN, G M
Jackson, Neville
GLASSCO, John
Bayer, Sylvia
Buffy
Colman, George
Colson-Haig, S
Davignon, Grace
Eady, W P R
Eddy, Albert
Gooch, Silas N
Henderson, George
Nudleman, Nordyk

Okada, Hideki
Saint-Luc, Jean de
Underwood, Miles
GLASSCOCK, Anne Bonner
Bonner, Michael
GLEADOW, Rupert
Case, Justin
GLEMSER, Bernard
Napier, Geraldine
GLEN, Duncan Munro
Foster, Simon
Munro, Ronald Eadie
GLENTON, Stella Lennox
King, Stella
GLIDDEN, Frederick Dilley
Short, Luke
GLIDDEN, Jonathan H
Dawson, Peter
GLIEWE, Unada G
Unada
GLOVER, Modwena
Sedgwick, Modwena
GLUCK, Sinclair
Danning, Melrod
GLUT, Don F
Jason, Johnny
Rogers, Mick
GOAMAN, Muriel
Cox, Edith
GODFREY, Frederick M
Cronheim, F G
GODFREY, Lionel Robert
Holcombe
Kennedy, Elliott
Mitchell, Scott
GODLEY, Robert
James, Franklin
GOETCHEUS, Carolyn
Lynn, Carol
GOGGAN, John Patrick
Patrick, John
GOHM, Douglas Charles
O'Connell, Robert Frank

GOLBERG, Harry
  Grey, Harry
GOLDBERG, Nathan Ralph
  Ralph, Nathan
GOLDEN, Dorothy
  Dennison, Dorothy
GOLDFRANK, *Mrs* Herbert
  Kay, Helen
GOLDIE, Kathleen Annie
  Fidler, Kathleen
GOLDIN, Kathleen McKinney
  Sky, Kathleen
GOLDING, Louise
  Davies, Louise
GOLDMAN, William
  Longbaugh, Harry
GOLDSTEIN, Arthur
  Ross, Albert
GOLDSTON, Robert
  Conroy, Robert
GOLLER, Celia Margaret
  Fremlin, Celia
GOLSWORTHY, Arnold
  Holcombe, Arnold
  Jingle
GOMPERTZ, Martin Louis Alan
  Ganpat
GOOD, Edward
  Oyved, Moysheh
GOODAVAGE, Joseph F
  Greystone, Alexander A
  Savage, Steve
GOODCHILD, George
  Dare, Alan
  Reid, Wallace Q
  Templeton, Jesse
GOODE, Arthur Russell
  Russell, Arthur
GOODEY, P E
  Condon, Patricia
GOODMAN, George Jerome W
  Smith, Adam

GOODMAN, George Jerome *and*
KNOWLTON, Winthrop
  Goodman, Winthrop
GOODSPEED, D J
  McLeish, Dougal
GOODWIN, Geoffrey
  Gemini
  Telstar
  Topicus
GOODWIN, Harold Leland
  Goodwin, Hal
  Savage, Blake
GOODWIN, Harold Leland *and*
HARKINS, Peter J
  Blaine, John
GOODWIN, Suzanne
  Ebel, Suzanne
GOODYEAR, Stephen Frederick
  Taylor, Sam
GOODYKOONTZ, William F
  Goode, Bill
GORDON, Alan Bacchus
  Ordon, A Lang
GORDON, *Reverend* Charles William
  Connor, Ralph
GORDON, Gordon *and*
GORDON, Mildred
  Gordons, The
GORDON, Jan
  Gore, William
GORDON, Richard
  Gordon, Stuart
  Stuart, Alex R
GORDON, Robert I
  London, Anne
  London, Robert
GOREY, Edward St John
  Blutig, Eduard
  Dowdy, Mrs Regera
  Grode, Redway
  Weary, Ogdred
  Wodge, Dreary

GOSLING, Veronica
  Henriques, Veronica
GOSLING, William Flower
  Fleur, William
GOSSMAN, Oliver
  Clyde, Craig
GOTTLIEBSEN, Ralph Joseph
  Scott, O R
GOTTSCHALK, Laura Riding
  Riding, Laura
GOULART, Ronald Joseph
  Goulart, Ron
  Kains, Josephine
  Lee, Howard
  Robeson, Kenneth
  Shawn, Frank S
  Steffanson, Con
GOVAN, Mary Christine
  Allerton, Mary
  Darby, J N
GOWING, Sidney Floyd
  Goodwin, John
GOYDER, Margot *and*
 JOSKE, Neville
  Neville, Margot
GOYNE, Richard
  Courage, John
GRABER, George Alexander
  Cordell, Alexander
GRAHAM, Charles
  Montrose, David
GRAHAM, Harry
  Streamer, *Col* D
GRAHAM, James Maxtone
  Anstruther, James
GRAHAM, *Dr* Joan
  Medica
GRAHAM, Maude Fitzgerald
  Graham, Susan
GRAINGER, Francis Edward
  Hill, Headon
GRAMONT, Sanche de
  Morgan, Ted

GRANICH, Irving
  Gold, Michael
GRANT, Donald *and*
 WILSON, William
  Ness, K T
GRANT, Hilda Kay
  Grant, Kay
  Hilliard, Jan
GRANT, James Miller
  Balfour, Grant
GRANT, John
  Gash, Jonathan
GRANT, M H
  Linesman
  Scolopax
GRANT, Neil
  Mountfield, David
GRANT, *Lady* Sybil
  Scot, Neil
GRANT, William
  Onlooker
GRAVELEY, G C
  Grayson, Daphne
GRAVES, Clotilda Inez Mary
  Dehan, Richard
GRAVES, Robert
  Doyle, John
GRAY, Clement
  Daybreak
GRAY, Dorothy K
  Haynes, Dorothy K
GRAY, K E
  Grant, Eve
GRAY, Lindsay Russell Nixon
  Lemon, Grey
GRAY, Terence J S
  Wei Wu Wei
GRAYDON, William Murray
  Gordon, William Murray
  Murray, William
GRAYLAND, Valerie M
  Belvedere, Lee
  Spanner, Valerie
  Subond, Valerie

GRAYSON, Albert Victor
Ethel

§ §

A good name is better than
precious ointment.
Bible. Ecclesiastes, 7.1

§ §

GREALEY, Tom
Southworth, Louis
GREAVES, Michael
Callum, Michael
GREEN, Alan Baer *and*
BRODIE, Julian Paul
Denbie, Roger
GREEN, Charles Henry
Sandhurst, B G
GREEN, Dorothy
Auchterlonie, Dorothy
GREEN, Elizabeth Sara
Tresilian, Liz
GREEN, Evelyn Everett
Adair, Cecil
GREEN, Lalage Isobel
March, Hilary
Pulvertaft, Lalage
GREEN, Maxwell
Cabby with camera
GREEN, Peter Morris
Delaney, Denis
GREEN, Peter *Canon*
Artifex
GREEN, T
Ramsey, Michael
GREENAWAY, Gladys
Manners, Julia
GREENBERG, Jack
Greenhill, Jack
GREENBERG, Joanne
Green, Hannah

GREENE, *Sir* **Hugh**
Eleigh, Sebastian
GREENE, Sigrid
De Lima, Sigrid
GREENE, Ward
Dudley, Frank
GREENER, William Oliver
Gerrare, Wirt
GREENHILL, Elizabeth Ann
Giffard, Ann
GREENHOOD, David
Sawyer, Mark
GREENLAND, W K
King, W Scott
GREENOUGH, William Parker
Montauban, G de
GREENWOOD, A E
Hawthorne, Marx
GREENWOOD, Augustus George
Archer, Owen
GREENWOOD, Julia E C
Askham, Francis
GREENWOOD, T E
McCabe, Rory
GREENWOOD, Thomas *and*
LANDE, Lawrence Montague
Verval, Alain
GREER, Germaine
Blight, Rose
GREGG, Hilda
Grier, Sydney C
GREIG, Maysie
Ames, Jennifer
Barclay, Ann
Thompson, Madeline
Warren, Mary D
GRESHAM, Elizabeth F
Grey, Robin
GRIBBEN, James
James, Vincent
GRIBBLE, Leonard Reginald
Browning, Sterry
Cody, Stetson
Denver, Lee

Grant, Landon
Grex, Leo
Grey, Louis
Marlowe, Piers
Muir, Dexter
Sanders, Bruce
GRIERSON, Edward
Stevenson, John P
GRIERSON, Walter
Enquiring Layman
GRIEVE, Alexander Haig
 Glanville
Glanville, Alec
GRIEVE, Christopher Murray
MacDiarmid, Hugh
GRIEVESON, Mildred
Flemming, Cardine
Mather, Anne
GRIFFIN, Robert John Thurlow
Griffin, Jonathan
Thurlow, Robert
GRIFFIN, Vivian Cory
Crosse, Victoria
GRIFFITH, Valeria W *and*
 EYERLY, Jeannette
Griffith, Jeannette
GRIFFITHS, Aileen Esther
Passmore, Aileen E
GRIFFITHS, Charles
Boardman, Charles
Bold, Ralph
GRIFFITHS, Jack
Griffith, Jack
GRIMM, Barbara Lockett
Wilder, Cherry
GRIMSTEAD, Hettie
Manning, Marsha
GRINDAL, Richard
Grayson, Richard
GRINGHUIS, Richard H
Gringhuis, Dirk
GROOM, Arthur William
Adamson, Graham
Anderson, George

Du Blane, Daphne
Grimsley, Gordon
Pembury, Bill
Stanstead, John
Templar, Maurice
Toonder, Martin
GROSSMAN, Judith
Hamilton, Ernest
Merril, Judith
Sharon, Rose
Thorstein, Eric
GROSSMAN, Judith *and*
 KORNBLUTH, Cyril M
Judd, Cyril
GROVES, Sheila
Durrant, Sheila
GRUBER, Frank
Acre, Stephen
Boston, Charles K
Vedder, John K
GUARIENTO, Ronald
Parks, Ron
GUEST, Enid
Quin, Shirland
GUEST, Francis Harold
Spenser, James
GUGGISBERG, *Sir* **F G**
Ubique
GUIGO, Ernest Philip
Holt, E Carleton
GUINNESS, Maurice
Brewer, Mike
Gale, Newton
GUIRDHAM, Arthur
Eaglesfield, Francis
GULICK, Grover C
Gulick, Bill
GUNN, John Angus Lancaster
Hall, B
GUTHRIE, Norman Gregor
Crichton, John
GUTHRIE, P R
Pain, Barry

GUTHRIE, Thomas Anstey
  Anstey, F
GUTHRIE, Woodrow Wilson
  Guthrie, Woody
GUYONVARCH, Irene
  Pearl, Irene
GWINN, Christine M
  Kelway, Christine
GWINN, William R
  Randall, William
GWYNN, Audrey
  Thomson, Audrey
GWYNN, Ursula Grace
  Leigh, Ursula
GYE, Harold Frederick Neville
  Gye, Hal
  Hackston, James

HAARER, Alec Ernest
  Shanwa
HADFIELD, Alan
  Dale, Robin
HAGAN, Stelia F
  Hawkins, John
HAIG, Emily Alice
  B L H
  E H
  Field, Robert à
  Hastings, Beatrice
  Longclothes, Ninon de
  Morning, Alice
  Tina, Beatrice
  Triformis, D
HALDANE, Robert Aylmer
  Square, Charlotte
HALDANE-STEVENSON, James
  Patrick
  Stevenson, J P
HALDEMAN, Joe
  Graham, Robert
HALE, Arlene
  Christopher, Louise
  Everett, Gail
  Tate, Mary Anne

HALE, Ethela Ruth
  (*Mrs* Fellowes)
  Hodgen, J T
HALE, Julian Anthony Stuart
  Stuart, Anthony
HALE, Kathleen
  McClean, Kathleen
HALE, Sylvia
  Barnard, Nancy
HALEY, W J
  Sell, Joseph
HALL, Bennie Caroline
  Hall, Bennet
  Marshall, Emily
HALL, Emma L
  St Claire, Yvonne
HALL, Frederick
  Hall, Patrick
HALL, Irene
  Gough, Irene
HALL, Josef Washington
  Close, Upton
HALL, Marie
  Boas, Marie
HALL, Norah E L
  Hall, Aylmer
HALL, Oakley Maxwell
  Manor, Jason
HALL, Verner
  Hustle, Hugh
HALLERAN, E E
  Broward, Donn
  Hall, Evan
HAMBLETON, Phyllis MacVean
  Vane, Phillipa
HAMILTON, Alex
  Pooter
HAMILTON, Cecily
  Hamilton, Max
  Rae, Scott
HAMILTON, Charles Harold
  St John
  Clifford, Martin
  Conquest, Owen

Redway, Ralph
Richards, Frank
Richards, Hilda
HAMILTON, Gerald
Weston, Patrick
**HAMILTON, *Sir* George
Rostrevor**
Rostrevor, George
HAMILTON, Leigh Brackett
Brackett, Leigh
HAMILTON, Mary A A
Iconoclast
**HAMILTON, Mary Margaret
Kaye**
Kaye, Mary Margaret
HAMILTON-WILKES, Edwin
Hamilton-Wilkes, Monty
Uncle Monty
HAMMERTON, J A
J A H
HAMMETT, Dashiell
Collinson, Peter
Dashiell, Samuel
Hammett, Mary Jane
HAMMOND, Lawrence
Francis, Victor
HAMMOND-INNES, Ralph
Hammond, Ralph
Innes, Hammond
HAMON, Louis *Count*
Cheiro
HAMPDEN, John
Montagu, Robert
HANKINSON, Charles J
Holland, Clive
HANLEY, Clifford
Calvin, Henry
HANLEY, Jack
Harvey, Gene
HANLEY, James
Bentley, James
Shone, Patric
HANNA, Frances
Nichols, Fan

HANNAY, James Owen
Birmingham, George A
HANSEN, Joseph
Brock, Rose
Colton, James
Coulton, James
HANZELON, Robert M
De Hart, Robert
HARBAGE, Alfred
Kyd, Thomas
HARBAUGH, Thomas Chalmers
Holmes, *Captain* Howard
HARBINSON-BRYANS, Robert
Bryans, Robin
Cameron, Donald
Harbinson, Robert
HARCOURT, Palma
Penn, John
HARDCASTLE, Michael
Clark, David
HARDING, Lee
Nye, Harold G
HARDINGE, George
Milner, George
HARDINGE, Rex
Capstan
HARDISON, O B
Bennett, H O
HARDWICK, Michael
Drinkrow, John
HARDWICK, Mollie
Atkinson, Mary
HARDWICK, Richard
Holmes, Rick
Honeycutt, Richard
HARDY, Jane
Boileau, Marie
HARDY, Marjorie
Hardy, Bobbie
HARE, Walter B
Burns, Mary
HARKINS, Peter
Adams, Andy

HARKINS, Peter J *and*
 GOODWIN, Harold Leland
   Blaine, John
HARKNETT, Terry
   Chandler, Frank
   Ford, David
   Gilman, George G
   Hardy, Adam
   Harman, Jane
   Hedges, Joseph
   James, William M
   Pine, William
   Russell, James
   Stone, Thomas H
   Terry, William
HARLAND, Henry
   Luska, Sidney
HARLING, Robert
   Drew, Nicholas
HARMAN, Richard
   Martin, Richard
HARPER, Edith
   Flamank, E
HARRELL, Irene Burk
   Amor, Amos
   Waylan, Mildred
HARRIS, *Mrs* Herbert
   Short, Francis
HARRIS, Ida Fraser
   Proctor, Ida
HARRIS, Joel Chandler
   Uncle Remus
HARRIS, John
   Hebden, Mark
   Hennessy, Max
HARRIS, John Wyndham Parkes
 Lucas Beynon
   Beynon, John
   Harris, John Beynon
   Parkes, Lucas
   Parkes, Wyndham
   Wyndham, John

HARRIS, Laurence Mark
   Blake, Alfred
   Blake, Andrew
   Harris, Larry Mark
   Janifer, Laurence M
   Wilson, Barbara
HARRIS, Marion Rose
   Charles, Henry
   Harriford, Daphne
   Rogers, Keith
   Young, Rose
HARRIS, Mark
   Wiggen, Henry W
HARRIS, Pamela
   Meinikoff, Pamela
HARRIS, Polly Anne Colver
   Colver, Anne
   Harris, Colver
HARRIS, Rona Olive
   O'Harris, Pixie
HARRIS, William
   Harris, Peter
HARRIS-BURLAND, John B
   Burland, Harris
HARRISON, Chester William
   Hickok, Will
HARRISON, Constance Cary
   Refugitta
HARRISON, *Mrs* E E
   Motte, Nel
HARRISON, Elizabeth C
   Cavanna, Betty
   Headley, Elizabeth
HARRISON, Harry
   Dempsey, Hank
HARRISON, J H
   Wynyard, John
HARRISON, John Gilbert
   Gilbert, John
HARRISON, Julia
   Richmond, Fiona
HARRISON, Michael
   Downes, Quentin
   Egremont, Michael

HARRISON, Philip
Carmichael, Philip
HARRISON, Richard Motte
Motte, Peter
HARRISON, Susie Frances
Seranus
HART, Caroline Horowitz
Winters, Mary K
HARTHOORN, Susanne
Hart, Suzanne
HARTIGAN, Patrick Joseph
O'Brien, John
HARTLEY, Ellen Raphael
Knauff, Ellen Raphael
HARTMANN, Helmut Henry
Seymour, Henry
HARVEY, Jean;
 BENNETT, Laura *and*
 MACKENZIE, Tina
Harlowe, Justine
HARVEY, John
Barton, Jon
Brady, William
Coburn, L J
Dancer, J B
Hart, Jon
McLaglen, John J
Mann, James
Ryder, Thom
Sandon, J D
White, Jonathan
HARVEY, Margaret Susan Janet
Michelmore, Susan
HARVEY, Nigel
Willoughby, Hugh
HARVEY, Peter Noel
Day, Adrian
Peters, Noel
HARVEY, William
Denovan, Saunders
HASKIN, Dorothy C
Clark, Howard

HASLAM, Nicky
Hopper, Sam
Parsons, Paul
HASSON, James
De Salignac, Charles
HASTINGS, Phyllis
Bedford, John
Hodge, E Chatterton
Land, Rosina
Mayfield, Julia
HASWELL, C J D
Foster, George
Haswell, Jock
HAUCK, Louise Platt
Landon, Louise
HAUSMAN, Leon Augustus
Poe, Bernand
HAUTZIG, Esther
Rudomin, Esther
HAVERS, Dora
Gift, Theo
HAWKINS, *Sir* Anthony Hope
A H
Hope, Anthony
HAWTON, Hector
Curzon, Virginia
HAYCRAFT, Anna
Ellis, Alice Thomas
HAYDEN, Eric William
Raikes, Robert
HAYES, Catherine E Simpson
Markwell, Mary
Yukon Bill
HAYES, Herbert Edward Elton
Elton, H E
HAYES, Joseph
Arnold, Joseph H
HAYMAN, Sheila
Trix, Mo
HAYNES, John Harold
Wake, G B
HAYNES DIXON, Margaret Rumer
Godden, Rumer

HAYS, Janice Nicholson
Loonie, Janice Hays
HAYS, Peter
Jeffries, Ian
HAZLEWOOD, Rex
Delta
Keneu
HEADLEY, Elizabeth
Allen, Betsy
HEAL, Edith
Page, Eileen
Powers, Margaret
HEALD, Tim
Lancaster, David
HEALEY, Benjamin James
Healey, Ben
Jeffreys, J G
Sturrock, Jeremy
HEARD, Henry Fitzgerald
Heard, Gerald
HEARNE, John *and*
 CARGILL, Morris
Morris, John
HEBERDEN, Mary Violet
Leonard, Charles L
HEBBLETHWAITE, Peter
Myddleton, Robert
HECKELMANN, Charles N
Lawton, Charles
HECTOR, Annie French
Alexander, Mrs
HECTOR, Barbara
Barrie, Hester
HEELIS, Beatrix
Potter, Beatrix
HEGEDUS, Adam de
Garland, Rodney
HEGEMAN, Mary Theodore
Sister Mary Theodore
HEILBRUN, Carolyn
Cross, Amanda
HEILESEN, Eileen De Lynn
De Lynn, Eileen

HEINEY, Donald William
Harris, Macdonald
HEINLEIN, Robert A
Macdonald, Anson
Monroe, Lyle
Riverside, John
Saunders, Caleb
HEISS, John Stanger
Asche, Oscar
HEITNER, Iris
James, Robert
HEMING, Dempster E
Dempster, Guy
HEMING, Jack C W
Western-Holt, J C
HEMINGWAY, Ernest
Hadley, John
HEMPSTEAD, Charles Edward
Charles, Edward
HENDERSON, Archibald
Steele, Erskine
HENDERSON, Donald Landels
Bridgwater, Donald
Landels, D H
Landels, Stephanie
HENDERSON, James Leal
Currier, Jay L
HENDERSON, James Maddock
Danvers, Peter
Jordan, Bryn
HENDERSON, Le Grand
Le Grand
HENDRY, Frank Coutts
Shalimar
HENHAM, Ernest George
Trevena, John
HENISSART, Martha *and*
 LATSIS, Mary J
Dominic, R B
Lathen, Emma
HENKLE, Henrietta
Buckmaster, Henrietta

HENLEY, Art
  Eric, Kenneth
  Jones, Webb
HENSLEY, Sophia Margaret
  Try-Davies, J
HEPBURN, Edith Alice Mary
  Wickham, Anna
HEPBURN, Thomas Nicoll
  Setoun, Gabriel
HEPPELL, Mary
  Clare, Marguerite
  Heppell, Blanche
HEPWORTH, James Michael
  Hepworth, Mike
HERAPATH, Theodora
  Capelle, Anne
HERBERT, *Sir* Alan Patrick
  A P H
  Haddock, Albert
HERBERT, John
  Simple, Peter
HERBERT, Robert Dudley
  Sidney Powys
  Adams, R D
  Alpha Crucis
  R D A
HERMAN, Alan
  Allan, Ted
HERN, Anthony
  Hope, Andrew
HERNDEN, Beryl *and*
  BALFOUR, Eve
  Hearnden, Balfour
HERON-ALLEN, Edward
  Blayre, Christopher
HERRICK, Marvin Theodore *and*
  HUDSON, Hoyt
  Smith, John
HERRON, Elsie Ellerington
  Elsey, J J
HERTZBERG, Nancy
  Keesing, Nancy
HESELTINE, Philip Arnold
  Warlock, Peter

HETHERINGTON, Keith James
  Conway, Keith
  Keith, James
HEUMAN, William
  Kramer, George
HEWETSON, Sara
  Dicant, V L
HEWETT, Anita
  Wellington, Anne
HEWISON, Robert John Petrie
  Petrie, John
HEWITT, Cecil Rolph
  Rolph, C H
HEWITT, Kathleen Douglas
  Martin, Dorothea
HEWSON, Irene Dale
  Ross, Jean
HEYDON, J K
  Trevarthen, Hal P
HEYER, Georgette
  Martin, Stella
HIBBERT, Eleanor Alice Burford
  Burford, Eleanor
  Carr, Philippa
  Ford, Elbur
  Holt, Victoria
  Kellow, Kathleen
  Plaidy, Jean
  Tate, Ellalice
HIBBS, John
  Blyth, John
HICKEN, Una
  Kindler, Asta
HICKEY, Madelyn E
  De Lacy, Louise
  Eastlund, Madelyn
  Hickey, Lyn
  Sullivan, Eric Harrison
HICKS, E L *Bishop of Lincoln*
  Quartus
HICKS, Tyler Gregory
  Murphy, Louis J

HIGGINBOTHAM, Anne D
Higginbotham, Anne T
McIntosh, Ann T
HIGGINS, Charles
Dall, Ian
HIGGINS, Margaret
O'Brien, Bernadette
HIGGINSON, Henry Clive
Theta, Eric Mark
HIGGS, Alec S
Stansbury, Alec
HIGHSMITH, Patricia
Morgan, Claire
HIGSON, Philip John Willoughby
Higson, Philip
Willoughby-Higson, Philip
HILDICK, E W
Hildick, Wallace
HILL, Brian
Magill, Marcus
HILL, Christopher
Holme, K E
HILL, Douglas
Hillman, Martin
HILL, *Mrs* E E
Southern Cross
HILL, Grace
MacDonald, Marcia
HILL, John Alexander
Skeever, Jim
HILL, Margaret
Bennett, Rachel
Thomas, Andrea
HILL, Mavis
Barrister, A
HILL, Pamela
Fiske, Sharon
HILL, Reginald
Morland, Dick
Ruell, Patrick
Underhill, Charles
HILLS, Frances E
Mercer, Frances

HILLSTROM, Joseph
Hill, Joe
HILLYARD, Mary Dorothea
Kellway, Mary D
HILTON, James
Trevor, Glen
HILTON, John Buxton
Greenwood, John
Stanley, Warwick
HINCKLEY, Helen
Jones, Helen
HINCKS, Cyril Malcolm
Coulsdon, John
Dayle, Malcolm
Gee, Osman
Howard, John M
Malcolm, Charles
Malcolm, Ronald
HINES, Dorothea
De Culwen, Dorothea
HIRD, Neville
Meyer, Henry J
HIRST, Gillian
Baxter, Gillian
HISCOCK, Eric
E H
Whitefriar
HISCOCK, Leslie
Marsh, Patrick
HITCHENS, Dolores
Birkley, Dolan
Burke, Noel
Olsen, D B
HITCHIN, Martin
Mewburn, Martin
HOAR, Peter
Amberley, Simon
HOAR, Roger Sherman
Farley, Ralph Milne
HOBSBAWM, E J
Newton, Francis
HODDER, Alfred
Walton, Francis

HODDER-WILLIAMS,
 Christopher
 Brogan, James
HODGE, Horace Emerton
 Hodge, Merton
HODGES, Barbara K
 Cambridge, Elizabeth
HODGES, Doris Marjorie
 Hunt, Charlotte
HOFDORP, Pim
 Geerlink, Will
HOFF, Harry Summerfield
 Cooper, William
HOFFENBERG, Mason
 Drake, Hamilton
 Perez, Faustino
HOFFENBERG, Mason *and*
 SOUTHERN, Terry
 Kenton, Maxwell
HOFFMAN, Anita
 Fettsman, Ann
HOFFMAN, Lee
 York, Georgia
HOGAN, Ray
 Ringold, Clay
HOGAN, Robert Jasper
 Cantrell, Wade B
 Jasper, Bob
HOGARTH, Grace
 Allen, Grace
 Gay, Amelia
HOGARTH, Grace *and*
 NORTON, André Alice
 Weston, Allen
HOGBEN, Lancelot Thomas
 Calvin, Kenneth
HOGBIN, Herbert
 Hogbin, Ian
HOGG, Beth
 Grey, Elizabeth
HOGG, Michael
 Simple, Peter
HOGUE, Wilbur Owings
 Shannon, Carl

HOKE, Helen L
 Sterling, Helen
 Troy, Alan
HOLBECHE, Philippa
 Shore, Philippa
HOLDAWAY, Marjorie F
 Japonica
HOLDAWAY, Neville Aldridge
 Temple-Ellis, N A
HOLDEN, J R
 Joystick
HOLDEN, Raymond
 Peckham, Richard
HOLLAND, Isabelle
 Hunt, Francesca
HOLLAND, James R
 Rand, R H
HOLLAND, Sheila
 Hardy, Laura
 Lamb, Charlotte
 Lancaster, Sheila
HOLLEY, Marietta
 Jemyma
 Josiah Allen's Wife
HOLLIDAY, Joseph
 Bosco, Jack
 Dale, Jack
HOLLIDAY, Robert Cortes
 Hill, Murray
HOLLIS, Christopher
 Somerset, Percy
HOLLOWS, Norman F *and*
 BRADLEY, Ian
 Duplex
HOLMES, Charles Henry
 Adams, Clayton
HOLMES, Daniel Henry
 Henry, Daniel Jr
HOLMES, Joseph Everett
 Holmes, Jay
HOLMES, Llewellyn Perry
 Hardin, Dave
 Stuart, Matt
 Westwood, Perry

61

HOLMES, Peter
  Fenwick, Peter
HOLMSTROM, John Eric
  Gellert, Roger
HOLROYD, Ethel Mary
  Cookridge, John Michael
  Marshall, Beverley
HOLT, Henry
  Hopkins, Stanley
HOLT, Margaret Van Vechten
  Holt, Rackham
HOLZAPFEL, Rudolf Patrick
  Holzapfel, Rudi
  Hurkey, Rooan
  Ward, R Patrick
HOME-GALL, Edward Reginald
  Clive, Clifford
  Dale, Edwin
  Hall, Rupert
  Home-Gall, Reginald
HOMERSHAM, Basil Henry
  Manningham, Basil
HOOD, Torrey
  Bevans, Torre
  Torrey, Marjorie
HOOK, Alfred Samuel
  Colton, A J
HOOK, H Clarke
  Harvey, Ross
HOOKE, Charles W
  Fielding, Howard
HOOKHAM, Margaret Evelyn
  Fonteyn, Margot
HOOVER, Helen
  Price, Jennifer
HOPE, Charles Evelyn Graham
  Pelham, Anthony
HOPE, Essex
  Smith, Essex
HOPE-MONCRIEFF, Ascott Robert
  Hope, Ascott R
HOPE-SIMPSON, Jacynth
  Dudley, Helen

HOPKINS, Kenneth
  Adams, Christopher
  Burney, Anton
  Mannon, Warwick
  Marsh, Paul
  Marshall, Edmund
  Meredith, Arnold
HOPKINS, Robert Sydney
  Rostand, Robert
HOPKINSON, *Sir* Henry Thomas
  Hopkinson, Tom
HOPLEY-WOOLRICH, Cornell George
  Hopley, George
  Irish, William
  Woolrich, Cornell
HOPP, Signe
  Zinken
HOPSON, William L
  Sims, John
HORKAN, Nelle Irwin
  Edwards, Ellen
HORLER, Sydney
  Cavendish, Peter
  Heritage, Martin
  Standish, J O
HORNBERGER, H Richard
  Hooker, Richard
HORNBY, John Wilkinson
  Brent, Calvin
  Grace, Joseph
  Hornby, John
  Summers, Gordon
HORNBY, Lesley
  Twiggy
HORNE, Geoffrey
  North, Gil
HORSFIELD, Richard Edward
  Gaunt, M B
HOSIE, Stanley William
  Stanley, Michael
HOSKEN, Alice Cecil Seymour
  Stanton, Coralie

HOSKEN, Clifford James
  Wheeler
  Keverne, Richard
HOSKIN, Cyril Henry
  Rampa, T Lobsang
HOSKINS, Bob
  Williams, Robert
HOSKINS, Robert
  Corren, Grace
  Gregory, John
  Jennifer, Susan
  Kerr, Michael
HOSSENT, Harry
  Savage, David
HOUGH, Richard Alexander
  Carter, Bruce
  Churchill, Elizabeth
  Stong, Pat
HOUGH, Stanley Bennett
  Gordon, Rex
  Stanley, Bennett
HOUNSFIELD, Joan
  Wheezy
HOUSEMAN, Lorna
  Westall, Lorna
HOVICK, Rose Louise
  Lee, Gypsy Rose
HOWARD, Felicity
  Longfield, Jo
HOWARD, Herbert Edmund
  Philmore, R
HOWARD, Hilda Glynn
  Glynn-Ward, H
  Glynn-Ward, Hilda
HOWARD, James Arch
  Fisher, Laine
HOWARD, Munroe
  St Clair, Philip
HOWARD, Peter;
  FOOT, Michael *and*
  OWEN, Frank
  Cato

HOWARD, Robert E
  Ervin, Patrick
  Taverel, John
  Walser, Sam
  Ward, Robert
HOWARD, Robert West
  Case, Michael
HOWARTH, Pamela
  Barrow, Pamela
HOWARTH, Patrick John
  Fielding
  Francis, C D E
HOWAT, Gerald
  Henderson-Howat, Gerald
HOWE, Doris Kathleen
  Munro, Mary
  Stewart, Kaye
HOWELL, Douglas Nayler
  Hancock, Robert
HOWITT, John Leslie Despard
  Despard, Leslie
HOYT, Edwin Palmer *Jr*
  Martin, Christopher
HUBBARD, Clifford Lionel Barry
  Canis
HUBBARD, Elbert
  Fra Elbertus
HUBBARD, Frank McKinney
  Hubbard, Kin
  Martin, Abe
HUBBARD, LaFayette Ronald
  Elron
  Engelhardt, Frederick
  Esterbrook, Tom
  Hubbard, L Ron
  La Fayette, Rene
  Northrop, *Captain* B A
  Rachen, Kurt von
HUBLER, Richard Gibson
  Gibson, Harry Clark
HUDLESTON, Gilbert Roger
  Pater, Roger
HUDSON, H Lindsay
  Lindsay, H

HUDSON, Hoyt *and*
HERRICK, Marvin Theodore
Smith, John
HUDSON, William Henry
Harford, Henry
HUEFFER, Ford Madox
Ford, Ford Madox
HUFF, Darrell
Hough, Don
Nelson, Chris
West, Mark
HUGGETT, Berthe
Brook, Esther
HUGHES, Ivy
Hay, Catherine
HUGHES, Valerie Anne
Carrington, V
HUGHES, Walter Dudley
Derventio
HUGHES, Walter Llewellyn
Walters, Hugh
HUGHES, William
Northerner
HUGILL, John Anthony
Crawford
Crawford, Anthony
HUGILL, Robert
Gill, Hugh
HULBERT, Joan
Rostron, Primrose
HULL, Richard
Sampson, Richard Henry
HUMM, Martin J
Nations, Opal L
HUMPHREYS, Eliza M J
Rita
HUMPHRIES, Adelaide
Harris, Kathleen
Way, Wayne
West, Token
HUMPHRIES, Barry
Barry
HUMPHRIES, Elsie Mary
Forrester, Mary

HUMPHRIES, Sydney
Vane, Michael
HUMPHRYS, Leslie George
Condray, Bruno
Humphrys, Geoffrey
HUNT, Anna Rebecca Gale
Berwick, Claude
Canadienne
HUNT, E Howard
Baxter, John
Davis, Gordon
Dietrich, Robert
St John, David
HUNT, Katherine Chandler
Nash, Chandler
HUNT-BODE, Gisele
Hunt, Diana
HUNTER, Alfred John
Addiscombe, John
Brenning, L H
Dax, Anthony
Drummond, Anthony
Hunter, Jean
Hunter, John
HUNTER, Bluebell Matilda
Guildford, John
HUNTER, Christine
Hunter, John
Steer, Charlotte
HUNTER, Eileen
Clements, E H
Laura
HUNTER, Elizabeth
Chace, Isobel
HUNTER, William R
Hagen, Brett
HUNTER BLAIR, Pauline *see*
BLAIR, Pauline Hunter
HUNTINGTON, Helen
Lynde, H H
HURLEY, John J
Rafferty, S S

HURLEY, Vic
  Duane, Jim
  Richards, Duane
HURREN, Bernard
  Nott, Barry
HURT, Edwin Franklin
  Franklin, E
HURWOOD, Bernhardt J
  Knight, Mallory
HUSKINSON, Richard King
  King, Richard
HUTCHIN, Kenneth
  Challice, Kenneth
  Family Doctor, A
  Travers, Kenneth
HUTCHINS, Francis Gilman
  Madison, Frank
HUTCHINSON, Barbara Beatrice
  Fearn, Roberta
HUTCHINSON, Juliet Mary Fox
  Phoenice, J
HUTCHINSON, Robert Hare
  Hare, Robert
HUTCHISON, Graham Seton
  Seton, Graham
HUTTON, Andrew Nielson
  Olympic
HUXLEY, Julian Sorrell
  Balbus
  J S H
HUXTABLE, Marjorie
  Dare, Simon
  Stewart, Marjorie
HUYGHUE, Douglas S
  Eugene
HYDE, Edmund Errol Claude
  Rejje, E
HYDE, Lavender Beryl
  Ashe, Elizabeth
HYLAND, Ann
  Ross, Laurence
  Trailrider
HYMERS, Laura M
  West, Laura M

HYNAM, John
  Kippax, John
HYNDMAN, Jane Andrews
  Wyndham, Lee
HYNDMAN, Robert Utley
  Wyndham, Robert
HYNE, Charles John
  Cutcliffe Wright
  Chesney, Weatherby
  Hyne, C J Cutcliffe
  Hyne, Cutcliffe

IAMS, Samuel H
  Iams, Jack
IBBOTT, Arthur Pearson
  Bertram, Arthur
IDELL, Albert Edward
  Rogers, Phillips
INGAMELLS, F G
  Home Guard
INGRAM-MOORE, Erica
  Marsden, June
INGRAMS, Richard *and*
  FANTONI, Barry
  Thribb, E J
INGRAMS, Richard *and*
  OSMOND, Andrew
  Reid, Philip
INHOFE, Susan Eloise
  Hinton, S E
IRISH, Betty M
  Arthur, Elisabeth
  Bell, Nancy
IRVING, Clifford
  Burkholz, Herbert
  Luckless, John
IRVING, John Treat
  Quod, John
IRWIN, Constance
  Frick, C H
ISAACS, Alan
  Valentine, Alec

IVISON, Elizabeth
Towers, Tricia
Wilson, Elizabeth

§ §

*Sam Johnson is hardly a name
for a great writer.*
– George Bernard Shaw

§ §

JACKSON, Ada Acraman
Ajax
JACKSON, Barbara A G S
Seagrave, Barbara Ann Garvey
JACKSON, Caary Paul
Lochions, Colin
Paulson, Jack
JACKSON, Charles Philip
 Castle Kains
Castle, Philip
Harmodius
P C
JACKSON, Kathryn
Hubbard, Joan
JACKSON, Lydia (Jiburtovich)
Fen, Elisaveta
JACOB, Anthony Dillingham
Anthony, Piers
JACOB, Naomi
Gray, Ellington
JACOBS, Charles
Humana, Charles
JACOBS, Helen Hull
Hull, H Braxton
JACOBS, Thomas Curtis Hicks
Carstairs, Kathleen
Curtis, Tom
Dower, Penn
Howard, Helen
Pender, Marilyn
Pendower, Jacques
Penn, Ann

JACOT DE BOLNOD, B L
Jacot, Bernard
JAFFE, Gabriel
Poole, Vivian
JAKES, John
Payne, Alan
Scotland, Jay
JAMES, Charles
Coronet
JAMES, Florence Alice Price
Warden, Florence
JAMES, Godfrey Warden
Broome, Adam
JAMES, J W G
Norham, Gerald
JAMES, Montague Rhodes
M R J
JAMESON, Annie Edith
Buckrose, J E
JAMESON, Storm
Hill, James
Lamb, William
JAMIESON, Kathleen Florence
Janes, Kathleen
Janes, Kathleen F
JANIFER, Laurence M *and*
 GARRETT, Randall
Phillips, Mark
JANNER, Greville
Mitchell, Ewan
JANSEN, Johanna *and*
 CAMPBELL, Margaret
Bayard, Fred
JANVIER, Margaret Thomson
Vandegrift, Margaret
JANVIER, Thomas Allibone
Black, Ivory
JAQUES, Edward Tyrell
Tearle, Christian
JARRETT, Cora
Keene, Faraday
JARVIS, Frederick G H
Gordon, Fritz

JAY, Geraldine
  Halls, Geraldine
  Jay, Charlotte
JAY, Marion
  Spalding, Lucille
JEFFCOATE, *Sir* Thomas
 Norman Arthur
  Jeffcoate, Norman
  Jeffcoate, T N A
JEFFERIES, Greg
  Collins, Geoffrey
JEFFERIES, Ira
  Morris, Ira J
JEFFERY, Graham
  Brother Graham
JEFFERY, Grant
  Turner, Peter Paul
JEFFREY-SMITH, May
  Aunt Maysie
  Thornton, Maimee
JEFFRIES, Bruce Graham
 Montague
  Bourne, Peter
  Graeme, Bruce
  Graeme, David
JEFFRIES, Gay
  Graeme, Linda
JEFFRIES, Roderic Graeme
  Alding, Peter
  Ashford, Jeffrey
  Draper, Hastings
  Graeme, Roderic
  Hastings, Graham
JELLY, George Oliver
  Fosse, Alfred
  Harsch, Hilya
  Jelly, Oliver
JENKINS, Alan Charles
  Bancroft, John
JENKINS, Richard
  Burton, Richard
JENKINS, Sara Lucile
  Sargent, Joan

JENKINS, William Fitzgerald
  Leinster, Murray
JENKS, George Charles
  Lawson, W B
JENNINGS, E C
  Jay
JENNINGS, Hilda *and others*
  Heptagon
JENNINGS, John Edward
  Baldwin, Bates
  Williams, Joel
JENNINGS, Richard
  W M
JEROME, Owen Fox
  Friend, Oscar Jerome
JERVIS, Vera Murdock Stuart
  England, Jane
JEWETT, Sarah Orne
  Eliot, Alice C
JOHN, Owen
  Bourne, John
JOHNS, Walter T
  Neby, Al
JOHNSON, Annabel I *and*
 JOHNSON, Edgar R
  Johnson, A E
JOHNSON, H
  Robertson, Muirhead
JOHNSON, Henry T
  Thomson, Neil
JOHNSON, Lilian Beatrice
  Johnson, Lee
JOHNSON, Marion
  Masson, Georgina
JOHNSON, Nancy Marr
  Marr, Nancy J
JOHNSON, Pamela Hansford *and*
 STEWART, Neil
  Lombard, Nap
JOHNSON, R V
  Johnson, Rob
JOHNSON, Ronald
  Chamberlain, Theodore

JOHNSON, Victor
Bell, John
JOHNSON, Virginia Wales
Cousin Virginia
JOHNSTON, Alexander
Smith, Spartacus
JOHNSTON, George Henry
Shane, Martin
JOHNSTON, Mable Annesley
Marney, Suzanne
JOHNSTON, Norma
St John, Nicole
JOHNSTON, Robert Thomson
Forsyth, R A
JONES, A Miles
Bullingham, Ann
JONES, Alice
John, Alix
JONES, David Robert
Bowie, David
JONES, Edward German
German, Edward
JONES, Frank H
Mentor
JONES, Harry Austin
Jons, Hal
JONES, Jack
Reynolds, Jack
JONES, Judith Anastasia
Maro, Judith
JONES, *Lady* Roderick
Bagnold, Enid
Lady of Quality
JONES, Le Roi
Baraka, Imamu Amiri
JONES, Maynard Benedict
Jones, Nard
JONES, P D
Denham, Peter
JONES, Robert Maynard
Jones, Bobi
Probert, Lowri
Siôn, Mari

JONES, Susan Carleton
Carleton-Milecete
Carleton, S
Milecete, Helen
JONES, Virgil Carrington
Jones, Pat
JORDAN, June
Meyer, June
JORDAN, Robert Furneaux
Player, Robert
JOSCELYN, Archie Lynn
Archer, A A
Cody, A R
Cody, Al
Holt, Tex
McKenna, Evelyn
Westland, Lynn
JOSEPH, James Herz
Adams, Lowell
JOSKE, Neville *and*
  GOYDER, Margot
Neville, Margot
JOSLIN, Sesyle
Gibson, Josephine
Kirtland, G B
JOURDAIN, Eleanor F
Lamont, Frances
JOYCE, James
Chanel
JUDD, Frederick
Lester-Rands, A
JUDD, Harrison
Garrett, Truman
JUDSON, Jeanne
Hancock, Frances Deane
JUNOR, *Sir* John
J J

KAGEY, Rudolf
Steel, Kurt
KAHANE, Jack
Barr, Cecil
Carr, Basil

KAHN, H S
Sackerman, Henry
KALER, James Otis
Otis, James
KALISCH, A
Crescendo
KAMPF, Harold Bertram
Kaye, Harold B
KANE, Frank
Boyd, Frank
KANE, Henry
McCall, Anthony
KAPLAN, Jean Caryl
Caryl, Jean
KAPP, Yvonne
Cloud, Yvonne
KARIG, Walter
Duncan, Julia K
Ferris, James Cody
Patrick, Keats
KARP, David
Singer, Adam
Ware, Wallace
KATCHAMAKOFF, Atanas
Shannon, Monica
KATZ, Menke
Hiat, Elchik
KATZIN, Olga
Sagittarius
KAUFMAN, Louis
Keller, Dan
KAY, Ernest
Ludlow, George
Random, Alan
KAY, Frederic George
Gee, Kenneth F
Howard, George
KAYE, Barrington
Kaye, Tom
KAYE, Mary Margaret
Hamilton, Mollie
KAYSER, Ronal
Clark, Dale

KEANE, Mary Nesta
Farrell, M J
. Keane, Molly
KEATING, Lawrence Alfred
Bassett, John Keith
Thomas, H C
KEATLEY, Sheila
Avon, Margaret
KECK, Maud *and*
ORBISON, Roy
Orbison, Keck
KEDDIE, Margaret Manson
Auntie Margaret
KEEGAN, Mary Constance
Heathcott, Mary
Merlin, Christina
Raymond, Mary
KEELE, Kenneth David
Cassils, Peter
KEELING, Jill Annette
Shaw, Jill A
KEEVILL, Henry John
Allison, Clay
Alvord, Burt
Bonney, Bill
Earp, Virgil
Harding, Wes
McLowery, Frank
Mossman, Burt
Reno, Mark
Ringo, Johnny
KELLEY, Audrey *and*
ROOS, William
Roos, Kelley
KELLIHER, Dan T *and*
SECRIST, W G
Secrist, Kelliher
KELLY, Elizabeth
Kellier, Elizabeth
Stevenson, Christine
KELLY, Harold Ernest
Carson, Lance
Glinto, Darcy
Toler, Buck

KELLY, Mrs T
Tennant, Carrie
KELLY, Tim
Bibolet, R H
KELTON, Elmer
Hawk, Alex
McElroy, Lee
KEMPF, Pat
Hunter, Pat
KEMPINSKI, Tom
Thomas, Gerrard
KENAFICK, Joseph
Kennedy, James
KENDALL, Carlton Waldo
Ladnek, Odlaw
KENDRICK, Baynard Hardwick
Hayward, Richard
KENNEDY, John McFarland
Verdad, S
KENNEDY, H A
H A K
KENNEDY, Joseph Charles
Kennedy, X J
KENNINGTON, Gilbert Alan
Grant, Alan
Kennington, Alan
KENSDALE, W E N
Norwood, Elliott
KENT, Arthur
Boswell, James
Bradwell, James
Du Bois, M
Granados, Paul
Karol, Alexander
Stamper, Alex
Vane, Brett
KENT, Ellen Louisa Margaret
Margaret
KENT, Louise Andrews
Tempest, Theresa
KENTON, Warren
Zev ben Shimon Halevi
KENWARD, Betty
Jennifer

KENYON, Fred
Cumberland, Gerald
KENYON, Michael
Forbes, Daniel
KEOGH, M J
Gumsucker
KERMOND, Evelyn Carolyn
Conway
Conway, E Carolyn
KERNER, Fred
Kerr, Frederick
Thaler, M N
KERR, D
Colt, Russ
KERR, Doris Boake
Boake, Capel
KERR, Graham
Galloping Gourmet, The
KERR, James Lennox
Dawlish, Peter
Kerr, Lennox
KERSHAW, John H D
D'Allenger, Hugh
KETCHUM, Philip
Saunders, Carl McK
KETTLE, Jocelyn
Kettle, Pamela
KEVIN, John William
Ferres, Arthur
KIDD, Walter E
Pendleton, Conrad
KIEFER, Warren *and*
MIDDLETON, Harry
Kiefer, Middleton
KIENZLE, Raymond N
Ray, Nicholas
KIMBRO, John
Ashton, Ann
Bramwell, Charlotte
Kimbro, Jean
Kimbrough, Katheryn
KING, Albert
Albion, Ken
Bannon, Mark

Brennan, Walt	**KING, Francis**
Brent, Catherine	Cauldwell, Frank
Bronson, Wade	**KING, Frank**
Cleveland, Jim	Conrad, Clive
Conrad, Paul	**KING, James Clifford**
Cooper, Craig	Fry, Pete
Creedi, Joel	King, Clifford
Dallas, Steve	**KING, John**
Doan, Reece	Boswell, John
Driscoll, Eli	Kildare, John
Ford, Wallace	**KING, Kay**
Foreman, Lee	Holt, Elizabeth
Foster, Evan	**KING-HALL, Stephen**
Gibson, Floyd	Etienne
Gifford, Matt	**KINGSLEY, Mary**
Girty, Simon	Malet, Lucas
Hammond, Brad	**KIRBY, Derek Amos**
Harlan, Ross	Ladwick, Marty
Harmon, Gil	**KIRK, Richard Edmund**
Hoffman, Art	Church, Jeffrey
Holland, Tom	**KIRKHAM, Nellie**
Howell, Scott	Myatt, Nellie
Hoyt, Nelson	**KIRKPATRICK, *Mrs* Helen**
Kane, Mark	Gemmill
Kelsey, Janice	**KIRKUP, James**
Kimber, Lee	Falconer, James
King, Ames	James, Andrew
King, Berta	Summerforest, Ivy B
King, Christopher	Terahata, Jun
Mason, Carl	Tsuyuki Shigeru
Muller, Paul	**KIRKWOOD, Joyce**
Ogden, Clint	Corlett, Joyce I
Owen, Ray	**KIRWAN, Molly**
Prender, Bart	Morrow, Charlotte
Ripley, Alvin	**KIRWAN-WARD, Bernard**
Santee, Walt	Ward, Kirwan
Scott, Grover	**KITCHIN, F H**
Shelby, Cole	Copplestone, Bennet
Taggart, Dean	**KLASS, Philip**
Tyler, Ellis	Tenn, William
Waldron, Simon	**KLEIN, Grace *and***
Wallace, Agnes	**COOPER, Mae Klein**
Wetzel, Lewis	Farewell, Nina
Yarbo, Steve	

KLEINHAUS, Theodore John
Littlejohn, Jon R
KNAPP, Clarence
Glutz, Ambrose
KNIGHT, Bernard
Picton, Bernard
KNIGHT, Eric
Hallas, Richard
KNIGHT, Francis Edgar
Knight, Frank
Salter, Cedric
KNIGHT, Kathleen Moore
Amos, Alan
KNIGHTS, Leslie
Leslie, Val
KNIPE, Emilie
Benson, Thérèse
KNIPSCHEER, James M W
Fox, James M
Holmes, Grant
KNOTT, William Cecil
Carol, Bill J
Evans, Tabor
Knott, Bill
Knott, Will C
St Giraud
Smith, Bryan
KNOTT, William Kilborn
Knott, Bill
KNOWLES, Mabel Winifred
Wynne, May
KNOWLTON, Edward Rogers
Rogers, Kerk
KNOWLTON, Winthrop *and*
GOODMAN, George Jerome
Goodman, Winthrop
KNOX, E V
Evoe
KNOX, William
Kirk, Michael
Knox, Bill
Macleod, Robert
Webster, Noah

KNUDSON, Margrethe
Knudson, Greta
KOEFED-NIELSEN, Carl
Nielsen, Koef
KOESTLER, Arthur
Costler, *Dr* A
KOFFLER, Camilla
Ylla
KOHLS, Olive N Allen
Allen, Dixie
KONINGSBERGER, Hans
Koning, Hans
KOONTZ, Dean R
Axton, David
Coffey, Brian
Dwyer, K R
KORMENDI, Ferenc
Julian, Peter
KORNBLUTH, Cyril M
Corwin, Cecil
Park, Jordan
KORNBLUTH, Cyril M *and*
GROSSMAN, Judith
Judd, Cyril
KORNBLUTH, Cyril M *and*
POHL, Frederick
Gottesman, S D
KORTNER, Peter
Hofer, Peter
KORZENIOWSKI, Jessie
Conrad, Jessie
**KORZENIOWSKI, Teodor Josef
Konrad**
Conrad, Joseph
KOSINSKI, Jerzy
Novak, Joseph
KOUYOUMDJIAN, Dikran
Arlen, Michael
KOVAR, Edith May
Lowe, Edith
KRAENZEL, Margaret Powell
Blue, Wallace
KRASNEY, Samuel A
Curzon, Sam

KRAUS, Robert
  Hippopotamus, Eugene H
KRECHNIAK, Joseph Marshall
  Marshall, Joseph
KREINER, George
  Bouverie
KRISHNAMURTI, Jiddu
  Alcyone
KRONMILLER, Hildegarde
  Lawrence, Hilda
KUBIS, Patricia Lou
  Scott, Casey
KULSKI, W W
  Coole, W W
  Knight-Patterson, W M
KUMMER, Frederick Arnold
  Fredericks, Arnold
KURLAND, Michael
  Plum, Jennifer
KURNITZ, Harry
  Page, Marco
KUSKIN, Karla Seidman
  Charles, Nicholas
KUTTNER, Henry
  Edmonds, Paul
  Gardner, Noel
  Garth, Will
  Hammond, Keith
  Hastings, Hudson
  Horn, Peter
  Kenyon, Robert O
  Liddell, C H
  Morgan, Scott
  Stoddard, Charles
KUTTNER, Henry *and*
BARNES, Arthur
  Kent, Kelvin
KUTTNER, Henry *and/or*
MOORE, C L
  O'Donnell, Lawrence
  Padgett, Lewis
KYLE, Duncan
  Meldrum, James

LACOSTE, Guy R *and*
BINGHAM, E A
  Berton, Guy
LA SPINA, Fanny Greye (Bragg)
  La Spina, Greye
  Putnam, Isra
LAFFEATY, Christina
  Carstens, Netta
  Fortina, Martha
LAFFIN, John
  Dekker, Carl
  Napier, Mark
  Sabre, Dirk
LAIDLER, Graham
  Pont
LAKE, Joe Barry
  Barry, Joe
LAKE, Kenneth Robert
  Boyer, Robert
  King, Arthur
  Market Man
  Mentor
  Roberts, Ken
  Soutter, Fred
  Xeno
LAKRITZ, Esther
  Collingswood, Frederick
  Marion, S T
LAMB, Antonia
  Hellerlamb, Toni
LAMB, Elizabeth Searle
  Mitchell, K L
LAMB, Geoffrey Frederick
  Balaam
LAMB, Mary Montgomerie *see*
CURRIE, *Lady*
LAMBERT, Derek
  Falkirk, Richard
LAMBERT, Eric
  Brennan, Frank
  Kay, George
LAMBERT, Hubert Steel
  Marle, T B

LAMBERT, Leslie Harrison
  Alan, A J
LAMBOT, Isobel Mary
  Ingham, Daniel
  Turner, Mary
LAMBURN, John Battersby
  Crompton
  Crompton, John
LAMBURN, Richmal Crompton
  Crompton, Richmal
L'AMOUR, Louis
  Burns, Tex
LAMPMAN, Evelyn
  Bronson, Lynn
LANDE, Lawrence Montague *and*
  GREENWOOD, Thomas
  Verval, Alain
LANDELLS, Anne
  Sibley, Lee
LANDELLS, Richard
  Baron, Paul
  Dryden, Keith
  Gaunt, Richard
  Lanzol, Cesare
  Pelham, Randolph
LANDESMAN, Irving Ned
  Landesman, Jay
LANDON, Melville de Lancy
  Lan
  Perkins, Eli
LANDWIRTH, Heinz
  Lind, Jakov
LANE, Kenneth Westmacott
  West, Keith
LANE, *Sir* Ralph Norman
  Angell
  Angell, Norman
LANE, Yoti
  Mayo, Mark
LANES, Selma G
  Gordon, Selma
LANGBEHN, Theo
  Lang, Theo
  Piper, Peter

LANGDON, John
  Gannold, John
LANGDON-DAVIES, John
  James, John
  Nada, John
  Stanhope, John
LANGE, John Frederick
  Norman, John
LANGLEY, Sarah
  Langley, Lee
LANGMAID, Kenneth Joseph
  Robb
  Graham, Peter
  Laing, Kenneth
LANGNER, Lawrence
  Child, Alan
LANIGAN, Richard
  Ex-Journalist
LARBALESTIER, Phillip George
  Archer, G Scott
LARCOMBE, Jennifer Geraldine
  Rees, J Larcombe
LARIAR, Lawrence
  Knight, Adam
  Stark, Michael
LARKIN, Rochelle
  Fairfield, Darrell
LARKINS, William
  Long, Gerry
LARRALDE, Romulo
  Brent, Romney
LASCHEVER, Barnett D
  Barnett, L David
LASH, William Quinlan
  Quinlan, William
LASKI, Marghanita
  Russell, Sarah
LASKY, Jesse L
  Love, David
  Smeed, Frances
LASSALLE, Caroline
  Cave, Emma

LATHAM, Alison *and*
 LATHAM, Esther
 Latham, Murray
LATHAM, Jean Lee
 Gard, Janice
 Lee, Julian
LATHROP, Lorin Andrews
 Gambier, Kenyon
LATIMER, Jonathan
 Coffin, Peter
LATSIS, Mary J *and*
 HENISSART, Martha
 Dominic, R B
 Lathen, Emma
LAUGHLIN, Virginia Carli
 Clarke, John
 Laklan, Carli
LAURENCE, Frances Elsie
 Field, Christine
LAVENDER, David Sievert
 Catlin, Ralph
LAVER, James
 Reval, Jacques
LAVRENCIC, Karl
 Sylvester, Anthony
LAW, Michael
 Kreuzenau, Michael
LAWLOR, Patrick
 Penn, Christopher
LAWRENCE, D H
 Davison, Lawrence H
LAWRENCE, Dulcie
 Hamilton, Judith
 Mace, Margaret
LAWRENCE, Elizabeth
 Bradburne, E S
LAWRENCE, James Duncan
 Lancer, Jack
LAWRENCE, T E
 C D
 C J G
 J C
 Ross, J H
 Shaw, T E

LAWSON, Alfred
 Torroll, G D
LAZARUS, Marguerite
 Gilbert, Anna
LAZENBY, Norman
 Norton, Jed
LAZEROWITZ, Alice Ambrose
 Ambrose, Alice
LE GALLIENNE, Richard
 Logroller
LE RICHE, P J
 Kish
LE ROI, David de Roche
 Roche, John
LEAF, Munro
 Calvert, John
 Mun
LEDERER, Esther Pauline
 Landers, Ann
LEE, Austin
 Austwick, John
 Callender, Julian
LEE, Henry David Cook
 Parios
LEE, Manfred B *and*
 DANNAY, Frederic
 Queen, Ellery
 Ross, Barnaby
LEE, Manning de Villeneuve
 Hatch, Robert
LEE, Marion Van Der Verr
 Lee, Babs
LEE, Maureen
 Northe, Maggie
LEE, Norman
 Armstrong, Raymond
 Corrigan, Mark
 Hobart, Robertson
LEE, Polly Jae
 Lee, Jae Gardiner
LEE, Wayne C
 Sheldon, Lee

LEE HOWARD, L A
Howard, Leigh
Krislov, Alexander
LEE-RICHARDSON, James
Dunne, Desmond
LEEMING, Jill
Chaney, Jill
LEFFINGWELL, Albert
Chambers, Dana
Jackson, Giles
LEGMAN, George Alexander
De La Glannege, Roger-Maxe
Legman, G
LEHMAN, Paul Evan
Evan, Paul
LEHMANN, R C
Toil, Cunnin
LEHNUS, Opal Hull
Hull, Opal I
LEHRBURGER, Egon
Larsen, Egon
LEIBER, Fritz
Lathrop, Francis
LEISK, David Johnson
Johnson, Crockett
LEISY, James Franklin
Lynn, Frank
LEITE, George Thurston *and*
SCOTT, Jody
Scott, Thurston
LEMIEUX, Kenneth
Orvis, Kenneth
LEMMON, Laura Lee
Wilson, Lee
LENANTON, *Lady*
Lenanton, C
Oman, Carola
LENGYEL, Cornel Adam
Adam, Cornel
LENT, Blair
Small, Ernest
LEON, Henry Cecil
Cecil, Henry
Maxwell, Clifford

LEONARD, John
Cyclops
LEONARD, Lionel Frederick
Lonsdale, Frederick
LESLEY, Peter
Allen, John W Jr
Lesley, J P
LESLIE, Cecilie
Macadam, Eve
LESLIE, Josephine A C
Dick, R A
LESLIE, *Sir* Shane
Ionicos, Ion
LESSER, Milton
Frazer, Andrew
Marlowe, Stephen
Ridgway, Jason
Thames, C H
L'ESTRANGE, C James *and*
ELY, George Herbert
Strang, Herbert
LESSING, Doris
Somers, Jane
LEVIN, Abraham
George, G S
LEVIN, Bernard
Battle, Felix
Cherryman, A E
Taper
LEVI, Peter
Tigar, Chad
LEVINE, Philip
Poe, Edgar
LEVINE, William
Levinrew, Will
LEVY, Julia Ethel
Juliet
LEVY, Newman
Flaccus
LEWIN, Michael Sultan
Furber, Douglas
LEWING, Anthony
Bannerman, Mark

LEWIS, Alfred Henry
  Quin, Dan
LEWIS, Charles Bertrand
  Quad, M
LEWIS, Clifford *and*
  LEWIS, Judith Mary
  Berrisford, Judith
LEWIS, Clive Staples
  Hamilton, Clive
LEWIS, J R
  Lewis, Roy
  Springfield, David
LEWIS, Lesley
  Lawrence, Lesley
LEWIS, Lydia T
  Lesbia
LEWIS, Mary Christianna
  Ashe, Mary Ann
  Berrisford, Mary
  Brand, Christianna
  Jones, Annabel
  Roland, Mary
  Thompson, China
LEWIS, Mildred
  De Witt, James
LEXAU, Joan M
  Nodset, Joan L
LEY, Willy
  Willey, Robert
LEYLAND, Eric
  Cleaver, Denis
  Felmersham, Michael
  Fielding, Anthony
  Grant, Nesta
  Little, Sylvia
  Lodge, John
  Patterson, Duke
  Strangeway, Mark
  Tarrant, Elizabeth
  Wyatt, Escott
L'HOTELLIER, Alf
  Outlaw, The
LIDDELOW, Marjorie Joan
  Law, Marjorie J

LIDDY, James
  Lynch, Brian
  O'Connor, Liam
  Reeves, Daniel
LIEBERS, Arthur
  Love, Arthur
LIEBLER, Jean Mayer
  Mather, Virginia
LIGHTHALL, William Douw
  Chateauclair, Wilfred
LIGHTNER, A M
  Hopf, Alice L
LILIENTHAL, David *Jr*
  Ely, David
LILLEY, Peter *and*
  STANSFIELD, Anthony
  Buckingham, Bruce
LILLIE, Gordon W
  Pawnee Bill
LINDARS, Frederick C
  Lindars, Barnabas
LINDHOLM, Anna Chandler
  Fay, Dorothy
LINDSAY, Barbara *and*
  STERNE, E G
  James, Josephine
LINDSAY, Jack
  Meadows, Peter
  Preston, Richard
LINDSAY, Kathleen
  Cameron, Margaret
  Richmond, Mary
LINDSAY, Maurice
  Brock, Gavin
LINDSAY, Rachel
  Leigh, Roberta
  Scott, Janey
LINEBARGER, Paul
  Smith, Cordwainer
LININGTON, Elizabeth
  Blaisdell, Anne
  Egan, Lesley
  O'Neill, Egan
  Shannon, Dell

LIPKIND, William
Will
LIPPINCOTT, Sara Jane
Greenwood, Grace
LIPSCHITZ, *Rabbi* Chaim
Yerushalmi, Chaim
LIST, Ilka Katherine
Macduff, Ilka
Obolensky, Ilka
LITTLE, Cecile Enid
Ashmore, Jane
LITTLE, Constance *and*
LITTLE, Gwenyth
Little, Conyth
LITTLE, D F
Wessex, Martin
LITTLE, Gwenyth *and*
LITTLE, Constance
Little, Conyth
LITTLE, Malcolm
Malcolm X
LIU, Wu-chi
Hsia, Hsiao
LIVERTON, Joan
Medhurst, Joan
LIVINGSTON, A D
Delano, Al
LIVINGSTONE, Harrison Edward
Fairfield, John
LLOYD, Richard Dafydd Vivian Llewellyn
Llewellyn, Richard
LOADER, William
Nash, Daniel
LOBAUGH, Elma K
Lowe, Kenneth
LOBLEY, Robert
Nong
LOCK, Arnold Charles Cooper
Cooper, Charles
LOCKHART, Arthur John
Pastor Felix

LOCKIE, Isobel
Knight, Isobel
LOCKRIDGE, Frances Louise *and*
LOCKRIDGE, Richard
Richards, Francis
LOCKWOOD, Frank
Circumlibra
LOCKYER, Roger Walter
Francis, Philip
LOEWENGARD, Heidi H F
Albrand, Martha
Holland, Katrin
Lambert, Christine
LOFTS, Norah
Astley, Juliet
Curtis, Peter
LOGAN, Olive
Chroniqueuse
LOGUE, Christopher
Vicarion, *Count* Palmiro
LOMBINO, Salvatore A
Cannon, Curt
Collins, Hunt
Hannon, Ezra
Hunter, Evan
McBain, Ed
Marsten, Richard
LOMER, Sydney Frederick McIllree
Oswald, Sydney
LOMNICKA, Josephine
Lom, Josephine
LONG, Amelia
Laing, Patrick
Reynolds, Adrian
Reynolds, Peter
LONG, Amelia *and*
McHUGH, Edna
Coxe, Kathleen Buddington
LONG, Gladys
Beaton, Jane
LONG, Leonard
Long, Shirley

LONG, Lily Augusta
Doubleday, Roman
LONG, Lois
Lipstick
LONGRIGG, Roger Erskine
Black, Laura
Drummond, Ivor
Erskine, Rosalind
LONGSTREET, Stephen
Burton, Thomas
Haggard, Paul
Ormsbee, David
Weiner, Henri
LOOKER, Samuel Joseph
Game Cock
Pundit, Ephraim
Wade, Thomas
LOOMIS, Noel Miller
Allison, Sam
Miller, Benj
Miller, Frank
Water, Silas
LORD, Doreen Mildred Douglas
Ireland, Doreen
Lord, Douglas
LORD, Phillips H
Parker, Seth
LORD, William Wilberforce
Langstaff, Tristram
LORDE, Andre Geraldin
Domini, Rey
LORDING, Rowland Edward
Tiveychoc, A
LORENZ, Frederic
Holden, Larry
LORIMER, Maxwell
Wall, Max
LORING, Emilie
Story, Josephine
LOTHROP, Harriet Mulford
Sidney, Margaret
LOTTICH, Kenneth
Conrad, Kenneth

LOUISE, *Princess, Duchess of Argyll*
Fontenoy, Myra
LOVESEY, Peter
Lear, Peter
LOW, Lois
Cass, Zoë
Low, Dorothy Mackie
Paxton, Lois
LOWELL, Jan *and*
LOWELL, Robert
Lowell, J R
LOWNDES, Marie Adelaide Belloc
Curtin, Philip
LOWRY, Joan
Catlow, Joanna
LOWTHER, Armstrong John
Laird
LU KUAN YU
Luk, Charles
LUARD, William Blaine
Luard, L
LUCAS, Beryl Llewellyn
Llewellyn
LUCAS, E V
E V L
V V V
LUCAS, Edgar Ernest
Goodson, Bill
LUCCHETTI, Anthony
Prescott, John
LUCCOCK, Halford Edward
Stylites, Simeon
LUCEY, James D
James, Matthew
Pierce, Matthew
LUCIE-SMITH, Edward
Kershaw, Peter
LUDLUM, Robert
Ryder, Jonathan
Shepherd, Michael
LUMSDEN, Jean
Swift, Rachelle

LUNN, *Sir* Arnold
  Croft, Sutton
  Rubicon
LUNN, Hugh Kingsmill
  Kingsmill, Hugh
LUTYENS, Mary
  Wyndham, Esther
LUTZ, Giles A
  Chaffin, James B
  Everett, Wade
  Hawk, Alex
  Ingram, Hunter
  Sullivan, Reese
  Thompson, Gene
LUXMORE, Robert
  Fesenmeyer
LYALL, James Robert
  Patroclus
LYBURN, *Dr* Eric Frederic
  St John
  Doctor Futuer
  Toller
LYLE-SMYTHE, Alan
  Caillou, Alan
LYND, Robert
  Y Y
LYNDS, Dennis
  Arden, William
  Carter, Nick
  Collins, Michael
  Crowe, John
  Dekker, Carl
  Grant, Maxwell
  Sadler, Mark
LYNE, Charles
  De Castro, Lyne
LYNES, Daisy Elfreda
  Glyn-Forest, D
LYNN, Elwyn
  Augustus
LYNNE, James Broom
  Quartermain, James
LYONS, John Benignus
  Fitzwilliam, Michael

LYTLE, *Mrs* W J A
  Berney, Beryl
LYTTLETON, Edith Joan
  Lancaster, G B

§ §

How public, like a frog
To tell your name the livelong day
To an admiring bog.
– Emily Dickinson. Collected
poems

§ §

MABBOTT, Thomas O
  Hunter, M O
McADAM, Constance
  Clyde, Constance
MACALLISTER, Alister
  Brock, Lynn
  Wharton, Anthony
McALMON, Robert
  Urquhart, Guy
MACARTHUR, David Wilson
  Wilson, David
MACAULAY, Fannie Caldwell
  Little, Frances
MACBETH, Madge Hamilton
  Dill, W S
  Knox, Gilbert
McBRIDE, Robert Medill
  Medill, Robert
  Reid, Marshall
McCAIG, Robert Jesse
  Engren, Edith
McCALL, Virginia
  Nielson, Virginia
McCARROLL, James
  Dubh, Scian
MACCARTHY, *Sir* Desmond
  Hawk, Affable

McCARTHY, Shaun
  Callas, Theo
  Cory, Desmond
McCARTNEY, R J
  Scott, Bruce
McCHESNEY, Mary F
  Rayter, Joe
McCLINTOCK, Marshall
  Duncan, Gregory
  Marshall, Douglas
  Starret, William
McCLOY, Helen
  Clarkson, Helen
MACCLURE, Victor
  Craig, Peter
McCONNELL, James Douglas
Rutherford
  Rutherford, Douglas
McCONNELL, James Douglas
Rutherford *and*
DURBRIDGE, Francis
  Temple, Paul
McCORMICK, Donald
  Deacon, Richard
McCORMICK, Wilfred
  Allison, Rand
  Dunlap, Lon
McCORQUODALE, Barbara
Hamilton
  Cartland, Barbara
McCUE, Lillian Bueno
  De la Torre, Lillian
  De la Torre-Bueno, Lillian
McCULLEY, Johnston
  Brien, Raley
  McAlpin, Grant
McCULLOCH, Derek
  Uncle Mac
McCULLOCH, Joseph
  Michaelhouse, John
McCUTCHAN, Philip D
  Galway, Robert Conington
  MacNeil, Duncan
  Wigg, T I G

McCUTCHEON, Hugh
  Davie-Martin, Hugh
McDERMOTT, John Richard
  Ryan, J M
McDONALD, Margaret Josephine
  McDonald, Jo
MACDONALD, Philip
  Lawless, Anthony
  Porlock, Martin
MACDONALD, Philip *and*
MACDONALD, Ronald
  Fleming, Oliver
MACDONALD, Susanne
  MacFarland, Anne
MACDONALD, Thomas Douglas
  MacColla, Fionn
MACDONNELL, A G
  Cameron, John
  Gordon, Neil
MACDONNELL, James Edmond
  Macnell, James
McDOUGALL, E Jean Taylor
  Rolyat, Jane
McDOUGALL, Margaret
  Norah
McELFRESH, Adeline
  Cleveland, John
  Scott, Jane
  Wesley, Elizabeth
McEVOY, Marjorie
  Bond, Gillian
  Harte, Marjorie
McEWEN, Jessie Evelyn
  Fisher, Agnes
McFARLANE, David
  Tyson, Teilo
MACFARLANE, George Gordon
  Miller, Patrick
McFAUL, Frances Elizabeth
  Grand, Sarah
McGARRY, William Rutledge
  Smythe, James P

McGAUGHY, Dudley Dean
  Dean, Dudley
  Owen, Dean
McGEOGH, Andrew
  Paul, Adrian
McGIVERN, William Peter
  Peters, Bill
MACGLASHAN, John
  Glashan, John
McGLOIN, Joseph Thaddeus
  O'Finn, Thaddeus
MACGREGOR, James Murdoch
  McIntosh, J T
MACGREGOR, Mary Esther
  Keith, Marian
MACGREGOR, Miriam
  Pegden, Helen
McGREW, Julia *and*
 FENN, Caroline K
  McGrew, Fenn
McGUINNESS, Bernard
  McGuinness, Brian
McHARGUE, Georgess
  Chase, Alice
  Usher, Margo Scegge
MACHEN, Arthur
  Siluriensis, Leolinus
MACHLIN, Milton
  Jason, William
  Roberts, McLean
McHUGH, Edna *and*
 LONG, Amelia
  Coxe, Kathleen Buddington
McILWAIN, David
  Maine, Charles Eric
  Rayner, Richard
  Wade, Robert
McILWRAITH, Jean Newton
  Forsyth, Jean
McILWRAITH, Maureen Mollie
 Hunter
  Hunter, Mollie
MACINTOSH, Joan
  Blaike, Avona

McINTOSH, Kinn Hamilton
  Aird, Catherine
MACINTYRE, John
  Brandane, John
MACINTYRE, John Thomas
  O'Neil, Kerry
MACK, Elsie Frances
  Moore, Frances Sarah
MACK, J C O
  Callum Beg
MACKAY, Fulton
  MacBride, Aeneas
MACKAY, James Alexander
  Angus, Ian
  Finlay, William
  Garden, Bruce
  Whittington, Peter
MACKAY, Lewis
  Matheson, Hugh
MACKAY, Louis Alexander
  Smalacombe, John
MACKAY, Minnie
  Corelli, Marie
MACKENZIE, *Sir* Edward
  Portsea
MACKENZIE, Joan
  Finnigan, Joan
MACKENZIE, Tina;
 HARVEY, Jean *and*
 BENNETT, Laura
  Harlowe, Justine
MACKEOWN, N R
  Giles, Norman
MACKESY, Leonora Dorothy
 Rivers
  Starr, Leonora
McKIBBIN, *Reverend* Archibald
  Cloie, Mack
McKIBBON, John
  Probyn, Elise
MACKIE, Albert David
  Macnib
McKILLOP, Norman
  Beg, Toram

MACKINLAY, Lelia A S
  Grey, Brenda
MACKINNON, Charles Roy
  Conte, Charles
  Donald, Vivian
  Macalpin, Rory
  Montrose, Graham
  Rose, Hilary
  Stuart, Charles
  Torr, Iain
MACKINTOSH, Elizabeth
  Daviot, Gordon
  Tey, Josephine
McLACHLAN, Dan
  McMud, Dok
MACLAREN, James Paterson
  Medicus
McLAREN, Moray David Shaw
  Murray, Michael
MACLEAN, Alistair
  Stuart, Ian
McLEAN, Kathryn
  Forbes, Kathryn
MACLEOD, Charlotte
  Craig, Alisa
  Hughes, Matilda
MACLEOD, Ellen
  Anderson, Ella
MACLEOD, Jean Sutherland
  Airlie, Catherine
MACLEOD, Joseph Todd
  Gordon
  Drinan, Adam
MACLEOD, Robert
  Knox, Bill
MACLEOD-SMITH, D
  Mariner, David
MACMANUS, Anna Johnston
  Carbery, Ethna
McMEEKIN, Isabel *and*
  CLARK, Dorothy
  McMeekin, Clark
McMILLAN, Donald
  Stuart, John Roy

MACMILLAN, Douglas
  Cary, D M
McMILLAN, James
  Coriolanus
McMORDIE, John Andrew
  Shan
McMORDIE, Taber
  Channing, Peter
MACMULLAN, Charles W
  Kirkpatrick
  Munro, C K
McNALLY, Mary Elizabeth
  O'Brien, Deirdre
McNAMARA, Barbara Willard
  O'Conner, Elizabeth
McNAMARA, Lena
  Mack, Evalina
McNAUGHT, Ann Boyce
  Gilmour, Ann
MACNEICE, Louis
  Malone, Louis
McNEILE, H C
  Sapper
McNEILLIE, John
  Niall, Ian
McNEILLY, Wilfred
  Ballinger, W A
McNEILLY, Wilfred *and*
  BAKER, William Howard
  Ballinger, W A
McPHEE, Hugh
  Phee, Hugh
MACPHERSON, A D L
  Seale, Sara
MACPHERSON, Jessie
  Kennie, Jessie
MACPHERSON, Thomas George
  Parsons, Tom
MACQUARRIE, Hector
  Cameron, Hector
MACQUEEN, James William
  Edwards, James G
MACRORY, Patrick
  Greer, Patrick

83

McSHANE, Mark
  Lovell, Marc
MACVEAN, Phyllis
  Greaves, Gillian
  Hambledon, Phyllis
MADDISON, Angela Mary
  Banner, Angela
MAGEE, James
  Taylor, John
MAGEE, William Kirkpatrick
  Eglinton, John
MAGENHEIMER, Cathryn Cecile
  Magenheimer, Kay
MAGRAW, Beatrice
  Padeson, Mary
MAGRILL, David S
  Dalheath, David
MAGUIRE, Robert A J
  Taaffe, Robert
MAHONEY, David
  Allen, Dave
MAHONEY, Elizabeth
  Mara, Thalia
MAIDEN, Cecil
  Cecil, Edward
MAINPRIZE, Don
  Rock, Richard
MAINWARING, Daniel
  Homes, Geoffrey
MAIR, George Brown
  Bok, Kooshti
  Macdouall, Robertson
MAIZEL, Clarice Louise
  Maizel, Leah
MAJOR, Charles
  Caskoden, *Sir* Edwin
MALERICH, Edward P
  Easton, Edward
MALLALIEU, J P W
  Pied Piper, The
MALLESON, Lucy
  Gilbert, Anthony
  Meredith, Anne

MALLETTE, Gertrude Ethel
  Gregg, Alan
MALONEY, Ralph Liston
  Liston, Jack
MALZBERG, Barry Norman
  Barry, Mike
  Dumas, Claudine
  Johnson, Mel
  Mason, Lee W
  Natale, Francine de
  O'Donnell, K M
  Watkins, Gerrold
MANCHEE, Carol M Cassidy
  Cole, Carol Cassidy
MANFRED, Frederick Feikema
  Feikema, Feike
MANLEY-TUCKER, Audrie
  Howard, Linden
MANN, E B
  Field, Peter
  Strong, Zachary
MANN, George
  Schwarz, Bruno
MANNES, Marya
  Sec
MANNING, Adelaide Frances
  Oke *and* COLES, Cyril Henry
  Coles, Manning
  Gaite, Francis
MANNING, Frederic
  Private 19022
MANNING, Rosemary
  Voyle, Mary
MANNOCK, Laura
  Adair, Sally
  Mannock, Jennifer
  Whetter, Laura
MANNON, Martha *and*
MANNON, Mary Ellen
  Mannon, M M
MANSELL, *Mrs* C B
  St Clair, Everett
MANTIBAND, James
  Keystone, Oliver

MANTLE, Winifred Langford
Fellowes, Anne
Lang, Frances
Langford, Jane
MAREK, Kurt W
Ceram, C W
MARKOV, Georgi *and*
PHILLIPS, David
St George, David
MARKS, Lilian Alicia
Markova, Alicia
MARLOWE, Stephen
Less, Milton
MARQUAND, John Phillips
Phillips, John
MARQUAND, Leopold
Burger, John
MARQUES, Susan Lowndes
Lowndes, Susan
MARRECO, Anne
Acland, Alice
MARRISON, Leslie William
Dowley, D M
MARSH, John
Davis, Julia
Elton, John
Harley, John
Lawrence, Irene
Marsh, Joan
Richmond, Grace
Sawley, Petra
Ware, Monica
Woodward, Lillian
MARSHALL, Arthur Hammond
Marshall, Archibald
MARSHALL, Charles Hunt *and*
YATES, George Worthing
Hunt, Peter
MARSHALL, Christabel
St John, Christopher
MARSHALL, Edison
Hunter, Hall
MARSHALL, Elizabeth Margaret
Sutherland, Elizabeth

MARSHALL, Evelyn
Bourne, Lesley
Marsh, J E
Marsh, Jean
MARSHALL, Margaret
Smith, Elvet
MARSHALL, Margaret Lenore
Wiley, Margaret L
MARSHALL, Marjorie
March, Stella
MARSTON, J E
Jeffrey, E Jeffrey
MARTEAU, F A
Bride, Jack
Rameaut, Maurice
MARTEN, J Chisholm
Lanark, David
MARTENS, Anne Louise
Kendall, Jane
MARTIN, Charles Morris
Martin, Chuck
MARTIN, Judith
Miss Manners
MARTIN, Kingsley
Critic
MARTIN, Malachi
Serafian, Michael
MARTIN, Netta
Ashton, Lucy
MARTIN, Patricia Miles
Miles, Miska
MARTIN, Reginald Alec
Cameron, Brett
Dixon, Rex
Eliott, E C
McCoy, Hank
Martin, Rex
Martin, Robert
Martin, Scott
MARTIN, Robert Bernard
Bernard, Robert
MARTIN, Robert Lee
Roberts, Lee

MARTIN, *Sir* Theodore
Bon Gaultier
MARTIN, Timothy
Tim
MARTIN, Violet Florence
Ross
Ross, Martin
MARTINEZ-DELGADO, Luis
Luimardel
MARTING, Ruth Lenore
Bailey, Hilea
MARTINN, Paul
Plaut, Martin
MARTYN, Wyndham
Grenvil, William
MASCHLER, Tom *and*
RAPHAEL, Frederic
Caine, Mark
MASCHWITZ, Eric
Marvel, Holt
MASON, Arthur Charles
Scrope, Mason
MASON, Douglas Rankine
Douglas, R M
Rankine, Douglas
Rankine, John
MASON, F Van Wyck
Coffin, Geoffrey
Mason, Frank W
Weaver, Ward
MASON, Madeline
Mason, Tyler
MASON, Michael
Blake, Cameron
MASON, Philip
Woodruff, Philip
MASON, Sydney Charles
Carr, Charles
Carr, Elaine
Hatton, Cliff
Hayes, Clanton
Henderson, Colt
Holmes, Caroline
Horn, Chester

Langley, John
Ledgard, Jake
Lee, Jesse
Lomax, Jeff
Maddern, Stan
Maine, Sterling
Mann, Stanley
Marlow, Phyllis
Masters, Steve
Merrick, Spencer
Stanley, Margaret
MASTERS, Anthony
Tate, Richard
MASTERS, Edgar Lee
Ford, Webster
MASTERS, Kelly
Ball, Zachary
MASTERTON, Graham
Luke, Thomas
MATCHA, Jack
Mitchel, Jackson
Tanner, John
MATHER, Anne
Fleming, Caroline
MATHERS, Edward Powys
Torquemada
MATHESON, Donald H
Harmston, Donald
MATHEWS, Albert
Siogvolk, Paul
MATTHEWMAN, Phyllis
Surrey, Kathryn
MATTHEWS, Clayton
Moore, Arthur
MATTHEWS, Edwin J
Saxon
MATTHEWS, James Brander
Matthews, Brander
Penn, Arthur
MATTHEWS, Margaret
Bryan
Goodyear, Susan

MATTHEWS, Patricia
  Brisco, P A
  Brisco, Patty
  Wylie, Laura
MATUSOW, Harvey Marshall
  Allenby, Gordon
  Matusow, Marshall
  Muldoon, Omar
  Sadballs, John
MAUGHAM, Robert Cecil
Romer *Viscount*
  Griffin, David
  Maugham, Robin
MAULE, Hamilton Bee
  Maule, Tex
MAVOR, Osborne Henry
  Bridie, James
MAXFIELD, Prudence
  Hill, Prudence
MAXTONE-GRAHAM, Joyce
  Struther, Jan
MAXWELL, Patricia Anne
  Blake, Jennifer
  Patrick, Maxine
  Ponder, Patricia
  Trchearne, Elizabeth
MAXWELL, Violet S
  Maxwell, C Bede
MAY, Elaine
  Dale, Esther
MAY, John
  Duffer, Allan
MAYER, Jane *and*
SPIEGEL, Clara E
  Jaynes, Clare
MAYNE, Ethel Colburn
  Huntly, Frances E
MAYNE, William J C *and*
CAESAR, Richard Dynely
  James, Dynely
MAZANI, Eric C F N
  Mars, E C

MAZURE, Alfred Leonardus
  Cullner, Lenard
  Maz
MAZZOCCO, Edward
  Maze, Edward
MEAD, Martha Norburn
  Norburn, Martha
MEAD, Sidney
  Moko
MEADOWCROFT, Ernest
  William, Arnold
MEAKER, Marijane
  Kerr, M E
  Packer, Vin
MEANS, Mary *and*
SAUNDERS, Theodore
  Scott, Denis
MEARES, John Willoughby
  Uncut Cavendish
MEARES, Leonard F
  Grover, Marshall
  McCoy, Marshall
MEE, Arthur
  Idris
MEESKE, Marilyn
  Crannach, Henry
MEGAW, Arthur Stanley
  Stanley, Arthur
MEGROZ, R L
  Cumberland, Roy
  Dimsdale, C D
MEHTA, Rustam
  Hartman, Roger
  Martin, R J
MEIGS, Cornelia Lynde
  Aldon, Adair
MEINZER, Helen Abbott
  Abbott, A C
MELIDES, Nicholas
  Macguire, Nicholas
MELLETT, John Calvin
  Brooks, Jonathan
MELLING, Leonard
  Lummins

MELONEY, W B *and*
FRANKEN, Rose
  Meloney, Franken
MENDELSSOHN, Oscar Adolf
  Milsen, Oscar
MENZEL, Donald H
  Howard, Don
MERCER, Cecil William
  Yates, Dornford
MERCER, Jessie
  Shannon, Terry
MEREDITH, Kenneth Lincoln
  Mayo, Arnold
MERRICK, Hugh
  Meyer, H A
MERTZ, Barbara G
  Michaels, Barbara
  Peters, Elizabeth
MERWIN, Samuel Kimball Jr
  Bennett, Elizabeth Deare
  Merwin, Sam
METHOLD, Kenneth
  Cade, Alexander
MEYER, Harold Albert
  Merrick, Hugh
MEYER, Jerome Sydney
  Jennings, S M
MEYERS, Roy
  Lethbridge, Rex
MEYNELL, Ester H
  Moorhouse, E Hallam
MEYNELL, Laurence Walter
  Baxter, Valerie
  Eton, Robert
  Ludlow, Geoffrey
  Tring, A Stephen
MEYNELL, Shirley Ruth
  Darbyshire, Shirley
MEYNELL, Wilfred
  Oldcastle, John
MICKLEWHITE, Maurice Joseph
  Caine, Michael

MIDDLETON, Harry *and*
KIEFER, Warren
  Kiefer, Middleton
MIDDLETON, Henry Clement
  Simplex, Simon
MIDDLETON, Maud Barbara
  Walker, Barbara
MIERS, Earl Schenk
  Meredith, David William
MILAM, Lorenzo W
  Allworthy, A W
MILKOMANE, George Alexis
Milkomanovich
  Bankoff, George
  Borodin, George
  Braddon, George
  Conway, Peter
  Redwood, Alec
  Sava, George
MILLAR, Kenneth
  Macdonald, John
  Macdonald, John Ross
  Macdonald, Ross
MILLAR, Minna
  Collier, Joy
MILLARD, Christopher S
  Mason, Stuart
MILLAY, Edna St Vincent
  Boyd, Nancy
MILLER, Albert
  Mills, Alan
MILLER, Charles Dean
  Von Mueller, Karl
MILLER, Charles Henry
  Muldor, Carl De
MILLER, Cincinnatus H
  Miller, Joaquin
MILLER, Harriet
  Miller, Olive Thorne
MILLER, J A
  Pook, Peter
MILLER, John Gordon
  Miller, Jon

MILLER, Lynn
  Captious Critic
MILLER, Mary
  Durack, Mary
MILLER, Mary Britton
  Bolton, Isabel
MILLER, R S
  Huston, Fran
MILLER, Warren
  Vail, Amanda
MILLER, William *and*
  WADE, Robert
  Daemer, Will
  Masterson, Whit
  Miller, Wade
  Wilmer, Dale
MILLER, Wright
  North, Mark
MILLETT, Nigel
  Oke, Richard
MILLIGAN, Elsie
  Burr, Elsie
MILLS, Algernon Victor
  Latimer, Rupert
MILLS, Hugh Travers
  Travers, Hugh
MILLS, Janet Melanie Ailsa
  Challoner, H K
MILLWARD, Pamela
  Midling, Perspicacity
MILNE, Charles
  Milne, Ewart
MILNER, Alfred, *Viscount Milner*
  M
MILNER, Marion
  Field, Joanna
MILSON, Charles Henry
  Weston, William
MILTON, Gladys Alexandra
  Carlyle, Anthony
M'ILWRAITH, Jean N
  Forsyth, Jean

MINES, Samuel
  Field, Peter
MINTO, Frances
  Cowen, Frances
  Hyde, Eleanor
  Munthe, Frances
MINTO, Mary
  Macqueen, Jay
MITCHELL, Clare May
  Canfield, Cleve
MITCHELL, Donald Grant
  Marvel, Ik
  Timon, John
MITCHELL, Gladys
  Hockaby, Stephen
  Torrie, Malcolm
MITCHELL, Isabel
  Plain, Josephine
MITCHELL, James
  Munro, James
MITCHELL, James Leslie
  Gibbon, Lewis Grassic
MITCHELL, John
  Slater, Patrick
MITCHELL, John Hanlon
  Hanlon, John
MITCHELL, Langdon Elwyn
  Varley, John Philip
MITRINOVIC, Dmitri
  Cosmoi, M M
MIZNER, Elizabeth Howard
  Howard, Elizabeth
MOBERLY, Charlotte Anne Elizabeth
  Morison, Elizabeth
MOCKLER, Gretchen
  Travis, Gretchen
MODELL, Merriam
  Piper, Evelyn
MOFFATT, James
  More, J J
MOGRIDGE, Stephen
  Stevens, Jill

MOHAN, Josephine Elizabeth
Jermonte
MOLESWORTH, *Mrs* Mary
Louisa Stewart
Graham, Ennis
MOLLOY, Edward
Jamieson, Thomas
Jones, H S
Ward, Herbert B S
MONGER, Ifor
Manngian, Peter
Richards, Peter
MONRO-HIGGS, Gertrude
Monro, Gavin
MONROE, Donald *and*
MONROE, Keith
Keith, Donald
MONTEFIORE, Caroline L
Eric
MONTGOMERY, Leslie
Alexander
Doyle, Lynn
MONTGOMERY, Robert Bruce
Crispin, Edmund
MONTGOMERY, Rutherford
George
Avery, Al
Elder, Art
Marshall, E P
Proctor, Everitt
MOORE, Bertha B
Cannon, Brenda
MOORE, Birkett
Allegro
MOORE, C L *and/or*
KUTTNER, Henry
O'Donnell, Laurence
Padgett, Lewis
MOORE, Doris Langley
Gentlewoman, A
MOORE, Harold William
Roome, Holdar
MOORE, John
Trotwood, John

MOORE, Mary McLeod
Pandora
MOORE, Rosalie
Brown, Bill
Brown, Rosalie
MOORHOUSE, Herbert Joseph
Moorhouse, Hopkins
MOORHOUSE, Hilda
Vansittart, Jane
MOORHOUSE, Sydney
Langdale, Stanley
Lyndale, Sydney M
MORANT, Harry H
Breaker, The .
MORDAUNT, Evelyn May
Mordaunt, Elinor
Riposte, A
MOREAU, David
Merlin, David
MORENO, Virginia
Pilè
MORETON, Douglas Arthur
Douglas, Arthur
MORETTI, Ugo
Drug, Victor
Gouttier, Maurice
Sherman, George
MOREWOOD, Sarah L
Hope, Noel
MORGAN, Brian Stanford
Morgan, Bryan
MORGAN, Charles
Menander
MORGAN, Diana
Blaine, Sara
MORGAN, Murray C
Murray, Cromwell
MORGAN, Thomas Christopher
Muir, John
MORIN, Claire
France, Claire
MORISON, John
Clergyman, A

MORLAND, Nigel
Dane, Mary
Donavan, John
Forrest, Norman
Garnett, Roger
McCall, Vincent
Shepherd, Neal
MORLEY, Leslie Reginald
William
Hutchins, Anthony
MORRIS, David
Hall, Martyn T
MORRIS, Jean
O'Hara, Kenneth
MORRIS, John
McGaw, J W
MORRISON, Alistair
Lauder, Afferbeck
MORRISON, Arthur
Hewitt, Martin
MORRISON, Eula A
Delmonico, Andrea
MORRISON, Margaret Mackie
Cost, March
Morrison, Peggy
MORRISON, Thomas
Muir, Alan
MORRISSEY, Joseph Lawrence
Richards, Henry
Saxon, Richard
MORSE, Anne Christensen
Head, Ann
MORSE, Martha
Wilson, Martha
MORTIMER, John
Lincoln, Geoffrey
MORTIMER, Penelope
Dimont, Penelope
Temple, Ann
MORTON, A Q
Kew, Andrew
MORTON, Guy Mainwaring
Traill, Peter

MORTON, J B
Beachcomber
MORUM, William *and*
DINNER, William
Smith, Surrey
MOSS, Robert Alfred
Moss, Nancy
Moss, Roberta
MOSTYN, Anita Mary
Fielding, Ann Mary
MOTLEY DE RENEVILLE,
Mary Margaret
Motley, Mary
MOTT, Edward Spencer
Gubbins, Nathaniel
Spencer, Edward
MOTT, J Moldon
Blackburn, John
MOTT, Michael
Alston, Charles
MOTTRAM, Ralph Hale
Marjoram, J
MOUNT, Thomas Ernest
Cody, Stone
King, Oliver
MOUNTBATTEN, *Lord* Louis
Marco
MOUNTCASTLE, Clara H
Sima, Caris
MOUNTFIELD, David
Grant, Neil
MOYNIHAN, Cornelius
Vivian
MUDDOCK, Joyce Emerson
Donovan, Dick
MUGGESON, Margaret
Dickinson, Margaret
Jackson, Everatt
MUIR, Augustus
Moore, Austin
MUIR, Edwin
Moore, Edward
MUIR, Kenneth Arthur
Finney, Mark

MUIR, Marie
  Blake, Monica
  Kaye, Barbara
MUIR, Wilhelmina Johnstone
  Muir, Willa
  Scott, Agnes Neill
MULHEARN, Winifred
  Grandma
MULLER, Charles George
  Geoffrey, Charles
MULLER, Robert
  Anatole
MUMFORD, A H
  Videns
MUMFORD, Ruth
  Dallas, Ruth
MUNBY, Arthur Joseph
  Brown, Jones
MUNRO, Hector Hugh
  Saki
MUNRO, Hugh
  Jason
MUNTZ, Isabelle Hope
  Langland, William
MURFREE, Mary Noailles
  Craddock, Charles Egbert
  Dembry, R Emmet
MURIEL, John
  Dewes, Simon
  Lindsey, John
MURPHY, Charlotte *and*
MURPHY, Lawrence
  Murphy, C L
MURPHY, Emily Gowan
(Ferguson)
  Canuck, Janey
  Ferguson, Emily
MURPHY, John *and*
CORLEY, Edwin
  Buchanan, Patrick
MURPHY, Lawrence *and*
MURPHY, Charlotte
  Murphy, C L

MURPHY, Lawrence D
  Lawrence, Steven C
MURRANKA, Mary
  McGrath, Mary
MURRAY, Andrew Nicholas
  Islay, Nicholas
MURRAY, Blanche
  Murray, Geraldine
MURRAY, Francis Edwin
  Mair, H Allen
MURRAY, Joan
  Blood, Joan Wilde
MURRAY, Ruth Hilary
  Finnegan, Ruth
MURRAY, Venetia Pauline *and*
BIRCH, Jack Ernest Lionel
  Flight, Francies
MURRAY, William Waldie
  Orderly Sergeant, The
MURRY, Colin Middleton
  Cowper, Richard
  Murry, Colin
MURRY, Violet
  Arden, Mary
MUSKETT, Netta Rachel
  Hill, Anne
MUSPRATT, Rosalie
  John, Jasper
MUSSI, Mary
  Edgar, Josephine
  Howard, Mary
MUSTO, Barry
  Simon, Robert
MYERS, Mary Cathcart
  Borer, Mary Cathcart
MYSTERY WRITERS OF
AMERICA INC: CALIFORNIA
CHAPTER
  Durrant, Theo

NAIR, K K
  Chaitanya, Krishna
NAISMITH, Robert Stevenson
  Stevenson, Robert

NASH, Vaughan *and*
SMITH, Llewellyn
Two East Londoners
NEAL, Adeline Phyllis
Grey, A F
NEEDHAM, Joseph
Holorenshaw, Henry
NEILD, James Edward
J E N
Jaques
Sly, Christopher
NELMS, Henning
Talbot, Hake
NELSON, Ethel
Nina
NELSON, Lawrence
Trent, Peter
NELSON, Radell Faraday
Elson, R N
Lord, Jeffrey
Nelson, Ray
NERNEY, Patrick W
Nudnick
NESMITH, Robert I
Clarke, *Captain* Jafah
NETTELL, Richard
Kenneggy, Richard
NETTZ, Julie
Julie
NEUBAUER, William Arthur
Arthur, William
Garrison, Joan
Marsh, Rebecca
Newcomb, Norma
NEVILLE, Alison
Candy, Edward
NEVILLE, Derek
Salt, Jonathan
NEWBY, Eric
Parker, James
NEWELL, Robert Henry
Kerr, Orpheus C
NEWLIN, Margaret
Rudd, Margaret

NEWMAN, Bernard
Betteridge, Don
NEWMAN, James Roy
Stryfe, Paul
NEWMAN, Lyn Lloyd
Irvine, Lyn
NEWMAN, Mona A J
Fitzgerald, Barbara
Newman, Barbara
Stewart, Jean
NEWMAN, Terence
O'Connor, Dermot
NEWNHAM, Don
Eden, Matthew
NEWTON, Dwight Bennett
Bennett, Dwight
Hardin, Clement
Logan, Ford
Mitchum, Hank
Temple, Dan
NEWTON, H Chance
Gawain
NEWTON, William
Jansen, Hank
Ross, Gene
NEWTON, William Simpson
Mitcham, Gilroy
Newton, Macdonald
NGUGI, J T
Ngugi, Wa Thiongio
NICHOLS, *Captain* G H F
Quex
NICHOLS, Mary Eudora
Brown, Eve
NICHOLSON, Joan
Craig, Alison
Weir, Jonnet
NICHOLSON, Margaret Beda
Yorke, Margaret
NICHOLSON, Violet
Hope, Lawrence
NICKSON, Arthur
Hodson, Arthur
Peters, Roy

NICKSON, Arthur (cont'd)
Saunders, John
Winstan, Matt
NICOL, Eric Patrick
Jabez
NICOLAEFF, Ariadne
Moore, Nicholas
NICOLE, Christopher
Cade, Robin
Grange, Peter
Logan, Mark
Nicholson, Christina
York, Andrew
NICOLL, *Sir* William Robertson
Clear, Claudius
Wace, W E
NIELSON, Helen Berniece
Giles, Kris
NILSON, Annabel
Nilson, Bee
NISBET, Ulric
Callaway, Hugh
NISOT, Mavis Elizabeth
Penmare, William
NOCK, Albert Jay
Historicus
Journeyman
NOLAN, Cynthia
Reed, Cynthia
NOLAN, Frederick
Christian, Frederick H
NOLAN, William F
Anmar, Frank
Cahill, Mike
Edwards, F E
Phillips, Michael
NOONAN, Robert
Tressall, Robert
Tressell, Robert
NORGATE, Walter
Le Grys, Walter
NORMAN, Barbara
Makanowitzky, Barbara

NORMAN, C H
Stanhope of Chester
NORTH, William
Rodd, Ralph
NORTHAM, Lois Edgell
Nelson, Lois
NORTHCOTT, Cecil
Miller, Mary
NORTHRUP, E F
Pseudoman, Akkad
NORTON, Alice Mary
North, Andrew
Norton, André
NORTON, Alice Mary *and* HOGARTH, Grace
Weston, Allen
NORTON, Marjorie
Ellison, Marjorie
NORTON, Olive Marion
Neal, Hilary
Noon, T R
Norton, Bess
Norway, Kate
NORWAY, Nevil Shute
Shute, Nevil
NORWOOD, Victor George Charles
Banton, Coy
Baxter, Shane V
Bowie, Jim
Brand, Clay
Brand, Victor
Clevinger, Paul
Cody, Walt
Colter, Shayne
Corteen, Craig
Corteen, Wes
Dangerfield, Clint
Dark, Johnny
Destry, Vince
Fargo, Doone
Fenton, Mark
Fisher, Wade
Gearing-Thomas, G

Hampton, Mark
Jansen, Hank
Karta, Nat
McCord, Whip
Rand, Brett
Regan, Brad
Russell, Shane
Shane, Mark
Shane, Rhondo
Shane, Victor
Tressidy, Jim
NOURSE, Alan E
Edwards, Al
NOVAK, Cornelius Dan
Zacharia
Zacharia, Dan
NOVIKOV, Olga
OK
NOWELL, Elizabeth Cameron
Clemons, Elizabeth
NUMANO, Allen
Corenanda, A L A
NUNN, William Curtis
Curtis, Will
Twist, Ananias
NURSE, Malcolm Ivan Meredith
Padmore, George
NUTT, Charles
Beaumont, Charles
Grantland, Keith
Lovehill, C V
McNutt, Charles
Phillips, Michael
Tenneshaw, S M
NUTT, David
Brand, David
NUTT, Lily Clive
Arden, Clive
NUTTALL, Anthony
Allyson, Alan
Bardsley, Michael
Curtis, Spencer
Lenton, Anthony
Tracey, Grant

Trent, Lee
Wells, Tracey
NYE, Nelson Coral
Colt, Clem
Denver, Drake C

OAKESHOTT, Edna
Peters, Jocelyn
OAKLEY, Eric Gilbert
Capon, Peter
Gregson, Paul
Scott-Morley, A
OAKLEY, John, *Dean of*
Manchester
Vicesimus
OBENCHAIN, Eliza Caroline
Hall, Eliza Calvert
O'BRIEN, Conor Cruise
O'Donnell, Donat
O'CASEY, Sean
Green Crow, The
O'Cathasaigh, P
O'CONNOR, Patrick Joseph
Fiacc, Padraic
O'CONNOR, Richard
Archer, Frank
Wayland, Patrick
O'CONNOR, T P
T P
O'DANIEL, Janet *and*
RESSLER, Lillian
Janet, Lillian
O'DONOGHUE, Elinor Mary
Oddie, E M
O'DONOVAN, Michael Francis
O'Connor, Frank
O'FARRELL, William
Grew, William
O'FERRALL, Ernest
Kodak
OGNALL, Leopold Horace
Carmichael, Harry
Howard, Harry
Howard, Hartley

95

O'GRADY, Elizabeth Anne
  Scollan, E A
O'GRADY, John P
  Culotta, Nino
  O'Grada, Sean
O'HARA, John
  Delaney, Franey
OLD, Phyllis Muriel Elizabeth
  Shiel-Martin
OLD COYOTE, Elnora A
  Old Coyote, Sally
  Wright, Elnora A
  Wright, Sally
OLDFIELD, Claude Houghton
  Houghton, Claude
OLDMEADOW, Ernest James
  Downman, Francis
O'LEARY, Liam
  O'Laoghaire, Liam
OLIVER, Amy Roberts
  Onions, Berta
  Ruck, Berta
OLIVER, Doris M
  Hughes, Alison
OLIVER, George
  Onions, Oliver
OLIVER, John Rathbone
  Roland, John
OLNEY, Ellen Warner
  Hayes, Henry
OLSEN, Theodore Victor
  Stark, Joshua
  Storm, Christopher
  Willoughby, Cass
OLSON, Herbert Vincent
  Olsen, Herb
O'MAHONY, Charles Kingston
  Kingston, Charles
O'MALLEY, *Lady*
  Bridge, Ann
O'MORE, Peggy
  Bowman, Jeanne
O'NEILL, Herbert Charles
  Strategicus

O'NEILL, Rose Cecil
  Latham, O'Neill
O'NOLAN, Brian
  An Broc
  Knowall, George
  Na gCopaleen, Myles
  O'Brien, Flann
OPPENHEIM, E Phillips
  Partridge, Anthony
OPPENHEIMER, Carlota
  Carlota
ORAGE, Alfred James
  A R O
  Congreve, R H
  Orage, A R
  R H C
ORBISON, Roy *and*
KECK, Maud
  Orbison, Keck
ORDE-WARD, F W
  Williams, F Harald
ORGA, Irfan
  Riza, Ali
ORGEL, Doris
  Adelberg, Doris
ORGILL, Douglas *and*
FISHMAN, Jack
  Gilman, J D
O'RIORDAN, Conal O'Connell
  Connell, Norreys
ORME, Eve
  Day, Irene
O'ROURKE, Frank
  Connor, Kevin
  O'Malley, Frank
  O'Malley, Patrick
ORRMONT, Arthur
  Hunter, Anson
ORTON, John Kingsley
  Orton, Joe
  Welthorpe, Edna
ORTON, Thora
  Colson, Thora

OSBERT, Reuben
Osborn, Reuben
OSBORNE, Dorothy Gladys
Arthur, Gladys
O'SHAUGHNESSY, Marjorie
Shaw, Adelaide
OSLER, Eric Richard
Dick, T
OSMOND, Andrew *and*
INGRAMS, Richard
Reid, Philip
OSTERGAARD, Geoffrey
Gerard, Gaston
OSTLERE, Gordon Stanley
Gordon, Richard
OSTLERE, Mary
Gordon, Mary
OSTRANDER, Isabel Egerton
Chipperfield, Robert Orr
Fox, David
Grant, Douglas
OURSLER, Fulton
Abbot, Anthony
OURSLER, William Charles
Gallagher, Gale
OUSELEY, G J R
Disciple of the Master, A
OVERHOLSER, Wayne D
Daniels, John S
Leighton, Lee
Morgan, Mark
Roberts, Wayne
Stevens, Dan J
Wayne, Joseph
OVERY, Jillian P J
Martin, Gil
Overy, Martin
ØVSTEDAL, Barbara
Laker, Rosalind
Paul, Barbara
OWEN, Dilys
Edwards, Olwen

OWEN, Frank; FOOT, Michael
and **HOWARD, Peter**
Cato
OWEN, Jack
Dykes, Jack
OWENS, Iris
Daimler, Harriet
OXMAN, Philip
Peachum, Thomas
OZAKI, Milton K
Saber, Robert O

§ §

*My name is legion: for we are
many.*
– *Bible. Mark, 5.9*

§ §

PADGETT, Ron
Dangerfield, Harlan
Veitch, Tom
PADLEY, Arthur
Winn, Patrick
PADLEY, Walter
Marcus Aurelius
PAGE, Evelyn *and*
BLAIR, Dorothy
Scarlett, Roger
PAGE, Gerald W
Grindle, Carleton
Pembrooke, Kenneth
PAGE, Norvell W
Stockbridge, Grant
PAGE, Patricia Kathleen
Cape, Judith
Irwin, P K
PAGE, Walter Hines
Worth, Nicholas
PAGET, Violet
Lee, Vernon
PAINE, Lauran Bosworth
Ainsworthy, Roy

PAINE, Lauran Bosworth
(cont'd)
  Allen, Clay
  Almonte, Rosa
  Andrews, A A
  Armour, John
  Bartlett, Kathleen
  Batchelor, Reg
  Beck, Harry
  Bedford, Kenneth
  Benton, Will
  Bosworth, Frank
  Bradford, Will
  Bradley, Concho
  Brennan, Will
  Carrel, Mark
  Carter, Nevada
  Cassady, Claude
  Clarke, Richard
  Clarke, Robert
  Custer, Clint
  Dana, Amber
  Dana, Richard
  Davis, Audrey
  Drexler, J F
  Duchesne, Antoinette
  Durham, John
  Fisher, Margot
  Fleck, Betty
  Frost, Joni
  Glendenning, Donn
  Glenn, James
  Gordon, Angela
  Gorman, Beth
  Hart, Francis
  Hayden, Jay
  Holt, Helen
  Houston, Will
  Howard, Elizabeth
  Howard, Troy
  Hunt, John
  Ingersol, Jared
  Kelley, Ray
  Ketchum, Jack

  Kilgore, John
  Liggett, Hunter
  Lucas, J K
  Lyon, Buck
  Martin, Bruce
  Martin, Tom
  Morgan, Angela
  Morgan, Arlene
  Morgan, Frank
  Morgan, John
  Morgan, Valerie
  O'Connor, Clint
  Pindell, Jon
  St George, Arthur
  Sharp, Helen
  Slaughter, Jim
  Standish, Buck
  Stuart, Margaret
  Thompson, Buck
  Thompson, Russ
  Thorn, Barbara
  Undine, P F
PAINTING, Norman
  Milna, Bruno
PALESTRANT, Simon
  Edward, Stephen
  Stevens, S P
  Strand, Paul E
PALMER, Cecil
  Ludlow, John
PALMER, John Leslie
  Haddon, Christopher
PALMER, John Leslie *and*
SAUNDERS, Hilary Aidan
St George
  Beeding, Francis
  Pilgrim, David
PALMER, John Williamson
  Coventry, John
PALMER, Madelyn
  Peters, Geoffrey
PALMER, Paul
  Downing, Century

PALMER, Ray
Gade, Henry
PALMER, Stuart
Stewart, Jay
PALMER-ARCHER, Laura M
Bushwoman
PANIKKAR, Kavalam
Putra, Kerala
PANOWSKI, Eileen Janet
Thompson, Eileen
PAPPAS, George S
Justificus
PARCELL, Norman Howe
Nicholson, John
PARES, Marion
Campbell, Judith
PARGETER, Edith Mary
Peters, Ellis
PARKER, Dorothy
Constant Reader
PARKER, Marion
Dominic, *Sister* Mary
Hope, Marion
PARKES, Frank
Dompo, Kwesi
PARKES, James W
Hadham, John
PARKES, Terence
Larry
PARKHILL, Forbes
Martinez, J D
Vloto, Otto
PARKINSON, Roger
Holden, Matthew
PARKS, Georgina
Gabrielle
PARR, Olive Katherine
Chase, Beatrice
PARRIS, John
Lascelles, Alison
PARRY, Hugh J
Cross, James
PARRY, Margaret G
Glyn, Megan

PARRY, Michel
Cassaba, Carlos
Fury, Nick
Lee, Steve
Lovecraft, Linda
Pendragon, Eric
PARSONS, Anthony
Nicholls, Anthony
PARSONS, Charles P
Craven Hill
PARTRIDGE, Bellamy
Bailey, Thomas
PARTRIDGE, Eric
Vigilans
PARTRIDGE, Kate Margaret
Partridge, Sydney
PATCHETT, Mary Elwyn
Bruce, David
PATERSON, W R
Swift, Benjamin
PATRICK, Keats
Karig, Walter
PATRY, M *and*
WILLIAMS, D F
Williams, Patry
PATTEN, Gilbert
Standish, Burt L
PATTERSON, Harry
Fallon, Martin
Graham, James
Higgins, Jack
Marlowe, Hugh
Patterson, Henry
PATTERSON, Isabella Innis
Patterson, Innis
PATTERSON, Peter
Terson, Peter
PATTINSON, James
Ryder, James
PATTINSON, Lee
Holland, Rosemary
Maxwell, Ann
Miller, Ellen

PATTINSON, Nancy
  Asquith, Nan
PATTISON, Andrew Seth P
  Seth, Andrew
PATTISON, Ruth
  Abbey, Ruth
PAUL, Elliot Harold
  Rutledge, Brett
PAUL, Maury
  Benedict, Billy
  Knickerbocker, Cholly
  Madison, Dolly
  Stuyvesant, Polly
PAWLEY, Martin Edward
  Noble, Charles
  Spade, Rupert
PAYNE, Charles J
  Snaffles
PAYNE, Donald Gordon
  Cameron, Ian
  Gordon, Donald
  Marshall, James Vance
PAYNE, Eileen Mary
  Mansell, C R
PAYNE, Pierre Stephen Robert
  Cargoe, Richard
  Horne, Howard
  Payne, Robert
  Young, Robert
PAYNE, Ronald Charles *and*
  GARROD, John William
  Castle, John
PAZ, Magdeleine
  Marx, Magdeleine
PEACH, Edward C
  Ophiel
PEARCE, Brian
  Hussey, Leonard
  Redman, Joseph
PEARCE, Melville Chaning
  Nicodemus
PEARCE, Raymond
  Maplesden, Ray

PEARSON, Katharine
  Gordon, Katharine
PEARSON, W T
  Pengreep, William
PECHEY, Archibald Thomas
  Cross, Mark
  Valentine
PECK, Leonard
  Brain, Leonard
PEDLAR, Ann
  Stafford, Ann
PEDRICK-HARVEY, Gale
  Pedrick, Gale
PEED, William Bartlett
  Peek, Bill
PEEL, Frederick *and*
  SIDDLE, Charles
  Slingsby, Rufus
PEEL, Hazel
  Hayman, Hazel
  Peel, Wallis
PEEPLES, Samuel Anthony
  Ward, Brad
PEERS, Edgar Allison
  Truscot, Bruce
PEISER, Maria Lilli
  Palmer, Lilli
PEMBER, William Leonard
  Monmouth, Jack
PEMBER-DEVEREUX, Margaret
  R R
  Devereux, Roy
PENDLETON, Donald Eugene
  Britain, Dan
  Gregory, Stephan
PENNER, Manola J
  Alexander, Jean
PENWARDEN, Helen
  Smith, Jessica
PEOPLE, Granville Church
  Church, Granville
PERELMAN, S J
  Namlerep, Sidney

PERKINS, Kenneth
  Phillips, King
PERRY, Clair Willard
  Perry, Clay
PERRY, James Black
  Weir, Logan
PERRY, Martin
  Martyn, Henry
PERRY, Ritchie John Allen
  Allen, John
PERRY, Robert
  Marquis, Don
PERSKE, Betty
  Bacall, Lauren
PETAJA, Emil
  Pine, Theodor
PETERS, Arthur A
  Peters, Fritz
PETERS, Maureen
  Black, Veronica
  Darby, Catherine
  Lloyd, Levanah
  Rothman, Judith
  Whitby, Sharon
PETERS, Robert Louis
  Bridge, John
PETERSON, Corinna
  Cochrane, Corinna
PETERSON, Margaret
  Green, Glint
PETRIE, Rhona
  Duell, Eileen-Marie
PETRONE, Jane Gertrude
  Muir, Jane
PEYTON, Kathleen Wendy *and*
PEYTON, Michael
  Herald, Kathleen
  Peyton, K M
PHILIPP, Elliot Elias
  Embey, Philip
  Havil, Anthony
  Tempest, Victor
PHILIPS, Judson Pentecost
  Pentecost, Hugh

PHILLIPS, David *and*
MARKOV, Georgi
  St George, David
PHILLIPS, David Graham
  Graham, John
PHILLIPS, Dennis John Andrew
  Challis, Simon
  Chambers, Peter
  Chester, Peter
PHILLIPS, Forbes Alexander
  Forbes, Athol
PHILLIPS, Gerald William
  Huntingdon, John
PHILLIPS, Gordon
  Lucio
PHILLIPS, Horace
  Stanton, Marjorie
PHILLIPS, Hubert
  Caliban
  Dogberry
  Ninespot
PHILLIPS, Hugh
  Hughes, Philip
PHILLIPS, James Atlee
  Atlee, Philip
PHILLIPS, Olga
  Olga
PHILLIPS, Pauline
  Van Buren, Abigail
PHILLIPS-BIRT, Douglas
  Argus
  Hextall, David
  Hogarth, Douglas
PHILLPOTTS, Eden
  Hext, Harrington
PHILPOT, Joseph H
  Lafargue, Philip
PHILPOTT, Alexis Robert
  Pantopuck
PHYSICK, Edward Harold
  Visiak, E H
PICKEN, Mary
  Wells, Jane Warren

PICKLES, Mabel Elizabeth
Burgoyne, Elizabeth
PIERCE, Mary Cunningham
Cunningham, Mary
PIGGOTT, William
Wales, Hubert
PIKE, Mary Hayden
Langdon, Mary
Story, Sydney A J
PILCHER, Rosamunde
Fraser, Jane
PILLEY, Phil
Lindley, Gerard
PINTO, Jacqueline
Blairman, Jacqueline
PIPER, David Towry
Towry, Peter
PIPER, Evelyn
Modell, Merriam
PITCAIRN, John James *and*
FREEMAN, R Austin
Ashdown, Clifford
PLACE, Marian Templeton
White, Dale
Whitinger, R D
PLATH, Sylvia
Lucas, Victoria
PLATT, Edward
Trent, Paul
PLOMER, William
D'Arfey, William
Pagan, Robert
PLUCKROSE, Henry Arthur
Cobbett, Richard
PLUMLEY, Ernest F
Clevedon, John
PLUMMER, Clare Emsley
Emsley, Clare
PLUMMER, Thomas Arthur
Sarne, Michael
POCOCK, Tom
Allcot, Guy
POHL, Frederik
MacCreigh, James

POHL, Frederik *and*
DEL REY, Lester
McCann, Edson
POHL, Frederik *and*
KORNBLUTH, Cyril M
Gottesman, S D
POLAND, Dorothy E H
Farely, Alison
Hammond, Jane
POLANSKY, Abraham *and*
WILLSON, Mitchell A
Hogarth, Emmett
POLIAKOFF, Vladimir
Augur
POLITELLA, Dario
Granite, Tony
Stewart, David
POLLAND, Madeleine Angela
Adrian, Frances
POLLEY, Judith Anne
Hagar, Judith
Kent, Helen
Luellen, Valentina
POLLOCK, Edith Caroline
Thorn, Ismay
POLWARTH, Gwendoline Mary
Polwarth, G Marchant
PONSONBY, Doris Almon
Rybot, Doris
Tempest, Sarah
POOLE, Reginald Heber
Heber, Austin
Heber, Reginald
Poole, Michael
POORTEN-SCHWARTZ, J M W
Van der
Maartens, Marten
PORN, Alice
Ali-Mar
PORTER, Barbara Conney
Conney, Barbara
PORTER, Edward
Harvey, Lyon

PORTER, Eleanor
 Stewart, Eleanor
PORTER, Harold Everett
 Hall, Holworthy
PORTER, Maurice
 Mouthpiece
PORTER, William Sydney
 Henry, O
POSNER, David Louis
 Bourchier, Jules
POSNER, Jacob D
 Dean, Gregory
POSNER, Richard
 Craig, Jonathan
 Foster, Iris
 Murray, Beatrice
 Todd, Paul
 Wine, Dick
POSSELT, Eric
 Palmer, Edgar A
POTTER, George William
 Withers, E L
POTTER, Heather
 Jenner, Heather
POTTER, Joanna
 Harvey, Caroline
 Trollope, Joanna
POTTER, Margaret
 Betteridge, Anne
 Melville, Anne
 Newman, Margaret
POU, Genevieve
 Holden, Genevieve
POUND, Ezra
 Adkins, M D
 Atheling, William
 B L
 Dias, B H
 Hall, John
 Helmholtz, Bastien von
 J L
 Janus, Hiram
 Llewmys, Weston

Maria, Hermann Karl Georg
 Jesus
 Saunders, Abel
 T J V
 Venison, Alfred
POURNELLE, Jerry
 Curtis, Wade
POWE, Bruce
 Portal, Ellis
POWELL, Eric
 Rusholm, Peter
POWELL, Talmage
 McCready, Jack
POWELL-SMITH, Vincent
 Elphinstone, Francis
 Justiciar
 Santa Maria
POWER, *Sir* D'Arcy
 D'A P
POWLEY, *Mrs* A A
 Gene, Marta
PRAFULLA, Das
 Subhadra-Nandan
PRATHER, Richard S
 Knight, David
 Ring, Douglas
PRATT, E B Atkinson
 Blake, Eleanor
PRATT, Fletcher
 Fretcher, George U
PRATT, John
 Winton, John
PRATT, Theodore
 Brace, Timothy
PRATT, William Henry
 Karloff, Boris
PRESBERG, Miriam
 Gilbert, Miriam
PRESLAND, John
 Bendit, Gladys
PREVOST-BATTERSBY, H F
 Prevost, Francis
PRICE, Beverly Joan
 Randell, Beverly

PRICE, Edgar Hoffman
Daly, Hamlin
PRICE, Jeremie
Lane, Marvyn
PRICE, Olive
Cherryholmes, Anne
PRICE-BROWN, John
Bohn, Eric
Price-Brown
PRICHARD, H Hesketh *and*
PRICHARD, Kate Hesketh
Heron, E *and* H
PRIESTLEY, Clive Ryland
Ryland, Clive
PRIESTLEY, John Boynton
Goldsmith, Peter
PRIMMER, Phyllis
Fredricks, P C
PRIOR, Mollie
Roscoe, Janet
PRITCHARD, John Wallace
Wallace, Ian
PRITCHARD, William Thomas
Dexter, William
PROCASSION, Michael
Cristofer, Michael
PRONZINI, Bill
Foxx, Jack
Saxon, Alec
PUDDEPHA, Derek
Quill
PUECHNER, Ray
Haddo, Oliver
Peekner, Ray
Victor, Charles B
PULLEIN-THOMPSON, Christine
Keir, Christine
PULLEIN-THOMPSON, Denis
Cannan, Denis
PULLEIN-THOMPSON, Josephine Mary
Cannan, Joanna
Mann, Josephine

PULLEN, George
Culpeper, Martin
PULLING, Albert Van Siclen
Pulling, Pierre
PUNNETT, Margaret *and*
PUNNETT, Ivor
Simons, Peter
Simons, Roger
PURCELL, Victor W W S
Buttle, Myra
PURDY, Ken
Prentiss, Karl
PURVES, Frederick
Lloyd, Joseph M
PUTLAND VAN SOMEREN, Elisabeth
Van Someren, Liesje
PYKE, John
Westlaw, Steven
PYKE, Lillian Maxwell
Maxwell, Erica

QUENTIN, Dorothy
Beverly, Linda
QUIBELL, Agatha
Pearce, A H
QUIGLEY, Aileen
Fabian, Ruth
Lindley, Erica
QUIGLEY, M C *and*
CLARK, Mary Elizabeth
Clark, Margery
QUIGLY, Elizabeth Pauline
Elisabeth
QUILLER-COUCH, *Sir* **Arthur**
A Q-C
Q

RABBETS, Thomas G
St Ebbar
RADCLIFFE, Garnett
Travers, Stephen

RADETZBY von RADETZ,
Countess
Harding, Bertita
RADFORD, Ruby Lorraine
Bailey, Matilda
Ford, Marcia
RAE, Hugh Crauford
Crawford, Robert
Houston, R B
McGrath, Morgan
Stern, Stuart
Stirling, Jessica
RAE, Margaret Doris
Rae, Doris
RAGG, Thomas Murray
Thomas, Murray
**RALEIGH-KING, Robin Victor
Lethbridge**
Graham, Robin
King, Robin
RAMAGE, Jennifer
Mason, Howard
RAME, Maria Louise
Ouida
RAMSAY, Allan
Zero
RAMSAY-LAYE, Elizabeth
Massary, Isabel
RAMSKILL, Valerie
Brooke, Carol
RANDALL, A E
Hope, John Francis
RANDOLPH, Georgiana Ann
Rice, Craig
Sanders, Daphne
Venning, Michael
RANDOLPH, Lowell King
Ran, Kip
RANSFORD, Oliver
Wylcotes, John
RANSOME, L E
Chester, Elizabeth
Melbourne, Ida

Ransome, Barbara
Stirling, Stella
RAPHAEL, Chaim
Davey, Jocelyn
RAPHAEL, Frederic *and*
MASCHLER, Tom
Caine, Mark
RASH, Dora
Wallace, Doreen
RAUBENHEIMER, George H
Harding, George
RAVENSCROFT, John R
Ravenscroft, Rosanne
RAWLEY, Callman
Rakosi, Carl
RAWSON, Clayton
Merlini, The Great
Towne, Stuart
RAYER, Francis G
Longdon, George
Scott, Milward
Worcester, Roland
RAYMOND, Rene
Chase, James Hadley
Docherty, James L
Grant, Ambrose
Marshall, Raymond
RAYMOND, Walter
Cobbleigh, Tom
RAYNER, Augustus Alfred
Hall, Whyte
RAYNER, Claire
Brandon, Sheila
Lynton, Ann
Martin, Ruth
REACH, James
Manning, Roy
West, Tom
READ, Anthony
Ferguson, Anthony
READ, James
Bacon, Jeremy
READ, John
Jan

READE, *Mrs* Frances
 Lawson
  Langworthy, Yolande
REAGAN, Thomas B
  Thomas, Jim
REANEY, James
  Spoonhill
REBACK, Marcus *and*
 CALDWELL, Janet Taylor
  Caldwell, Taylor
  Reiner, Max
REDMAN, Ben Ray
  Lord, Jeremy
REDMAN, William Xavier
  Scarlet, Will
REDMON, Lois
  Rogers, Rachel
REECE, Alys
  Wingfield, Susan
REED, Alexander Wyclif
  Harlequin
REED, Blair
  Ring, Adam
REEDER, Russell P
  Reeder, *Colonel* Red
REEMAN, Douglas
  Kent, Alexander
REES, Helen
  Oliver, Jane
REES, Joan
  Avery, June
  Bedford, Ann
  Strong, Susan
REEVE, Winifred Babcock
  Watanna, Onoto
REEVE-JONES, Alan
  Lunchbasket, Roger
REEVES, John Morris
  Reeves, James
REEVES, Joyce
  Gard, Joyce
REID, John
  Caliban
  Toulmin, David

REID, Phillipa
  Sise, Annie
REID, Whitelaw
  Agate
REILLY, Helen K
  Abbey, Kieran
REINFELD, Fred
  Young, Edward
RENEVILLE, Mary Margaret
 Motley de
  Motley, Mary
RENFREW, A
  Patterson, Shott
RENNIE, James Alan
  Denver, Boone
RENTOUL, T Laurence
  Gage, Gervais
RESIDE, W J
  Raeside, Juks
RESSICH, John S M *and*
 DE BANZIE, Eric
  Baxter, Gregory
RESSLER, Lillian *and*
 O'DANIEL, Janet
  Janet, Lillian
REY, Hans Augusto
  Uncle Gus
REY, Lester Del *and*
 POHL, Frederik
  McCann, Edson
REYNOLDS, Dallas McCord
  Harding, Todd
  Reynolds, Mack
  Reynolds, Maxine
REYNOLDS, Helen Mary
 Greenwood Dickson
  Dickson, Helen
  Reynolds, Dickson
REYNOLDS, John E
  Dexter, Ross
RICCI, Lewis Anselm da Costa
  Bartimeus
RICE, Brian Keith
  Vigilans

RICE, Dorothy
  Borne, D
  Vicary, Dorothy
RICE, Joan
  Hallam, Jay
RICHARDS, Allen
  Rosenthal, Richard A
RICHARDS, James
  Cladpole, Jim
RICHARDS, Ronald C W
  Saddler, K Allen
RICHARDSON, Eileen
  Shane
RICHARDSON, Ethel Henrietta
  Richardson, Henry Handel
RICHARDSON, Gladwell
  Blacksnake, George
  Jones, Calico
  Kent, Pete
  Kildare, Maurice
  O'Riley, Warren
  Warner, Frank
  Winslowe, John R
RICHARDSON, Mary Kathleen
  Norton, S H
RICHARDSON, Midge Turk
  Turk, Midge
RICHARDSON, Robert S
  Latham, Philip
RIDDELL, *Mrs* J H
  Hawthorne, Rainey
  Trafford, F G
RIDDLESTON, Charles H
  Drongo, Luke
RIDDOLLS, Brenda H
  English, Brenda H
RIDEAUX, Charles
  Chancellor, John
RIDGE, William Pett
  Simpson, Warwick
RIDING, Laura
  Rich, Barbara
RIEFE, Alan
  Riefe, Barbara

RIFKIN, Shepard
  Logan, Jake
  Michaels, Dale
RIGONI, Orlando Joseph
  Ames, Leslie
  Bell, Carolyn
  Wesley, James
RIGSBY, Howard
  Howard, Vechel
RILEY, James Whitcomb
  Johnson, Benjamin F
RIMANOCZY, A
  Eland, Charles
RISTER, Claude
  Billings, Buck
  Holt, Tex
RITCHIE, Claire
  Heath, Sharon
RITCHIE, L Edwin
  Lewis, Voltaire
RIVETT, Edith Caroline
  Carnac, Carol
  Lorac, E C R
ROARK, Garland
  Garland, George
ROBBINS, Clarence Aaron
  Robbins, Tod
ROBBINS, June
  Julie of Colorado Springs
ROBERTS, Ann Lewis
  Clwyd, Ann
ROBERTS, Cecil
  Beresford, Russell
ROBERTS, Dorothy James
  Mortimer, Peter
ROBERTS, E N
  Newman, Ernest
ROBERTS, Eric
  Robin
ROBERTS, Irene
  Carr, Roberta
  Harle, Elizabeth
  Roberts, I M
  Roberts, Ivor

ROBERTS, Irene (cont'd)
Rowland, Iris
Shaw, Irene
ROBERTS, James
Horton, Robert J
ROBERTS, Janet Louise
Bronte, Louisa
Dante, Rebecca
Radcliffe, Janette
ROBERTS, Keith J K
Bevan, Alistair
ROBERTS, Ursula
Miles, Susan
ROBERTSHAW, James Denis
Gaunt, Michael
ROBERTSON, Constance Noyes
Scott, Dana
ROBERTSON, Eileen Arbuthnot
Robertson, E Arnot
ROBERTSON, Frank Chester
Crane, Robert
Field, Frank Chester
Hill, King
ROBERTSON, James Logie
Haliburton, Hugh
ROBERTSON, James Robin
Connell, John
ROBERTSON, Keith
Keith, Carlton
ROBERTSON, Margery Ellen
Thorp, Ellen
Thorp, Morwenna
ROBERTSON, Walter George
Werrerson, Talbot
ROBERTSON, William
Strathearn-Hay
ROBEY, Timothy Lester Townsend
Townsend, Timothy
ROBINETT, Stephen
Hallus, Tak
ROBINS, Denise
Chesterton, Denise
French, Ashley

Gray, Harriet
Hamilton, Hervey
Kane, Julia
Wright, Francesca
ROBINS, Elizabeth
Raimond, C E
ROBINSON, Derek
Robson, Dirk
ROBINSON, H
Madeoc
ROBINSON, Joan Gale
Thomas, Joan Gale
ROBINSON, Julien Louis
Vedey, Julian
ROBINSON, Lewis George
Limnelius, George
ROBINSON, Patricia *and* STEVENSON, Ferdinan
Macomber, Daria
ROBINSON, Richard Blundell
Leaderman, George
ROBINSON, Sheila
Radley, Sheila
Rowan, Hester
ROBSON, Norman
Robb, John
ROBY, Mary Linn
D'Arcy, Pamela
Grey, Georgina
Welles, Elizabeth
Wilson, Mary
ROCHE, Thomas
Yes Tor
ROCHESTER, George Ernest
Gaunt, Jeffrey
ROCKEY, Howard
Panbourne, Oliver
RODDA, Charles
Holt, Gavin
RODDA, Charles *and* AMBLER, Eric
Reed, Eliot
RODRIGUEZ, Judith G
Green, Judith G

ROE, Eric
  Roe, Tig
ROE, F Gordon
  Uncle Gordon
ROE, Ivan
  Savage, Richard
ROETHKE, Theodore
  Rothberg, Winterset
ROGERS, Rosemary
  Mayson, Marina
ROGERS, Ruth
  Alexander, Ruth
ROGERS, Samuel Shepard
  Shepard, Sam
ROGERSON, James
  Hamilton, Roger
ROHEN, Edward
  Connors, Bruton
ROHLFS, *Mrs* Anna
  Greene, Anna Katharine
ROHRBACH, Peter Thomas
  Cody, James
ROLFE, Edwin
  Fuller, Lester
ROLFE, Frederick
  Corvo, *Baron*
ROLLINS, Kathleen *and*
  DRESSER, Davis
  Debrett, Hal
ROLLINS, William
  Stacy, O'Connor
ROMANOFF, Alexander
  Nicholayevitch
  Abdullah, Achmed
ROMLEY, Frederick J
  Romley, Derek
ROOME, Gerald Antony
  Leslie, Colin
ROOS, William
  Rand, William
ROOS, William *and*
  KELLEY, Audrey
  Roos, Kelley

ROPER, Laura Wood
  Wood, Laura Newbold
ROPES, Arthur Reed
  Ross, Adrian
ROSCOE, John *and*
  RUSO, Michael
  Roscoe, Mike
ROSE, Alfred
  Reade, Rolf S
ROSE, Alvin Emmanuel
  Pruitt, Alan
ROSE, Elizabeth Jane
  Elizabeth
ROSE, Evelyn Gita
  Davis, Gita
ROSE, Graham
  Graham, John
ROSE, Ian
  Drachman, Wolf
  Rose, Robert
ROSE, Mary H
  Maizie
ROSE, Nancy A
  Sweetland, Nancy Rose
ROSEN, Michael
  Landgrave of Hesse
ROSENBERG, Ethel
  Clifford, Eth
  Penn, Ruth Bonn
ROSENBERG, Henrietta
  Keating, Walter S
ROSENKRANTZ, Linda
  Damiano, Laila
ROSENQUIST, Fingal
  Südorf, Fingal von
ROSENTHAL, Michael D H
  Ross, Michael D H
ROSENTHAL, Richard Allen
  Richards, Allen
ROSMAN, Alice Grant
  Rosna
ROSS, Charles
  Francis, James

109

ROSS, Frank Xavier
Frank, R Jr
ROSS, Isaac
Ross, George
ROSS, W W Eustace
E R
ROSS, William Edward Daniel
Ames, Leslie
Brooks, Laura Frances
Colby, Alice
Colby, Lydia
Dana, Rose
Daniels, Jan
Daniels, Jane
Dorset, Ruth
Gilmer, Ann
McCormack, Charlotte
Randolph, Ellen
Randolph, Jane
Roberts, Dan
Ross, Clarissa
Ross, Dan
Ross, Dana
Ross, Marilyn
Ross, W E D
Rossiter, Jane
Steele, Tex
Williams, Rose
ROSS, Zola Helen
Arre, Helen
Iles, Bert
Ross, Z H
ROSS-MACDONALD, Malcolm
Macdonald, Malcolm
Ross, Malcolm
ROSSITER, John
Ross, Jonathan
ROSSNER, Robert
Ross, Ivan T
ROSTEN, Leo C
Ross, Leonard Q
ROTH, Arthur
McGurk, Slater

ROTH, Holly
Ballard, K G
Merrill, P J
ROTHERAY, Geoffrey Neville
Rooke, Dennis
ROTHERY, Brian
Dyer, Brian
ROTHWEILER, Paul R
Ruyerson, James Paul
Scofield, Jonathan
ROTHWELL, Henry Talbot
Talbot, Henry
ROTSLER, William
Arrow, William
Hall, John Ryder
ROUSSEAU, Leon
Strydom, Len
ROWE, John Gabriel
Rowe, Alice E
Walters, T B
ROWE, Vivian Claud
Hooton, Charles
ROWLAND, Donald Sydney
Adams, Annette
Bassett, Jack
Baxter, Hazel
Benton, Karla
Berry, Helen
Brant, Lewis
Bray, Alison
Brayce, William
Brockley, Fenton
Bronson, Oliver
Buchanan, Chuck
Caley, Rod
Carlton, Roger
Cleve, Janita
Court, Sharon
Craig, Vera
Craile, Wesley
Dryden, John
Fenton, Freda
Field, Charles
Kroll, Burt

Langley, Helen
Lansing, Henry
Lant, Harvey
Lynn, Irene
McHugh, Stuart
Madison, Hank
Mason, Chuck
Murray, Edna
Page, Lorna
Patterson, Olive
Porter, Alvin
Random, Alex
Rimmer, W J
Rix, Donna
Rockwell, Matt
Roscoe, Charles
Rossetti, Minerva
Scott, Norford
Scott, Valerie
Segundo, Bart
Shaul, Frank
Spurr, Clinton
Stan, Roland
Stevens, J D
Suttling, Mark
Talbot, Kay
Travers, Will
Vinson, Elaine
Walters, Rick
Webb, Neil
RUBEL, James Lyon
Hayes, Timothy
Macrae, Mason
RUBENSTEIN, Stanley Jack
Ar, Esjay
RUBINS, Harold
Robbins, Harold
RUCHLIS, Hyman
Barrow, George
RUDNYCKYJ, Jaroslav B
Bij-Bijchenko
RUMBOLD-GIBBS, Henry St John C
Gibbs, Henry

Harvester, Simon
Saxon, John
RUNBECK, Margaret Lee
McKinley, Karen
RUNDLE, Anne
Lamont, Marianne
Manners, Alexandra
Marshall, Joanne
Sanders, Jeanne
RUNYAN, Alfred Damon
Runyon, Damon
RURIC, Peter
Cain, Paul
RUSH, Noel
Garnett, David S
Lee, David
RUSO, Michael *and*
ROSCOE, John
Roscoe, Mike
RUSSELL, Elizabeth Mary
Countess
Elizabeth
RUSSELL, George William
A E
Russell, Henry George
Minicam
RUSSELL, Shirley
King, Stephanie
Vernon, Marjorie
RUSSELL, Ursula D'Ivry
D'Ivry, Ursula
RUSTERHOLTZ, Winsome Lucy
Turvey, Winsome
RUTLEDGE, Nancy
Bryson, Leigh
RYALL, William Bolitho
Bolitho, William
RYAN, John D
Brother Ernest
RYAN, Paul William
Finnegan, Robert
RYDBERG, Ernie
Brouillette, Emil
McCary, Reed

RYDELL, Helen *and*
FORBES, Deloris Stanton
  Rydell, Forbes
RYDELL, Wendy
  Rydell, Wendell
RYDER, M L
  Lawson, Michael
RYDER, Vera
  Cook, Vera
  Mortimer, June
RYNNE, Alice
  Curtayne, Alice
RYWELL, Martin
  Hemingway, Taylor
  Sears, Deane

SABRE, Mel R *and*
EIDEN, Paul
  Stagg, Delano
SADGROVE, Sidney Henry
  Torrance, Lee
SAINT, Dora Jessie
  Read, Miss
SAINT-HILAIRE, P B
  Pavitra
SAINT INNOCENT, *Marquis of*
  Kahler, Woodland
ST JOHN, Wylly Folk
  Fox, Eleanor
  Larson, Eve
  Pierce, Katherine
  Vincent, Mary Keith
  Williams, Michael
SAKLATVALA, Beram
  Marsh, Henry
SALMON, Annie Elizabeth
  Ashley, Elizabeth
  Martin, Nancy
SALMON, Geraldine Gordon
  Sarasin, J G
SALMON, P R
  Panlake, Richard
SALSBURY, Nate
  Ireland, Baron

SALTZMANN, Sigmund
  Salten, Felix
SAMACHSON, Joseph
  Miller, John
  Morrison, William
SAMBROT, William Anthony
  Ayes, Anthony
SAMMAN, Fern
  Powell, Fern
SAMPSON, Richard Henry
  Hull, Richard
SAMUELSON-SANDVID,
Dorothy
  Dorfy
SANBORN, Duane
  Bradley, Duane
SANCTUARY, Brenda
  Campbell, Bridget
SANDERS, Dorothy Lucie
  Dean, Shelley
  Walker, Lucy
SANDERSON, Douglas
  Brett, Martin
  Douglas, Malcolm
SANDES, John
  Oriel
SANDFORD, Christopher
  Dansdorf, Chrysilla von
SANDFORD, Matthew
  Matt
SANDOZ, Mari
  Macumber, Mari
SANDS, Leo G
  Craig, Lee
  Helmi, Jack
  Herman, Jack
  Meuron, Skip
SARGENT, Genevieve
  Ginger
SASSOON, Siegfried
  Kain, Saul
  Lyre, Pinchbeck
  S S
  Sigma Sashûn

SATHERLEY, David *and*
  WHITEHAND, James
  Whitehand, Satherley
SAUNDERS, Ann Loreille
  Cox-Johnson, Ann
SAUNDERS, Cicely
  Strode, Mary
SAUNDERS, Hilary Aidan St
  George *and* PALMER, John
  Leslie
  Beeding, Francis
  Pilgrim, David
SAUNDERS, Jean
  Blake, Sally
  Innes, Jean
  Summers, Rowena
SAUNDERS, Margaret Bell
  Bell, Margaret
SAUNDERS, Margaret Marshall
  Saunders, Marshall
SAUNDERS, Theodore *and*
  MEANS, Mary
  Scott, Denis
SAVAGE, Lee
  Stewart, Logan
SAVAGE, Mildred
  Barrie, Jane
SAWKINS, Raymond Harold
  Forbes, Colin
  Raine, Richard
SAWYER, John *and*
  SAWYER, Nancy
  Buckingham, Nancy
  John, Nancy
  Quest, Erica
SAXON, Sophia
  Jarrett, Kay
SAYER, Nancy Margetts
  Bradfield, Nancy
SAYER, Walter William
  Quiroule, Pierre
SAYERS, Dorothy L
  Leigh, Johanna

SAYERS, James D
  James, Dan
SCHAAF, M B
  Goffstein, M B
SCHIFF, Sydney
  Hudson, Stephen
SCHISGALL, Oscar
  Hardy, Stuart
SCHLESINGER, Eleanor Medill
  Gizycka, Eleanor M
SCHMIDT, James Norman
  Norman, James
SCHNEIDER, B V H
  Humphreys, B V
SCHNEIDER, Daniel Edward
  Taylor, Daniel
SCHNEIDER, Monica Maria
  Oliver, Frances
SCHOENFELD, Eugene L
  Pocrates, *Dr* Hip
SCHOFIELD, Sylvia Anne
  Matheson, Sylvia A
  Mundy, Max
SCHOLEFIELD, Alan
  Jordan, Lee
SCHONFIELD, Hugh Joseph
  Fielding, Hubert
  Hegesippus
SCHREIBER, Hermann O L
  Bassermann, Lujo
SCHREINER, Olive Emilie
  Albertina
  Iron, Ralph
SCHUBE, Purcell G
  Mee
SCHÜTZE, Gladys Henrietta
  Leslie, Henrietta
  Mendl, Gladys
SCHWARTZ, F *and*
  SEAMAN, Sylvia Sybil
  Sylvin, Francis
SCOBIE, Stephen Arthur Cross
  Waverley, John

113

SCORTIA, Thomas Nicholas
Kurz, Artur R
McDow, Gerald
Nichols, Scott
SCOTT, Elise Aylen
Aylen, Elise
SCOTT, Evelyn
Souza, Ernest
SCOTT, Hilda R
Smith, Harriet
SCOTT, Hugh Stowell
Merriman, Henry Seton
SCOTT, Jody *and*
 LEITE, George Thurston
Scott, Thurston
SCOTT, Leslie
Cole, Jackson
Leslie, A
Leslie, A Scott
Scott, Bradford
SCOTT, Marian Gallagher
Oliver, Gail
SCOTT, Mary E
Graham, Jean
SCOTT, Peter Dale
Greene, Adam
Sproston, John
SCOTT, Rose Laure
Buckley, Eunice
SCOTT, William Matthew
Scott, Will
Watt, William
SCOTT, Winifred Mary
Wynne, Pamela
SCOTT-HANSEN, Olive
Murrell, Shirley
SCROGGIE, Marcus Graham
Cathode Ray
SEAMAN, Elizabeth C
Bly, Nellie
SEAMAN, *Sir* Owen
Nauticus
O S

SEAMAN, Sylvia Sybil *and*
 SCHWARTZ, F
Sylvin, Francis
SEARLE, M E
Eirene
M E S
SEAVER, Richard
Mole, Oscar
SEAWELL, Molly Elliot
Davis, Foxcroft
SEBENTHALL, Roberta
Kruger, Paul
SEBLEY, Frances Rae
Jeffs, Rae
SECCOMBE, Thomas
T S
SECRIST, W G *and*
 KELLIHER, Dan T
Secrist, Kelliher
SEDGEMORE, Brian Charles
 John
Forthemoney, Justinian
SEE, Carolyn
Highland, Monica
SEEDO, Sonia
Fuchs, Sonia
SEID, Ruth
Sinclair, Jo
SELCAMM, George
Machlis, Joseph
SELDES, Gilbert Vivian
Johns, Foster
SELDON TRUSS, Leslie
Selmark, George
SERAILLIER, Anne
Rogers, Anne
SERNER, Gunnar
Heller, Frank
SERVADIO, Gaia
Mostyn-Owen, Gaia
SERWICHER, Kurt
Kasznar, Kurt
SETH-SMITH, Leslie James
Brabazon, James

SEUFFERT, Muriel
 Faulkner, Mary
 Seuffert, Muir
SEWALL, Robert
 Abbott, Bruce
 Lamont, Wood C
SEWELL, Brocard
 Jerome, Joseph
SHACKLETON, Edith
 Heald, Edith
SHAFFER, Anthony *and*
 SHAFFER, Peter
 Anthony, Peter
SHAMBROOK, Rona
 Randall, Rona
SHANN, Renée
 Gaye, Carol
 Pent, Katherine
SHAPIRO, Samuel
 Falcon, Richard
SHAPPIRO, Herbert Arthur
 Arthur, Herbert
 Herbert, Arthur
SHARKEY, Jack
 Johnson, Mike
SHAROT, Angela
 Lansbury, Angela
SHARP, *Sir* Henry
 Ainsworth, Oliver
SHARP, Ian
 Judge, The
SHARP, William
 Macleod, Fiona
SHAW, Bynum G
 Gillette
SHAW, Charles
 Singer, Bant
SHAW, Felicity
 Morice, Anne
SHAW, George Bernard
 Corno di Bassetto
 G B S
SHAW, Howard
 Howard, Colin

SHAW, Jane
 Gillespie, Jane
SHEA, Michael
 Sinclair, Michael
SHEA, Patrick
 Laughlin, P S
SHECKLEY, Robert
 O'Donnevan, Finn
SHELDON, Alice B
 Sheldon, Raccoona
 Tiptree, James *Jr*
SHELDON, Peter
 Gaddes, Peter
SHELLABARGER, Samuel
 Esteven, John
 Loring, Peter
SHEPPARD, John Hamilton
 George
 Creek, Nathan
SHERIDAN, Elsie Lee
 Cromwell, Elsie
 Gordon, Jane
 Lee, Elsie
SHERIDAN, H B
 Sherry, Gordon
SHERMAN, Frank Dempster
 Carmen, Felix
SHIEL, M P *and*
 TRACY, Louis
 Holmes, Gordon
SHIELDS, George Oliver
 Coquina
SHIPLEY, Joseph Twadell
 Goliard, Roy
SHIPMAN, Natalie
 Arthur, Phyllis
SHIRAS, Wilmar H
 Howes, Jane
SHIRLEY, Edith
 Australia Jane
SHIRREFFS, Gordon D
 Donalds, Gordon
 Gordon, Stewart
 Maclean, Art

SHOLL, Anna McClure
  Corson, Geoffrey
SHORTT, Charles Rushton
  Rushton, Charles
SHUMSKY, Zena Feldman
  Collier, Jane
  Collier, Zena
SHUTE, Evan Vere
  Jameson, Vere
SIDDLE, Charles *and*
  PEEL, Frederick
  Slingsby, Rufus
SIDEBOTHAM, Herbert
  Candidus
  Scrutator
  Student of Politics, A
  Student of War, A
SIEGEL, Benjamin
  Benn, Matthew
SIEGEL, Doris
  Wells, Susan
SIEPMANN, Mary
  Wesley, Mary
SILLER, Hilda van
  Siller, Van
SILVERBERG, Robert
  Chapman, Walker
  Drummond, Walter
  Jorgenson, Ivar
  Knox, Calvin
  Knox, Calvin M
  Osborne, David
  Randall, Robert
  Sebastian, Lee
SILVERBERG, Robert *and*
  GARRETT, Randall
  Randall, Robert
SILVETTE, Herbert
  Dogbolt, Barnaby
SIM, Katharine Phyllis
  Nuraini
SIMMONDS, Michael Charles
  Essex, Frank
  Simmonds, Mike

SIMMONS, J S A
  Cromie, Stanley
  Montgomery, Derek
SIMONDS, Peter
  Greaves, Richard
SIMONS, Katherine Drayton
  Mayrant
  Mayrant, Drayton
SIMPSON, Anthony McVay
  Warren, Tony
SIMPSON, Bertram L
  Weale, B Putnam
SIMPSON, Evan John
  John, Evan
SIMPSON, John Frederick
  Norman Hampson
  Hampson, John
SIMPSON, Keith
  Bailey, Guy
SIMS, George Robert
  Dagonet
SIMSON, Eric Andrew
  Kirk, Laurence
SINCLAIR, Bertha Muzzy
  Bower, B M
SINCLAIR, Kathleen Henrietta
  Knight, Brigid
SINCLAIR, Olga Ellen
  Clare, Ellen
SINGER, Isaac Bashevis
  Bashevis, Isaac
  Warshofsky, Isaac
SINGER, James Hyman
  Singer, Burns
SINGH, Gopal
  Dardi
SIZER, Laurence
  Laurier, Don
SKIDELSKY, Simon Jasha
  Simon, S J
SKINNER, Conrad Arthur
  Maurice, Michael

SKINNER, June O'Grady
  Carleon, A
  O'Grady, Rohan
SKRINE, Agnes Higginson
  O'Neill, Moira
SKUES, George Edward
  Mackenzie
  Seaforth
SLADEK, John Thomas *and*
  DISCH, Thomas M
  Demijohn, Thom
  Knye, Cassandra
SLANEY, George Wilson
  Woden, George
SLATER, Ernest
  Gwynne, Paul
SLATER, James
  Capitalist
SLATER, Montagu
  Johns, Richard
SLAUGHTER, Frank Gill
  Terry, C V
SLAVITT, David
  Sutton, Henry
SLESAR, Henry
  Leslie, O H
SLOCUM, Edward Mark
  Edwinson, Edmund
SLOGGETT, Nellie
  Cornwall, Nellie
SLUNG, Louis Scheaffer
  Sheaffer, Louis
SMALL, Austin J
  Seamark
SMITH, Alfred Aloysius
  Horn, Trader
SMITH, Barbara Herrnstein
  Herrnstein, Barbara
SMITH, Charles H
  Arp, Bill
SMITH, Dorothy Gladys
  Anthony, C L
  Smith, Dodie

SMITH, Edgar
  Mason, Michael
SMITH, Edward Ernest
  Lindall, Edward
SMITH, Edward Percy
  Percy, Edward
SMITH, Elizabeth Thomasina
  Meade
  Meade, L T
SMITH, Ernest Bramah
  Bramah, Ernest
SMITH, Evelyn E
  Lyons, Delphine C
SMITH, Florence Margaret
  Smith, Stevie
SMITH, Frances C
  Smith, Jean
SMITH, Frank E
  Craig, Jonathan
SMITH, Frederick E
  Farrell, David
SMITH, Frederick William Robin,
  Earl of Birkenhead
  Furneaux, Robin
SMITH, G M
  Grey, Steele
SMITH, George
  Smith, Clyde
SMITH, George H
  Hudson, Jan
  Jason, Jerry
  Summers, Diana
SMITH, George H *and*
  SMITH, M Jane Deer
  Deer, M J
SMITH, Goldwin
  Bystander, A
SMITH, H Everard
  Everard, Henry
SMITH, Helen Zenna
  Price, Evadne
SMITH, John
  Smith, C Busby

SMITH, June Johns
  Johns, June
SMITH, Lillian M
  Warner, Leigh
SMITH, Lily
  Wanderer
SMITH, Llewellyn *and*
  NASH, Vaughan
  Two East Londoners
SMITH, Margaret Ruth
  Seranne, Ann
SMITH, Marjorie Seymour
  Fearn, Elena
SMITH, Mary
  Drewery, Mary
SMITH, Norman Edward Mace
  Sheraton, Neil
  Shore, Norman
SMITH, Robert
  Chattan, Robert
SMITH, Robert Charles
  Charles, Robert
  Leader, Charles
SMITH, Rodney Collin *see*
  COLLIN SMITH, Rodney
SMITH, Sarah
  Stretton, Hesba
SMITH, Sidney Wallace
  Brodie, Gordon
SMITH, Walter Chalmers
  Knott, Hermann
  Orwell
SMITHELLS, Doreen
  Boscawen, Linda
SMITHERS, Leonard
  Neaniskos
SMITHIES, Muriel
  Howe, Muriel
  Nash, Newlyn
  Redmayne, Barbara
SMITTER, Eliott-Burton
  Hadley, Leila

SNODGRASS, W D
  Gardons, S S
  McConnell, Will
  Prutkov, Kozma
SNOW, Donald Clifford
  Fall, Thomas
SNOW, Charles Horace
  Averill, H C
  Ballew, Charles
  Hardy, Russ
  Lee, Ranger
  Marshall, Gary
  Smith, Wade
  Wills, Chester
SNOW, Helen Foster
  Wales, Nym
SNYDER, Louis Leo
  Nordicus
SODERBERG, Percy Measday
  Archer, S E
SOHL, Gerald Allen
  Butler, Nathan
  Sohl, Jerry
  Sullivan, Sean Mei
SOLOMON, Samuel
  Britindian
  Moolson, Melusa
SOMERVILLE, Edith Oenone
  Graham, Viva
  Herring, Geilles
  Somerville
SONTUP, Daniel
  Clarke, John
  Saunders, David
SOUSTER, Raymond
  Holmes, John
  Holmes, Raymond
SOUTER, Helen Greig
  Aunt Kate
SOUTHERN, Terry *and*
  HOFFENBERG, Mason
  Kenton, Maxwell

SOUTHWOLD, Stephen
  Bell, Neil
  Martens, Paul
  Miles
SPALDING, Keith
  Spalt, Karl Heinz G
SPALDING, Ruth
  Jay, Marion
SPECK, Gerald Eugene
  Kepps, Gerald
  Science Investigator
  Stone, Eugene
SPEICHER, Helen Ross *and*
 BORLAND, Kathryn K
  Abbott, Alice
  Land, Jane *and* Ross
SPENCE, William Duncan
  Bowden, Jim
  Ford, Kirk
  Rogers, Floyd
  Spence, Duncan
SPENDER, Stephen
  S H S
SPEWACK, Samuel
  Abbott, A A
SPICER, Bart *and*
 SPICER, Betty Coe
  Barbette, Jay
SPIEGEL, Clara E *and*
 MAYER, Jane
  Jaynes, Clare
SPILLANE, Frank Morrison
  Spillane, Mickey
SPINELLI, Grace
  Spinelli, Marcos
SPIRO, Edward H
  Cookridge, E H
SPOONER, Peter Alan
  Mellor, Michael
  Peters, Alan
  Rennie, Jack
  Underwood, Keith
SPRATLING, Walter Norman
  Sparlin, W

SPRIGG, Christopher St John
  Caudwell, Christopher
SPRING, Howard
  R H S
SPROAT, Iain Macdonald
  Penn, Richard
SPROULE, Howard
  Sproule, Wesley
SQUIBBS, H W Q
  Quirk
SQUIRE, *Sir* John Collings
  Eagle, Solomon
STACEY, P M de Cosqueville
  De Cosqueville, Pierre
  Shelton, Michael
STAFFORD, Muriel
  Sauer, Muriel S
STAMP, Roger
  Mingston, R Gresham
STANIER, Maida
  Culex
STANLEY, Nora Kathleen Begbie
  Stange, Nora K
STANNARD, Eliza Vaughan
  Winter, John Strange
STANSFIELD, Anthony *and*
 LILLEY, Peter
  Buckingham, Bruce
STANTON-HOPE, W E
  Hope, Stanton
STAPLES, Reginald Thomas
  Brewster, Robin
  Sinclair, James
  Stevens, Robert Tyler
STARK, Raymond
  Norwood, John
STARKEY, James Sullivan
  O'Sullivan, Seumas
STARR, Richard
  Essex, Richard
  Richards, Stella
STATON-BEVAN, William Norman
  Abbey, Staton

STEAD, Thistle Yolette
Harris, Thistle Y
STEARN, John Theodor
Stern, John
STEARNS, Myron Morris
Amid, John
STEEGMULLER, Francis
Keith, David
Steele, Byron
STEELE, Harwood Elmes Robert
Steele, Howard
STEELE, Mary Quintard Govan
Gage, Wilson
STEELE, Patricia M V
Joudry, Patricia
STEELE, Robert V P
Thomas, Lately
STEFFAN, Alice Jacqueline
Steffan, Jack
STEFFENS, Arthur Joseph
Hardy, Arthur S
STEIN, Aaron Marc
Bagby, George
Bagby, George A
Stone, Hampton
STEIN, Gertrude
Toklas, Alice B
STEPHEN, Joyce Alice
Thomas, J Bissell
STEPHENS, Donald Ryder
Sinderby, Donald
STEPHENS, Eve
Anthony, Evelyn
STEPHENS, James
Esse, James
STERN, David
Sterling, Peter
STERN, Elisabeth Gertrude
Morton, Leah
STERN, Frederick Martin
Martin, Frederick
STERN, James
St James, Andrew

STERN, Philip Van Doren
Storme, Peter
STERNE, E G
Broun, Emily
STERNE, E G *and*
LINDSAY, Barbara
James, Josephine
STEVENS, Frances Moyer
Hale, Christopher
STEVENS, Henry Charles
Garry, Stephen
Mann, John
STEVENSON, Edward I P
Mayne, Xavier
STEVENSON, Ferdinan *and*
ROBINSON, Patricia
Macomber, Daria
STEVENSON, Florence
Colt, Zandra
Curzon, Lucia
Faire, Zabrina
STEVENSON, James Patrick
Radyr, Tomos
STEWART, Alfred Walter
Connington, J J
STEWART, Dorothy Mary
Elgin, Mary
STEWART, James L
Granger, Stewart
STEWART, John Innes
Mackintosh
Innes, Michael
STEWART, Kenneth Livingston
Livingston, Kenneth
STEWART, Neil *and*
JOHNSON, Pamela Hansford
Lombard, Nap
STICKLAND, Louise Annie
Beatrice
Somers, J L
STICKLAND, M E
Stand, Marguerite
STINE, George Harry
Correy, Lee

STITT, James M
  Brunswick, James
STOBO, *Reverend* Edward
John
  Aletheia
STOCKFORD, Lela E
  Hamilton-Stockford, Joan
STOCKS, Mary *and others*
  Heptagon
STODDARD, Charles Warren
  Pepperwood, Pip
STODDARD, William Osborn
  Forrest, *Colonel* Cris
STODDART, Jane T
  Lorna
STOE, M
  Bazagonov, M S
STOFFER, Edith G
  Ross, Deborah
STOKER, Alan
  Evans, Alan
STOKES, Francis William
  Everton, Francis
STOKES, Manning Lee
  Ludwell, Bernice
  Manning, Lee
STOLL, Dennis Gray
  Craig, Denys
STONE, Grace Zaring
  Vance, Ethel
STONE, Irving
  Tennenbaum, Irving
STONEBRAKER, Florence
  Shepard, Fern
  Stuart, Florence
STONEHAM, Charles Thurley
  Thurley, Norgrove
STONEHOUSE, Patricia Ethel
  Russell, Lindsay
STONIER, George
  Fanfarlo
  Whitebait, William
STONOR, Oliver
  Bishop, Morchard

STOPPARD, Tom
  Boot, William
STORY, Rosamond Mary
  Jeskins, Richard
  Lee, Charles H
  Lindsay, Josephine
  Tracy, Catherine
  Woods, Ross
STOTT, Mary
  Jacques
STOUTENBURG, Adrien
  Kendall, Lace
STRACHAN, Gladys Elizabeth
  Bill
STRAITON, Edward Cornock
  Vet, T V
STRAKER, J F
  Rosse, Ian
STRATEMEYER, Edward
  Appleton, Victor
  Bonehill, Ralph
  Winfield, Allen
  Winfield, Arthur M
STRATTON, Rebecca
  Gillen, Lucy
STREATFIELD, Noel
  Scarlett, Susan
STREET, Cecil John Charles
  Burton, Miles
  Rhode, John
STRONG, Anna Louise
  Anise
STRONG, Charles Stanley
  Stanley, Chuck
STRUNSKY, Simeon
  Patient Observer, The
STUART, Dorothy Margaret
  D M S
STUART, Hector A
  Caliban
STUART, Vivian Alex
  Allen, Barbara
  Finlay, Fiona
  Long, William Stuart

STUART, Vivian Alex (cont'd)
  Stuart, Alex
  Stuart, V A
STUART-HEATON, Peter
  Heaton, Peter
STUART-JERVIS, Charles Edward
  Coysh, Edward
STUBBS, Harry Clement
  Clement, Hal
STUBBS, Jean
  Darby, Emma
  March, Emma
STUDDERT, Annie
  Rixon, Annie
STURE-VASA, Mary
  O'Hara, Mary
STURGES, Mary d'Este
  Virakam, Soror
STURGIS, Justin
  Burgess, Gelett
STURT, George
  Bourne, George
STURTZEL, Howard Allison
  Annixter, Paul
STURTZEL, Jane L
  Annixter, Jane
  Comfort, Jane Levington
STYLES, Showell
  Carr, Glyn

§ §

*What song the Syrens sang, or
what name Achilles assumed,
though puzzling questions, are
not beyond all conjecture.
— Sir Thomas Browne. Urn burial*

§ §

SUDDABY, William Donald
  Griff, Alan

SULLIVAN, Edward Alan
  Murray, Sinclair
SULLIVAN, Marion F
  Brooks, James M
SUMMERS, Hollis
  Hollis, Jim
SUMMERSCALES, Rowland
  Gaines, Robert
SUMMERTON, Margaret
  Roffman, Jan
SUTHERLAND, Robert Garioch
  Garioch, Robert
SUTTON, Graham
  Marsden, Anthony
SUTTON, Phyllis Mary
  Riches, Phyllis
SUTTON, Rachel Irene Beebe
  Ray, Irene
  Sutton, Rachel B
SVEINSSON, Solveig
  Rivers, Ronda
SWALLOW, Norman
  Leather, George
SWAN, Annie S
  Lyall, David
  Orchard, Evelyn
SWARD, Robert S
  Dr Soft
SWATRIDGE, Irene M M
  Chandos, Fay
  Lance, Leslie
  Mossop, Irene
  Storm, Virginia
  Tempest, Jan
SWATRIDGE, Irene M M *and*
SWATRIDGE, Charles John
  Charles, Theresa
SWEET, John
  Kim
SWETENHAM, Violet Hilda
  Drummond, Violet Hilda
SWINNERTON, Frank
  Pure Simon

SWINTON, *Sir* Ernest Dunlop
Backsight-Forethought
O'le, Luk-Oie
SYMINGTON, David
Halliday, James
SYMONDS, E M
Paston, George
SYMONS, Dorothy G
Groves, Georgina

TABER, Clarence Wilbur
Job, Modern
TABORI, Paul
Hefner, Paul
Stafford, Peter
Stevens, Christopher
TAIT, Dorothy
Fairburn, Ann
TAIT, Euphemia Margaret
Ironside, John
TAIT, George B
Barclay, Alan
TAMES, Richard Lawrence
Lawrence, James
TANN, Jennifer
Booth, Geoffrey
TANNER, Edward Everett
Dennis, Patrick
Rowans, Virginia
TATE, George
Armstrong, George
TATHAM, Laura
Martin, John
Phipps, Margaret
TATTERSALL, Muriel Joyce
Wand, Elizabeth
TAYLOR, Bert Leston
B L T
TAYLOR, Constance Lindsay
Cullingford, Guy
TAYLOR, Deems
Smeed
TAYLOR, Kamala
Markandaya, Kamala

TAYLOR, Margaret Stewart
Collier, Margaret
TAYLOR, Phoebe Atwood
Tilton, Alice
TAYLOR, Roland
Gill, Stanley
TAYLOR, Stephana Vere
Benson, S Vere
TAYLOR, Sybil
Tremayne, Sydney
TAYLOR, Thomas Hillhouse
Taylor, Toso
TEAGUE, John Jessop
Gerard, Morice
TEGNER, Henry
Northumbrian Gentleman
Ruffles
TEILHET, Darwin le Ora
Fisher, Cyrus
Fisher, Cyrus T
TELENGA, Suzette
Yorke, Susan
TELLER, Neville
Owen, Edmund
TENNANT, Emma
Aydy, Catherine
TENNYSON, Margaret
Forrest, Carol
TERHUNE, Mary Virginia
Harland, Marion
TERKEL, Louis
Terkel, Studs
TETLEY, Edith Madeline
Weetwood, E M
TETTMAR, Betty Eileen
Spence, Betty E
THAYER, Emma Redington
Thayer, Lee
THAYER, Tiffany Ellsworth
Doe, John
Ellsworth, Elmer
THEODORACOPULOS, Peter
Taki

THIMBLETHORPE, June
Thorpe, Sylvia
THIRKELL, Angela
Parker, Leslie
THOM, William Albert Strang
Morrison, J Strang
THOMAS, Charles
Trevelyan, Percy
THOMAS, Craig
Grant, David
THOMAS, Edward
Eastaway, Edward
THOMAS, Edward Llewellyn Gordon
Gordon, Don
THOMAS, Ernest Lewys
Vaughan, Richard
THOMAS, Eugene
Grey, Donald
THOMAS, John Oram
Oram, John
THOMAS, Mary
Thomas, Tay
THOMAS, Reg
Preston, Jane
THOMAS, Robert Richard
Howerd, Gareth
THOMAS, Ronald Wills
Wills, Ronald
THOMAS, Ross
Bleeck, Oliver
THOMAS, Stanley A C
Wyandotte, Steve
THOMAS, Walter Dill Jr
Dill, Walter
THOMASHOWER, Dorothy
Thomas, Dorothy
THOMPSON, A M
Dangle
THOMPSON, Antony Allert
Alban, Antony
THOMPSON, Arthur Leonard Bell
Clifford, Francis

THOMPSON, Edward Anthony
Lejeune, Anthony
THOMPSON, George Selden
Selden, George
THOMPSON, Harlan
Holt, Stephen
THOMPSON, J W M
Quince, Peter
THOMPSON, Phyllis
Morgan, Phyllis
Rose, Phyllis
THOMSON, Christine Campbell
Alexander, Dair
THOMSON, Daisy
Roe, M S
Thomson, Jon H
THOMSON, Derick S
MacThomas, Ruaraidh
THORNE, Isabel Mary
Villiers, Elizabeth
THORNETT, Ernest Basil Charles
Penny, Rupert
THORP, Joseph
T
THORPE, John
Campbell, Duncan
Centaur
Scott, Douglas
THORPE-CLARK, Mavis
Latham, Mavis
TICHBORNE, Henry
Sundowner
TIERNEY, John
James, Brian
TILLETT, Dorothy Stockbridge
Strange, John Stephen
TILLEY, E D
Tilley, Gene
TILSLEY, Frank
X Y Z
TINDALL, William York
Yorick, A P

TINNE, Dorothea
  Strover, Dorothea
  Tinne, E D
TIRBUTT, Honoria
  Page, Emma
TITUS, Eve
  Lord, Nancy
TODD, Barbara Euphan
  Euphan
TODD, John Murray
  Fox, John
TODD, Ruthven Campbell
  Campbell, R T
TOFANI, Louise E
  Theophany
TOMALIN, Ruth
  Leaver, Ruth
TOMLIN, Eric
  Stuart, Frederick
TOMLINSON, Joshua Leonard
  Linson
TOMPKINS, Julia
  Neilson, Marguerite
TONKIN, C B
  Pledger, P J
TOOHEY, Barbara *and*
 BIERMANN, June
  Bennett, Margaret
TORDAY, Ursula
  Allardyce, Paula
  Blackstock, Charity
  Blackstock, Lee
  Keppel, Charlotte
TORREY, Ware
  Crosby, Lee
TORSVAN, Traven
  Traven, B
TOWNSEND, George Alfred
  Gath
TOWNSEND, Joan
  Pomfret, Joan
TOWNSEND, Mary Ashley
  Ashley, Mary
  Xariffa

TRACY, Donald Fiske
  Fuller, Roger
TRACY, Louis *and*
  SHIEL, M P
  Holmes, Gordon
TRALINS, S Robert
  Bixby, Ray Z
  King, Norman A
  Miles, Keith
  O'Shea, Sean
  O'Toole, Rex
  Sydney, Cynthia
  Tracy, Leland
  Tralins, Bob
  Tralins, Robert S
  Trainor, Richard
  Traube, Ruy
  Verdon, Dorothy
TRANTER, Nigel
  Tredgold, Nye
TRASK, Kate Nichols
  Trask, Katrina
TRENT, Ann
  Carlton, Ann
  Crosse, Elaine
  Desana, Dorothy
  Sernicoli, Davide
TREWIN, J C
  J C T
TRIEM, Paul Ellsworth
  Ellsworth, Paul
TRIMBLE, Chloe Maria
  Gartner, Chloe
TRIMBLE, Louis
  Brock, Stuart
  Travis, Gerry
TRIMMER, Eric
  Jameson, Eric
  Lawson, Dr Philip
TRIPP, H Alker
  Hoe, Lee
TRIPP, Kathleen
  Loewenthal, Karen

TRIPP, Miles Barton
  Brett, John Michael
  Brett, Michael
TRIPPE, Peter
  Peters, Geoffrey
TROCCHI, Alexander
  De Las Lunas, Carmencita
  Lengel, Frances
TROTTER, Grace Violet
  Paschal, Nancy
TROUBETZKOI, *Princess*
  Rives, Amelia
TROWBRIDGE, John Townsend
  Creyton, Paul
TRUAX, Rhoda
  Wyngard, Rhoda
TRUMAN, Marcus George
  Beckett, Mark
TRUMBO, Dalton
  Abbott, *Dr* John
  Demaine, C F
  Doyle, Emmett
  Fincher, Beth
  Flexman, Theodore
  Jackson, Sam
  Rich, Robert
TRUPO, Anthony
  Norvell, Anthony
TRUSS, Leslie Seldon *see*
  SELDON TRUSS, Leslie
TUBB, E C
  Adams, Chuck
  Cary, Jud
  Clarkson, J F
  Farrow, James S
  Fenner, James R
  Graham, Charles S
  Grey, Charles
  Gridban, Volsted
  Guthrie, Alan
  Holt, George
  Hunt, Gill
  Jackson, E F
  Kern, Gregory

  Lang, King
  Lantry, Mike
  Lawrence, P
  Lawson, Chet
  MacLean, Arthur
  Maddox, Carl
  Powers, M L
  Schofield, Paul
  Shaw, Brian
  Sheldon, Roy
  Stevens, John
  Thomson, Edward
  West, Douglas
  Wilding, Eric
TUCCI, Niccolo
  Stravolgi, Bartolomeo
TUCK, John Erskine
  Erskine, John T
TUCKER, Agnes
  Carruth, Agnes K
TUCKER, James
  Craig, David
TUCKER, William Joseph
  Scorpio
TULLETT, Denis John
  Dee, John
  Melmoth
  Sutton, John
TUNLEY, Roul
  Boyd, Edward
TURNBULL, Dora Amy
  Wentworth, Patricia
TURNER, John Victor
  Hume, David
TURNER, Judy
  Saxton, Judith
TURNER, Lida Larrimore
  Larrimore, Lida
TURNER, Philip
  Chance, Stephen
TURNER, W Price
  Turner, Bill
TURNGREN, Annette
  Hopkins, A T

TURTON-JONES, Edith
 Gillespie, Susan
TUTE, Warren
 Warren, Andrew
TYLER-WHITTLE, Michael
 Sidney
 Oliver, Mark
 Whittle, Tyler

UHR, Elizabeth
 Stern, Elizabeth
ULLYETT, Kenneth
 Bentley, W J
UNDERWOOD, Mavis Eileen
 Kilpatrick, Sarah
UNETT, John
 Preston, James
UNWIN, David Storr
 Severn, David
UPCHURCH, Boyd
 Boyd, John
UPTON, George Putnam
 Pickle, Peregrine
UPWARD, Edward Falaise
 Chalmers, Allen
URCH, Elizabeth
 Brogan, Elise
URELL, William Francis
 Francis, William
UREN, Malcolm
 Malcolm, John
 Matelot
URIS, Auren
 Auren, Paul
URQUHART, Macgregor
 Hart, Max
USHER, Frank Hugh
 Franklin, Charles
 Lester, Frank
USHER, John Gray
 Gray, Christopher
UTTLEY, Alice Jane
 Uttley, Alison

VACZEK, Louis C
 Hardin, Peter
VAHEY, John George Haslette
 Clandon, Henrietta
 Haslette, John
 Lang, Anthony
 Loder, Vernon
 Mowbray, John
 Proudfoot, Walter
VALLEE, Hubert Prior
 Vallee, Rudy
VAN ATTA, Winfred Lowell
 Ryerson, Lowell
VAN DEURS, George
 Shepard, Stratton
VAN DEVENTER, Emma M
 Lynch, Lawrence L
VAN ESSEN, W
 Serjeant, Richard
VAN ZELLER, Claud H
 Brother Choleric
 Venning, Hugh
VANCE, John Holbrook
 Held, Peter
 Holbrook, Jack
 Holbrook, John
 Vance, Jack
 Wade, Alan
VANCE, William E
 Cassidy, George
VANN, Gerald
 Oke, Simon
VAUGHAN, *Lady* Auriel
 Malet, Oriel
VAUGHAN, Owen
 Rhoscomyl, Owen
VAUGHAN WILLIAMS, Ursula
 Wood, Ursula
VEITCH, Thomas
 Kentigern, John
VENABLES, Terry *and*
 WILLIAMS, Gordon Maclean
 Yuill, P B

VENN, Mary Eleanor
  Adrian, Mary
VENNARD, Alexander Vindex
  Bowyang, Bill
  Reid, Frank
VERNER, Christopher Stuart
  Chase, Lesley
VERNON, Kathleen Rose
  Dixon, Lesley
  Vernon, Kay
VERRAL, Charles Spain
  Eaton, George L
VERWER, Johanne
  Johanson, Elizabeth
  Verwer, Hans
VESEY, Ernest Blakeman
  Lewis, Ernest
VICKERS, Roy
  Durham, David
  Kyle, Sefton
  Spencer, John
VICTOR, Metta Victoria Fuller
  Regester, Seeley
VIDAL, Gore
  Box, Edgar
VIERECK, George Sylvester
  Corners, George F
VILLIERS, David Hugh
  Buckingham, David
VINCIGUERRA, Frances
  Winwar, Francis
VINING, Charles A M
  R T L
VINING, Elizabeth Gray
  Gray, Elizabeth Janet
VINSQN, Rex Thomas
  King, Vincent
VINTER, Helen
  Smith, Naomi
VIVIAN, Evelyn Charles H
  Cannell, Charles
  Mann, Jack
  Vivian, E Charles

VLASTO, John Alexander
  Alexander, John
  Remenham, John
VOELKER, John Donaldson
  Traver, Robert
VOLK, Gordon
  Knotts, Raymond
VOSS, Vivian
  Vee, Roger
VULLIAMY, Colwyn Edward
  Rolls, Anthony
  Teg, Twm

WACE, M A
  Golden Gorse
WADDEL, Charles Carey
  Carey, Charles
WADDELL, Evelyn Margaret
  Cook, Lyn
WADDELL, Martin
  Sefton, Catherine
WADDELL, Samuel
  Mayne, Rutherford
WADDINGTON, Miriam
  Merritt, E B
WADE, Robert *and*
  MILLER, William
  Daemer, Will
  Masterson, Whit
  Miller, Wade
  Wilmer, Dale
WADE, Rosalind
  Carr, Catharine
WAGENKNECHT, Edward
  Charles
  Forrest, Julian
WAGNER, Margaret Dale
  Wagner, Peggy
WAGNER, Sharon Blythe
  Stephens, Casey
WAINHOUSE, Austryn
  Audiart
  Casavini, Pieralissandro

WAINWRIGHT, Gordon Ray
  Gordon, Ray
WAINWRIGHT, John
  Ripley, Jack
WAKEMAN, Frederic Evans
  Wakeman, Evans
WALDO, Edward Hamilton
  Ewing, Frederick R
  Hunter, E Waldo
  Queen, Ellery
  Sturgeon, Theodore
  Waldo, E Hunter
WALDRON, Corbin A
  Cal, Dakota
WALKER, David Esdaile
  Esdaile, David
WALKER, Edith
  Trafford, Jean
  Walker, Jean Brown
WALKER, Emily Kathleen
  Ash, Pauline
  Barry, Eileen
  Devon, Sara
  Durham, Anne
  Ellis, Louise
  Foster, Delia
  Lawson, Christine
  Lester, Jane
  Mayne, Cora
  Murray, Jill
  Tilbury, Quenna
  Treves, Kathleen
  Vincent, Heather
  Vincent, Honor
  Winchester, Kay
WALKER, Irma Ruth
  Walker, Ira
WALKER, John
  Thirlmere, Rowland
WALKER, Kenneth Macfarlane
  Macfarlane, Kenneth
WALKER, Lucy
  Sanders, Dorothy Lucy

WALKER, Peter Norman
  Coram, Christopher
  Ferris, Tom
  Manton, Paul
WALKER, Rowland
  Kenworthy, Hugh
WALKER, Roy
  Oliver, Roy
WALKER, Stella Archer
  Archer-Batten, S
WALKER, W Sylvester
  Coo-ee
WALKERLEY, Rodney L de
Burgh
  Athos
WALL, John W
  Sarban
WALLACE, Elizabeth Virginia
  Wallace, Betty
WALLACE, Henry
  Uncle Henry
WALLACE, John
  Texas Ranger
WALLACE, Lewis Alexander
  M B Oxon
WALLACE, Penelope
  Halcrow, Penelope
WALLACE-CLARKE, George
  Jaffa, George
WALLER, Leslie
  Cody, C S
  Mann, Patrick
WALLIS, Geraldine
  Campbell, Hope
WALLIS, Peter
  York, Peter
WALMSLEY, Arnold
  Roland, Nicholas
WALSH, James Morgan
  Carew, John
  Hill, H Haverstock
WALSH, Sheila
  Leyton, Sophie

WALTER, Dorothy Blake
Blake, Katherine
Blake, Kay
Ross, Katherine
Walter, Katherine
Walter, Kay
WALTON, John *and*
BRIGHOUSE, Harold
Conway, Olive
WALZ, Audrey
Bonnamy, Francis
WANNAN, John Fearn
Fearn, John
WARBURG, James Paul
Paul, James
WARD, Arthur Sarsfield
Rohmer, Sax
WARD, Robert Spencer
King, Evan
WARD, Elizabeth Honor
Leslie, Ward S
WARE, Eugene Fitch
Ironquill
WARNER, Anna Bartlett
Lothrop, Amy
WARNER, Geoffrey John
Johns, Geoffrey
WARNER, Susan Bogert
Wetherell, Elizabeth
WARREN, Edward Perry
Raile, Arthur Lyon
WARREN, John Russell
Coverack, Gilbert
WARRINER, Thurman
Kersey, John
Troy, Simon
WASHINGTON, Solomon
Gladden, Washington
WATERHOUSE, Keith *and*
DEGHY, Guy
Froy, Herald
Gibb, Lee
WATERS, John
Warner, Jack

WATERS, Rosemary Elizabeth
Horstmann, Rosemary
WATFORD, Joel
Essex, Jon
WATKINS, Alex
Linklater, Lane
WATKINS-PITCHFORD, Denys
James
B B
WATNEY, Bernard
Dolley, Marcus J
WATSON, Adam
Scipio
WATSON, Albert Ernest
Watson, Andrew
WATSON, Elliot Grant
Lovegood, John
WATSON, Jack Charles
Wauchope
Chrystie, Edward M
WATSON, James Wreford
Wreford, James
WATSON, John
Maclaren, Ian
WATSON, Julia
De Vere, Jane
Fitzgerald, Julia
Hamilton, Julia
WATSON, R A
Cromarty, Deas
WATT, Alexander Peter Fordham
Fraser, Peter
WATT, Esme
Jeans, Angela
WATTS, Edgar John Palmer
Palmer, John
WATTS, Mabel Pizzey
Lynn, Patricia
WATTS, Peter Christopher
Chisholm, Matt
James, Cy
Jones, Luke
Mackinloch, Duncan
Owen, Tom

WAUGH, Auberon
St Crispian, Crispin de
WAUGH, Hillary Baldwin
Grandower, Elissa
Taylor, H Baldwin
Walker, Harry
WAY, Elizabeth Fenwick
Fenwick, Elizabeth
WAYE, Ellen
Jose, Ellen J
WEALE, Anne
Blake, Andrea
WEAVER, Harriet Shaw
Wright, Josephine
WEBB, Charles Henry
Paul, John
WEBB, Dorothy Anna
March, Jermyn
WEBB, Godfrey E C
England, Norman
Godfrey, Charles
WEBB, Jack
Farr, John
Grady, Tex
WEBB, Jean Frances
Hamill, Ethel
Morrison, Roberta
Willoughby, Lee Davis
WEBB, Richard Wilson *and*
WHEELER, Hugh Callingham
Patrick, Q
Quentin, Patrick
Stagge, Jonathan
WEBB, Robert Forrest *and*
ELIADES, David
Forrest, David
WEBB, Ruth Enid
Morris, Ruth
WEBBE, Gale Dudley
Cole, Stephen
WEBER, Nancy
Harmston, Olivia
Rose, Jennifer
West, Lindsay

**WEBSTER, Alice Jane
Chandler**
Webster, Jean
WEBSTER, Owen
Pilgrim, Adam
WEEKES, Agnes Russell
Pryde, Anthony
WEEKS, *Lady* Constance Avard
Tomkinson, Constance
WEES, Frances Shelley
Shelley, Frances
WEHEN, Joy De Weese
Wade, Jennifer
WEI, Rex
Williams, Rex
WEIGHTMAN, Archibald John
Stuart, Alan
WEINBAUM, Stanley Grauman
Jessel, John
Stanley, Marge
WEINER, Margery
Lake, Sarah
WEINRICH, Anna Katharina H
Aquinas, Sister Mary
WEINSTEIN, Nathan Wallenstein
West, Nathanael
WEIR, Rosemary
Bell, Catherine
Green, R
WELCH, Colin
Simple, Peter
WELDON, A E
Macnamara, Brinsley
WELLMAN, Manly Wade
Field, Gans T
WELLS, Carolyn
Wright, Rowland
WELLS, H G
Bliss, Reginald
WELLS, Helen
Lewis, Francine
WELLS, Lee Edwin
Poole, Richard

WENZ, Paul
  Warrego, Paul
WERNER, Elsa Jane
  Bedford, A N
  Bedford, Annie North
  Hill, Monica
  Nast, Elsa Ruth
  Werner, Jane
WERNER, Victor Emile
  Dallas, Vincent
WERTENBAKER, Lael Tucker
  Tucker, Lael
WEST, Betty Bowen
  Bowen, Betty
WEST, G A
  Kap-o-Kaslo
WEST, Gertrude
  West, Trudy
WEST, Joyce
  Gilbert, Manu
WEST, Morris
  East, Morris
  Morris, Julian
WEST-WATSON, Keith Campbell
  Campbell, Keith
WESTHEIMER, David
  Smith, Z Z
WESTLAKE, Donald Edwin
  Clark, Curt
  Coe, Tucker
  Culver, Timothy J
  Stark, Richard
WESTMARLAND, Ethel Louisa
  Courtney, Christine
  Elliott, Ellen
WESTMORELAND, Vera
Gertrude
  Elysian, Anne
WETHERELL-PEPPER, Joan
Gertrude
  Alexander, Joan
WHALLEY, Dorothy
  Cowlin, Dorothy

WHARMBY, Margot
  Winn, Alison
WHARTON, Michael
  Simple, Peter
WHEAR, Rachel
  Low, Rachel
WHEELER, Hugh Callingham
and WEBB, Richard Wilson
  Patrick Q
  Quentin, Patrick
  Stagge, Jonathan
WHEEN, Francis
  House, Patricia
WHELAN, Jerome Bernard
  Brien, R N
WHELAN, John
  O'Faolain, Sean
WHELPTON, Eric
  Lyte, Richard
WHEWAY, John
  Armitage, Hazel
WHIBLEY, Charles
  Thersites
WHISH, Violet E
  Swift, Stella
WHISTLER, Penelope
  Evans, Margiad
WHITAKER, Peter
  Proteus
WHITAKER, Rod
  Seare, Nicholas
  Trevanian
WHITBY, Anthony Charles
  Lesser, Anthony
WHITE, Alan
  Fraser, James
WHITE, Celia
  Tustin, Elizabeth
WHITE, Frank James
  Stewart-Hargreaves, E H I
WHITE, Herbert Oliver
  Martyn, Oliver
WHITE, Pauline Arnold
  Arnold, Pauline

WHITE, Stanhope
 Dan Bana
 Sabiad
WHITE, Stanley
 Krull, Felix
 White, James Dillon
WHITE, Theodore Edwin
 Archer, Ron
 Edwards, Norman
 White, Ted
WHITE, William Anthony P
 Boucher, Anthony
 Holmes, H H
WHITE, William Hale
 Rutherford, Mark
WHITEHAND, James *and*
 SATHERLEY, David
 Whitehand, Satherley
WHITEHOUSE, Arthur George
 Joseph
 Whitehouse, Arch
WHITEING, Richard
 Thorn, Whyte
WHITEMAN, William Meredith
 Turner, C John
WHITEFIELD, John
 Pilio, Gerone
WHITFIELD, Raoul
 Decolta, Ramon
WHITFORD, Joan
 Ford, Barry
 Oldham, Hugh R
WHITLOCK, Ralph
 Reynolds, John
 Reynolds, Madge
WHITNEY, Julie
 Yulya
WHITSON, John Harvey
 Garland, Luke
 Hazelton, *Captain*
 Hazelton, *Colonel*
 Merriwell, Frank
 Sewell, Arthur
 Sims, *Lieut* A K

Steel, Robert
Steele, Addison
Stevens, Maurice
Williams, Russell
WHITTEN, Wilfred
 John o'London
WHITTET, George Sorley
 Kerr, John O'Connell
 Monkland, George
WHITTINGTON, Harry
 Carter, Ashley
 Harrison, Whit
 Holland, Kel
 Myers, Harriet Kathryn
 Philips, Steve
 Stevens, Blaise
 Stuart, Clay
 Wells, Hondo
 White, Harry
 Whitney, Hallam
WIBBERLEY, Leonard Patrick
 O'Connor
 Holton, Leonard
 O'Connor, Patrick
 Webb, Christopher
WICKER, Tom
 Connolly, Paul
WICKSTEED, Margaret Hope
 Hope, Margaret
WIDGERY, Jeanne-Ann
 Widgery, Jan
WIEDENBECK, Emilie Agnes
 Mable, Peter
WIGGINS, David
 Priestley, Robert
WIGGLESWORTH, Martin
 Worth, Martin
WIGHT, J A
 Herriot, James
WILBY, Basil
 Knight, Gareth
WILCOX, Collin
 Wick, Carter

WILCOX, Harry
Derby, Mark
WILCOXEN, Harriett
Harriett
WILD, Dora Mary
Broome, Dora
WILD, Reginald
Edwards, Leonard
WILDING, Philip
Fraser, Jefferson
Haynes, John Robert
Marshall, Lloyd
Russell, Erle
Stanton, Borden
Stewart, Logan
Stuart, Logan
WILKES-HUNTER, Richard
Douglas, D
Douglas, Shane
Farr, C
Gray, Adrian
Mitchell, Kerry
WILKINS, Mary Louise
Calhoun, Mary
WILKINSON, A G
Desor, Réné
WILKINSON, Louis Umfreville
Marlow, Louis
WILKINSON, Percy F H
Wilkinson, Tim
WILLANS, Angela
Grant, Mary
WILLARD, Josiah Flynt
Flynt, Josiah
WILLEFORD, Charles
Charles, Will
WILLETT, Franciscus
McKern, Pat
WILLIAMS, Carol Elizabeth
Fenner, Carol
WILLIAMS, D F *and*
PATRY, M
Williams, Patry

WILLIAMS, Dorian (Joseph George)
Loriner
WILLIAMS, Edward John
Farrer, E Maxwell
WILLIAMS, Gordon Maclean *and*
VENABLES, Terry
Yuill, P B
WILLIAMS, Guy Richard Owen
Guinness, Owen
Woolland, Henry
WILLIAMS, Jay
Delving, Michael
WILLIAMS, Jeanne
Creasey, Jeanne
Crecy, Jeanne
Michaels, Kristin
Rowan, Deirdre
Williams, J R
WILLIAMS, Kathryn
Vinson, Kathryn
WILLIAMS, Margaret Wetherby
Erskine, Margaret
Williams, Wetherby
WILLIAMS, Meurig
Carrington, Michael
WILLIAMS, Ned
Harbin, Robert
WILLIAMS, Peggy Eileen Arabella
Evans, Margiad
WILLIAMS, Robert Moore
Browning, John S
WILLIAMS, Ursula Vaughan
see **Vaughan Williams, Ursula**
WILLIAMSON, Ellen DOUGLAS
Douglas, Ellen
WILLIAMSON, Ethel
Veheyne, Cherry
WILLIAMSON, Jack
Stewart, Will
WILLIAMSON, Leila Isobel
Orme, Eve

WILLIAMSON, Lydia Buckland
Sorace, Richard
WILLIAMSON, Thames Ross
Dagonet, Edward
Fleming, Waldo
Morgan, De Wolfe
Saltar the Mongol
Smith, S S
Trent, Gregory
WILLIS, Corinne
Denning, Patricia
**WILLIS, George Anthony
Armstrong**
A A
Armstrong, Anthony
WILLIS, Priscilla D
Adams, Mary Scott
**WILLOUGHBY-HIGSON, Philip
John**
Higson, P J W
WILLSON, Mitchell A *and*
POLANSKY, Abraham
Hogarth, Emmett
WILMOT, Frank Leslie Thomson
Maurice, Furnley
WILMOT, James Reginald
Trevor, Ralph
WILSON, Albert
Wilson, Yates
WILSON, Alec
Ulster Imperialist
WILSON, Andrew James
Wilson, Snoo
WILSON, Arthur
Dalry
WILSON, Desemea
Patrick, Diana
WILSON, Florence Roma Muir
Marichaud, Alphonse
Wilson, Romer
WILSON, Guthrie
Paolotti, John
WILSON, Helen
Wilson, Holly

WILSON, John
Stripper
**WILSON, John Anthony
Burgess**
Burgess, Anthony
Kell, Joseph
Wilson, John Burgess
WILSON, Joyce Muriel
Stranger, Joyce
WILSON, Robert McNair
Wynne, Anthony
WILSON, Sandra
Heath, Sandra
WILSON, Viva
Viva
WILSON, William *and*
GRANT, Donald
Ness, K T
WILTON, Charles Edward
Anglo-Austral
**WIMHURST, Cecil Gordon
Eugene**
Brent, Nigel
WINCHELL, Prentice
Collans, Dev
De Bekker, Jay
Dean, Spencer
St Clair, Dester
Sterling, Stewart
WINDER, Mavis Areta
Areta, Mavis
Winder, Mavis
Wynder, Mavis Areta
WINDSOR, Patricia
Daniel, Colin
WINKWORTH, Derek W
5029
WINNINGTON, Richard
Ross, John
WINSTON, Sarah
Lorenz, Sarah E
WINTER, Bevis
Bocca, Al
Cagney, Peter

WINTER, Bevis (cont'd)
Hill, Bennet
Shayne, Gordon
WINTER, C H
Riverina
WINTERFIELD, Henry
Michael, Manfred
WINTERS, Bayla
Winters, Bernice
WINTERTON, Paul
Bax, Roger
Garve, Andrew
Somers, Paul
WINTHROP, Bud Robert
Flanagan, Bud
WINTRINGHAM, Tom
Gracchus
WIRT, Mildred
Bell, Frank
Clark, Joan
West, Dorothy
WISE, Arthur
McArthur, John
WITCOMBE, Rick
Marker, Clare
WODEHOUSE, Pelham Graham
Powys, Stephen
WOHL, Ludwig von
De Wohl, Louis
WOLFF, William
Martindale, Spencer
WOLFSON, Victor
Dodge, Langdon
WOLLHEIM, Donald A
Grinnell, David
WOOD, Christopher
Dixon, Rosie
Grape, Oliver
Lea, Timothy
May, Jonathan
WOOD, Edgar Allardyce
Wood, Kerry

WOOD, Grace Ashley
Ancilla
WOOD, James
McLeod, Finlay
Stuart, Gordon
WOOD, John James O'Hara
Dee, R K
WOOD, Lilian Catherine
Cymry Bach
WOOD, Patricia E W
Ross, Patricia
WOOD, Samuel Andrew
Temple, Robin
WOOD, Violet
Wood, Quality
WOODCOCK, E Page
Uncle Reg
WOODFORD, Irene-Cecile
Barrie, Jane
Goff, Madeleine
Lee, Veronica
Woodford, Cecile
WOODHAM-SMITH, Cecil
Gordon, Janet
WOODHOUSE, Martin
Charlton, John
WOODRICH, Mary Neville
Neville, Mary
WOODROFFE, *Sir* John G
Avalon, Arthur
WOODS, Margery Hilton
Hilton, Margery
WOODS, Olwen
Woods, Jonah
WOOLFOLK, Josiah Pitts
Britt, Sappho Henderson
Kennedy, Howard
Sayre, Gordon
Woodford, Jack
WOOLLEY, Catherine
Thayer, Jane
WOOLSEY, Sarah Chauncey
Coolidge, Susan

WORBOYS, Annette Isobel
  Eyre, Annette
  Maxwell, Vicky
  Worboys, Anne Eyre
WORDINGHAM, James A
  Dare, Michael
WORNER, Philip A I
  Incledon, Philip
  Sylvester, Philip
WORNUM, Miriam
  Dennis, Eve
WORRELL, Everil
  Monett, Lireve
WORSLEY, T C
  Lister, Richard
WORTHINGTON-STUART,
  Brian Arthur
  Meredith, Peter
  Stuart, Brian
WORTHLEY, R G
  Viola
WORTHY, Brian Johnson
  Johnson, Brian
WORTIS, Avi
  Avi
WORTS, George F
  Brent, Loring
WRAITH, W J
  Alexander, Walter
WRIGHT, Elinor
  Lyon, Elinor
WRIGHT, George T
  Wright, Ted
WRIGHT, John
  Wright, Wade
WRIGHT, Marjory Beatrice
  Pilgrim
WRIGHT, Mary
  Bawn, Mary
WRIGHT, Patricia
  Napier, Mary
WRIGHT, R L Gerard
  Bristowe, Edwin

WRIGHT, Ronald Selby
  Radio Padre
WRIGHT, Sydney Fowler
  Fowler, Sydney
WRIGHT, Willard Huntington
  Van Dine, S S
WUNSCH, Josephine M
  McLean, J Sloan
WURMBRAND, Richard
  Moses, Ruben
WYLER, Rose
  Thayer, Peter
WYLLIE, James McLeod
  Barras Seer
WYND, Oswald
  Black, Gavin
WYNDHAM LEWIS, D B
  Beachcomber
  Shy, Timothy
WYNNE-TYSON, Esme
  De Morny, Peter

YARBRO, Chelsea Quinn
  Pryor, Vanessa
YARDUMIAN, Miryam
  Miryam
YATES, Alan Geoffrey
  Brown, Carter
YATES, George Worthing *and*
  MARSHALL, Charles Hunt
  Hunt, Peter
YATES, Raymond Francis
  Hall, Borden
YAUKEY, Grace
  Spencer, Cornelia
YEAKLEY, Marjory Hall
  Blair, Lucile
  Hall, Marjory
  Morse, Carol
YELLOT, Barbara Leslie
  Jordan, Barbara Leslie
YIN, Leslie Charles Bowyer
  Charteris, Leslie

YOCKEY, Francis Parker
Varange, Ulick
YONGE, Charlotte Mary
Aunt Charlotte
YORKE, Henry Vincent
Green, Henry
YOSELOFF, Thomas
Young, Thomas
YOUD, Samuel
Christopher, John
Ford, Hilary
Godfrey, William
Graaf, Peter
Nichols, Peter
Rye, Anthony
YOUNG, Agnes
Young, Agatha
YOUNG, Chesley Virginia
Barnes, C V
YOUNG, Eric Brett
Leacroft, Eric
YOUNG, Ernest
Gilcraft
YOUNG, Ernest A
Rockwood, Harry
YOUNG, Janet Randall *and*
  YOUNG, Robert William
Randall, Janet
Young, Bob
Young, Jan
YOUNG, Nedrick
Douglas, Nathan
YOUNG, Phyllis Brett
Young, Kendal
YOUNG, Robert
Hill, Rabin
YOUNG, Robert William *and*
  YOUNG, Janet Randell
Randell, Janet
Young, Bob
Young, Jan
YOUNGER, Elizabeth
Hely, Elizabeth

YOUNGER, William Anthony
Mole, William

ZACHARY, Hugh
Gorman, Ginny
Hughes, Elizabeth
Hughes, Zach
Kanto, Peter
Pilgrim, Derral
Rangely, E R
Rangely, Olivia
Van Heller, Marcus
ZAFFO, George J
Stewart, Scott
ZALBERG, Daniel
Daniel, S
ZARCHY, Harry
Lewis, Roger
ZEHNDER, Meinrad
Martin, Anthony
ZEIGER, Henry Anthony
Peterson, James
ZELAZNY, Roger
Denmark, Harrison
ZILLIACUS, Konni
Covenanter
Diplomaticus
Vigilantes
Williams, Roth
ZIM, Sonia
Bleeker, Sonia
ZIMMER, Maude Files
Baird, Maude F
Fileman, Nan
ZIMMERMAN, Robert Allen
Dylan, Bob
ZINBERG, Len
Lacy, Ed
ZINSSER, Hans
R S
ZOLL, Donald Atwell
Winslow, Donald
ZONIK, Eleanor Dorothy
Glaser, Eleanor Dorothy

ZORZA, Victor
  Kremlinologist

ZUBER, Mary E L
  Rowlands, Lesley

Pseudonyms

A A
Willis, George Anthony Armstrong

A A B
Baumann, Arthur A

A E
Russell, George William

A H
Hawkins, *Sir* Anthony Hope

A H G
Girdleston, A H

A L O M
Frank, *Mrs* M J

A P H
Herbert, *Sir* Alan Patrick

A Q-C
Quiller-Couch, *Sir* Arthur

A R O
Orage, Alfred James

ABBEY, Kieran
Reilly, Helen K

ABBEY, Ruth
Pattison, Ruth

ABBEY, Staton
Staton-Bevan, William Norman

ABBOT, Anthony
Oursler, Fulton

ABBOTT, A A
Spewack, Samuel

ABBOTT, A C
Meinzer, Helen Abbott

ABBOTT, Alice
Borland, Kathryn K *and*
Speicher, Helen Ross

ABBOTT, Bruce
Sewall, Robert

ABBOTT, *Dr* John
Trumbo, Dalton

ABBOTT, Johnston
Ashworth, Edward Montague

ABDULLAH, Achmed
Romanoff, Alexander Nicholayevitch

ABERCROMBIE, Patricia Barnes
Barnes, Patricia

ABHAVANANDA
Crowley, Edward Alexander

ACHAD, Haan
Ginzberg, Asher

ACHARYA, Pundit
Bhattacharya, Basudeb

ACLAND, Alice
Marreco, Anne

ACRE, Stephen
Gruber, Frank

ADAIR, Cecil
Green, Evelyn Everett

ADAIR, Dennis
Cronin, Bernard
ADAIR, Hazel
Addis, Hazel Iris
ADAIR, Sally
Mannock, Laura
ADAM, Cornel
Lengyel, Cornel Adam
ADAMS, Andy
Harkins, Peter
ADAMS, Annette
Rowland, Donald Sydney
ADAMS, Bart
Bingley, David Ernest
ADAMS, Christopher
Hopkins, Kenneth
ADAMS, Chuck
Tubb, E C
ADAMS, Clayton
Holmes, Charles Henry
ADAMS, Justin
Cameron, Lou
ADAMS, Lowell
Joseph, James Herz
ADAMS, Mary Scott
Willis, Priscilla D
ADAMS, Perseus
Adams, Peter Robert Charles
ADAMS, R D
Herbert, Robert Dudley
Sidney Powys
ADAMSON, Graham
Groom, Arthur William
ADDIO, E I
Fantoni, Barry
ADDISCOMBE, John
Hunter, Alfred John
ADDISON, Carol
Clarke, J Calvitt
ADALBERG, Doris
Orgel, Doris
ADELER, Max
Clark, Charles Heber

ADKINS, M D
Pound, Ezra
ADRIAN, Frances
Polland, Madeleine Angela
ADRIAN, Mary
Venn, Mary Eleanor
AGAR, Brian
Ballard, Willis Todhunter
AGARD, H E
Evans, Hilary Agard
AGATE
Reid, Whitelaw
AHERNE, Owen
Cassill, Ronald Verlin
AINSWORTH, Harriet
Cadell, Elizabeth
AINSWORTH, Oliver
Sharp, *Sir* Henry
AINSWORTH, Patricia
Bigg, Patricia Nina
AINSWORTH, Ruth
Gilbert, Ruth Gallard
AINSWORTHY, Roy
Paine, Laura Bosworth
AIRD, Catherine
McIntosh, Kinn Hamilton
AIRLIE, Catherine
Macleod, Jean Sutherland
AJAX
Jackson, Ada Acraman
AKENS, Floyd
Baum, Lyman Frank
AKERS, Alan Burt
Bulmer, Henry Kenneth
ALAIN
Brustlein, Daniel
ALAN, A J
Lambert, Leslie Harrison
ALAN, Jane
Chisholm, Lilian
ALAN, Marjorie
Bumpus, Doris Marjorie
ALBAN, Antony
Thompson, Antony Allert

ALBERT, Ned
Braun, Wilbur
ALBION, Ken
King, Albert
ALBRAND, Martha
Loewengard, Heidi H F
ALCYONE
Krishnamurti, Jiddu
ALDA, Frances
Davis, Frances
ALDEN, Jack
Barrows, Marjorie
ALDEN, Sue
Francis, Dorothy Brenner
ALDING, Peter
Jeffries, Roderic Graeme
ALDON, Adair
Meigs, Cornelia Lynde
ALETHEIA
Stobo, *Reverend* Edward John
ALEXANDER, Dair
Thomson, Christine Campbell
ALEXANDER, Jean
Penner, Manola J
ALEXANDER, Joan
Wetherell-Pepper, Joan
Gertrude
ALEXANDER, John
Vlasto, John Alexander
ALEXANDER, L G
Ftyaras, Louis George
ALEXANDER, Martin
Daventry, Leonard John
ALEXANDER, Mrs
Hector, Annie French
ALEXANDER, Ruth
Rogers, Ruth
ALEXANDER, Walter
Wraith, W J
ALGOL
Bretherton, C H
ALI-MAR
Porn, Alice

ALIEN
Baker, Louise Alice
ALIKI
Brandenberg, Alyce Christina
ALIUNAS
Baronas, Aloyzas
ALLABEN, Anne E
Farrell, Anne Elisabeth
ALLAN, Dennis
Denniston, Elinore
ALLAN, Luke
Amy, William Lacey
ALLAN, Ted
Herman, Alan
ALLARDYCE, Paula
Torday, Ursula
ALLBEURY, Ted
Allbeury, Theo Edward le
Bouthillier
ALLCOT, Guy
Pocock, Tom
ALLEGRO
Moore, Birkett
ALLEN, Adam
Epstein, Beryl *and*
Epstein, Samuel
ALLEN, Allyn
Eberle, Irmengarde
ALLEN, Barbara
Stuart, Vivian Alex
ALLEN, Betsy
Headley, Elizabeth
ALLEN, Clay
Paine, Lauran Bosworth
ALLEN, Dave
Mahoney, David
ALLEN, Dixie
Kohls, Olive N Allen
ALLEN, Eric
Allen-Ballard, Eric
ALLEN, F M
Downey, Edmund
ALLEN, Grace
Hogarth, Grace

ALLEN, John
Perry, Ritchie John Allen
ALLEN, John W Jr
Lesley, Peter
ALLEN, Ronald
Ayckbourne, Alan
ALLEN, Steve
Allen, Stephen Valentine
ALLENBY, Gordon
Matusow, Harvey Marshall
ALLERTON, Mark
Cameron, William Ernest
ALLERTON, Mary
Govan, Mary Christine
ALLISON, Clay
Keevil, Henry John
ALLISON, Rand
McCormick, Wilfred
ALLISON, Sam
Loomis, Noel Miller
ALLWORTHY, A W
Milam, Lorenzo W
ALLYSON, Alan
Nuttall, Anthony
ALMEDINGEN, E M
Almedingen, Martha Edith von
ALMONTE, Rosa
Paine, Lauran Bosworth
ALPHA CRUCIS
Herbert, Robert Dudley
Sidney Powys
ALPHA OF THE PLOUGH
Gardiner, Alfred George
ALSTON, Charles
Mott, Michael
ALTHEA
Braithwaite, Althea
ALVORD, Burt
Keevill, Henry John
AMBERLEY, Richard
Bourquin, Paul
AMBERLEY, Simon
Hoar, Peter

AMBROSE, Alice
Lazerowitz, Alice Ambrose
AMES, Felicia
Burden, Jean
AMES, Jennifer
Greig, Maysie
AMES, Leslie
Rigoni, Orlando Joseph
AMES, Leslie
Ross, William Edward Daniel
AMICUS CURIAE
Fuller, Edmund
AMID, John
Stearns, Myron Morris
AMIS, Breton
Best, Rayleigh Breton Amis
AMOR, Amos
Harrell, Irene Burk
AMOS, Alan
Knight, Kathleen Moore
AMPHIBIAN
Aston, *Sir* George
AMPLEGIRTH, Anthony
Dent, Anthony
AN BROC
O'Nolan, Brian
ANATOLE
Muller, Robert
ANAUTA
Blackmore, Anauta
ANCILLA
Wood, Grace Ashley
ANDERS, Rex
Barrett, Geoffrey John
ANDERSON, Ella
Macleod, Ellen
ANDERSON, George
Groom, Arthur William
ANDERSON, Rachel
Bradby, Rachel
ANDOM, R
Barrett, Alfred Walter
ANDREWS, A A
Paine, Lauran Bosworth

ANDREWS, Lucilla
Crichton, Lucilla Matthew
ANDRÉZEL, Pierre
Blixen-Finecke, Karen Christine
Baroness
ANGELL, Norman
Lane, *Sir* Ralph Norman Angell
ANGLO-AUSTRAL
Wilton, Charles Edward
ANGUS, Ian
Mackay, James Alexander
ANISE
Strong, Anna Louise
ANMAR, Frank
Nolan, William F
ANNIXTER, Jane
Sturtzel, Howard Allison
ANNIXTER, Paul
Sturtzel, Howard Allison
ANSTEY, F
Guthrie, Thomas Anstey
ANSTRUTHER, James
Graham, James Maxtone
ANTHONY, C L
Smith, Dorothy Gladys
ANTHONY, Charles
Akerman, Anthony Charles
ANTHONY, Evelyn
Stephens, Eve
ANTHONY, John
Beckett, Ronald Brymer
ANTHONY, John
Connor, Tony
ANTHONY, Peter
Shaffer, Anthony *and*
Shaffer, Peter
ANTHONY, Piers
Jacob, Anthony Dillingham
ANTONINUS, BROTHER
Everson, William Oliver
ANVIL, Christopher
Crosby, Harry C
AP EVANS, Humphrey
Drummond, Humphrey

APPLETON, Victor
Stratemeyer, Edward
AQUARIUS
Allen, John E
AQUINAS, *Sister* Mary
Weinrich, Anna Katharina H
AR, Esjay
Rubinstein, Stanley Jack
ARCHER, A A
Joscelyn, Archie
ARCHER, Frank
O'Connor, Richard
ARCHER, G Scott
Larbalestier, Phillip George
ARCHER, Owen
Greenwood, Augustus George
ARCHER, Ron
White, Theodore Edwin
ARCHER, S E
Soderberg, Percy Measday
ARCHER-BATTEN, S
Walker, Stella Archer
ARCHESTRATUS
Driver, Christopher
ARDEN, Clive
Nutt, Lily Clive
ARDEN, J E M
Conquest, Robert
ARDEN, Mary
Murry, Violet
ARDEN, William
Lynds, Dennis
ARESBYS, The
Bamberger, Helen R *and*
Bamberger, Raymond S
ARETA, Mavis
Winder, Mavis Areta
ARGUS
Phillips-Birt, Douglas
ARGUS, M K
Eisenstadt-Jeleznov, Mikhail
ARIEL
Arden, Adrian

ARION
Chesterton, G K
ARLEN, Michael
Kouyoumdjian, Dikran
ARLEY, Catherine
D'Arley, Catherine
ARMITAGE, Hazel
Wheway, John
ARMOUR, John
Paine, Lauran Bosworth
ARMSTRONG, Anthony
Willis, George Anthony
Armstrong
ARMSTRONG, George
Tate, George
ARMSTRONG, Raymond
Lee, Norman
ARMSTRONG, Sybil
Edmondson, Sybil
ARMSTRONG, Warren
Bennett, William E
ARNOLD, Joseph H
Hayes, Joseph
ARNOLD, L J
Cameron, Lou
ARNOLD, Pauline
White, Pauline Arnold
ARNOLD, Wilcox
Aitken, Andrew
ARP, Bill
Smith, Charles H
ARRE, Helen
Ross, Zola Helen
ARROW, William
Rotsler
ARSDALE, Wirt Van
Davis, Martha Wirt
ARTHUR, Burt
Arthur, Herbert
ARTHUR, Elisabeth
Irish, Betty M
ARTHUR, Frank
Ebert, Arthur Frank

ARTHUR, Gavin
Arthur, Chester Alan
ARTHUR, Gladys
Osborne, Dorothy Gladys
ARTHUR, Herbert
Shappiro, Herbert Arthur
ARTHUR, Phyllis
Shipman, Natalie
ARTHUR, William
Baker, William Howard
ARTHUR, William
Neubauer, William Arthur
ARTIFEX
Green, *Canon* Peter
ASCHE, Oscar
Heiss, John Stanger
ASCOTT, Adelie
Bobin, John W
ASH, Fenton
Atkins, Frank A
ASH, Pauline
Walker, Emily Kathleen
ASHDOWN, Clifford
Freeman, R Austin *and*
Pitcairn, John James
ASHE, Douglas
Bardin, John Franklin
ASHE, Elizabeth
Hyde, Lavender Beryl
ASHE, Gordon
Creasey, John
ASHE, Mary Ann
Lewis, Mary Christianna
ASHE, Susan
Best, Carol Anne
ASHFORD, Jeffrey
Jeffries, Roderic Graeme
ASHLEY, Elizabeth
Salmon, Annie Alizabeth
ASHLEY, Fred
Atkins, A
ASHLEY, Gladys
Ewens, Gwendoline Wilson

ASHLEY, Mary
Townsend, Mary Ashley
ASHMORE, Jane
Little, Cecile Enid
ASHTON, A B
Basch, Ernst
ASHTON, Ann
Kimbro, John
ASHTON, E B
Basch, Ernst
ASHTON, E E
Basch, Ernst
ASHTON, Lucy
Martin, Netta
ASKHAM, Francis
Greenwood, Julia E C
ASQUITH, Nan
Pattinson, Nancy
ASSIAC
Fraenkel, Heinrich
ASTLEY, Juliet
Lofts, Norah
ATHELING, William
Pound, Ezra
ATHELING, William *Jr*
Blish, James
ATHOS
Walkerley, Rodney L de Burgh
ATKINSON, Mary
Hardwick, Mollie
ATLEE, Philip
Phillips, James Atlee
ATTHILL, Robin
Atthill, Robert Anthony
AUBREY, Frank
Atkins, Frank A
AUCHTERLONIE, Dorothy
Green, Dorothy
AUDIART
Wainhouse, Austryn
AUGUR
Poliakoff, Vladimir
AUGUST, John
De Voto, Bernard Augustine

AUGUSTUS
Lynn, Elwyn
AULD, Philip
Burns, Bernard
AUMBRY, Alan
Bayley, Barrington John
AUNT CHARLOTTE
Yonge, Charlotte Mary
AUNT DAISY
Basham, Daisy
AUNT EVA
Bilsky, Eva
AUNT FRIENDLY
Baker, Sarah S T
AUNT KATE
Souter, Helen Greig
AUNT MAYSIE
Jeffrey-Smith, May
AUNTIE MARGARET
Keddie, Margaret Manson
AUREN, Paul
Uris, Auren
AUSTIN, Brett
Floren, Lee
AUSTIN, Frank
Faust, Frederick
AUSTIN, Hugh
Evans, Hugh Austin
AUSTRALIA JANE
Shirley, Edith
AUSTRALIANUS
Back, Karl John
AUSTWICK, John
Lee, Austin
AVALON
Blaser, Robin
AVALON, Arthur
Woodroffe, *Sir* John G
AVERILL, H C
Snow, Charles Horace
AVERY, Al
Montgomery, Rutherford
George

AVERY, June
Rees, Joan
AVERY, Lynn
Cole, Lois Dwight
AVERY, Richard
Cooper, Edmund
AVI
Wortis, Avi
AVON, Margaret
Keatley, Sheila
AWDRY, R C
Charles, Richard
AXTON, David
Koontz, Dean R
AYDY, Catherine
Tennant, Emma
AYE, John
Atkinson, John
AYES, Anthony
Sambrot, William Anthony
AYLEN, Elise
Scott, Elise Aylen
AYRE, Jessica
Appignanesi, Lisa
AYRES, Paul
Aarons, Edward Sidney
AYSCOUGH, John
Bickerstaffe-Drew, Alexander
Francis

§   §

*'The case of the prisoner Leon
Trotsky – which', he said, giving
Sippy the eye again, 'I am strongly
inclined to think an assumed and
fictitious name – is more serious.'
– P.G. Wodehouse. Carry on,
Jeeves*

§   §

B B
Watkins-Pitchford, Denys James

B B B
Buckham, Bernard
B L
Pound, Ezra
B L H
Haig, Emily Alice
B L T
Taylor, Bert Leston
BAB
Gilbert, William Schwenck
BABBITT, Robert
Bangs, Robert Babbitt
BACALL, Lauren
Perske, Betty
BACH, Sebastian
Andrews, John Arthur
BACHELOR OF ARTS, A
Bentley, Phyllis
BACK-BACK
Brown, Kay
BACKSIGHT-FORETHOUGHT
Swinton, *Sir* Ernest Dunlop
BACON, J D
Dodge, Josephine Daskam
BACON, Jeremy
Read, James
BAGBY, George
Stein, Aaron Marc
BAGBY, George A
Stein, Aaron Marc
BAGNOLD, Enid
Jones, *Lady* Roderick
BAILEY, Guy
Simpson, Keith
BAILEY, Hilea
Marting, Ruth Lenore
BAILEY, Matilda
Radford, Ruby Lorraine
BAILEY, Temple
Bailey, Irene Temple
BAILEY, Thomas
Partridge, Bellamy
BAIN, Bruce
Findlater, Richard

147

BAIRD, Maude F
Zimmer, Maude Files
BAKER, Asa
Dresser, Davis
BALAAM
Lamb, Geoffrey Frederick
BALBUS
Huxley, Julian Sorell
BALDRY, Enid
Citovich, Enid
BALDWIN, Bates
Jennings, John Edward
BALDWIN, Faith
Cuthrell, Faith Baldwin
BALDWIN, Gordo
Baldwin, Gordon C
BALFOUR, Grant
Grant, James Miller
BALL, Zachary
Masters, Kelly
BALLARD, K G
Roth, Holly
BALLARD, P D
Ballard, Willis Todhunter
BALLARD, Todhunter
Ballard, Willis Todhunter
BALLENTINE, John
Da Cruz, Daniel
BALLEW, Charles
Snow, Charles Horace
BALLINGER, W A
Baker, William Howard
BALLINGER, W A
Baker, William Howard *and*
McNeilly, Wilfred
BALLINGER, W A
NcNeilly, Wilfred
BAMFYLDE, Walter
Bevan, Tom
BANA, Dan
White, Stanhope
BANCROFT, John
Jenkins, Alan Charles

BANKOFF, George
Milkomane, George Alexis
Milkomanovich
BANNATYNE, Jack
Gaston, William J
BANNER, Angela
Maddison, Angela Mary
BANNERMAN, Mark
Lewing, Anthony
BANNON, Mark
King, Albert
BANNON, Peter
Durst, Paul
BANTON, Coy
Norwood, Victor George
Charles
BARAK, Michael
Bar-Zohar, Michael
BARAKA, Imamu Amiri
Jones, Le Roi
BARBELLION, W N P
Cummings, Bruce Frederick
BARBER, Antonia
Anthony, Barbara
BARBETTE, Jay
Spicer, Bart and
Spicer, Betty Coe
BARCLAY, Alan
Tait, George B
BARCLAY, Ann
Greig, Maysie
BARCYNSKA, Hélène *Countess*
Evans, Marguerite Florence
BARDSLEY, Michael
Nuttall, Anthony
BARKER, Jack
Barker, Michael
BARLAY, Bennett
Crossen, Kendell Foster
BARLING, Charles
Barling, Muriel Vere
BARNARD, Nancy
Hale, Sylvia

BARNES, C V
Young, Chesley Virginia
BARNES, Susan
Crosland, Susan
BARNETT, Adam
Fast, Julius
BARNETT, L David
Laschever, Barnett D
BARNWELL, J O
Caruso, Joseph
BARON, Alexander
Bernstein, Alec
BARON MIKAN
Barba, Harry
BARON, Paul
Landells, Richard
BARON, Peter
Clyde, Leonard Worswick
BARON, Willie
Bryant, Baird
BARR, Cecil
Kahane, Jack
BARR, Elisabeth
Edward, Irene
BARRACLOUGH, Howard
Fell, Barry
BARRAS SEER
Wyllie, James McLeod
BARRATT, Robert
Beeton, D R
BARRIE, Hester
Hector, Barbara
BARRIE, Jane
Savage, Mildred
BARRIE, Jane
Woodford, Irene-Cecile
BARRINGTON, E
Beck, Lily Adams
BARRINGTON, Maurice
Brogan, Denis
BARRINGTON, P V
Barling, Muriel Vere
BARRINGTON, Pamela
Barling, Muriel Vere

BARRISTER, A
Hill, Mavis
BARROW, George
Ruchlis, Hyman
BARROW, Pamela
Howarth, Pamela
BARRY
Humphries, Barry
BARRY, Ann
Byers, Amy
BARRY, Charles
Bryson, Charles
BARRY, Eileen
Walker, Emily Kathleen
BARRY, Jocelyn
Bowden, Jean
BARRY, Joe
Lake, Joe Barry
BARRY, Mike
Malzberg, Barry Norman
BARTHOLOMEW, Jean
Beatty, Patricia
BARTIMEUS
Ricci, Lewis Anselm da Costa
BARTLETT, Kathleen
Paine, Lauran Bosworth
BARTLETT, Laura
Baum, Lyman Frank
BARTON, Jack
Chadwick, Joseph
BARTON, Jon
Harvey, John
BARTON, Lee
Fanthorpe, Robert Lionel
BASHEVIS, Isaac
Singer, Isaac Bashevis
BASS, T J
Bassler, Thomas J
BASSERMANN, Lujo
Schreiber, Hermann O L
BASSETT, Jack
Rowland, Donald Sydney
BASSETT, John Keith
Keating, Lawrence Alfred

BASUDEB, Sree
Bahttacharya, Basudeb
BATCHELOR, Reg
Paine, Lauran Bosworth
BATTLE, Felix
Levin, Bernard
BAWN, Mary
Wright, Mary
BAX, Roger
Winterton, Paul
BAXTER, George Owen
Faust, Frederick
BAXTER, Gillian
Hirst, Gillian
BAXTER, Gregory
Ressich, John S M *and*
De Banzie, Eric
BAXTER, Hazel
Rowland, Donald Sydney
BAXTER, John
Hunt, E Howard
BAXTER, Olive
Eastwood, Helen B
BAXTER, Shane V
Norwood, Victor George
Charles
BAXTER, Valerie
Meynell, Laurence Walter
BAYARD, Fred
Campbell, Margaret *and*
Jansen, Johanna
BAYER, Oliver Weld
Bayer, Eleanor *and*
Bayer, Leo
BAYER, Sylvia
Glassco, John
BAYLISS, Timothy
Baybars, Taner
BAZAGANOV, M S
Stoe, M
BEA, Empy
Babcock, Maurice P
BEACHCOMBER
Morton, J B

BEACHCOMBER
Wyndham Lewis, D B
BEAMISH, Noel de Vic
Beamish, Annie O'Meara de Vic
BEAR, Bullen
Donnelly, Augustine
BEAR, I D
Douglass, Percival Ian
BEATON, George
Brenan, Edward Fitzgerald
BEATON, Jane
Long, Gladys
BEATTY, Baden
Casson, Frederick
BEAUMONT, Charles
Nutt, Charles
BECK, Allen
Cave, Hugh Barnett
BECK, Christopher
Bridges, Thomas Charles
BECK, Harry
Paine, Lauran Bosworth
BECKET, Lavinia
Course, Pamela
BECKETT, Mark
Truman, Marcus George
BECKWITH, Lillian
Comber, Lillian
BEDFORD, A N
Werner, Elsa Jane
BEDFORD, Ann
Rees, Joan
BEDFORD, Annie North
Werner, Elsa Jane
BEDFORD, Donald F
Bedford-Jones, Henry;
Friede, Donald *and*
Fearing, Kenneth
BEDFORD, John
Hastings, Phyllis
BEDFORD, Kenneth
Paine, Lauran Bosworth
BEE
Boshell, Gordon

BEECH, Margaret
Barclay, Vera C
BEECH, Webb
Butterworth, William Edmund
BEEDING, Francis
Saunders, Hilary Aidan St
George *and*
Palmer, John Leslie
BEER, Lisl
Beer, Eloise
BEG, Callum
Mack, J C O
BEG, Toram
McKillop, Norman
BELCHEM, David
Belchem, Ronald Frederick King
BELL, Carolyn
Rigoni, Orlando Joseph
BELL, Catherine
Weir, Rosemary
BELL, Frank
Wirt, Mildred
BELL, John
Johnson, Victor
BELL, Josephine
Ball, Doris Bell Collier
BELL, Leigh
Bell, Alison Clare Harvey
BELL, Margaret
Saunders, Margaret Bell
BELL, Nancy
Irish, Betty M
BELL, Neil
Southwold, Stephen
BELLAIRS, George
Blundell, Harold
BELLMAN, Walter
Barrett, Hugh Gilchrist
BELVEDERE, Lee
Grayland, Valerie M
BENARY-ISBERT, Margot
Benary, Margot
BENDER, Jay
Deindorfer, Robert G

BENDIT, Gladys
Presland, John
BENEDICT, Billy
Paul, Maury
BENKO, Nancy
Atkinson, Nancy
BENN, Matthew
Siegel, Benjamin
BENNETT, Dwight
Newton, Dwight Bennett
BENNETT, Elizabeth Deare
Merwin, Samuel Kimball
BENNETT, H O
Hardison, O B
BENNETT, Margaret
Toohey, Barbara *and*
Biermann, June
BENNETT, Rachel
Hill, Margaret
BENNEY, Mark
Degras, Henry Ernest
BENSON, Adam
Bingley, David Ernest
BENSON, Daniel
Cooper, Colin Symons
BENSON, S Vere
Taylor, Stephana Vere
BENSON, Thérèse
Knipe, Emilie
BENTINCK, Ray
Best, Rayleigh Breton Amis
BENTLEY, James
Hanley, James
BENTLEY, W J
Ullyett, Kenneth
BENTON, Karla
Rowland, Donald Sydney
BENTON, Will
Paine, Lauran Bosworth
BERCH, William O
Coyne, Joseph E
BERESFORD, Russell
Roberts, Cecil

BERG, Ila
Garber, Nellia B
BERGER, Helen
Bamberger, Helen R
BERKELEY, Anthony
Cox, A B
BERKLEY, Tom
Geen, Clifford
BERLIN, Irving
Baline, Israel
BERNARD
Boggs, Helen
BERNARD, Robert
Martin, Robert Bernard
BERNE, Leo
Davies, Leslie Purnell
BERNEY, Beryl
Lytle, *Mrs* W J A
BERRINGTON, John
Brownjohn, Alan
BERRISFORD, Judith
Lewis, Clifford *and*
Lewis, Judith May
BERRISFORD, Mary
Lewis, Mary Christianna
BERRY, Erick
Best, Allena
BERRY, Helen
Rowland, Donald Sydney
BERRY, Matilda
Beauchamp, Kathleen
Mansfield
BERTIN, Jack
Germano, Peter B
BERTON, Guy
La Coste, Guy R *and*
Bingham, E A
BERTRAM, Arthur
Ibbott, Arthur Pearson
BERWICK, Claude
Hunt, Anna Rebecca Gale
BETHUNE, Mary
Clopet, Liliane M C

BETTERIDGE, Anne
Potter, Margaret
BETTERIDGE, Don
Newman, Bernard
BETTINA
Ehrlich, Bettina
BEVAN, Alistair
Roberts, Keith J K
BEVANS, Torre
Hood, Torrey
BEVERLY, Linda
Quentin, Dorothy
BEXAR, Phil
Borg, Philip Anthony John
BEY, Isabelle
Bosticco, Mary
BEYNON, John
Harris, John Wyndham
Parkes Lucas Beynon
BHATIA, June
Bhatia, Jamunadevi
BIBOLET, R H
Kelly, Tim
BICKERDYKE, John
Cooke, C H
BIELY, Andrey
Bugaev, Boris Nikolaevich
BIJ-BIJCHENKO, B
Rudnyckyj, Jaroslav B
BILL
Strachan, Gladys Elizabeth
BILL, Margaret
Saunders, Margaret Bill
BILLINGS, Buck
Rister, Claude
BINDER, Eando
Binder, Otto
BINGHAM, Carson
Cassiday, Bruce
BIRD, Brandon
Evans, George *and*
Evans, Kay
BIRD, Lilian
Barradell-Smith, Walter

BIRD, Richard
Barradell-Smith, Walter
BIRKENHEAD, Edward
Birkenhead, Elijah
BIRKLEY, Dolan
Hitchens, Dolores
BIRMINGHAM, George A
Hannay, James Owen
BIRO, Val
Biro, Balint Stephen
BISHOP, Morchard
Stonor, Oliver
BISONIUS
Allen, John E
BIXBY, Ray Z
Tralins, S Robert
BIZET, George
Bisset-Smith, G T
BLACK, Gavin
Wynd, Oswald
BLACK, Ivory
Janvier, Thomas Allibone
BLACK, Jack
Ames, R F
BLACK, Jett
Black, Oliver
BLACK, Kitty
Black, Dorothy
BLACK, Laura
Longrigg, Roger Erskine
BLACK, Lionel
Barker, Dudley
BLACK, Mansell
Dudley-Smith, Trevor
BLACK, Veronica
Peters, Maureen
BLACKBURN, John
Mott, J Moldon
BLACKBURN, Martin
Allfree, P S
BLACKER, Hereth
Chalke, Herbert
BLACKLIN, Malcolm
Chambers, Aidan

BLACKSNAKE, George
Richardson, Gladwell
BLACKSTOCK, Charity
Torday, Ursula
BLACKSTOCK, Lee
Torday, Ursula
BLACKWELL, John
Collings, Edwin
BLAIKE, Avona
Macintosh, Joan
BLAINE, James
Avallone, Michael Angelo *Jr*
BLAINE, Jeff
Barrett, Geoffrey John
BLAINE, John
Goodwin, Harold Leland *and*
Harkins, Peter J
BLAINE, Sara
Morgan, Diana
BLAIR
Blair-Fish, Wallace Wilfred
BLAIR, Frank
Buckby, Samuel
BLAIR, Lucile
Yeakley, Marjory Hall
BLAIRMAN, Jacqueline
Pinto, Jacqueline
BLAISDELL, Anne
Linington, Elizabeth
BLAKE
Adam, Ronald
BLAKE, Alfred
Harris, Laurence Mark
BLAKE, Andrea
Weale, Anne
BLAKE, Andrew
Harris, Laurence Mark
BLAKE, Cameron
Mason, Michael
BLAKE, Eleanor
Pratt, E B Atkinson
BLAKE, Jennifer
Maxwell, Patricia Anne

BLAKE, Justin
Bowen, John *and*
Bullmore, Jeremy
BLAKE, Katherine
Walter, Dorothy Blake
BLAKE, Kay
Walter, Dorothy Blake
BLAKE, Ken
Bulmer, Henry Kenneth
BLAKE, Monica
Muir, Marie
BLAKE, Nicholas
Day Lewis, Cecil
BLAKE, Patrick
Egleton, Clive
BLAKE, Robert
Davies, Leslie Purnell
BLAKE, Sally
Saunders, Jean
BLAKE, Vanessa
Brown, May
BLAKE, Walker E
Butterworth, William Edmund
BLAKE, William
Blech, William James
BLAKE, William James
Blech, William James
BLANCHAN, Neltje
Doubleday, Neltje
BLAND, E
Bland, *Mrs* Edith (Nesbit)
BLAND, Fabian
Bland, *Mrs* Edith (Nesbit)
and Bland, Hubert
BLAND, *Mrs* Hubert
Bland, *Mrs* Edith (Nesbit)
BLAND, Jennifer
Bowden, Jean
BLAUTH, Christopher
Blauth-Muszkowski, Peter
BLAYRE, Christopher
Heron-Allen, Edward
BLEECK, Oliver
Thomas, Ross

BLEEKER, Sonia
Zim, Sonia
BLIGHT, Rose
Greer, Germaine
BLINDERS, Belinda
Coke, Desmond
BLINKHOALIE
Allison, William
BLISS, Adam
Burkhardt, Eve *and*
Burkhardt, Robert Ferdinand
BLISS, Reginald
Wells, H G
BLIXEN, Karen
Blixen-Finecke, Karen
Christence *Baroness*
BLOOD, Joan Wilde
Murray, Joan
BLOOD, Matthew
Dresser, Davis
BLOOMFIELD, Robert
Edgley, Leslie
BLUE, Wallace
Kraenzel, Margaret Powell
BLUNDELL, Peter
Butterworth, Frank Nestle
BLUNT, Don
Booth, Edwin
BLUTIG, Eduard
Gorey, Edward St John
BLY, Nellie
Seaman, Elizabeth C
BLYTH, John
Hibbs, John
BOAKE, Capel
Kerr, Doris Boake
BOARDMAN, Charles
Griffiths, Charles
BOAS, Marie
Hall, Marie
BOCCA, Al
Winter, Bevis
BODEN, Hilda
Bodenham, Hilda

BOGLE, Charles
Dukenfield, William Claude
BOHN, Eric
Price-Brown, John
BOILEAU, Marie
Hardy, Jane
BOK, Kooshti
Mair, George Brown
BOLD, Ralph
Griffiths, Charles
BOLDREWOOD, Rolf
Browne, Thomas Alexander
BOLES, Hal
Boles, Harold Wilson
BOLITHO, Ray D
Blair, Dorothy
BOLITHO, William
Ryall, William Bolitho
BOLSTER, Evelyn
Bolster, *Sister* M Angela
BOLT, Ben
Binns, Ottwell
BOLT, Lee
Faust, Frederick
BOLTON, Isabel
Miller, Mary Britton
BON GAULTIER
Martin, *Sir* Theodore
BON VIVEUR
Cradock, Phyllis Nan Sortain
and Cradock, John
BOND, Gillian
McEvoy, Marjorie
BONEHILL, Ralph
Stratemeyer, Edward
BONETT, Emery
Carter, Felicity Winifred
BONETT, John
Coulson, John
BONNAMY, Francis
Walz, Audrey
BONNER, Michael
Glasscock, Anne Bonner

BONNER, Parker
Ballard, Willis Todhunter
BONNEY, Bill
Keevill, Henry John
BOON, August
Breton-Smith, Clare
BOONE, Pat
Boone, Charles Eugene
BOOT, Rosie
Brown, Tina
BOOT, William
Stoppard, Tom
BOOTH, Geoffrey
Tann, Jennifer
BORDEN, Lee
Deal, Borden
BORDEN, Leigh
Deal, Borden
BORER, Mary Cathcart
Myers, Mary Cathcart
BORG, Jack
Borg, Philip Anthony John
BORLAND, Hal
Borland, Harold Glen
BORNE, D
Rice, Dorothy
BORODIN, George
Milkomane, George Alexis
Milkomanovich
BORTH, Willan G
Bosworth, Willan George
BOSCAWEN, Linda
Smithells, Doreen
BOSCO, Jack
Holliday, Joseph
BOSTON, Charles K
Gruber, Frank
BOSWELL, James
Kent, Arthur
BOSWELL, John
King, John
BOSWORTH, Frank
Paine, Lauran Bosworth

BOUCHER, Anthony
White, William Anthony P
BOUNDER, THE
Fay, E F
BOURCHIER, Jules
Posner, David Louis
BOURNE, George
Sturt, George
BOURNE, John
John, Owen
BOURNE, Lesley
Marshall, Evelyn
BOURNE, Peter
Jeffries, Bruce Graham
Montague
BOUVERIE
Kreiner, George
BOVEE, Ruth
Paine, Lauran Bosworth
BOWDEN, Jim
Spence, William
BOWEN, Betty
West, Betty Bowen
BOWEN, Elenore Sith
Bohannan, Laura M Smith
BOWEN, Marjorie
Campbell, Gabrielle Margaret
Vere
BOWER, B M
Sinclair, Bertha Muzzy
BOWERS, *Mrs* J Milton
Bierce, Ambrose
BOWIE, David
Jones, David Robert
BOWIE, Jim
Norwood, Victor George
Charles
BOWIE, Sam
Ballard, Willis Todhunter
BOWMAN, Jeanne
O'More, Peggy
BOWOOD, Richard
Daniell, Albert Scott

BOWYER, Nina
Conarain, Alice Nina
BOX, Edgar
Vidal, Gore
BOY
Fowkes, Aubrey
BOWYANG, Bill
Vennard, Alexander Vindex
BOYD, Alamo
Bosworth, Allan R
BOYD, Edward
Tunley, Roul
BOYD, Frank
Kane, Frank
BOYD, John
Upchurch, Boyd
BOYD, Nancy
Millay, Edna St Vincent
BOYD, Neil
De Rosa, Peter
BOYD, Prudence
Gibbs, Norah
BOYER, Robert
Lake, Kenneth Robert
BRABAZON, James
Seth-Smith, Leslie
BRACE, Timothy
Pratt, Theodore
BRACKEN, Steve
Farris, John Lee
BRACKETT, Leigh
Hamilton, Leigh Brackett
BRADBURNE, E S
Lawrence, Elizabeth
BRADDON, George
Milkomane, George Alexis
Milkomanovich
BRADEN, Walter
Finney, Jack
BRADFIELD, Nancy
Sayer, Nancy Margetts
BRADFORD, De Witt
Blossom, D Bradford

BRADFORD, Will
Paine, Lauran Bosworth
BRADLEY, Concho
Paine, Lauran Bosworth
BRADLEY, Duane
Sanborn, Duane
BRADLEY, Shelland
Birt, Francis Bradley
BRADWELL, James
Kent, Arthur
BRADY, William S
Harvey, John
BRAHMS, Caryl
Abrahams, Doris Caroline
BRAIN, Leonard
Peck, Leonard
BRAMAH, Ernest
Smith, Ernest Bramah
BRAMWELL, Charlotte
Kimbro, John
BRAND, Christianna
Lewis, Mary Christianna
BRAND, Clay
Norwood, Victor George
Charles
BRAND, David
Nutt, David
BRAND, Max
Faust, Frederick
BRAND, Mona
Fox, Mona Alexis
BRAND, Victor
Norwood, Victor George
Charles
BRANDANE, John
Macintyre, John
BRANDON, Bruce
Braun, Wilbur
BRANDON, Curt
Bishop, Curtis Kent
BRANDON, Joe
Davis, Robert Prunier
BRANDON, Sheila
Rayner, Claire

BRANDT, Tom
Dewey, Thomas Blanchard
BRANT, Lewis
Rowland, Donald Sydney
BRAY, Alison
Rowland, Donald Sydney
BRAYCE, William
Rowland, Donald Sydney
BREAKER, THE
Morant, Harry H
BRECK, Vivian
Breckenfeld, Vivian Gurney
BRENAN, Gerald
Brenan, Edward Fitzgerald
BRENDA
Castle Smith, *Mrs* G
BRENNAN, Walt
King, Albert
BRENNAN, Will
Paine, Lauran Bosworth
BRENNAND, Frank
Lambert, Eric
BRENNING, L H
Hunter, Alfred John
BRENT, *of Bin Bin*
Franklin, Stella Maria Sarah
Miles
BRENT, Calvin
Hornby, John Wilkinson
BRENT, Catherine
King, Albert
BRENT, Loring
Worts, George F
BRENT, Nigel
Wimhurst, Cecil Gordon
Eugene
BRENT, Romney
Larralde, Romulo
BREOLA, Tjalmar
De Jong, David Cornel
BRETT, John Michael
Tripp, Miles Barton
BRETT, Martin
Sanderson, Douglas

BRETT, Michael
Brett, Leslie Frederick
BRETT, Michael
Tripp, Miles Barton
BRETT, Molly
Brett, Mary Elizabeth
BRETT, Rosalind
Blair, Kathryn
BREWER, Mike
Guinness, Maurice
BREWSTER, Benjamin
Elting, Mary
BREWSTER, Benjamin
Folsom, Franklin Brewster
BREWSTER, Franklin
Folsom, Franklin Brewster
BREWSTER, Robin
Staples, Reginald Thomas
BRIARTON, Grendel
Bretnor, Reginald
BRIDE, Jack
Marteau, F A
BRIDGE, Ann
O'Malley, *Lady*
BRIDGE, John
Peters, Robert Louis
BRIDGEMAN, Richard
Davies, Leslie Purnell
BRIDGER, Adam
Bingley, David Ernest
BRIDGES, Tom
Bridges, Thomas Charles
BRIDGES, Victor
De Freyne, George
BRIDGWATER, Donald
Henderson, Donald Landels
BRIDIE, James
Mavor, Osborne Henry
BRIEN, R N
Whelan, Jerome Bernard
BRIEN, Raley
McCulley, Johnston
BRIGGS, Philip
Briggs, Phyllis

BRINSMEAD, H F
Brinsmead, Hesba
BRIONY, Henry
Ellis, Oliver
BRISCO, P A
Matthews, Patricia
BRISCO, Patty
Matthews, Patricia
BRISTOWE, Edwin
Wright, R L Gerrard
BRITAIN, Dan
Pendleton, Donald Eugene
BRITINDIAN
Solomon, Samuel
BRITT, Sappho Henderson
Woolfolk, Josiah Pitts
BROCK, Gavin
Lindsay, Maurice
BROCK, Lynn
Macallister, Alister
BROCK, Rose
Hansen, Joseph
BROCK, Stuart
Trimble, Louis
BROCKLEY, Fenton
Rowland, Donald Sydney
BRODIE, Gordon
Smith, Sidney Wallace
BROGAN, Elise
Urch, Elizabeth
BROGAN, James
Hodder-Williams, Christopher
BRONSON, Lynn
Lampman, Evelyn
BRONSON, Oliver
Rowland, Donald Sydney
BRONSON, Wade
King, Albert
BRONTE, Louisa
Roberts, Janet Louise
BROOK, Barnaby
Brooks, Collin
BROOK, Esther
Huggett, Berthe

BROOK, Peter
Chovil, Alfred Harold
BROOKE, Carol
Ramskill, Valerie
BROOKER, Clark
Fowler, Kenneth A
BROOKS, James M
Sullivan, Marion F
BROOKS, Jonathan
Mellett, John Calvin
BROOKS, Laura Frances
Ross, William Edward Daniel
BROOKS, W A
Fryefield, Maurice P
BROOKS, William Allan
Fryefield, Maurice P
BROOME, Adam
James, Godfrey Warden
BROOME, Dora
Wild, Dora Mary
BROTHER ANTONINUS
Everson, William Oliver
BROTHER CHOLERIC
Van Zeller, Claud H
BROTHER ERNEST
Ryan, John D
BROTHER FLAVIUS
Ellison, James
BROTHER GRAHAM
Jeffrey, Graham
BROUILLETTE, Emil
Rydberg, Ernie
BROUN, Emily
Sterne, E G
BROWARD, Donn
Halleran, E E
BROWN, Bill
Moore, Rosalie
BROWN, Carter
Yates, Alan Geoffrey
BROWN, Douglas
Gibson, Walter Brown
BROWN, Eve
Nichols, Mary Eudora

BROWN, Evelyn Berger
Berger, Evelyn Miller
BROWN, Jones
Munby, Arthur Joseph
BROWN, Mandy
Brown, May
BROWN, Marel
Brown, Margaret Elizabeth Snow
BROWN, Rosalie
Moore, Rosalie
BROWN, Will C
Boyles, Clarence Scott
BROWNE, Barum
Dennis, Geoffrey Pomeroy
BROWNE, Courtney
Courtney-Browne, Reginald D S
BROWNING, John
Brown, John
BROWNING, John S
Williams, Robert Moore
BROWNING, Sterry
Gribble, Leonard Richard
BROWNING, Vivienne
Baly, Elaine
BRUCE, Charles
Francis, Arthur Bruce Charles
BRUCE, David
Patchett, Mary Elwyn
BRUCE, Leo
Croft-Cooke, Rupert
BRUIN, John
Brutus, Dennis
BRUNSWICK, James
Stitt, James M
BRYAN, John
Delves-Broughton, Josephine
BRYANS, Robin
Harbinson-Bryans, Robert
BRYHER
Ellerman, Annie Winifred
BRYHER, Winifred
Ellerman, Annie Winifred

159

BRYSON, Leigh
Rutledge, Nancy
BUCHANAN, Chuck
Rowland, Donald Sydney
BUCHANAN, Patrick
Corley, Edwin *and*
Murphy, John
BUCHANAN, William
Buck, William Ray
BUCKINGHAM, Bruce
Lilley, Peter *and*
Stansfield, Anthony
BUCKINGHAM, David
Villiers, David Hugh
BUCKINGHAM, Nancy
Sawyer, John *and*
Sawyer, Nancy
BUCKLEY, Eunice
Scott, Rose Laure
BUCKMASTER, Henrietta
Henkle, Henrietta
BUCKROSE, J E
Jameson, Annie Edith
BUDD, Jackson
Budd, William John
**BUFFALO CHILD LONG
LANCE**
Clarke, Sylvestre
BUFFY
Glassco, John
BUGY, Oly
Buggie, Olive M
BULLEN BEAR
Donnelly, Augustine
BULLINGHAM, Ann
Jones, A Miles
BULMER, Kenneth
Bulmer, Henry Kenneth
BUNKER, *Capt* Moss
Brackman, Arnold C
BUPP, Walter
Garrett, Randall
BURCHELL, Mary
Cook, Ida

BURFIELD, Eva
Ebbett, Eve
BURFORD, Eleanor
Hibbert, Eleanor Alice Burford
BURGEON, G A L
Barfield, Arthur Owen
BURGER, John
Marquand, Leopold
BURGESS, Anthony
Wilson, John Anthony Burgess
BURGESS, Gelett
Sturgis, Justin
BURGESS, Sally
Burgess, Mary
BURGESS, Trevor
Dudley-Smith, Trevor
BURGOYNE, Elizabeth
Pickles, Mabel Elizabeth
BURKE, Edmund
Boggs, Winifred
BURKE, Fielding
Dargan, Olive
BURKE, Jonathan
Burke, John Frederick
BURKE, Leda
Garnett, David
BURKE, Michael
Farrell, Michael
BURKE, Noel
Hitchens, Dolores
BURKE, Owen
Burke, John
BURKE, Shifty
Benton, Peggie
BURLAND, Harris
Harris-Burland, John B
BURKHOLZ, Herbert
Irving, Clifford
BURNABY, Nigel
Ellett, Harold Pincton
BURNEY, Anton
Hopkins, Kenneth
BURNS, Bobby
Burns, Vincent

BURNS, Elizabeth
Behanna, Gertrude Florence
BURNS, Mary
Hare, Walter B
BURNS, Sheila
Bloom, Ursula
BURNS, Tex
L'Amour, Louis
BURR, Elsie
Milligan, Elsie
BURROUGHS, Margaret
Feldman, Eugene P R
BURROWAY, Janet
Eysselinck, Janet Gay
BURTON, Conrad
Edmundson, Joseph
BURTON, Miles
Street, Cecil John Charles
BURTON, Richard
Jenkins, Richard
BURTON, Thomas
Longstreet, Stephen
BUSHWOMAN
Palmer-Archer, Laura M
BUSTOS DOMECQ, Honorio
Borges, Jorge Luis *and*
Bioy-Casares, Adolfo
BUTLER, Ivan
Beuttler, Edward I O
BUTLER, Joan
Alexander, Robert William
BUTLER, Nathan
Sohl, Gerald Allen
BUTLER, Richard
Allbeury, Theo Edward le
Bouthillier
BUTLER, Richard
Butler, Arthur Ronald
BUTLER, Walter C
Faust, Frederick
BUTTERS, Dorothy Gilman
Gilman, Dorothy
BUTTLE, Myra
Purcell, Victor W W S

BYRNE, Donn
Donn-Byrne, Brian Oswald
BYROM, James
Bramwell, James Guy
BYSTANDER, A
Smith, Goldwin

C
Cuthbertson, James Lister
C D
Lawrence, T E
C J G
Lawrence, T E
C O
Collinson Owen, H
CABBY WITH CAMERA
Green, Maxwell
CABLE, Boyd
Ewart, Ernest Andrew
CABOCHON, Francis
Allan, Philip Bertram Murray
CADE, Alexander
Methold, Kenneth
CADE, Robin
Nicole, Christopher
CADWALLADER
Clemens, Paul

§ §

*A self-made man may prefer a
self-made name.*
– Judge Learned Hand

§ §

CAGNEY, Peter
Winter, Bevis
CAHILL, Mike
Nolan, William F
CAILLOU, Alan
Lyle-Smythe, Alan
CAILLOUX, Pousse
Bethell, Leonard Arthur

CAIN, Paul
Ruric, Peter
CAINE, Mark
Maschler, Tom *and*
Raphael, Frederic
CAINE, Michael
Micklewhite, Maurice Joseph
CAL, Dakota
Waldron, Corbin A
CALDECOTT, Veronica
Cohen, Victor
CALDWELL, Elinor
Breton-Smith, Clare
CALDWELL, Taylor
Caldwell, Janet Taylor *and*
Reback, Marcus
CALEHAS
Garvin, J L
CALEY, Rod
Rowland, Donald Sydney
CALHOUN, Mary
Wilkins, Mary Louise
CALIBAN
Phillips, Hubert
CALIBAN
Reid, John
CALIBAN
Stuart, Hector A
CALLAHAN, John
Chadwick, Joseph
CALLAHAN, William
Gallun, Raymond Z
CALLAS, Theo
McCarthy, Shaun
CALLAWAY, Hugh
Nisbet, Ulric
CALLENDER, Julian
Lee, Austin
CALLISTHENES
Costa, Gabriel
CALLUM, Michael
Greaves, Michael
CALLUM BEG
Mack, J C O

CALVERT, John
Leaf, Munro
CALVERT, Mary
Danby, Mary
CALVIN, Henry
Hanley, Clifford
CALVIN, Kenneth
Hogben, Lancelot Thomas
CAM
Campbell, Barbara Mary
CAMBRIDGE, Elizabeth
Hodges, Barbara K
CAMDEN, Richard
Beeston, L J
CAMERON, Brett
Martin, Reginald Alec
CAMERON, D Y
Cook, Dorothy Mary
CAMERON, Donald
Harbinson-Bryans, Robert
CAMERON, Hector
Macquarrie, Hector
CAMERON, Ian
Payne, Donald Gordon
CAMERON, John
Macdonell, A G
CAMERON, Julie
Cameron, Lou
CAMERON, Lorna
Fraser, Anthea
CAMERON, Margaret
Lindsay, Kathleen
CAMPBELL, Berkeley
Duddington, Charles Lionel
CAMPBELL, Bridget
Sanctuary, Brenda
CAMPBELL, Bruce
Epstein, Samuel
CAMPBELL, Colin
Christie, Douglas
CAMPBELL, Duncan
Thorpe, John
CAMPBELL, Hope
Wallis, Geraldine

CAMPBELL, Judith
Pares, Marion
CAMPBELL, Karen
Beaty, Betty
CAMPBELL, Keith
West-Watson, Keith Campbell
CAMPBELL, R T
Todd, Ruthven Campbell
CAMPBELL, Scott
Davis, Frederick William
CAMPBELL, Stuart
Campbell, Sydney George
CAMPION, Sarah
Alpers, Mary Rose
CANADIENNE
Hunt, Anna Rebecca Gale
CANAWAY, Bill
Canaway, W H
CANDIDUS
Brogan, Colm
CANDIDUS
Sidebotham, Herbert
CANDY, Edward
Neville, Alison
CANFIELD, Cleve
Mitchell, Clare May
CANFIELD, Dorothy
Fisher, Dorothea F C
CANIS
Hubbard, Clifford Lionel Barry
CANNAN, Denis
Pullein-Thompson, Denis
CANNAN, Joanna
Pullein-Thompson, Josephine
Mary
CANNELL, Charles
Vivian, Evelyn Charles H
CANNING, Effie
Carlton, Effie Crockett
CANNON, Brenda
Moore, Bertha B
CANNON, Curt
Lombino, Salvatore A

CANNON, Elliott
Elliott-Cannon, Arthur Elliott
CANTRELL, Wade B
Hogan, Robert Jasper
CANUCK, Abe
Bingley, David Ernest
CANUCK, Janey
Murphy, Emily Gowan
(Ferguson)
CANUSI, Jose
Barker, S Omar
CANYON, Claudia
Anderson, Betty
CAPE, Judith
Page, Patricia Kathleen
CAPELLE, Anne
Herapath, Theodora
CAPITALIST
Slater, James
CAPON, Peter
Oakley, Eric Gilbert
CAPP, Al
Caplin, Alfred Gerald
CAPSTAN
Hardinge, Rex
CAPTIOUS CRITIC
Miller, Lynn
CARBERY, Ethna
MacManus, Anna Johnston
CARDER, Michael
Fluharty, Vernon L
CAREW, Jean
Corby, Jane
CAREW, John
Walsh, James Morgan
CAREW, Tim
Carew, John Mohun
CAREY, Charles
Waddel, Charles Carey
CAREY, James
Carew-Slater, Harold James
CARFAX, Catherine
Fairburn, Eleanor

CARGOE, Richard
Payne, Pierre Stephen Robert
CARLEON, A
Skinner, June O'Grady
CARLETON, Janet
Adam Smith, Janet Buchanan
CARLETON, S
Jones, Susan Carleton
CARLETON-MILECETE
Jones, Susan Carleton
CARLISLE, D M
Cook, Dorothy Mary
CARLOTA
Oppenheimer, Carlota
CARLTON, Ann
Trent, Ann
CARLTON, Roger
Rowland, Donald Sydney
CARLYLE, Anthony
Milton, Gladys Alexandra
CARMAN, Dulce
Drummond, Edith
CARMEN, Felix
Sherman, Frank Dempster
CARMICHAEL, Harry
Ognall, Leopold Horace
CARMICHAEL, Philip
Harrison, Philip
CARNAC, Carol
Rivett, Edith Caroline
CARNEGIE, Sacha
Carnegie, Raymond Alexander
CAROL, Bill J
Knott, William Cecil
CARP, Augustus
Bashford, *Sir* Henry Howarth
CARR, Basil
Kahane, Jack
CARR, Catherine
Wade, Rosalind
CARR, Charles
Mason, Sydney Charles
CARR, Christopher
Benson, Arthur Christopher

CARR, Elaine
Mason, Sydney Charles
CARR, Glyn
Styles, Showell
CARR, H D
Crowley, Edward Alexander
CARR, Philippa
Hibbert, Eleanor Alice Burford
CARR, Roberta
Roberts, Irene
CARREL, Mark
Paine, Lauran Bosworth
CARRICK, Edward
Craig, Edward Anthony
CARRICK, John
Crosbie, Hugh Provan
CARRINGTON, Michael
Williams, Meurig
CARRINGTON, V
Hughes, Valerie Anne
CARROLL, Martin
Carr, Margaret
CARRUTH, Agnes K
Tucker, Agnes
CARSON, Anthony
Brooke, Peter
CARSON, Lance
Kelly, Harold Ernest
CARSON, Sylvia
Dresser, Davis
CARSTAIRS, Kathleen
Jacobs, Thomas Curtis Hicks
CARSTAIRS, Rod
Dalton, Gilbert
CARSTENS, Netta
Laffeaty, Christina
CARTER, Ann
Brooks, Ann
CARTER, Anne
Brooks, Ann
CARTER, Ashley
Whittington, Harry
CARTER, Avis Murton
Allen, Kenneth Sydney

CARTER, Bruce
Hough, Richard Alexander
CARTER, Diana
Copper, Dorothy
CARTER, John L
Carter, Compton Irving
CARTER, Nevada
Paine, Lauran Bosworth
CARTER, Nick
Avallone, Michael Angelo *Jr*
CARTER, Nick
Ballard, Willis Todhunter
CARTER, Nick
Carter, Bryan
CARTER, Nick
Lynds, Dennis
CARTER, Phyllis Ann
Eberle, Irmengarde
CARTIER, Steve
Cameron, Lou
CARTLAND, Barbara
McCorquodale, Barbara
Hamilton
CARTON, Richard Claude
Critchett, Richard Claude
CARVER, Dave
Bingley, David Ernest
CARY, Arthur
Cary, Joyce
CARY, D M
Macmillan, Douglas
CARY, Jud
Tubb, E C
CARYL, Jean
Kaplan, Jean Caryl
CASAVINI, Pieralessandro
Wainhouse, Austryn
CASE, Justin
Cave, Hugh Barnett
CASE, Justin
Gleadow, Rupert
CASE, Michael
Howard, Robert West

CASEY, Mart
Casey, Michael T *and*
Casey, Rosemary
CASEY, T
Cordes, Theodor K
CASKODEN, *Sir* Edwin
Major, Charles
CASS, Zoë
Low, Lois
CASSABA, Carlos
Parry, Michel
CASSADY, Claude
Paine, Lauran Bosworth
CASSANDRA
Connor, *Sir* William
CASSELLS, John
Duncan, William Murdoch
CASSIDY, George
Vance, William E
CASSILIS, Robert
Edwardes, Michael
CASSILS, Peter
Keele, Kenneth David
CASSIUS
Foot, Michael
CASTLE, Douglas
Brown, John Ridley
CASTLE, John
Payne, Ronald Charles *and*
Garrod, John William
CASTLE, Philip
Jackson, Charles Philip
Castle Kains
CASTLEMON, Harry
Fosdick, Charles Austin
CASWELL, Anne
Denham, Mary Orr
CATALAN, Henri
Dupuy-Mazuel, Henri
CATHODE RAY
Scroggie, Marcus Graham
CATLIN, Ralph
Lavender, David Sievert

165

CATLOW, Joanna
Lowry, Joan
CATO
Foot, Michael;
Howard, Peter *and*
Owen, Frank
CATTO, Max
Catto, Maxwell Jeffrey
CAUDWELL, Christopher
Sprigg, Christopher St John
CAULDWELL, Frank
King, Francis
CAUSEWAY, Jane
Cork, Barry
CAVANNA, Betty
Harrison, Elizabeth C
CAVE, Emma
Lassalle, Caroline
CAVENDISH
Brown, E
CAVENDISH, Peter
Horler, Sydney
CECIL, Edward
Maiden, Cecil
CECIL, Henry
Leon, Henry Cecil
CELTICUS
Bevan, Aneurin
CENSOR
Bunce, Oliver Bell
CENTAUR
Thorpe, John
CERAM, C W
Marek, Kurt W
CHABER, M E
Crossen, Kendell Foster
CHACE, Isobel
Hunter, Elizabeth
CHAFFIN, James B
Lutz, Giles A
CHAITANYA, Krishna
Nair, K K
CHALLICE, Kenneth
Hutchin, Kenneth Charles

CHALLIS, George
Faust, Frederick
CHALLIS, Simon
Phillips, Dennis John Andrew
CHALLONER, H K
Mills, Janet Melanie Ailsa
CHALMERS, Allen
Upward, Edward Falaise
CHALON, Jon
Chaloner, John Seymour
CHAMBERLAIN, Theodore
Johnson, Ronald
CHAMBERS, Dana
Leffingwell, Albert
CHAMBERS, Peter
Phillips, Dennis John Andrew
CHANAIDH, Fear
Campbell, John Lorne

§ §

Chance is but the pseudonyme of God for those particular cases which he does not choose to subscribe openly with his own sign manual. – De Quincey. The Spanish military nun

§ §

CHANCE, Jonathan
Chance, John Newton
CHANCE, Stephen
Turner, Philip
CHANCELLOR, John
Rideaux, Charles
CHANDLER, Frank
Harknett, Terry
CHANDOS, Fay
Swatridge, Irene M M
CHANEL
Joyce, James
CHANEY, Jill
Leeming, Jill

CHANNEL, A R
Catherall, Arthur
CHANNING, Peter
McMordie, Taber
CHAPMAN, Lee
Bradley, Marion Z
CHAPMAN, Mariston
Chapman, Mary I *and*
Chapman, John Stanton
CHAPMAN, Walker
Silverberg, Robert
CHARLES, Anita
Barrie, Susan
CHARLES, Edward
Hempstead, Charles Edward
CHARLES, Franklin
Adams, Cleve Franklin
CHARLES, Frederick
Ashford, F C
CHARLES, Henry
Harris, Marion Rose
CHARLES, Nicholas
Kuskin, Karla Seidman
CHARLES, Richard
Awdry, Richard Charles
CHARLES, Robert
Smith, Robert Charles
CHARLES, Theresa
Swatridge, Charles John *and*
Swatridge, Irene M M
CHARLES, Will
Willeford, Charles
CHARLTON, John
Woodhouse, Martin
CHARQUES, Dorothy
Emms, Dorothy
CHARTERIS, Leslie
Yin, Leslie Charles Bowyer
CHASE, Alice
McHargue, Georgess
CHASE, Beatrice
Parr, Olive Katherine
CHASE, James Hadley
Raymond, Rene

CHASE, Lesley
Verner, Christopher Stuart
CHATEAUCLAIR, Wilfred
Lighthall, William Douw
CHATHAM, Larry
Bingley, David Ernest
CHATTAN, Robert
Smith, Robert
CHEETHAM, Hal
Cheetham, James
CHEIRO
Hamon, Louis *Count*
CHELTON, John
Durst, Paul
CHERNICHEWSKI, Vladimir
Duff, Charles
CHERRYH, C J
Cherry, Carolyn Janice
CHERRYHOLMES, Anne
Price, Olive
CHERRYMAN, A E
Levin, Bernard
CHESHAM, Henry
Bingley, David Ernest
CHESHIRE, Giff
Cheshire, Gifford Paul
CHESNEY, Weatherby
Hyne, Charles John Cutliffe
Wright
CHESTER, Elizabeth
Ransome, L E
CHESTER, Peter
Phillips, Dennis John Andrew
CHESTER, Tom
Cheshire, David Frederick
CHESTERTON, Denise
Robins, Denise
CHESTOR, Rui
Courtier, Sidney Hobson
CHICHESTER
Drummond, Edith Victoria
CHILD, Alan
Langner, Laurence

CHILD, Charles B
Frost, C Vernon
CHIPPERFIELD, Robert Orr
Ostrander, Isabel Egerton
CHISHOLM, Matt
Watts, Peter Christopher
CHOLERIC, BROTHER
Van Zeller, Claude H
CHRISTIAN, Frederick
Gehman, Richard Boyd
CHRISTIAN, Frederick H
Nolan, Frederick
CHRISTIAN, Jill
Dilcock, Noreen
CHRISTIAN, John
Dixon, Roger
CHRISTOPHER, John
Youd, Samuel
CHRISTOPHER, Louise
Hale, Arlene
CHRONIQUEUSE
Logan, Olive
CHRYSTIE, Edward M
Watson, Jack Charles
Wauchope
CHU FENG
Blofeld, John
CHUB, Sergeant
Abrahamson, Maurice Noel
CHURCH, Granville
People, Granville Church
CHURCH, Jeffrey
Kirk, Richard Edmund
CHURCHILL, Elizabeth
Hough, Richard Alexander
CHURCHILL, Luanna
Dughman, John Karl *and*
Dughman, Frieda Mae
CIRCUIT BREAKER
Baker, C
CIRCUMLIBRA
Lockwood, Frank
CLADPOLE, Jim
Richards, James

CLAIRE, Keith
Andrews, Claire *and*
Andrews, Keith
CLANDON, Henrietta
Vahey, John George Haslette
CLAPP, Patricia
Cone, P C L
CLARE, Elizabeth
Cook, Dorothy Mary
CLARE, Ellen
Sinclair, Olga Ellen
CLARE, Helen
Blair, Pauline Hunter
CLARE, Marguerite
Heppell, Mary
CLARK, Curt
Westlake, Donald Edwin
CLARK, Dale
Kayser, Ronal
CLARK, David
Hardcastle, Michael
CLARK, Howard
Haskin, Dorothy C
CLARK, Joan
Wirt, Mildred
CLARK, Margery
Clark, Mary Elizabeth *and*
Quigley, M C
CLARK, Mary Lou
Clark, Maria
CLARKE, Hockley
Clarke, Henry Charles
CLARKE, *Captain* Jafah
Nesmith, Robert I
CLARKE, John
Laughlin, Virginia Carli
CLARKE, John
Sontup, Daniel
CLARKE, Merle
Gessner, Lynne
CLARKE, Pauline
Blair, Pauline Hunter
CLARKE, Richard
Paine, Lauran Bosworth

CLARKE, Robert
Paine, Lauran Bosworth
CLARKSON, Helen
McCloy, Helen
CLARKSON, J F
Tubb, E C
CLAUDE
Forde, Claude Marie
CLAUGHTON-JAMES, James
Bentley, James W B
CLAY, Bertha M
Braeme, Charlotte Monica
CLAY, Weston
Ford, T W
CLAYMORE, Tod
Clevely, Hugh Desmond
Claymore
CLEAR, Claudius
Nicoll, *Sir* William Robertson
CLEAVER, Denis
Leyland, Eric
CLEMENT, Hal
Stubbs, Harry Clement
CLEMENTIA
Feehan, *Sister* Mary Edward
CLEMENTS, E H
Hunter, Eileen
CLEMO, Jack
Clemo, Reginald John
CLEMONS, Elizabeth
Nowell, Elizabeth Cameron
CLEO ET ANTHONY
Anthony, Edward
CLERGYMAN, A
Morison, John
CLERIHEW, E
Bentley, Edmund Clerihew
CLEVE, Janita
Rowland, Donald Sydney
CLEVEDON, John
Plumley, Ernest F
CLEVELAND, Jim
King, Albert

CLEVELAND, John
McElfresh, Adeline
CLEVINGER, Paul
Norwood, Victor George
Charles
CLIFFORD, Eth
Rosenberg, Ethel
CLIFFORD, Francis
Thompson, Arthur Leonard Bell
CLIFFORD, John
Bayliss, John Clifford
CLIFFORD, Martin
Hamilton, Charles Harold
St John
CLINTON, Jeff
Bickham, Jack Miles
CLISSMANN, Anne
Clune, Anne
CLIVE, Clifford
Home-Gall, Edward Reginald
CLIVE, William
Bassett, Ronald
CLOIE, Mack
McKibbin, *Reverend*
Archibald
CLOSE, Upton
Hall, Josef Washington
CLOUD, Yvonne
Kapp, Yvonne
CLWYD, Ann
Roberts, Ann
CLYDE, Constance
MacAdam, Constance
CLYDE, Craig
Gossman, Oliver
COALFLEET, Pierre
Davison, Frank Cyril Shaw
COBBER, Lance Corporal
Adcock, A St John
COBBETT, Richard
Pluckrose, Henry Arthur
COBBLEIGH, Tom
Raymond, Walter

COBURN, L J
Harvey, John
COCHRAN, Jeff
Durst, Paul
COCHRANE, Corinna
Peterson, Corinna
COCKIN, Joan
Burbridge, Edith Joan
CODY, A R
Joscelyn, Archie Lynn
CODY, Al
Joscelyn, Archie Lynn
CODY, C S
Waller, Leslie
CODY, James R
Rohrbach, Peter Thomas
CODY, Stetson
Gribble, Leonard Reginald
CODY, Stone
Mount, Thomas Ernest
CODY, Walt
Norwood, Victor George
Charles
COE, Douglas
Epstein, Beryl *and*
Epstein, Samuel
COE, Tucker
Westlake, Donald Edwin
COFFEY, Brian
Koontz, Dean R
COFFIN, Geoffrey
Mason, F Van Wyck
COFFIN, Peter
Latimer, Jonathan
COIGNARD, John
Barach, Alvan Leroy
COLAM, Lance
Cooper, Gordon
COLBERE, Hope
Coolbear, Marian H
COLBY, Alice
Ross, William Edward Daniel
COLBY, Lydia
Ross, William Edward Daniel

COLE, Ann Kilborn
Callahan, Claire
COLE, Carol Cassidy
Manchee, Carol M Cassidy
COLE, Davis
Elting, Mary
COLE, Douglas
Cole, G(eorge) D(ouglas)
H(oward)
COLE, Jackson
Scott, Leslie
COLE, Richard
Barrett, Geoffrey John
COLE, Stephen
Webbe, Gale Dudley
COLEMAN, Lonnie
Coleman, William Lawrence
COLERIDGE, John
Binder, Otto
COLES, Manning
Manning, Adelaide Frances Oke
and Coles, Cyril Henry
COLIN, Jean
Bell, Joyce
COLLANS, Dev
Winchell, Prentice
COLLIER, Douglas
Fellowes-Gordon, Ian
COLLIER, Jane
Shumsky, Zena Feldman
COLLIER, Joy
Millar, Minna
COLLIER, Margaret
Taylor, Margaret Stewart
COLLIER, Zena
Shumsky, Zena Feldman
COLLIN, Rodney
Collin Smith, Rodney
COLLINGS, Jillie
Collings, I J
COLLINGSWOOD, Frederick
Lakritz, Esther
COLLINS, D
Bulleid, H A V

COLLINS, Geoffrey
Jefferies, Greg
COLLINS, Hunt
Lombino, Salvatore A
COLLINS, Joan
Collins, Mildred
COLLINS, Michael
Lynds, Dennis
COLLINS, Tom
Furphy, Joseph
COLLINSON, Peter
Hammett, Dashiell
COLLYER, Doric
Fellows, Dorothy Alice
COLMAN, George
Glassco, John
COLSON, Thora
Orton, Thora
COLSON-HAIG, S
Glassco, John
COLT, Clem
Nye, Nelson Coral
COLT, Russ
Kerr, D
COLT, Zandra
Stevenson, Florence
COLTER, Shayne
Norwood, Victor George
Charles
COLTMAN, Will
Bingley, David Ernest
COLTON, A J
Hook, Alfred Samuel
COLTON, James
Hansen, Joseph
COLTON, Mel
Braham, Hal
COLUMBINE
Ferguson, Rachel
COLVER, Anne
Harris, Polly Anne Colver
COMFORT, Jane Levington
Sturtzel, Jane L

COMFORT, Montgomery
Campbell, Ramsay
COMPERE, Mickie
Davidson, Margaret
COMPTON, Frances Snow
Adams, Henry
COMPTON, Guy
Compton, D G
COMRADE, Robert W
Brooks, Edwy Searles
COMYNS, Barbara
Carr, Barbara Irene Veronica
Comyns
CONARAIN, Nina
Conarain, Alice Nina
CONDON, Patricia
Gooden, P E
CONDRAY, Bruno
Humphrys, Leslie George
CONGREVE, R H
Orage, Alfred James
CONISTON, Ed
Bingley, David Ernest
CONNELL, John
Robertson, James Robin
CONNELL, Norreys
O'Riordan, Conal O'Connell
CONNEY, Barbara
Porter, Barbara Conney
CONNINGTON, J J
Stewart, Alfred Walter
CONNOLLY, Paul
Wicker, Tom
CONNOR, Kevin
O'Rourke, Frank
CONNOR, Patrick Reardon
Conner, Reardon
CONNOR, Ralph
Gordon, *Reverend* Charles
William
CONNORS, Bruton
Rohen, Edward

CONQUEST, Owen
  Hamilton, Charles Harold
  St John
CONRAD, Brenda
  Brown, Zenith
CONRAD, Clive
  King, Frank
CONRAD, Con
  Dober, Conrad K
CONRAD, Jack
  Conrad, Isaac
CONRAD, Jessie
  Korzeniowski, Jessie
CONRAD, Joseph
  Korzeniowski, Teodor Józef
  Konrad
CONRAD, Kenneth
  Lottich, Kenneth
CONRAD, Paul
  King, Albert
CONROY, Jim
  Chadwick, Joseph
CONROY, Robert
  Goldston, Robert
CONSTANT READER
  Parker, Dorothy
CONSTANT, Stephen
  Daneff, Stephen Constantin
CONTE, Charles
  Mackinnon, Charles Roy
CONWAY, Celine
  Blair, Kathryn
CONWAY, E Carolyn
  Kermond, Evelyn Carolyn
  Conway
CONWAY, Hugh
  Fargus, Frederick John
CONWAY, Keith
  Hetherington, Keith James
CONWAY, Laura
  Ansle, Dorothy Phoebe
CONWAY, Olive
  Walton, John *and*
  Brighouse, Harold

CONWAY, Peter
  Gautier-Smith, Peter Claudius
CONWAY, Peter
  Milkomane, George Alexis
  Milkomanovich
CONWAY, Troy
  Avallone, Michael Angelo *Jr*
COO-EE
  Walker, W Sylvester
COOK, John Estes
  Baum, Lyman Frank
COOK, Lyn
  Waddell, Evelyn Margaret
COOK, Robin
  Cook, Robert W A
COOK, Vera
  Ryder, Vera
COOK, Will
  Cook, William Everett
COOKE, M E
  Creasey, John
COOKE, Margaret
  Creasey, John
COOKRIDGE, E H
  Spiro, Edward H
COOKRIDGE, John Michael
  Holroyd, Ethel Mary
COOLE, W W
  Kulski, W W
COOLIDGE, Susan
  Woolsey, Sarah Chauncey
COOMBS, Murdo
  Davis, Frederick Clyde
COOPER, Charles
  Lock, Arnold Charles Cooper
COOPER, Craig
  King, Albert
COOPER, Henry St John
  Creasey, John
COOPER, Jeff
  Cooper, John Dean
COOPER, Jefferson
  Fox, Gardner F

COOPER, Lynna
Fox, Gardner F
COOPER, William
Hoff, Harry Summerfield
COPPLESTONE, Bennet
Kitchin, F H
COQUINA
Shields, George Oliver
CORAM, Christopher
Walker, Peter Norman
CORBY, Dan
Catherall, Arthur
CORD, Barry
Germano, Peter
CORDELL, Alexander
Graber, George Alexander
CORELLI, Marie
Mackay, Minnie
CORENANDA, A L A
Numano, Allen
CORIOLANUS
McMillan, James
CORK, Patrick
Cockburn, Claud Francis
CORLETT, Joyce I
Kirkwood, Joyce
CORLEY, Ernest
Bulmer, Henry Kenneth
CORNERS, George F
Viereck, George Sylvester
CORNING, Kyle
Gardner, Erle Stanley
CORNO DI BASSETTO
Shaw, George Bernard
CORNWALL, Nellie
Sloggett, Nellie
CORONET
James, Charles
CORREN, Grace
Hoskins, Robert
CORREY, Lee
Stine, George Harry
CORRIGAN, Mark
Lee, Norman

CORSON, Geoffrey
Sholl, Anna McClure
CORTEEN, Craig
Norwood, Victor George
Charles
CORTEEN, Wes
Norwood, Victor George
Charles
CORVO, *Baron*
Rolfe, Frederick
CORWIN, Cecil
Kornbluth, Cyril M
CORY, Caroline
Freeman, Kathleen
CORY, Desmond
McCarthy, Shaun
COSMOI, M M
Mitrinovič, Dmitrí
COST, March
Morrison, Margaret Mackie
COSTLER, *Dr* A
Koestler, Arthur
COSTS
Booth, John Bennion
COTTERELL, Brian
Dingle, Aylward Edward
COULSDON, John
Hincks, Cyril Malcolm
COURAGE, John
Goyne, Richard
COURT, Sharon
Rowland, Donald Sydney
COURTLAND, Roberta
Dern, Erolie Pearl
COURTNEY, Christine
Westmarland, Ethel Louisa
COURTNEY, John
Cournos, John
COUSIN VIRGINIA
Johnson, Virginia Wales
COVENANTER
Zilliacus, Konni
COVENTRY, John
Palmer, John Williamson

173

COVERACK, Gilbert
Warren, John Russell
COWAN, Alan
Gilchrist, Alan
COWEN, Frances
Minto, Frances
COWLIN, Dorothy
Whalley, Dorothy
COWPER, Richard
Murry, Colin Middleton
COX, Edith
Goaman, Muriel
COX, Jack
Cox, John
COX, Lewis
Cox, Euphrasia Emeline
COXE, Kathleen Buddington
Long, Amelia R *and*
McHugh, Edna
COX-JOHNSON, Ann
Saunders, Ann Loreille
COYSH, Edward
Stuart-Jervis, Charles Edward
CRAD, Joseph
Ansell, Edward Clarence
Trelawney
CRADDOCK, Charles Egbert
Murfree, Mary Noailles
CRADOCK, Fanny
Cradock, Phyllis Nan Sortain
CRAIG, A A
Anderson, Poul
CRAIG, Alisa
MacLeod, Charlotte
CRAIG, Alison
Nicholson, Joan
CRAIG, David
Tucker, James
CRAIG, Denys
Stoll, Dennis Gray
CRAIG, Georgia
Dern, Erolie Pearl
CRAIG, Jennifer
Brambleby, Ailsa

CRAIG, John Eland
Chipperfield, Joseph E
CRAIG, Jonathan
Posner, Richard
CRAIG, Jonathan
Smith, Frank E
CRAIG, Lee
Sands, Leo G
CRAIG, M S
Craig, Mary
CRAIG, Peter
MacClure, Victor
CRAIG, Vera
Rowland, Donald Sydney
CRAIGIE, David
Craigie, Dorothy M
CRAILE, Wesley
Rowland, Donald Sydney
CRANE, Henry
Douglass, Percival Ian
CRANE, Robert
Robertson, Frank Chester
CRANNACH, Henry
Meeske, Marilyn
CRANSTON, Edward
Fairchild, William
CRAVEN HILL
Parsons, Charles P
CRAWFORD, Anthony
Hugill, John Anthony Crawford
CRAWFORD, Robert
Rae, Hugh Cranford
CRECY, Jeanne
Williams, Jeanne
CREEDI, Joel
King, Albert
CREEK, Nathan
Sheppard, John Hamilton
George
CREIGHTON, Don
Drury, Maxine Cole
CRESCENDO
Kalisch, A

CRESSY, Edward
Creasey, Clarence Hamilton
CRESTON, Dormer
Baynes, Dorothy Julia
CREYTON, Paul
Trowbridge, John Townsend
CRIBLECOBLIS, Otis
Dukenfield, William Claude
CRICHTON, John
Guthrie, Norman Gregor
CRICKETER
Cardus, *Sir* Neville
CRISP, Tony
Crisp, Anthony Thomas
CRISPIE
Crisp, S E
CRISPIN, Edmund
Montgomery, Robert Bruce
CRISPIN, Suzy
Cartwright, Justin
CRISTOFER, Michael
Procassion, Michael
CRISTY, R J
De Cristoforo, R J
CRITCHIE, Estil
Burks, Arthur J
CRITIC
Martin, Kingsley
CROFT, Sutton
Lunn, *Sir* Arnold
CROFT, Taylor
Croft-Cooke, Rupert
CROMARTY, Deas
Watson, R A
CROMIE, Stanley
Simmons, J S A
CROMPTON, John
Lamburn, John Battersby
Crompton
CROMPTON, Richmal
Lamburn, Richmal Crompton
CROMWELL, Elsie
Sheridan, Elsie Lee

CRONHEIM, F G
Godfrey, Frederick M
CRONIN, Michael
Cronin, Brendan Leo
CROSBIE, Elizabeth
Ewer, Monica
CROSBIE, Provan
Crosbie, Hugh Provan
CROSBY, Lee
Torrey, Ware
CROSS, Amanda
Heilbrun, Carolyn
CROSS, Brenda
Colloms, Brenda
CROSS, James
Parry, Hugh J
CROSS, Mark
Pechey, Archibald Thomas
CROSS, Nancy
Baker, Anne
CROSS, T T
Da Cruz, Daniel
CROSS, Victor
Coffman, Virginia
CROSSE, Elaine
Trent, Ann
CROSSE, Victoria
Griffin, Vivian Cory
CROSSEN, Ken
Crossen, Kendell Foster
CROWE, John
Lynds, Dennis
CROWLEY, Aleister
Crowley, Edward Alexander
CRUMPET, Peter
Buckley, Fergus Reid
CRUNDEN, Reginald
Cleaver, Hylton Reginald
CULEX
Stanier, Maida
CULLINGFORD, Guy
Taylor, Constance Lindsay
CULLNER, Lenard
Mazure, Alfred Leonardus

CULOTTA, Nino
O'Grady, John P
CULPEPER, Martin
Pullen, George
CULVER, Kathryn
Dresser, Davis
CULVER, Timothy J
Westlake, Donald Edwin
CUMBERLAND, Gerald
Kenyon, Fred
CUMBERLAND, Roy
Mégroz, R L
CUMMINGS, Richard
Gardner, Richard
CUNNINGHAM, Cathy
Cunningham, Chet
CUNNINGHAM, E V
Fast, Howard
CUNNINGHAM, Mary
Pierce, Mary Cunningham
CUNNINGHAM, Ray
Arthur, Frances Browne
CURLING, Audrey
Clark, Marie Catherine Audrey
CURNOW, Frank
Atkinson, Frank
CURRIER, Jay L
Henderson, James Leal
CURRY, Avon
Bowden, Jean
CURTAYNE, Alice
Rynne, Alice
CURTIN, Philip
Lowndes, Marie Adelaide
Belloc
CURTIS, Peter
Lofts, Norah
CURTIS, Spencer
Nuttall, Anthony
CURTIS, Tom
Jacobs, Thomas Curtis Hicks
CURTIS, Wade
Pournelle, Jerry

CURTIS, Will
Nunn, William Curtis
CURZON, Clare
Buchanan, Marie
CURZON, Lucia
Stevenson, Florence
CURZON, Sam
Krasney, Samuel A
CURZON, Virginia
Hawton, Hector
CUSTER, Clint
Paine, Lauran Bosworth
CYCLOPS
Leonard, John
CYMRY BACH
Wood, Lilian Catherine
CYNICUS
Anderson, Martin

§ §

Why 'WM'? No-one knows. But
those were the initials Richard
Jennings chose to write under
and used for forty years.
Perhaps he was paying respects
to William Morris.
— Hugh Cudlipp. Publish and
be damned

§ §

D'A P
Power, *Sir* D'Arcy
D M S
Stuart, Dorothy Margaret
DAEDALUS
Cordes, Theodor K
DAEMER, Will
Wade, Robert *and*
Miller, William
DAGONET
Sims, George Robert

DAGONET, Edward
Williamson, Thames Ross
DAIMLER, Harriet
Owens, Iris
DAINTON, Courtney
Dainton, William
DALE, Edwin
Home-Gall, Edward Reginald
DALE, Esther
May, Elaine
DALE, Frances
Cradock, Phyllis Nan Sortain
DALE, Jack
Holliday, Joseph
DALE, Laura
Cheshire, David Frederick
DALE, Maxine
Covert, Alice Lent
DALE, Norman
Denny, Norman George
DALE, Robin
Hadfield, Alan
DALEY, Bill
Appleman, John Alan
DALHEATH
Magrill, David S
DALL, Ian
Higgins, Charles
D'ALLARD, Hunter
Ballard, Willis Todhunter
DALLAS, John
Duncan, William Murdoch
DALLAS, Ruth
Mumford, Ruth
DALLAS, Steve
King, Albert
DALLAS, Vincent
Werner, Victor Emile
D'ALLENGER, Hugh
Kershaw, John H D
DALRY
Wilson, Arthur
DALTON, Clive
Clark, Frederick Stephen

DALTON, Priscilla
Avallone, Michael Angelo *Jr*
DALY, Hamlin
Price, Edgar Hoffman
DALZEL, Peter
Dalzel-Job, Patrick
D'AMBROSIO, Raymond
Brosia, D M
DAMIANO, Laila
Rosenkrantz, Linda
DAN BANA
White, Stanhope
DANA, Amber
Paine, Lauran Bosworth
DANA, Richard
Paine, Lauran Bosworth
DANA, Rose
Ross, William Edward Daniel
DANBY, Frank
Frankau, Julia Davis
DANCER, J B
Harvey, John
DANE, Clemence
Ashton, Winifred
DANE, Eva
Dawes, Edna
DANE, Joel Y
Delany, Joseph Francis
DANE, Mark
Avallone, Michael Angelo *Jr*
DANE, Mary
Morland, Nigel
DANFORTH, Paul M
Allen, John E
DANGERFIELD, Clint
Norwood, Victor George
Charles
DANGERFIELD, Harlan
Padgett, Ron
DANGLE
Thompson, A M
DANIEL, Colin
Windsor, Patricia

DANIEL, S
Zalberg, Daniel
DANIELL, David Scott
Daniell, Albert Scott
DANIELS, Jan
Ross, William Edward Daniel
DANIELS, Jane
Ross, William Edward Daniel
DANIELS, John S
Overholser, Wayne D
DANIELS, Max
Gellis, Roberta
DANNING, Melrod
Gluck, Sinclair
DANSDORF, Chrysilla von
Sandford, Christopher
DANTON, Rebecca
Roberts, Janet Louise
DANVERS, Jack
Casseleyr, Camille
DANVERS, Peter
Henderson, James Maddock
DARBY, Catherine
Peters, Maureen
DARBY, Emma
Stubbs, Jean
DARBY, J N
Govan, Mary Christine
DARBYSHIRE, Shirley
Meynell, Shirley Ruth
D'ARCY, Pamela
Roby, Mary Linn
DARDI
Singh, Gopal
DARE, Alan
Goodchild, George
DARE, Michael
Wordingham, James A
DARE, Simon
Huxtable, Marjorie
D'ARFEY, William
Plomer, William
DARK, Johnny
Norwood, Victor George Charles

DARLING, V H
Dryhurst, Michael John
DARLINGTON, Con
Best, Carol Anne
DARRICH, Sybah
Di Prima, Diane
DASHIELL, Samuel
Hammett, Dashiell
DATALLER, Roger
Eaglestone, Arthur Archibald
DAVEY, Jocelyn
Raphael, Chaim
DAVID, Jay
Adler, Bill
DAVIDSON, Mickie
Davidson, Margaret
DAVIE-MARTIN, Hugh
McCutcheon, Hugh
DAVIES, Christie
Davies, John Christopher
Hughes
DAVIES, Louise
Golding, Louise
DAVIES, Lucian
Beeston, L J
DAVIGNON, Grace
Glassco, John
DAVIOT, Gordon
Mackintosh, Elizabeth
DAVIS, Audrey
Paine, Lauran Bosworth
DAVIS, David
Davis, William Eric
DAVIS, Don
Dresser, Davis
DAVIS, Foxcroft
Seawell, Molly Elliot
DAVIS, Gita
Rose, Evelyn Gita
DAVIS, Gordon
Dietrich, Robert S
DAVIS, Gordon
Hunt, E Howard

DAVIS, Julia
Marsh, John
DAVIS, Rosemary L
Davis, Lily May *and*
Davis, Rosemary
DAVIS, Stratford
Bolton, Miriam
DAVISON, Lawrence H
Lawrence, D H
DAWLISH, Peter
Kerr, James Lennox
DAWSON, Elizabeth
Geach, Christine
DAWSON, Jane
Critchlow, Dorothy
DAWSON, Michael
Boyle, John Howard Jackson
DAWSON, Oliver
Coxall, Jack Arthur
DAWSON, Peter
Faust, Frederick
DAWSON, Peter
Glidden, Jonathan H
DAX, Anthony
Hunter, Alfred John
DAY, Adrian
Harvey, Peter Noel
DAY, Harvey
Cleary, C V H
DAY, Irene
Orme, Eve
DAY, Lionel
Black, Ladbroke Lionel Day
DAY, Max
Cassiday, Bruce
DAY, Michael
Dempewolff, Richard F
DAYBREAK
Gray, Clement
DAYLE, Malcolm
Hincks, Cyril Malcolm
DE BEKKER, Jay
Winchell, Prentice

DE CASTRO, Lyne
Lyne, Charles
DE COSQUEVILLE, Pierre
Stacey, P M de Cosqueville
DE CULWEN, Dorothea
Hines, Dorothea
DE FACCI, Liane
De Bellet, Liane
DE GRAEFF, Allen
Blaustein, Albert P
DE HART, Robert
Hanzelon, Robert M
DE KIRILINE, Louise
De Kiriline Lawrence, Louise
DE LA GLANNEGE, Roger-Maxe
Legman, George Alexander
DE LA TORRE, Lillian
McCue, Lillian Bueno
DE LA TORRE-BUENO, Lillian
McCue, Lillian Bueno
DE LACY, Louise
Hickey, Madelyn E
DE LAS LUNAS, Carmencita
Trocchi, Alexander
DE LAUBE
Cardena, Clement
DE LIMA, Sigrid
Greene, Sigrid
DE LYNN, Eileen
Heilesen, Eileen De Lynn
DE MORNY, Peter
Wynne-Tyson, Esme
DE PRE, Jean-Anne
Avallone, Michael Angelo *Jr*
DE SALIGNAC, Charles
Hasson, James
DE VERE, Jane
Watson, Julia
DE WITT, James
Lewis, Mildred
DE WOHL, Louis
Wohl, Ludwig von
DEACON, Richard
McCormick, Donald

DEAN, Dudley
McGaughy, Dudley Dean
DEAN, Gregory
Posner, Jacob D
DEAN, Lyn
Garret, Winifred Selina
DEAN, Shelley
Sanders, Dorothy Lucie
DEAN, Spencer
Winchell, Prentice
DEANE, Norman
Creasey, John
DEBORAH, Leonard
Abbott, Harold Daniel
DEBRETT, Hal
Dresser, Davis *and*
Rollins, Kathleen
DECOLTA, Ramon
Whitfield, Raoul
DEE, John
Tullett, Denis John
DEE, R K
Wood, John James O'Hara
DEER, M J
Smith, George H *and*
Smith, M Jane Deer
DEHAN, Richard
Graves, Clotilda Inez Mary
DEKKER, Carl
Laffin, John
DEKKER, Carl
Lynds, Dennis
DELAFIELD, E M
De la Pasture, Edmée E M
DELANEY, Denis
Green, Peter Morris
DELANEY, Franey
O'Hara, John
DELANO, Al
Livingston, A D
DELL, Belinda
Bowden, Jean
DELMONICO, Andrea
Morrison, Eula A

DELTA
Hazlewood, Rex
DELVING, Michael
Williams, Jay
DEMAINE, C F
Trumbo, Dalton
DEMAREST, Anne
Bond, Florence D F
DEMAREST, Doug
Barker, Will
DEMARIS, Ovid
Desmarais, Ovide E
DEMBRY, R Emmet
Murfree, Mary Noailles
DEMIJOHN, Thom
Disch, Thomas *and*
Sladek, John
DEMPSEY, Hank
Harrison, Harry
DEMPSTER, Guy
Heming, Dempster E
DENBIE, Roger
Brodie, Julian Paul *and*
Green, Alan Baer
DENDER, Jay
Deindorfer, Robert G
DENHAM, Peter
Jones, P D
DENMARK, Harrison
Zelazny, Roger
DENNING, Patricia
Willis, Corinne
DENNIS, Eve
Wornum, Miriam
DENNIS, Patrick
Tanner, Edward Everett
DENNISON, Dorothy
Golden, Dorothy
DENOVAN, Saunders
Harvey, William
DENVER, Boone
Rennie, James Alan
DENVER, Drake C
Nye, Nelson Coral

DENVER, Lee
Gribble, Leonard Reginald
DERBY, Mark
Wilcox, Harry
DERMOTT, Stephen
Bradbury, Parnell
DERN, Peggy
Dern, Erolie Pearl
DERVENTIO
Hughes, Walter Dudley
DESANA, Dorothy
Trent, Ann
DESOR, René
Wilkinson, A G
DESPARD, Leslie
Howitt, John Leslie Despard
DESTRY, Vince
Norwood, Victor George
Charles
DEVEREUX, Roy
Pember-Devereux, Margaret
R R
DEVINE, D M
Devine, David McDonald
DEVINE, Dominic
Devine, David McDonald
DEVON, Sara
Walker, Emily Kathleen
DEWDNEY, Peter
Brock, Alan St Hill
DEWES, Simon
Muriel, John
DEXTER, John
Bradley, Marion Z
DEXTER, Martin
Faust, Frederick
DEXTER, Ross
Reynolds, John E
DEXTER, William
Pritchard, William Thomas
DIAS, B H
Pound, Ezra
DICANT, V L
Hewetson, Sara

DICK, Alexandra
Dick-Erikson, Cicely Sibyl
Alexandra
DICK, R A
Leslie, Josephine A C
DICK, T
Osler, Eric Richard
DICKENS, Irene
Copper, Dorothy
DICKINSON, Frankie
Brownlee, Frances
DICKINSON, Margaret
Muggeson, Margaret
DICKSON, Carr
Carr, John Dickson
DICKSON, Carter
Carr, John Dickson
DICKSON, Frank C
Danson, Frank Corse
DICKSON, Helen
Reynolds, Helen Mary
Greenwood Dickson
DIETRICH, Robert
Hunt, E Howard
DIGGES, Jeremiah
Berger, Josef
DILL, W S
Macbeth, Madge Hamilton
DILL, Walter
Thomas, Walter Dill *Jr*
DIMONT, Penelope
Mortimer, Penelope
DIMSDALE, C D
Mégroz, R L
DINESEN, Isak
Blixen-Finecke, Karen
Christence *Baroness*
DINGWALL, Peter
Forsythe, Robin
DIPLOMAT
Carter, John Franklin
DIPLOMATICUS
Zilliacus, Konni

DISCIPLE OF THE MASTER, A
Ouseley, G J R
DITTON, James
Clark, Douglas
DIVINE, David
Divine, Arthur Durham
D'IVRY, Ursula
Russell, Ursula D'Ivry
DIX, Dorothy
Gilmer, Elizabeth Meriwether
DIXON, Lesley
Vernon, Kathleen Rose
DIXON, Paige
Corcoran, Barbara
DIXON, Rex
Martin, Reginald Alec
DIXON, Rosie
Wood, Christopher
DIXON, Ruth
Barrows, Marjorie
DOAN, Reece
King, Albert
DOCHERTY, James L
Raymond, Rene
DR A
Asimov, Isaac
DOCTOR FUTUER
Lyburn, *Dr* Eric Frederic
St John
DR SEUSS
Geisel, Theodor Seuss
DR SOFT
Sward, Robert S
DODGE, Langdon
Wolfson, Victor
DODGE, Steve
Becker, Stephen David
DOE, John
Thayer, Tiffany Ellsworth
DOGBERRY
Phillips, Hubert
DOGBOLT, Barnaby
Silvette, Herbert

DOLBERG, Alexander
Burg, David
DOLLEY, Marcus J
Watney, Bernard
DOMINI, Rey
Lorde, Andre Geraldin
DOMINIC, *Sister* Mary
Parker, Marion
DOMINIC, R B
Latis, Mary J *and*
Henissart, Martha
DOMPO, Kwesi
Parkes, Frank
DONALD, Vivian
Mackinnon, Charles Roy
DONALDS, Gordon
Shirreffs, Gordon D
DONAVAN, John
Morland, Nigel
DONNE, Jack
Bloom, Jack Don
DONNE, Maxim
Duke, Madelaine
DONOVAN, Dick
Muddock, Joyce Emerson
DOOLEY, Martin
Dunne, Finley Peter
DOR, Ana
Ceder, Georgiana Dorcas
DORFY
Samuelson-Sandvid, Dorothy
DORLAND, Henry
Ash, Brian
DORMAN, Luke
Bingley, David Ernest
DORS, Diana
Fluck, Diana
DORSET, Ruth
Ross, William Edward Daniel
DORSETT, Danielle
Daniels, Dorothy
DOUBLEDAY, Roman
Long, Lily Augusta

DOUGLAS, Albert
Armstrong, Douglas
DOUGLAS, Arthur
Moreton, Douglas Arthur
DOUGLAS, Colin
Currie, Colin Thomas
DOUGLAS, D
Wilkes-Hunter, Richard
DOUGLAS, Ellen
Williamson, Ellen Douglas
DOUGLAS, George
Brown, George Douglas
DOUGLAS, George
Fisher, Douglas George
DOUGLAS, Malcolm
Sanderson, Douglas
DOUGLAS, Michael
Bright, Robert
DOUGLAS, Michael
Crichton, Michael *and*
Crichton, Douglas
DOUGLAS, Nathan
Young, Nedrick
DOUGLAS, Noel
Chetham-Strode, Warren
DOUGLAS, O
Buchan, Anna
DOUGLAS, R M
Mason, Douglas Rankine
DOUGLAS, Shane
· Wilkes-Hunter, Richard
DOUGLAS, Theo
Everett, *Mrs* H D
DOWDY, *Mrs* Regera
Gorey, Edward St John
DOWER, Penn
Jacobs, Thomas Curtis Hicks
DOWLEY, D M
Marrison, Leslie William
DOWNES, Quentin
Harrison, Michael
DOWNING, Century
Palmer, Paul

DOWNMAN, Francis
Oldmeadow, Ernest James
DOYLE, Emmett
Trumbo, Dalton
DOYLE, John
Graves, Robert
DOYLE, Lynn
Montgomery, Leslie Alexander
DOYLE, Mike
Doyle, Charles
DRACHMAN, Wolf
Rose, Ian
DRACO, F
David, Julia
DRAKE, Hamilton
Hoffenberg, Mason
DRAKE, Joan
Davies, Joan Howard
DRAKE, Lisl
Beer, Eloise
DRAKE, Winifred
Bryant, Denny
DRAPER, Hastings
Jeffries, Roderic Graeme
DRAX, Peter
Addis, E E
DREW, Kenneth
Cockburn, Claud Francis
DREW, Nicholas
Harling, Robert
DREWERY, Mary
Smith, Mary
DREXLER, J F
Paine, Lauran Bosworth
DRINAN, Adam
Macleod, Joseph Todd Gordon
DRINKROW, John
Hardwick, Michael
DRISCOLL, Eli
King, Albert
DRONGO, Luke
Riddleston, Charles H
DRUG, Victor
Moretti, Ugo

DRUMMOND, Anthony
Hunter, Alfred John
DRUMMOND, Ivor
Longrigg, Roger Erskine
DRUMMOND, John
Chance, John Newton
DRUMMOND, Violet Hilda
Swetenham, Violet Hilda
DRUMMOND, Walter
Silverberg, Robert
DRURY, C M
Abrahall, Clare Hoskyns
DRURY, Clare
Abrahall, Clare Hoskyns
DRYDEN, John
Rowland, Donald Sydney
DRYDEN, Keith
Landells, Richard
DU BLANE, Daphne
Groom, Arthur William
DU BOIS, M
Kent, Arthur
DU VAUL, Virginia
Coffman, Virginia
DU VAUL, Virginia C
Coffman, Virginia
DUANE, Jim
Hurley, Vic
DUBH, Scian
McCarroll, James
DUCHESNE, Antoinette
Paine, Lauran Bosworth
DUDLEY, Ernest
Coltman-Allen, Ernest Vivian
DUDLEY, Frank
Greene, Ward
DUDLEY, Helen
Hope-Simpson, Jacynth
DUDLEY, Nancy
Cole, Lois Dwight
DUELL, Eileen-Marie
Petrie, Rhona
DUFFER, Allan
May, John

DUFFIELD, Anne
Duffield, Dorothy Dean
DUKA, Ivo
Duchacek, Ivo D
DUKE, Margaret
Dunk, Margaret
DUKE, Will
Gault, William Campbell
DUMAS, Claudine
Malzberg, Barry Norman
DUNCAN, A H
Cleary, C V H
DUNCAN, Alex
Duke, Madelaine
DUNCAN, George
Davison, Geoffrey
DUNCAN, Gregory
McClintock, Marshall
DUNCAN, Jane
Cameron, Elizabeth Jane
DUNCAN, Julia K
Karig, Walter
DUNCAN, Lois
Cardozo, Lois S
DUNLAP, Lon
McCormick, Wilfred
DUNN, Harris
Doerffler, Alfred
DUNNE, Desmond
Lee-Richardson, James
DUNNE, Lyell
Bundey, Ellen Milne
DUPLEX
Bradley, Ian *and*
Hollows, Norman F
DUPONT, Paul
Frewin, Leslie Ronald
DURACK, Mary
Miller, Mary
DURHAM, Anne
Walker, Emily Kathleen
DURHAM, David
Vickers, Roy

DURHAM, John
Paine, Lauran Bosworth
DURIE, Lynn
Christie, Douglas
DURRANT, Sheila
Groves, Sheila
DURRANT, Theo
Mystery Writers of America
Inc; California Chapter
DUVAL, Jeanne
Coffman, Virginia
DWIGHT, Allan
Cole, Lois Dwight
DWYER, K R
Koontz, Dean R
DYER, Brian
Rothery, Brian
DYKES, Jack
Owen, Jack
DYLAN, Bob
Zimmerman, Robert Allen
DYMOKE, Juliet
De Schanschieff, Juliet Dymoke

E H
Haig, Emily Alice
E H
Hiscock, Eric
E H A
Aitken, E H
E M B
Barton, Emily Mary
E R
Ross, W W Eustace
E V L
Lucas, E V
EADY, W P R
Glassco, John
EAGLE, Solomon
Squire, *Sir* John Collings
EAGLESFIELD, Francis
Guirdham, Arthur
EARLE, Olive L
Daughtrey, Olive Lydia

EARP, Virgil
Keevill, Henry John
EAST, Michael
West, Morris
EAST, Roger
Burford, Roger d'Este
EASTAWAY, Edward
Thomas, Edward
EASTERTIDE
Blagbrough, Harriet
EASTLUND, Madelyn
Hickey, Madelyn E
EASTON, Edward
Malerich, Edward P
EATON, George L
Verral, Charles Spain
EBEL, Suzanne
Goodwin, Suzanne
EDDY, Albert
Glassco, John
EDEN, Rob
Burkhardt, Eve *and*
Burkhardt, Robert Ferdinand
EDEN, Matthew
Newnham, Don
EDGAR, Icarus Walter
Bishop, Stanley
EDGAR, Josephine
Mussi, Mary
EDMONDS, Charles
Carrington, Charles Edmund
EDMONDS, Paul
Kuttner, Henry
EDMONDSON, G C
Edmondson y Cotton, José
Mario Garry Ordonez
EDSON, George Alden
Ernst, Paul F
EDWARD, Stephen
Palestrant, Simon
EDWARDS, Al
Nourse, Alan E
EDWARDS, Albert
Bullard, Arthur

185

EDWARDS, Charman
Edwards, Frederick Anthony
EDWARDS, Ellen
Horkan, Nelle Irwin
EDWARDS, F E
Nolan, William F
EDWARDS, James G
Macqueen, James William
EDWARDS, June
Bhatia, Jamunadevi
EDWARDS, Laurence
Edwards, Florence
EDWARDS, Leonard
Wild, Reginald
EDWARDS, Norman
Carr, Terry
EDWARDS, Norman
White, Theodore Edwin
EDWARDS, Olwen
Owen, Dilys
EDWARDS, Samuel
Gerson, Noel Bertram
EDWINSON, Edmund
Slocum, Edward Mark
EFF, B
Carney, Jack
EGAN, Lesley
Linington, Elizabeth
EGBERT, H M
Emanuel, Victor Rousseau
EGERTON, Denise
Duggan, Denise Valerie
EGERTON, George
Bright, Mary C
EGLINTON, John
Magee, William Kirkpatrick
EGOMET
Fowler, Henry Watson
EGREMONT, Michael
Harrison, Michael
EIRENE
Searle, M E
ELAND, Charles
Rimanoczy, A

ELDER, Art
Montgomery, Rutherford
George
ELDERSHAW, M Barnard
Barnard, Marjorie Faith *and*
Eldershaw, Flora Sydney
ELEIGH, Sebastian
Greene, *Sir* Hugh
ELGIN, Mary
Stewart, Dorothy Mary
ELIOT, Alice C
Jewett, Sarah Orne
ELIOT, Anne
Cole, Lois Dwight
ELIOTT, E C
Martin, Reginald Alec
ELISABETH
Quigley, Elizabeth Pauline
ELIZABETH
Rose, Elizabeth Jane
ELIZABETH
Russell, Elizabeth Mary
Countess
ELIZABETH, Anne
Fleur, Anne Elizabeth
ELIZABETH VON S
Freeman, Gillian
ELLIOTT, Charles
Ewart-Biggs, Christopher
ELLIOTT, Ellen
Westmarland, Ethel Louisa
ELLIS, Alice Thomas
Haycraft, Anna
ELLIS, Kathy
Bentley, Margaret
ELLIS, Louise
Walker, Emily Kathleen
ELLIS, Olivia
Francis, Anne
ELLISON, Marjorie
Norton, Marjorie
ELLSWORTH, Elmer
Thayer, Tiffany Ellsworth

ELLSWORTH, Paul
Trien, Paul Ellsworth
ELPHINSTONE, Francis
Powell-Smith, Vincent
ELRON
Hubbard, Lafayette Ronald
ELSEY, J J
Herron, Elsie Ellerington
ELSNA, Hebe
Ansle, Dorothy Phoebe
ELSON, R N
Nelson, Radell Faraday
ELTON, H E
Hayes, Herbert Edward Elton
ELTON, John
Marsh, John
ELWART, Joan Potter
Elwart, Joan Frances
ELY, David
Lilienthal, David *Jr*
ELYSIAN, Anne
Westmoreland, Vera Gertrude
EMMETT STREET
Behan, Brendan
EMBEY, Philip
Philipp, Elliot Elias
EMSLEY, Clare
Plummer, Clare Emsley
ENGELHARDT, Frederick
Hubbard, Lafayette Ronald
ENGLAND, Edith M
Anders, Edith Mary
ENGLAND, Jane
Jervis, Vera Murdock Stuart
ENGLAND, Norman
Webb, Godfrey E C
ENGLISH, Brenda H
Riddolls, Brenda H
ENGREN, Edith
McCaig, Robert Jesse
ENQUIRING LAYMAN
Grierson, Walter

ENRIGHT, Elizabeth
Gillham, Elizabeth Wright
Enright
EPERNAY, Mark
Galbraith, J K
EPHESIAN
Bechoffer Roberts, C E
ERIC
Montefiore, Caroline L
ERIC, Kenneth
Henley, Art
ERICSON, Sybil
Dick-Erikson, Cicely Sybil
Alexandra
ERICSON, Walter
Fast, Howard
ERIKSON, Charlotte
Dick-Erikson, Cicely Sibyl
Alexandra
ERIMUS
Fall, William E
ERMINE, Will
Drago, Harry Sinclair

§ §

'My own Ernest! I felt from the start that you could have no other name.' – Oscar Wilde. The Importance of being Ernest

§ §

ERNEST, Paul
Focke, E P W
ERSKINE, Douglas
Buchan, John Stuart
ERSKINE, John T
Tuck, John Erskine
ERSKINE, Margaret
Williams, Margaret Wetherby
ERSKINE, Rosalind
Longrigg, Roger Erskine

ERSKINE-GRAY
Cordes, Theodor K
ERVIN, Patrick
Howard, Robert E
ESDAILE, David
Walker, David Esdaile
ESMOND, Harriet
Burk, John Frederick
ESSE, James
Stephens, James
ESSEX, Frank
Simmonds, Michael Charles
ESSEX, Jon
Watford, Joel
ESSEX, Mary
Bloom, Ursula
ESSEX, Richard
Starr, Richard
ESTERBROOK, Tom
Hubbard, Lafayette Ronald
ESTERHAZY, Louise J
Fairchild, John
ESTEVEN, John
Shellabarger, Samuel
ESTORIL, Jean
Allan, Mabel Esther
ETHEL
Grayson, Albert Victor
ETIENNE
King-Hall, Stephen
ETON, Robert
Meynell, Laurence Walter
EUGENE
Huyghue, Douglas S
EUPHAN
Todd, Barbara Euphan
EUSTACE, Robert
Barton, Eustace Robert
EVAN, Evin
Faust, Frederick
EVAN, Paul
Lehman, Paul Evan
EVANS, Alan
Stoker, Alan

EVANS, Cherry
Drummond, Cherry
EVANS, Evan
Faust, Frederick
EVANS, Frances
Carter, Frances Monet
EVANS, Harris
Evans, George *and*
Evans, Kay
EVANS, John
Browne, Howard
EVANS, Jonathan
Freemantle, Brian
EVANS, Margiad
Whistler, Penelope
EVANS, Margiad
Williams, Peggy Eileen Arabella
EVANS, Morgan
Davies, Leslie Purnell
EVANS, Tabor
Knott, William Cecil
EVELETH, Stanford
Dickson, Emma Wells
EVERARD, Henry
Smith, H Everard
EVERETT, Gail
Hale, Arlene
EVERETT, Wade
Cook, William Everett
EVERETT, Wade
Lutz, Giles A
EVERMAY, March
Eiker, Mathilde
EVERTON, Francis
Stokes, Francis William
EVOE
Knox, E V
EWING, Frederick R
Waldo, Edward Hamilton
EX-JOURNALIST
Lanigan, Richard
EX-PRIVATE X
Burrage, Alfred M

EXCELLENT, Matilda
Farson, Daniel
EYE WITNESS
Archibald, Edith Jessie
EYRE, Annette
Worboys, Anne Isobel

F P A
Adams, Franklin Pierce
FABIAN, Ruth
Quigley, Aileen
FABIAN, Warner
Adams, Samuel Hopkins
FABRIZIUS, Peter
Fabry, Joseph B
FAGYAS, Maria
Bush-Fekete, Marie Ilona
FAID, Mary
Dunn, Mary
FAIR, A A
Gardner, Erle Stanley
FAIRBURN, Ann
Tait, Dorothy
FAIRE, Zabrina
Stevenson, Florence
FAIRFIELD, Darrell
Larkin, Rochelle
FAIRFIELD, John
Livingstone, Harrison Edward
FAIRLESS, Michael
Barber, Margaret Fairless
FAIRWAY, Sidney
Daukes, Sidney Herbert
FALCON, Richard
Shapiro, Samuel
FALCONER, James
Kirkup, James
FALK, Elsa
Escherlich, Elsa Antonie
FALKIRK, Richard
Lambert, Derek
FALL, Thomas
Snow, Donald Clifford

FALLON, George
Bingley, David Ernest
FALLON, Martin
Patterson, Harry
FAMILY DOCTOR, A
Hutchin, Kenneth Charles
FAN-FAN
Blackburn, Victoria Grace
FANE, Bron
Fanthorpe, Robert Lionel
FANE, Violet
Currie, *Lady*
FANFARLO
Stonier, G W
FANSHAWE, Caroline
Cust, Barbara Kate
FARELY, Alison
Poland, Dorothy E H
FAREWELL, Nina
Klein, Grace *and*
Cooper, Mae Klein
FARGO, Doone
Norwood, Victor George
Charles
FARLEY, Ralph Milne
Hoar, Roger Sherman
FARMER, Wendell
Davis, Lavinia
FARNDALE, James
Farndale, W A J
FARQUHARSON, Martha
Finley, Martha Farquharson
FARR, C
Wilkes-Hunter, Richard
FARR, John
Webb, Jack
FARRELL, Ben
Cebulash, Mel
FARRELL, David
Smith, Frederick E
FARRELL, M J
Keane, Mary Nesta
FARRER, E Maxwell
Williams, Edward John

189

FARROW, James S
Tubb, E C
FAULKNER, Mary
Seuffert, Muriel
FAULKNER, Nancy
Faulkner, Anne Irvin
FAWCETT, Catherine
Cookson, Catherine
FAWKES, Guy
Benchley, Robert
FAY, Dorothy
Lindholm, Anna Chandler
FEARN, Elena
Smith, Marjorie Seymour
FEARN, John
Wannan, John Fearn
FEARN, Roberta
Hutchinson, Barbara Beatrice
FECAMPS, Elise
Creasey, John
FEIKEMA, Feike
Manfred, Frederick Feikema
FELIX, Pastor
Lockhart, Arthur John
FELLOWES, Anne
Mantle, Winifred Langford
FELMERSHAM, Michael
Leyland, Eric
FEMORA
Brodey, Jim
FEN, Elisaveta
Jackson, Lydia Jiburtovich
FENIX, *Comte de*
Crowley, Edward Alexander
FENNER, Carol
Williams, Carol Elizabeth
FENNER, James R
Tubb, E C
FENNIMORE, Stephen
Collins, Dale
FENTON, Freda
Rowland, Donald Sydney
FENTON, Mark
Norwood, Victor George Charles

FENWICK, Elizabeth
Way, Elizabeth Fenwick
FENWICK, Peter
Holmes, Peter
FERGUS, Dyjan
Ferguson, Ida May
FERGUSON, Anthony
Read, Anthony
FERGUSON, Emily
Murphy, Emily Gowan
(Ferguson)
FERGUSON, Helen
Edmonds, Helen
FERN, Edwin
Cryer, Neville
FERNWAY, Peggy
Braun, Wilbur
FERRAND, Georgina
Castle, Brenda
FERRARS, E X
Brown, Morna D
FERRARS, Elizabeth
Brown, Morna D
FERRES, Arthur
Kevin, John William
FERRIS, James Cody
Karig, Walter
FERRIS, Tom
Walker, Peter Norman
FESENMEYER
Luxmore, Robert
FETHERSTON, Patrick
Fetherstonhaugh, Patrick
William Edward
FETTSMAN, Ann
Hoffman, Anita
FEW, Betty
Few, Eunice Beatty
FIACC, Padraic
O'Connor, Patrick Joseph
FICKLING, G G
Fickling, Forrest E *and*
Fickling, Gloria

FIDLER, Kathleen
Goldie, Kathleen Annie
FIELD, Charles
Rowland, Donald Sydney
FIELD, Christine
Laurence, Frances Elsie
FIELD, Frank Chester
Robertson, Frank Chester
FIELD, Gans T
Wellman, Manly Wade
FIELD, Hill
Fielding, Molly Hill
FIELD, Joanna
Milner, Marion
FIELD, Michael
Bradley, Katherine H *and*
Cooper, Edith E
FIELD, Peter
Mann, E B
FIELD, Peter
Mines, Samuel
FIELD, Robert à
Haig, Emily Alice
FIELDING, A E
Feilding, Dorothy
FIELDING, Ann Mary
Mostyn, Anita Mary
FIELDING, Anthony
Leyland, Eric
FIELDING, Dorothy
Fielding, Archibald
FIELDING, Gabriel
Barnsley, Alan G
FIELDING, Howard
Hooke, Charles W
FIELDING, Hubert
Schonfield, Hugh Joseph
FIELDING, Xan
Fielding, Alexander
FIELDS, W C
Dukenfield, William Claude
FILEMAN, Nan
Zimmer, Maude Files

FINCH, John
Cooper, John
FINCH, Matthew
Fink, Merton
FINCH, Merton
Fink, Merton
FINCHER, Beth
Trumbo, Dalton
FINDLATER, Richard
Bain, Kenneth Bruce Findlater
FINDLEY, Ferguson
Frey, Charles Weiser
FINK, Brat
Davis, Gwen
FINKELL, Max
Catto, Maxwell Jeffrey
FINLAY, Fiona
Stuart, Vivian Alex
FINLAY, William
Mackay, James Alexander
FINLEY, Scott
Clark, Winifred
FINNEGAN, Robert
Ryan, Paul William
FINNEGAN, Ruth
Murray, Ruth Hilary
FINNEY, Mark
Muir, Kenneth Arthur
FINNIGAN, Joan
Mackenzie, Joan
FISHER, A E
Fisher, Edward
FISHER, Agnes
McEwen, Jessie Evelyn
FISHER, Clay
Allen, Henry
FISHER, Cyrus T
Teilhet, Darwin le Ora
FISHER, Laine
Howard, James Arch
FISHER, Margot
Paine, Lauran Bosworth
FISHER, Steve
Fisher, Stephen Gould

FISHER, Wade
Norwood, Victor George
Charles
FISKE, Sharon
Hill, Pamela
FISKE, Tarleton
Bloch, Robert
FITT, Mary
Freeman, Kathleen
FITZALAN, Roger
Dudley-Smith, Trevor
FITZGERALD, Barbara
Newman, Mona A J
FITZGERALD, Errol
Clarke, *Lady*
FITZGERALD, *Capt* Hugh
Baum, Lyman Frank
FITZGERALD, Julia
Watson, Julia
FITZWILLIAM, Michael
Lyons, John Benignus
5029
Winkworth, Derek W
FLACCUS
Levy, Newman
FLAMANK, E
Harper, Edith
FLANAGAN, Bud
Winthrop, Bud Robert
FLANNEL, J C
Fantoni, Barry
FLAVIUS, BROTHER
Ellison, James
FLECK, Betty
Paine, Lauran Bosworth
FLEMING, Caroline
Mather, Anne
FLEMING, George
Fletcher, Constance
FLEMING, Harry
Bird, William Henry Fleming
FLEMING, Oliver
MacDonald, Philip *and*
MacDonald, Ronald

FLEMING, Rhoda
Fleming, Ronald
FLEMING, Waldo
Williamson, Thames Ross
FLEMMING, Cardine
Grieveson, Mildred
FLEMMING, Sarah
Gilderdale, Michael
FLETCHER, Adam
Flexner, Stuart
FLETCHER, David
Barber, Dulan Friar
FLETCHER, George U
Pratt, Fletcher
FLETCHER, John
Fletcher, Harry L Verne
FLEUR, William
Gosling, William Flower
FLEXMAN, Theodore
Trumbo, Dalton
FLIGHT, Francies
Birch, Jack Ernest Lionel *and*
Murray, Venetia Pauline
FLYING OFFICER X
Bates, Herbert Ernest
FLYNT, Josiah
Willard, Josiah Flynt
FODA, Aun
Foxe, Arthur Norman
FOLEY, Helen
Fowler, Helen
FOLEY, Rae
Denniston, Elinore
FOLEY, Scott
Dareff, Hal
FOLKE, Will
Bloch, Robert
FONTENOY, Myra
Louise, *Princess of Gt Britain,*
Duchess of Argyll
FONTEYN, Margot
Hookham, Margaret Evelyn
FORBES, Athol
Phillips, Forbes Alexander

FORBES, Colin
Sawkins, Raymond Harold
FORBES, Daniel
Kenyon, Michel
FORBES, Kathryn
McLean, Kathryn
FORBES, Stanton
Forbes, Deloris Stanton
FORD, Barry
Whitford, Joan
FORD, David
Harknett, Terry
FORD, Elbur
Hibbert, Eleanor Alice
Burford
FORD, Ford Madox
Hueffer, Ford Madox
FORD, Fred
Doerffler, Alfred
FORD, Hilary
Youd, Samuel
FORD, Kirk
Spence, William Duncan
FORD, Langridge
Coleman-Cooke, John C
FORD, Leslie
Brown, Zenith
FORD, Marcia
Radford, Ruby Lorraine
FORD, Norrey
Dilcock, Noreen
FORD, Wallace
King, Albert
FORD, Webster
Masters, Edgar Lee
FORDE, Nicholas
Elliott-Cannon, Arthur Elliott
FORDEN, James
Barlow, James
FOREMAN, Lee
King, Albert
FORREST, Carol
Tennyson, Margaret

FORREST, *Colonel* Cris
Stoddard, William Osborn
FORREST, David
Denholm, David
FORREST, David
Eliades, David *and*
Webb, Robert Forrest
FORREST, Julian
Wagenknecht, Edward
FORREST, Norman
Morland, Nigel
FORRESTER, Helen
Bhatia, Jamunadevi
FORRESTER, Mary
Humphries, Elsie Mary
FORSTER, Christine
Forte, Christine
FORSYTH, Jean
McIlwraith, Jean Newton
FORSYTH, R A
Johnston, Robert Thomson
FORSYTHE, Robert
Crichton, Kyle
FORTHEMONEY, Justinian
Sedgemore, Brian Charles
FORTINA, Martha
Laffeaty, Christina
FORTUNE, Dion
Firth, Violet Mary
FOSSE, Alfred
Jelly, George Oliver
FOSTER, Delia
Walker, Emily Kathleen
FOSTER, Evan
King, Albert
FOSTER, George
Haswell, C J D
FOSTER, Iris
Posner, Richard
FOSTER, Richard
Crossen, Kendell Foster
FOSTER, Simon
Glen, Duncan Munro

FOUGASSE
Bird, Cyril Kenneth
FOWLER, Sydney
Wright, Sydney Fowler
FOX, Anthony
Fullerton, Alexander
FOX, David
Ostrander, Isabel Egerton
FOX, Eleanor
St John, Wylly Folk
FOX, James M
Knipscheer, James M W
FOX, John
Todd, John Murray
FOX, Petronella
Balogh, Penelope
FOX, Sebastian
Bullett, Gerald
FOXX, Jack
Pronzini, Bill
FRA ELBERTUS
Hubbard, Elbert
FRANCE, Claire
Morin, Claire
FRANCE, Evangeline
France-Hayhurst, Evangeline
FRANCHON, Lisa
Floren, Lee
FRANCIS, C D E
Howarth, Patrick John Fielding
FRANCIS, James
Ross, Charles
FRANCIS, Philip
Lockyer, Roger Walter
FRANCIS, Victor
Hammond, Lawrence
FRANCIS, William
Urell, William Francis
FRANK, R Jr
Ross, Frank Xavier
FRANK, Theodore
Gardiner, Dorothea Frances
FRANKLIN, Charles
Usher, Frank Hugh

FRANKLIN, E
Hurt, Edwin Franklin
FRANKLIN, Eugene
Bandy, Eugene Franklin *Jr*
FRANKLIN, Jay
Carter, John Franklin
FRANKLIN, Max
Deming, Richard
FRASER, Alex
Brinton, Henry
FRASER, James
White, Alan
FRASER, Jane
Pilcher, Rosamunde
FRASER, Jefferson
Wilding, Philip
FRASER, Peter
Coles, Phoebe Catherine
FRASER, Peter
Watt, Alexander Peter Fordham
FRATER PERDURABO
Crowley, Edward Alexander
FRAZER, Andrew
Lesser, Milton
FRAZER, Martin
Clarke, Percy A
FRAZER, Renee
Fleming, Ronald
FRAZER, Robert Caine
Creasey, John
FRAZER, Shamus
Frazer, James Ian Arbuthnot
FRAZIER, Arthur
Bulmer, Henry Kenneth
FRECKLES
Dietz, Howard
FREDERIC, Mike
Cox, William Robert
FREDERICK, Dick
Dempewolff, Richard F
FREDERICK, John
Faust, Frederick
FREDERICKS, Arnold
Kummer, Frederick Arnold

FREDERICKS, Frank
Franck, Frederick S
FREDERICKS, Vic
Fell, Frederick Victor
FREDERICS, Jocko
Frede, Richard
FREDRICKS, P C
Primmer, Phyllis
FREEMAN, Cynthia
Feinberg, Bea
FREEMAN, Larry
Freeman, Graydon La Verne
FREEMAN, Thomas
Fehrenbach, T R
FREMLIN, Celia
Goller, Celia Margaret
FRENCH, Ashley
Robins, Denise
FRENCH, Ellen Jean
English, Jean Ellen
FRENCH, Fergus
Friedlander, Peter
FRENCH, Paul
Asimov, Isaac
FRESHFIELD, Mark
Field, M J
FREUGON, Ruby
Ashby, Rubie Constance
FREYER, Frederic
Ballinger, William Sanborn
FRICK, C H
Irwin, Constance
FRIEDMAN, Elias
Friedman, Jacob Horace
FRIEDMAN, John
Friedman, Jacob Horace
FRIEDMAN, Rosemary
Friedman, Eve Rosemary
FRIEND, Oscar Jerome
Jerome, Owen Fox
FRIENDLY, Aunt
Baker, Sarah S T
FROEST, Frank
Dilnot, George

FROME, David
Brown, Zenith
FROST, Frederick
Faust, Frederick
FROST, Joni
Paine, Lauran Bosworth
FROY, Herald
Deghy, Guy *and*
Waterhouse, Keith
FRY, Jane
Drew, Jane B
FRY, Pete
King, James Clifford
FUCHS, Sonia
Seedo, Sonia
FULLER, Ed
Fuller, Harold Edgar
FULLER, Lester
Rolfe, Edwin
FULLER, Roger
Tracy, Donald Fiske
FULMAN, Al
Fuller, Harold Edgar
FURBER, Douglas
Lewin, Michael Sultan
FURNEAUX, Robin
Smith, Frederick William
Robin, *Earl of Birkenhead*
FURY, Nick
Parry, Michel
FUTUER, *Dr*
Lyburn, *Dr* Eric St John
FYVEL, T R
Feiwel, Raphael Joseph

G B S
Shaw, George Bernard
G K C
Chesterton, G K
GABRIELLE
Parks, Georgina
GADDES, Peter
Sheldon, Peter

195

GADDIS, Peggy
Dern, Erolie Pearl
GADE, Henry
Palmer, Ray
GAGE, Gervais
Rentoul, T Laurence
GAGE, Wilson
Steele, Mary Quintard Govan
GAINES, Robert
Summerscales, Rowland
GAINHAM, Sarah
Ames, Sarah Rachel
GAITE, Francis
Manning, Adelaide Frances
Oke *and* Coles, Cyril Henry
GALE, John
Gaze, Richard
GALE, Newton
Guinness, Maurice
GALLAGHER, Gale
Oursler, William Charles
GALLOPING GOURMET, THE
Kerr, Graham
GALWAY, Robert Conington
McCutchan, Philip D
GAME COCK
Looker, Samuel Joseph
GAMBIER, Kenyon
Lathrop, Lorin Andrews
GANNOLD, John
Langdon, John
GANPAT
Gompertz, Martin Louis Alan
GANT, Jonathan
Adams, Clifton
GANT, Richard
Freemantle, Brian
GARD, Janice
Latham, Jean Lee
GARD, Joyce
Reeves, Joyce
GARDEN, Bruce
Mackay, James Alexander

GARDEN, John
Fletcher, Harry L Verne
GARDNER, Nancy Bruff
Bruff, Nancy
GARDNER, Jeffrey
Fox, Gardner
GARDNER, Miriam
Bradley, Marion Z
GARDNER, Noel
Kuttner, Henry
GARDONS, S S
Snodgrass, W D
GARFORD, James
Blackburn, James Garford
GARIOCH, Robert
Sutherland, Robert Garioch
GARLAND, Bennett
Garfield, Brian
GARLAND, George
Roark, Garland
GARLAND, Lisette
Gibbs, Norah
GARLAND, Luke
Whitson, John Harvey
GARLAND, Madge
Ashton, *Lady*
GARLAND, Rodney
Hegedus, Adam de
GARNETT, David S
Rush, Noel
GARNETT, Roger
Morland, Nigel
GARRATT, Teddie
Garratt, Alfred
GARRETT, Truman
Judd, Harrison
GARRISON, Joan
Neubauer, William Arthur
GARRITY, Calli Goran
Garrity, David James
GARRY, Stephen
Stevens, Henry Charles
GARSTANG, Basil
Brereton, John Le Gay

GARTH, Cecil
  Carlton, Grace
GARTH, Will
  Kuttner, Henry
GARTNER, Chloe
  Trimble, Chloe Maria
GARVE, Andrew
  Winterton, Paul
GASH, Jonathan
  Grant, John
GASKELL, Jane
  Denvil, Jane Gaskell
GASKET, Bamber
  Fantoni, Barry
GAST, Kelly P
  Edmondson y Cotton, José
  Mario Garry Ordonez
GASTON, Bill
  Gaston, William J
GATE, A G
  Anthony, Edward
GATH
  Townsend, George Alfred
GAULT, Mark
  Cournos, John
GAUNT, Jeffrey
  Rochester, George Ernest
GAUNT, M B
  Horsfield, Richard Edward
GAUNT, Michael
  Robertshaw, James Denis
GAUNT, Richard
  Landells, Richard
GAVIN, Amanda
  Fry, Clodagh Micaela Gibson
GAWAIN
  Newton, H Chance
GAWSWORTH, John
  Fytton-Armstrong, T I
GAY, Amelia
  Hogarth, Grace
GAY, Noel
  Armitrage, Reginald

GAYE, Carol
  Shann, Renée
GAYLE, Emma
  Fairburn, Eleanor
GAYLE, Newton
  Guinness, Maurice
GEACH, Christine
  Wilson, Christine
GEARING-THOMAS, G
  Norwood, Victor George
  Charles
GEARON, John
  Flagg, John
GEE, Kenneth F
  Kay, Frederick George
GEE, Osman
  Hincks, Cyril Malcolm
GEERLINK, Will
  Hofdorp, Pim
GEISEL, Eva
  Bornemann, Eva
GELLERT, Roger
  Holmstrom, John Eric
GEMINI
  Goodwin, Geoffrey
GEMMILL
  Kirkpatrick, *Mrs* Helen
GENE, Marta
  Powley, *Mrs* A A
GENET
  Flanner, Janet
**GENTLEMAN OF THE
UNIVERSITY OF CAMBRIDGE**
  Crowley, Edward Alexander
**GENTLEMAN WITH A
DUSTER**
  Begbie, Harold
GENTLEWOMAN, A
  Moore, Doris Langley
GEOFFREY, Charles
  Muller, Charles George
GEORGE, Daniel
  Bunting, D G

GEORGE, Eugene
Chevalier, Paul Eugene George
GEORGE, G S
Levin, Abraham
GEORGE, Jonathan
Burke, John Frederick
GEORGE, Vicky
Collings, I J
GERAINT, George
Evans, George
GERALD, Daryl
Fitzgerald, Desmond
GERARD, Gaston
Ostergaard, Geoffrey
GERARD, Morice
Teague, John Jessop
GERARDY, *Trooper*
Gerard, Edwin
GERMAN, Edward
Jones, Edward German
GERRARE, Wirt
Greener, William Oliver
GIBB, Lee
Deghy, Guy *and*
Waterhouse, Keith
GIBBON, Lewis Grassic
Mitchell, James Leslie
GIBBS, Henry
Rumbold-Gibbs, Henry St
John C
GIBBS, Lewis
Cove, Joseph Walter
GIBBS, Mary Ann
Bidwell, Marjory Elizabeth
Sarah
GIBSON, Floyd
King, Albert
GIBSON, Harry Clark
Hubler, Richard Gibson
GIBSON, Josephine
Joslin, Sesyle
GIFFARD, Ann
Greenhill, Elizabeth Ann

GIFFIN, Frank
Carter, Ernest
GIFFORD, Matt
King, Albert
GIFT, Theo
Havers, Dora
GILBERT, Anna
Lazarus, Marguerite
GILBERT, Anthony
Malleson, Lucy
GILBERT, John
Harrison, John Gilbert
GILBERT, Manu
West, Joyce
GILBERT, *Sister* Mary
DeFrees, Madeline
GILBERT, Miriam
Presberg, Miriam
GILBERT, Nan
Gilbertson, Mildred
GILCHRIST, John
Gardner, Jerome
GILCRAFT
Young, Ernest
GILDEN, K B
Gilden, Katya *and*
Gilden, Bert
GILES, Gordon A
Binder, Otto
GILES, Kris
Nielson, Helen Berniece
GILES, Norman
Mackeown, N R
GILL, Hugh
Hugill, Robert
GILL, Patrick
Creasey, John
GILL, Stanley
Taylor, Roland
GILLEN, Lucy
Stratton, Rebecca
GILLESPIE, Jane
Shaw, Jane

GILLESPIE, Susan
Turton-Jones, Edith C
GILLETTE, Bob
Shaw, Bynum G
GILMAN, Dorothy
Butters, Dorothy Gilman
GILMAN, George G
Harknett, Terry
GILMAN, J D
Fishman, Jack *and*
Orgill, Douglas
GILMAN, Robert Cham
Coppel, Alfred
GILMER, Ann
Ross, William Edward Daniel
GILMOUR, Ann
McNaught, Ann Boyce
GILROONEY
Cassidy, Robert John
GINGER
Sargent, Genevieve
GIRTY, Simon
King, Albert
GIZYCKA, Eleanor M
Schlesinger, Eleanor Medill
GLADDEN, Washington
Washington, Solomon
GLANVILLE, Alec
Grieve, Alexander Haig
Glanville
GLASER, Comstock
Glaser, Kurt
GLASER, Eleanor Dorothy
Zonik, Eleanor Dorothy
GLASHAN, John
MacGlashan, John
GLASS, Justine
Corrall, Alice Enid
GLENDENNING, Donn
Paine, Lauran Bosworth
GLENELG
Frost, J W
GLENN, James
Paine, Lauran Bosworth

GLINTO, Darcy
Kelly, Harold Ernest
GLUTZ, Ambrose
Knapp, Clarence
GLYN, Megan
Parry, Margaret G
GLYN-FOREST, D
Lynes, Daisy Elfreda
GLYNN-WARD, Hilda
Howard, Hilda Glynn
GLYNN-WARD, H
Howard, Hilda Glynn
GOAMAN, Muriel
Cox, Edith Muriel
GODDEN, Rumer
Haynes Dixon, Margaret
Rumer
GODEY, John
Freedgood, Morton
GODFREY, Charles
Webb, Godfrey E C
GODFREY, William
Youd, Samuel
GOFF, Madeleine
Woodford, Irene-Cecile
GOFFSTEIN, M B
Schaaf, M B
GOFORTH, Ellen
Francis, Dorothy Brenner
GOLD, Michael
Granich, Irving
GOLDEN GORSE
Wace, M A
GOLDSMITH, Peter
Priestley, John Boynton
GOLIARD, Roy
Shipley, Joseph Twadell
GOOCH, Silas N
Glassco, John
GOODE, Bill
Goodykoontz, William F
GOODMAN, Winthrop
Goodman, George Jerome
and Knowlton, Winthrop

GOODSON, Bill
Lucas, Edgar Ernest
GOODWIN, Hal
Goodwin, Harold Leland
GOODWIN, John
Gowing, Sidney Floyd
GOODWIN, Suzanne
Ebel, Suzanne
GOODYEAR, Susan
Matthews, Margaret Bryan
GORDON, Alex
Cutler, Gordon
GORDON, Angela
Paine, Lauran Bosworth
GORDON, David
Garrett, Randall
GORDON, Diana
Andrews, Lucilla
GORDON, Don
Thomas, Edward Llewellyn
Gordon
GORDON, Donald
Payne, Donald Gordon
GORDON, Fritz
Jarvis, Frederick G H
GORDON, Gary
Edmonds, Ivy Gordon
GORDON, Glenda
Beadle, Gwyneth Gordon
GORDON, Ian
Fellowes-Gordon, Ian
GORDON, Jane
Sheridan, Elsie Lee
GORDON, Janet
Woodham-Smith, Cecil
GORDON, Katharine
Pearson, Katharine
GORDON, Keith
Bailey, Gordon
GORDON, Lew
Baldwin, Gordon C
GORDON, Mary
Ostlere, Mary

GORDON, Neil
Macdonell, A G
GORDON, Ray
Wainwright, Gordon Ray
GORDON, Rex
Hough, Stanley Bennett
GORDON, Richard
Ostlere, Gordon Stanley
GORDON, Selma
Lanes, Selma G
GORDON, Stewart
Shirreffs, Gordon D
GORDON, Stuart
Gordon, Richard
GORDON, UNCLE
Roe, F Gordon
GORDON, William Murray
Graydon, William Murray
GORDONS, THE
Gordon, Gordon *and*
Gordon, Mildred
GORE, William
Gordon, Jan
GORHAM, Michael
Folsom, Franklin Brewster
GORMAN, Beth
Paine, Lauran Bosworth
GORMAN, Ginny
Zachary, Hugh
GOTTESMAN, S D
Kornbluth, Cyril M *and*
Pohl, Frederik
GOUGH, Irene
Hall, Irene
GOULART, Ron
Goulart, Ronald Joseph
GOULD, Alan
Canning, Victor
GOULD, Stephen
Fisher, Stephen Gould
GOUTTIER, Maurice
Moretti, Ugo
GOYNE, Richard
Courage, John

GRAAF, Peter
Youd, Samuel
GRACCHUS
Wintringham, Tom
GRACE, Joseph
Hornby, John Wilkinson
GRADY, Tex
Webb, Jack
GRAEME, Bruce
Jeffries, Bruce Graham
Montague
GRAEME, David
Jeffries, Bruce Graham
Montague
GRAEME, Linda
Jeffries, Gay
GRAEME, Roderic
Jeffries, Roderic Graeme
GRAFTON, Garth
Duncan, Sara Jeanette
GRAHAM, BROTHER
Jeffrey, Graham
GRAHAM, Charles S
Tubb, E C
GRAHAM, Ennis
Molesworth, *Mrs* Mary Louisa
Stewart
GRAHAM, Harvey
Flack, Isaac Harvey
GRAHAM, James
Patterson, Harry
GRAHAM, Jean
Scott, Mary E
GRAHAM, John
Phillips, David Graham
GRAHAM, John
Rose, Graham
GRAHAM, Neill
Duncan, William Murdoch
GRAHAM, Peter
Abraham, Peter L
GRAHAM, Peter
Langmaid, Kenneth Joseph
Robb

GRAHAM, Ramona
Cook, Ramona Graham
GRAHAM, Robert
Haldeman, Joe
GRAHAM, Robin
Raleigh-King, Robin Victor
Lethbridge
GRAHAM, Scott
Black, Hazleton
GRAHAM, Susan
Graham, Maud Fitzgerald
GRAHAM, Vanessa
Fraser, Anthea
GRAHAM, Viva
Somerville, Edith Oenone
GRAMMATICUS
Blaiklock, Edward
GRANADOS, Paul
Kent, Arthur
GRAND, Sarah
McFaul, Frances Elizabeth
GRANDMA
Mulhearn, Winifred
GRANDOWER, Elissa
Waugh, Hillary Baldwin
GRANGE, Ellerton
Fraser-Harris, D
GRANGE, Peter
Nicole, Christopher
GRANGER, Stewart
Stewart, James L
GRANITE, Tony
Politella, Dario
GRANT, Alan
Kennington, Gilbert Alan
GRANT, Ambrose
Raymond, Rene
GRANT, Anthony
Campbell, Judith
GRANT, Carol
Copper, Dorothy
GRANT, David
Thomas, Craig

GRANT, Douglas
Ostrander, Isabel Egerton
GRANT, Eve
Gray, K E
GRANT, Jane
Blackburn, Barbara
GRANT, Kay
Grant, Hilda Kay
GRANT, Landon
Gribble, Leonard Reginald
GRANT, Margaret
Franken, Rose *and*
Meloney, W B
GRANT, Marjorie
Cook, Marjorie Grant
GRANT, Mary
Willans, Angela
GRANT, Maxwell
Gibson, Walter Brown
GRANT, Maxwell
Lynds, Dennis
GRANT, Neil
Mountfield, David
GRANT, Nesta
Leyland, Eric
GRANT, Richard
Clarke, J Calvitt
GRANTLAND, Keith
Nutt, Charles
GRAPE, Oliver
Wood, Christopher
GRAVELEY, George
Edwards, George Graveley
GRAVES, Valerie
Bradley, Marion Z
GRAY, Adrian
Wilkes-Hunter, Richard
GRAY, Angela
Daniels, Dorothy
GRAY, Berkeley
Brooks, Edwy Searles
GRAY, Christopher
Usher, John Gray

GRAY, Elizabeth Janet
Vining, Elizabeth Gray
GRAY, Ellington
Jacob, Naomi
GRAY, Harriet
Robins, Denise
GRAY, Jane
Evans, Constance May
GRAY, Jonathan
Adams, Herbert
GRAY, Russell
Fischer, Bruno
GRAY, Simon
Davidson, Simon
GRAYSON, Daphne
Graveley, G C
GRAYSON, David
Baker, Ray Stannard
GRAYSON, Richard
Grindal, Richard
GREAVES, Gillian
Macvean, Phyllis
GREAVES, Richard
Simonds, Peter
GREEN, Charles M
Gardner, Erle Stanley
GREEN, Glint
Peterson, Margaret
GREEN, Hannah
Greenberg, Joanne
GREEN, Henry
Yorke, Henry Vincent
GREEN, Judith
Rodriguez, Judith G
GREEN, Linda
Copper, Dorothy
GREEN, O O
Durgnat, Raymond Eric
GREEN, R
Weir, Rosemary
GREEN CROW, THE
O'Casey, Sean
GREENE, Adam
Scott, Peter Dale

GREENE, Anna Katharine
Rohlfs, *Mrs* Anna
GREENE, Robert
Deindorfer, Robert G
GREENFIELD, Bernadette
Darby, Edith M
GREENHALGH, Katherine
Bobin, John W
GREENHILL, Jack
Greenberg, Jack
GREENWOOD, Grace
Lippincott, Sara Jane
GREENWOOD, John
Hilton, John Buxton
GREER, Patrick
Macrory, Patrick
GREGG, Alan
Mallette, Gertrude Ethel
GREGORY, Hilton
Ferguson, Charles W
GREGORY, John
Hoskins, Robert
GREGORY, Stephan
Pendleton, Donald Eugene
GREGSON, Paul
Oakley, Eric Gilbert
GREIG, Charles
Cruickshank, Charles Greig
GREIG, Maysie
Ames, Jennifer
GRENDON, Stephen
Derleth, August William
GRENVIL, William
Martyn, Wyndham
GREW, William
O'Farrell, William
GREX, Leo
Gribble, Leonard Reginald
GREY, A F
Neal, Adeline Phyllis
GREY, Brenda
Mackinlay, Lelia A S
GREY, Charles
Tubb, E C

GREY, Donald
Thomas, Eugene
GREY, Elizabeth
Hogg, Beth
GREY, Georgina
Roby, Mary Linn
GREY, Harry
Golberg, Harry
GREY, Louis
Gribble, Leonard Reginald
GREY, Robin
Gresham, Elizabeth F
GREY, Rowland
Brown, L Rowland
GREY, Steele
Smith, G M
GREY OWL
Belaney, Archie
GREYSTONE, Alexander A
Goodavage, Joseph F
GRIDBAN, Volsted
Tubb, E C
GRIER, Sydney C
Gregg, Hilda
GRIFF, Alan
Suddaby, William Donald
GRIFFIN, David
Maugham, Robert Cecil Romer
GRIFFIN, John
Clay, Michael John
GRIFFIN, Jonathan
Griffin, Robert John Thurlow
GRIFFITH, Jack
Griffiths, Jack
GRIFFITH, Jeannette
Eyerly, Jeannette *and*
Griffith, Valeria W
GRILE, Dod
Bierce, Ambrose
GRIMSLEY, Gordon
Groom, Arthur William
GRINDLE, Carleton
Page, Gerald W

GRINGHUIS, Dirk
Gringhuis, Richard H
GRINNELL, David
Wollheim, Donald A
GRISWOLD, George
Dean, Robert George
GRODE, Redway
Gorey, Edward St John
GROSS, Gene
Edmonds, Ivy Gordon
GROUPE, Darryl R
Bunch, David R
GROVE, Will O
Brister, Richard
GROVER, Marshall
Meares, Leonard F
GROVES, Georgina
Symons, Dorothy G
GUBBINS, Nathaniel
Mott, Edward Spencer
GUILDFORD, John
Hunter, Bluebell Matilda
GUINNESS, Owen
Williams, Guy Richard
GULICK, Bill
Gulick, Grover C
GULLIVER, Lemuel
Farrell, Michael
GUMSUCKER
Keogh, M J
GUN BUSTER
Austin, John *and*
Austin, Richard
GUNN, Victor
Brooks, Edwy Searles
GURNEY, David
Bair, Patrick
GUTHRIE, Alan
Tubb, E C
GUTHRIE, David
Allen, Hubert Raymond
GUTHRIE, Hugh
Freeman, John Crosby

GUTHRIE, John
Brodie, John
GUTHRIE, Woody
Guthrie, Woodrow Wilson
GWYNNE, Arthur
Evans, Gwynfil Arthur
GWYNNE, Nell
Boggs, Helen
GWYNNE, Paul
Slater, Ernest
GYE, Hal
Gye, Harold Frederick Neville

§ §

Caro nome che il mio cor
Festi primo palpitar.
– G. Verdi; F. Piave. Rigoletto

§ §

H A K
Kennedy, H A
H D
Doolittle, Hilda
HAAS, Carola
Catalani, Victoria
HACKSTON, James
Gye, Harold Frederick Neville
HADDO, Oliver
Puechner, Ray
HADDOCK, Albert
Herbert, *Sir* Alan Patrick
HADDON, Christopher
Palmer, John Leslie
HADDOW, Leigh
Best, Rayleigh Breton Amis
HADHAM, John
Parkes, James W
HADLEY, John
Hemingway, Ernest
HADLEY, Leila
Smitter, Eliott-Burton

HAEFER, Hanna
Condon, Madeline B
HAGAR, Judith
Polley, Judith Anne
HAGEN, Brett
Hunter, William R
HAGGARD, Paul
Longstreet, Stephen
HAGGARD, William
Clayton, Richard H M
HAGON, Priscilla
Allan, Mabel Esther
HALCROW, Penelope
Wallace, Penelope
HALE, Christopher
Stevens, Frances Moyer
HALE, Hope
Davis, Hope Hale
HALE, Katherine
Garvin, Amelia Beers
(Warnock)
HALE, Michael
Bullock, Michael Hale
HALES, Joyce
Coombs, Joyce
HALEVI, Zev ben Shimon
Kenton, Warren
HALIBURTON, Hugh
Robertson, James Logie
HALIFAX, Clifford
Beaumont, *Dr* Edgar
HALL, Adam
Dudley-Smith, Trevor
HALL, Aylmer
Hall, Norah E L
HALL, B
Gunn, John Angus Lancaster
HALL, Bennett
Hall, Bennie Caroline
HALL, Borden
Yates, Raymond Francis
HALL, Claudia
Floren, Lee

HALL, Eliza Calvert
Obenchain, Eliza Caroline
HALL, Evan
Halleran, E E
HALL, Holworthy
Porter, Harold Everett
HALL, John
Pound, Ezra
HALL, John Ryder
Rotsler, William
HALL, Marjory
Yeakley, Marjory Hall
HALL, Martyn T
Morris, David
HALL, Patrick
Hall, Frederick
HALL, Rupert
Home-Gall, Edward Reginald
HALL, Whyte
Rayner, Augustus Alfred
HALLAM, Jay
Rice, Joan
HALLARD, Peter
Catherall, Arthur
HALLAS, Richard
Knight, Eric
HALLER, Bill
Bechko, Peggy Anne
HALLIDAY, Brett
Dresser, Davis
HALLIDAY, Dorothy
Dunnett, Dorothy
HALLIDAY, James
Symington, David
HALLIDAY, Michael
Creasey, John
HALLS, Geraldine
Jay, Geraldine
HALLUS, Tak
Robinett, Stephen
HAMBLEDON, Phyllis
Macvean, Phyllis
HAMILL, Ethel
Webb, Jean Frances

HAMILTON, Clive
Lewis, Clive Staples
HAMILTON, Ernest
Grossman, Judith
HAMILTON, Hervey
Robins, Denise
HAMILTON, Judith
Lawrence, Dulcie
HAMILTON, Julia
Watson, Julia
HAMILTON, Kay
De Leeuw, Cateau W
HAMILTON, Max
Hamilton, Cecily
HAMILTON, Michael
Chetham-Strode, Warren
HAMILTON, Mollie
Kaye, Mary Margaret
HAMILTON, Paul
Dennis-Jones, Harold
HAMILTON, Priscilla
Gellis, Roberta
HAMILTON, Roger
Rogerson, James
HAMILTON, Wade
Floren, Lee
HAMILTON, William
Canaway, W H
HAMILTON-STOCKFORD, Joan
Stockford, Lela E
HAMILTON-WILKES, Monty
Hamilton-Wilkes, Edwin
HAMMETT, Mary Jane
Hammett, Dashiell
HAMMOND, Brad
King, Albert
HAMMOND, Jane
Poland, Dorothy E H
HAMMOND, Keith
Kuttner, Henry
HAMMOND, Ralph
Hammond-Innes, Ralph

HAMPSON, John
Simpson, John Frederick
Norman Hampson
HAMPTON, Mark
Norwood, Victor George
Charles
HAN SUYIN
Comber, Elizabeth
HANCOCK, Frances Deane
Judson, Jeanne
HANCOCK, Robert
Howell, Douglas Nayler
HANLON, John
Mitchell, John Hanlon
HANNAFORD, Justin
Fitz-Gerald, S J A
HANNON, Ezra
Lombino, Salvatore A
HARBIN, Robert
Williams, Ned
HARBINSON, Robert
Harbinson-Bryans, Robert
HARDEN, Verna Loveday
Bentley, Verna Bessie
HARDIN, Clement
Newton, Dwight Bennett
HARDIN, Dave
Holmes, Llewellyn Perry
HARDIN, Mitch
Gerrity, David James
HARDIN, Peter
Vaczek, Louis C
HARDING, Bertita
Radetzby von Radetz, *Countess*
HARDING, George
Raubenheimer, George H
HARDING, Matt
Floren, Lee
HARDING, Matthew Whitman
Floren, Lee
HARDING, Richard
Boulton, A Harding
HARDING, Todd
Reynolds, Dallas McCord

HARDING, Wes
Keevill, Henry John
HARDWICK, Sylvia
Doherty, Ivy Ruby
HARDY, Adam
Harknett, Terry
HARDY, Arthur S
Steffens, Arthur Joseph
HARDY, Bobbie
Hardy, Marjorie
HARDY, Laura
Holland, Sheila
HARDY, Russ
Snow, Charles Horace
HARDY, Stuart
Schisgall, Oscar
HARE, Cyril
Clark, Alfred Alexander
Gordon
HARE, Martin
Girling, Zoë
HARE, Robert
Hutchinson, Robert Hare
HARFORD, Henry
Hudson, William Henry
HARGIS, Pauline
Dillard, Polly Hargis
HARGIS, Polly
Dillard, Polly Hargis
HARGRAVE, Leonie
Disch, Thomas
HARLAN, Glen
Cebulash, Mel
HARLAN, Ross
King, Albert
HARLAND, Marion
Terhune, Mary Virginia
HARLE, Elizabeth
Roberts, Irene
HARLEQUIN
Reed, Alexander Wyclif
HARLEY, John
Marsh, John

HARLOWE, Justine
Bennett, Laura; Harvey, Jean
and Mackenzie, Tina
HARMAN, Jane
Harknett, Terry
HARMODIUS
Jackson, Charles Philip Castle
Kains
HARMON, Gill
King, Albert
HARMSTON, Donald
Matheson, Donald H
HARMSTON, Olivia
Weber, Nancy
HARPER, Daniel
Brossard, Chandler
HARPOLE, James
Abraham, James Johnston
HARRIETT
Wilcoxen, Harriett
HARRIFORD, Daphne
Harris, Marion Rose
HARRIS, Christopher
Fry, Christopher
HARRIS, Colver
Harris, Polly Anne Colver
HARRIS, John Beynon
Harris, John Wyndham Parkes
Lucas Beynon
HARRIS, Kathleen
Humphries, Adelaide
HARRIS, Larry Mark
Harris, Laurence Mark
HARRIS, Macdonald
Heiney, Donald William
HARRIS, Peter
Harris, William
HARRIS, Thistle Y
Stead, Thistle Yolette
HARRISON, Chip
Block, Lawrence
HARRISON, Whit
Whittington, Harry

HARSCH, Hilya
Jelly, George Oliver
HART, Francis
Paine, Lauran Bosworth
HART, Jon
Harvey, John
HART, Max
Urquhart, Macgregor
HART, R W
Ferneyhough, Roger Edmund
HART, Susanne
Harthoorn, Susanne
HARTE, Marjorie
McEvoy, Marjorie
HARTFORD, Via
Donson, Cyril
HARTMAN, Roger
Mehta, Rustam
HARTWELL, Nancy
Callahan, Claire Wallis
HARVESTER, Simon
Rumbold-Gibbs, Henry St
John C
HARVEY, Caroline
Potter, Joanna
HARVEY, Gene
Hanley, Jack
HARVEY, Lyon
Porter, Edward
HARVEY, Rachel
Bloom, Ursula
HARVEY, Ross
Hook, H Clarke
HASLETTE, John
Vahey, John George Haslette
HASSAN i SABBAH
Butler, Bill
HASTINGS, Beatrice
Haig, Emily Alice
HASTINGS, Brook
Edgley, Leslie *and*
Edgley, Mary
HASTINGS, Graham
Jeffries, Roderic Graeme

HASTINGS, Hudson
Kuttner, Henry
HASWELL, Jock
Haswell, C J D
HATCH, Robert
Lee, Manning de Villeneuve
HATRED, Peter
Douglas, Keith
HATTON, Cliff
Mason, Sydney Charles
HAVIL, Anthony
Philipp, Elliot Elias
HAWK, Affable
MacCarthy, *Sir* Desmond
HAWK, Alex
Garfield, Brian
HAWK, Alex
Kelton, Elmer
HAWK, Alex
Lutz, Giles A
HAWKES, John
Burne, Clendennin Talbot
HAWKEYE
Carlisle, R H
HAWKINS, John
Hagan, Stelia F
HAWTHORNE, E M D
Dolbey, Ethel M
HAWTHORNE, Ernest H
Dawson, William Henry
HAWTHORNE, Marx
Greenwood, A E
HAWTHORNE, Rainey
Riddell, *Mrs* J H
HAY, Catherine
Hughes, Ivy
HAY, Frances
Dick-Erikson, Cicely Sibyl
Alexandra
HAY, Ian
Beith, John Hay
HAY, John
Dalrymple-Hay, Barbara *and*
Dalrymple-Hay, John

HAYDEN, Jay
Paine, Lauran Bosworth
HAYES, Clanton
Mason, Sydney Charles
HAYES, Evelyn
Bethell, Mary
HAYES, Henry
Olney, Ellen Warner
HAYES, Timothy
Rubel, James Lyon
HAYMAN, Hazel
Peel, Hazel
HAYNES, Dorothy K
Gray, Dorothy K
HAYNES, John Robert
Wilding, Philip
HAYWARD, Richard
Kendrick, Baynard Hardwick
HAZARD, Jack
Booth, Edwin
HAZARD, Laurence
Barr, Patricia
HAZELTON, Alexander
Armstrong, William Alexander
HAZELTON, Captain
Whitson, John Harvey
HAZELTON, Colonel
Whitson, John Harvey
HEAD, Ann
Morse, Anne Christensen
HEAD, Matthew
Canaday, John
HEADLEY, Elizabeth
Harrison, Elizabeth C
HEALD, Edith
Shackleton, Edith
HEALEY, Ben
Healey, Benjamin James
HEARD, Gerald
Heard, Henry Fitzgerald
HEARNDEN, Balfour
Balfour, Eve *and*
Hernden, Beryl

HEATH, Eldon
Derleth, August W
HEATH, Sandra
Wilson, Sandra
HEATH, Sharon
Ritchie, Claire
HEATH, Veronica
Blackett, Veronica
HEATHCOTT, Mary
Keegan, Mary Constance
HEATON, Peter
Stuart-Heaton, Peter
HEBDEN, Mark
Harris, John
HEBER, Austin
Poole, Reginald Heber
HEBER, Reginald
Poole, Reginald Heber
HEDGES, Joseph
Harknett, Terry
HEDLEY, Frank
Barker, Clarence Hedley
HEFNER, Paul
Tabori, Paul
HEGESIPPUS
Schonfield, Hugh Joseph
HELD, Peter
Vance, John Holbrook
HELLER, Frank
Serner, Gunnar
HELLERLAMB, Toni
Lamb, Antonia
HELLEY, Denis
Allen, Hubert Raymond
HELMHOLTZ, Bastien von
Pound, Ezra
HELMI, Jack
Sands, Leo G
HELVICK, James
Cockburn, Claud
HELY, Elizabeth
Younger, Elizabeth
HEMINGWAY, Percy
Addleshaw, Percy

209

HEMINGWAY, Taylor
Rywell, Martin
HENDERSON, Colt
Mason, Sydney Charles
HENDERSON, George
Glassco, John
HENDERSON, Paul
France, Ruth
HENDERSON, Sylvia
Ashton-Warner, Sylvia
HENDERSON-HOWAT, Gerald
Howat, Gerald
HENNESSEY, Hugh
Donovan, John
HENNESSY, Max
Harris, John
HENRIQUES, Veronica
Gosling, Veronica
HENRY, B A
Abrahams, Henry B
HENRY, Daniel *Jr*
Holmes, Daniel Henry
HENRY, Lewis C
Copeland, Lewis
HENRY O
Porter, William Sydney
HENRY, Will
Allen, Henry
HEPPELL, Blanche
Heppell, Mary
HEPPLE, Anne
Dickinson, Anne Hepple
HEPTAGON
Charlton, Joan;
Falk, Katherine;
Falk, Millicent; Fox, Winifred;
Gill, Winifred; Jennings, Hilda
and Stocks, Mary
HEPWORTH, Mike
Hepworth, James Michael
HERALD, Kathleen
Peyton, Kathleen Wendy *and*
Peyton, Michael

HERBERT, Arthur
Shappiro, Herbert Arthur
HERBERT, John
Brundage, John Herbert
HEREFORD, John
Fletcher, Harry L Verne
HERITAGE, A J
Addis, Hazel Iris
HERITAGE, Martin
Horler, Sydney
HERMAN, Jack
Sands, Leo G
HERMAN, William
Bierce, Ambrose
HERMES
Canaway, W H
HERNE, Eric
Garvey, Eric William
HERNE, Huxley
Brooker, Bertram
HERON, E *and* **H**
Prichard, H Hesketh *and*
Prichard, Kate Hesketh
HERRING, Geilles
Somerville, Edith Oenone
HERRIOT, James
Wight, J A
HERRNSTEIN, Barbara
Smith, Barbara Herrnstein
HESSING, Dennis
Dennis-Jones, Harold
HEWES, Cady
De Voto, Bernard Augustine
HEWETT, Anita
Duke, Anita
HEWITT, Martin
Morrison, Arthur
HEXT, Harrington
Phillpotts, Eden
HEXTALL, David
Phillips-Birt, Douglas
HIAT, Elchik
Katz, Menke

HICKEY, Lyn
Hickey, Madelyn E
HICKOK, Will
Harrison, Chester William
HICKS, Eleanor
Coerr, Eleanor Beatrice
HIGGINBOTHAM, Anne T
Higginbotham, Anne D
HIGGINS, Jack
Patterson, Harry
HIGHLAND, Dora
Avallone, Michael Angelo *Jr*
HIGHLAND, Monica
See, Carolyn
HIGSON, P J W
Willoughby-Higson, Philip John
HIGSON, Philip
Higson, Philip John Willoughby
HILDICK, Wallace
Hildick, E W
HILL, Alexis
Craig, Mary
HILL, Anne
Muskett, Netta Rachel
HILL, Bennet
Winter, Bevis
HILL, Craven
Parsons, Charles P
HILL, H Haverstock
Walsh, James Morgan
HILL, Headon
Grainger, Francis Edward
HILL, James
Jameson, Storm
HILL, Joe
Hillstrom, Joseph
HILL, King
Robertson, Frank Chester
HILL, Monica
Werner, Elsa Jane
HILL, Murray
Holliday, Robert Cortes
HILL, Prudence
Maxfield, Prudence

HILL, Rabin
Young, Robert
HILLIARD, Jan
Grant, Hilda Kay
HILLMAN, Martin
Hill, Douglas
HILTON, Margery
Woods, Margery Hilton
HIN ME GEONG
Armitage, John
HINDE, Thomas
Chitty, *Sir* Thomas Willes
HINDIN, Nathan
Bloch, Robert
HINTON, S E
Inhofe, Susan Eloise
HIPPOPOTAMUS, Eugene H
Kraus, Robert
HISTORICUS
Nock, Albert Jay
HOBART, Robertson
Lee, Norman
HOBBES, John Oliver
Craigie, Pearl Mary Teresa
HOBSON, Polly
Evans, Julia
HOCKABY, Stephen
Mitchell, Gladys
HODEMART, Peter
Audemars, Pierre
HODGE, E Chatterton
Hastings, Phyllis
HODGE, Merton
Hodge, Horace Emerton
HODGEN, J T
Hale, Ethela Ruth (*Mrs* Fellowes)
HODSON, Arthur
Nickson, Arthur
HOE, Leigh
Tripp, H Alker
HOFER, Peter
Kortner, Peter

HOFFMAN, Art
King, Albert
HOFFMAN, Louise
Fitzgerald, Beryl
HOFFNER, Dorothy
Doane, Pelagie
HOFMEYER, Hans
Fleischer, Anthony
HOGAN, David
Gallagher, Frank
HOGARTH, Charles
Creasy, John
HOGARTH, Douglas
Phillips-Birt, Douglas
HOGARTH, Emmett
Wilson, Mitchell *and*
Polansky, Abraham
HOGARTH, John
Finnin, Mary
HOGBIN, Ian
Hogbin, Herbert
HOLBROOK, Jack
Vance, John Holbrook
HOLBROOK, John
Vance, John Holbrook
HOLCOMBE, Arnold
Golsworthy, Arnold
HOLDEN, Genevieve
Pou, Genevieve
HOLDEN, Joanne
Corby, Jane
HOLDEN, Larry
Lorenz, Frederic
HOLDEN, Matthew
Parkinson, Roger
HOLLAND, Clive
Hankinson, Charles J
HOLLAND, Elizabeth
Baxter, Elizabeth
HOLLAND, Katrin
Loewengard, Heidi H F
HOLLAND, Kel
Whittington, Harry

HOLLAND, Rosemary
Pattinson, Lee
HOLLAND, Tom
King, Albert
HOLLIDAY, James
Davidson, Simon
HOLLIS, Jim
Summers, Hollis
HOLME, K E
Hill, Christopher
HOLMES, Arnold W
Fryefield, Maurice P
HOLMES, *Captain* Howard
Harbaugh, Thomas Chalmers
HOLMES, Caroline
Mason, Sydney Charles
HOLMES, Gordon
Shiel, M P *and* Tracy, Louis
HOLMES, Grant
Fox, James
HOLMES, Grant
Knipscheer, James M W
HOLMES, H H
White, William Anthony P
HOLMES, Jay
Holmes, Joseph Everett
HOLMES, John
Souster, Raymond
HOLMES, Kenyon
Derleth, August W
HOLMES, Raymond
Souster, Raymond
HOLMES, Rick
Hardwick, Richard
HOLORENSHAW, Henry
Needham, Joseph
HOLT, E Carleton
Guigo, Ernest Philip
HOLT, Elizabeth
King, Kay
HOLT, Gavin
Rodda, Charles
HOLT, George
Tubb, E C

HOLT, Helen
Paine, Lauran Bosworth
HOLT, Rackham
Holt, Margaret Van Vechten
HOLT, Stephen
Thompson, Harlan
HOLT, Tex
Joscelyn, Archie Lynn
HOLT, Tex
Rister, Claude
HOLT, Victoria
Hibbert, Eleanor Alice Burford
HOLTON, Leonard
Wibberley, Leonard Patrick
O'Connor
HOLZAPFEL, Rudi
Holzapfel, Rudolf Patrick
HOME, Michael
Bush, Christopher
HOME-GALL, Reginald
Home-Gall, Edward Reginald
HOME GUARD
Ingamells, F G
HOMES, Geoffrey
Mainwaring, Daniel
HON MEMBER FOR X
De Chair, Somerset
HONEYCUTT, Richard
Hardwick, Richard
HONEYMAN, Brenda
Clarke, Brenda
HOOKER, Richard
Hornberger, H Richard
HOOLEY, Teresa
Butler, Teresa Mary
HOOTON, Charles
Rowe, Vivian Claud
HOPE, Andrew
Hern, Anthony
HOPE, Anthony
Hawkins, *Sir* Anthony Hope
HOPE, Ascott R
Hope-Moncrieff, Ascott Robert

HOPE, Brian
Creasey, John
HOPE, Edward
Coffey, Edward Hope
HOPE, John Francis
Randall, A E
HOPE, Lawrence
Nicholson, Violet
HOPE, Margaret
Wicksteed, Margaret Hope
HOPE, Marion
Parker, Marion
HOPE, Noel
Morewood, Sarah L
HOPE, Stanton
Stanton-Hope, W E
HOPF, Alice
Lightner, A M
HOPKINS, A T
Turngreen, Annette
HOPKINS, Lyman
Folsom, Franklin Brewster
HOPKINS, Stanley
Holt, Henry
HOPKINSON, Tom
Hopkinson, *Sir* Henry Thomas
HOPLEY, George
Hopley-Woolrich, Cornell
George
HOPPER, Sam
Haslam, Nicky
HORN, Chester
Mason, Sydney Charles
HORN, Peter
Kuttner, Henry
HORN, Trader
Smith, Alfred Aloysius
HORNBROOKE, Obadiah
Comfort, Alex
HORNBY, John
Hornby, John Wilkinson
HORNE, Howard
Payne, Pierre Stephen Robert

213

HORSLEY, David
Bingley, David Ernest
HORSTMANN, Rosemary
Waters, Rosemary Elizabeth
HORTON, Felix Lee
Floren, Lee
HORTON, Robert J
Roberts, James
HOUGH, Don
Huff, Darrell
HOUGHTON, Claude
Oldfield, Claude Houghton
HOUGHTON, Elizabeth
Gilzean, Elizabeth Houghton
HOUSE, Brant
Chadwick, Paul
HOUSE, Patricia
Wheen, Francis
HOUSTON, R B
Rae, Hugh Cranford
HOUSTON, Will
Paine, Lauran Bosworth
HOWARD, Colin
Shaw, Howard
HOWARD, Don
Menzel, Donald H
HOWARD, Elizabeth
Mizner, Elizabeth Howard
HOWARD, Elizabeth
Paine, Lauran Bosworth
HOWARD, George
Kay, Frederic George
HOWARD, Harry
Ognall, Leopold Horace
HOWARD, Hartley
Ognall, Leopold Horace
HOWARD, Helen
Jacobs, Thomas Curtis Hicks
HOWARD, John M
Hincks, Cyril Malcolm
HOWARD, Keble
Bell, John Keble
HOWARD, Leigh
Lee Howard, L A

HOWARD, Linden
Manley-Tucker, Audrie
HOWARD, Mary
Mussi, Mary
HOWARD, Troy
Paine, Lauran Bosworth
HOWARD, Vechel
Rigsby, Howard
HOWE, Muriel
Smithies, Muriel
HOWELL, Scott
King, Albert
HOWELL, Virginia Tier
Ellison, Virginia Howell
HOWERD, Gareth
Thomas, Robert Richard
HOWES, Jane
Shiras, Wilmar H
HOY, Elizabeth
Conarain, Alice Nina
HOYT, Nelson
King, Albert
HSIA, HSIAO
Liu, Wu-chi
HUBBARD, Joan
Jackson, Kathryn
HUBBARD, Kin
Hubbard, Frank McKinney
HUBBARD, L Ron
Hubbard, Lafayette Ronald
HUBERT
Bland, Hubert
HUDSON, Jan
Smith, George H
HUDSON, Jeffrey
Crichton, Michael
HUDSON, Stephen
Schiff, Sydney
HUGGINS, Ruth Mabel
Arthur, Ruth M
HUGHES, Alison
Oliver, Doris M
HUGHES, Brenda
Colloms, Brenda

HUGHES, Colin
Creasey, John
HUGHES, Elizabeth
Zachary, Hugh
HUGHES, Matilda
Macleod, Charlotte
HUGHES, Philip
Phillips, Hugh
HUGHES, Terence
Best, Rayleigh Breton Amis
HUGHES, Valerina
Coleman, John
HUGHES, Zach
Zachary, Hugh
HUGO, Grant
Cable, James
HULL, H Braxton
Jacobs, Helen Hull
HULL, Opal I
Lehnus, Opal Hull
HULL, Richard
Sampson, Richard Henry
HUMANA, Charles
Jacobs, Charles
HUME, David
Turner, John Victor
HUME, Frances
Buckland-Wright, Mary
HUMPHREYS, B V
Schneider, B V H
HUMPHRYS, Geoffrey
Humphrys, Leslie George
HUNT, Charlotte
Hodges, Doris Marjorie
HUNT, Diana
Hunt-Bode, Gisele
HUNT, Dorothy
Fellows, Dorothy Alice
HUNT, Francesca
Holland, Isabelle
HUNT, Gill
Tubb, E C
HUNT, Harrison
Ballard, Willis Todhunter

HUNT, John
Paine, Lauran Bosworth
HUNT, Kyle
Creasey, John
HUNT, Peter
Yates, George Worthing *and*
Marshall, Charles Hunt
HUNTER, Alison
Blair, Norma Hunter
HUNTER, Anson
Orrmont, Arthur
HUNTER, E Waldo
Waldo, Edward Hamilton
HUNTER, Evan
Lombino, Salvatore
HUNTER, George
Ballard, Willis Todhunter
HUNTER, Hall
Marshall, Edison
HUNTER, Jean
Hunter, Alfred John
HUNTER, John
Ballard, Willis Todhunter
HUNTER, John
Hunter, Alfred John
HUNTER, John
Hunter, Christine
HUNTER, M O
Mabbott, Thomas O
HUNTER, Mollie
McIlwraith, Maureen Mollie
Hunter
HUNTER, Pat
Kempf, Pat
HUNTINGDON, John
Phillips, Gerald William
HUNTLY, Frances E
Mayne, Ethel Colborn
HUNTON, Mary
Gilzean, Elizabeth Houghton
HURGERFORD, Pixie
Brinsmead, Hesba
HURKEY, Rooan
Holzapfel, Rudolf Patrick

HUSSEY, Leonard
Pearce, Brian
HUSSINGTREE, Martin
Baldwin, Oliver
HUSTLE, Hugh
Hall, Verner
HUSTON, Fran
Miller, R S
HUTCHINS, Anthony
Morley, Leslie Reginald William
HUTCHINSON, Anne
Burnett, Hallie
HUTCHINSON, Patricia
Fullbrook, Gladys
HYDE, Eleanor
Minto, Frances
HYNE, C J Cutliffe
Hyne, Charles John Cutliffe
Wright
HYNE, Cutliffe
Hyne, Charles John Cutliffe
Wright

I B
Brown, Ivor
IAMS, Jack
Iams, Samuel H
ICONOCLAST
Hamilton, Mary A A
IDRIS
Mee, Arthur
IFANS, Glyn
Evans, Glyn
IGNOTUS
Fuller, James Franklin
ILES, Bert
Ross, Zola Helen
ILES, Francis
Cox, A B
INCLEDON, Philip
Worner, Philip A I
INGERSOL, Jared
Paine, Lauran Bosworth

INGHAM, Daniel
Lambot, Isobel Mary
INGRAM, Hunter
Lutz, Giles A
INGRAM, Martin
Campbell, Alice Ormond
INNES, Hammond
Hammond-Innes, Ralph
INNES, Jean
Saunders, Jean
INNES, Michael
Stewart, John Innes Mackintosh
IONICUS, Ion
Leslie, *Sir* Shane
IOTA
Caffyn, Kathleen M
IRELAND, Baron
Salsbury, Nate
IRELAND, Doreen
Lord, Doreen Mildred Douglas
IRELAND, Michael
Figgis, Darrell
IRELAND, Noelle
Gibbs, Norah
IRISH, William
Hopley-Woolrich, Cornell
George
IRISHMAN, AN
Clayton, *Reverend* F H
IRON, Ralph
Schreiner, Olive Emilie
Albertina
IRONBARK
Gibson, G H
IRONQUILL
Ware, Eugene Fitch
IRONSIDE, John
Tait, Euphemia Margaret
IRVINE, Lyn
Newman, Lyn Lloyd
IRVING, Robert
Adler, Irving
IRWIN, P K
Page, Patricia Kathleen

ISLAY, Nicholas
Murray, Andrew Nicholas
IVES, John
Garfield, Brian
IVES, Morgan
Bradley, Marion Z

J A H
Hammerton, J A
J C
Lawrence, T E
J C T
Trewin, J C
J E N
Neild, James Edward
J F-K
Fitzmaurice-Kelly, James
J J
Junor, *Sir* John
J L
Pound, Ezra
J S H
Huxley, Julian Sorell
JABEZ
Nicol, Eric Patrick
JACKS, Oliver
Gandley, Kenneth Royce
JACKSON, E F
Tubb, E C
JACKSON, Everatt
Muggeson, Margaret
JACKSON, Giles
Leffingwell, Albert
JACKSON, Joyce
Crounse, Helene Louise
JACKSON, Neville
Glaskin, Gerald Marcus
JACKSON, Sam
Trumbo, Dalton
JACKSON, Wallace
Budd, William John
JACKSTAFF
Bennett, J J

JACOB, Herbert Mathias
Davies, D Jacob
JACOBS, Leah
Gellis, Roberta
JACOT, Bernard
Jacot de Bolnod, B L
JACQUES
Stott, Mary
JAFFA, George
Wallace-Clarke, George
JAMES, Andrew
Kirkup, James
JAMES, Brian
Tierney, John
JAMES, Cy
Watts, Peter Christopher
JAMES, Dan
Sayers, James D
JAMES, Dynely
Mayne, William J C *and*
Caesar, Richard Dynely
JAMES, Franklin
Godley, Robert
JAMES, James
Adams, Arthur Henry
JAMES, John
Langdon-Davies, John
JAMES, Josephine
Lindsay, Barbara *and*
Sterne, E G
JAMES, Margaret
Bennetts, Pamela
JAMES, Matthew
Lucey, James D
JAMES, Robert
Heitner, Iris
JAMES, Vincent
Gribben, James
JAMES, William M
Harknett, Terry
JAMESON, Eric
Trimmer, Eric
JAMESON, Vere
Shute, Evan Vere

217

JAMIESON, Thomas
Molloy, Edward
JAN
Read, John
JANES, Kathleen
Jamieson, Kathleen Florence
JANES, Kathleen F
Jamieson, Kathleen Florence
JANET, Lillian
O'Daniel, Janet *and*
Ressler, Lillian
JANICE
Brustlein, Janice
JANIFER, Laurence M
Harris, Laurence Mark
JANSEN, Hank
Newton, William
JANSEN, Hank
Norwood, Victor George
Charles
JANSEN, Jared
Cebulash, Mel
JANSON, Hank
Frances, Stephen Daniel
JANUS, Hiram
Pound, Ezra
JAPONICA
Holdaway, Marjorie F
JAQUES
Neild, James Edward
JARDIN, Rex
Burkhardt, Eve *and*
Burkhardt, Robert Ferdinand
JARRETT, Kay
Saxon, Sophia
JASON
Craine, John Henry
JASON
Munro, Hugh
JASON, Jerry
Smith, George H
JASON, Johnny
Glut, Don F

JASON, Stuart
Floren, Lee
JASON, William
Machlin, Milton
JASPER, Bob
Hogan, Robert Jasper
JAY
Jennings, E C
JAY, Charlotte
Jay, Geraldine
JAY, Joan
Davies, Edith
JAY, Marion
Spalding, Ruth
JAY, Simon
Alexander, Colin James
JAYNES, Clare
Spiegel, Clara E *and*
Mayer, Jane
JEANS, Angela
Watt, Esme
JEEVES, Mahatma Kane
Dukenfield, William Claude
JEFFCOATE, Norman
Jeffcoate, *Sir* Thomas Norman
Arthur
JEFFCOATE, T N A
Jeffcoate, *Sir* Thomas Norman
Arthur
JEFFERIES, Ian
Hays, Peter
JEFFERIS, Jeff
Curry, Thomas Albert
JEFFERSON, Ian
Davies, Leslie Purnell
JEFFERSON, Sarah
Farjeon, Eve
JEFFERY, E Jeffery
Marston, J E
JEFFORD, Bat
Bingley, David Ernest
JEFFREYS, J G
Healey, Benjamin James

JEFFRIES, Jeff
Boatfield, Jeffrey
JEFFS, Rae
Sebley, Frances Rae
JELLY, Oliver
Jelly, George Oliver
JEMONTE
Mohan, Josephine Elizabeth
JEMYMA
Holley, Marietta
JENNER, Heather
Potter, Heather
JENNIFER
Kenward, Betty
JENNIFER, Susan
Hoskins, Robert
JENNINGS, D
Frazee, Steve
JENNINGS, S M
Meyer, Jerome Sydney
JENNY WREN
Cruttenden, Nellie
JEREMY, Richard
Fox, Charles
JEROME, Joseph
Sewell, Brocard
JEROME, Owen Fox
Friend, Oscar Jerome
JESKINS, Richard
Story, Rosamond Mary
JESSE, Michael
Baldwin, Michael
JESSEL, John
Weinbaum, Stanley Grauman
JINGLE
Golsworthy, Arnold
JOB, Modern
Taber, Clarence Wilbur
JOCELYN, Richard
Clutterbuck, Richard
JODY, J M
Edmundson, Joseph
JOHANSON, Elizabeth
Verwer, Johanne

JOHN, A SUFFOLK HERD BOY
Brundle, John
JOHN, Alix
Jones, Alice
JOHN, Evan
Simpson, Evan John
JOHN, Jasper
Muspratt, Rosalie
JOHN, Nancy
Sawyer, John *and*
Sawyer, Nancy
JOHN, Salisbury
Caute, David
JOHN O'LONDON
Whitten, Wilfred
JOHN O'THE NORTH
Browne, Harry T
JOHNS, Avery
Cousins, Margaret
JOHNS, Foster
Seldes, Gilbert Vivian
JOHNS, Frederick
Cheshire, David Frederick
JOHNS, Geoffrey
Warner, Geoffrey John
JOHNS, Hilary
Barraud, E M
JOHNS, June
Smith, June Johns
JOHNS, Kenneth
Bulmer, Henry Kenneth
JOHNS, Richard
Slater, Montagu
JOHNSON, A E
Johnson, Annabel J *and*
Johnson, Edgar R
JOHNSON, Benjamin F
Riley, James Whitcomb
JOHNSON, Brian
Worthy, Brian Johnson
JOHNSON, Crockett
Leisk, David Johnson
JOHNSON, Lee
Johnson, Lilian Beatrice

JOHNSON, Marigold
Gilles, Daniel
JOHNSON, Mel
Malzberg, Barry Norman
JOHNSON, Mike
Sharkey, Jack
JOHNSON, Rob
Johnson, R V
JOHNSON, W Bolingbroke
Bishop, Morris Gilbert
JOLLY, Susan
Edwards, Florence
JONES, Annabel
Lewis, Mary Christianna
JONES, Bobi
Jones, Robert Maynard
JONES, Bradshaw
Bradshaw-Jones, Malcolm
Henry
JONES, Calico
Richardson, Gladwell
JONES, Clara
Baldwin, Dorothy
JONES, Joanna
Burke, John Frederick
JONES, H S
Molloy, Edward
JONES, Helen
Hinckley, Helen
JONES, Llewellyn
Allen, Hubert Raymond
JONES, Luke
Watts, Peter Christopher
JONES, Melville
Bander, Peter
JONES, Nard
Jones, Maynard Benedict
JONES, Pat
Jones, Virgil Carrington
JONES, Webb
Henley, Art
JONS, Hal
Jones, Harry Austin

JORDAN, Barbara Leslie
Yellot, Barbara Leslie
JORDAN, Bryn
Henderson, James Maddock
JORDAN, Gail
Dern, Erolie Pearl
JORDAN, Lee ⋅
Scholefield, Alan
JORDAN, Neill
Barker, E M
JORGENSON, Ivar
Silverberg, Robert
JOSE, Ellen J
Waye, Ellen
JOSIAH ALLEN'S WIFE
Holley, Marietta
JOUDRY, Patricia
Steele, Patricia M V
JOURNEYMAN
Nock, Albert Jay
JOYCE, Thomas
Cary, Joyce
JOYSTICK
Holden, J R
JUBILATE
Coppage, George Herman
JUDD, Cyril
Grossman, Judith *and*
Kornbluth, Cyril M
JUDGE, THE
Sharp, Ian
JULIA
Cox, Julia
JULIAN, Peter
Körmendi, Ferens
JULIE
Nettz, Julie
JULIE OF COLORADO
SPRINGS
Robbins, June
JULIET
Levy, Julia Ethel
JUNE, Jenny
Croly, Jane Cunningham

JUNIOR SUB
Beith, John Hay
JUSTICIAR
Powell-Smith, Vincent
JUSTIFICUS
Pappas, George S

K B
Baker, Kate
KAHLER, Woodland
Saint Innocent, *Marquis of*
KAIN, Saul
Sassoon, Siegfried
KAINS, Josephine
Goulart, Ronald Joseph
KAJAR
Bowen, Reuben
KANE, Jim
Germano, Peter
KANE, Julia
Robins, Denise
KANE, Mark
King, Albert
KANE, Wilson
Bloch, Robert
KANTO, Peter
Zachary, Hugh
KAP-O-KASLO
West, G A
KARAGEORGE, Michael
Anderson, Poul
KARIG, Walter
Patrick, Keats
KARLOFF, Boris
Pratt, William Henry
KAROL, Alexander
Kent, Arthur
KARTA, Nat
Norwood, Victor George
Charles
KASZNAR, Kurt
Serwicher, Kurt
KAVAN, Anna
Edmonds, Helen

KAVANAGH, Dan
Barnes, Julian
KAVANAGH, Paul
Block, Lawrence
KAVANAUGH, Cynthia
Daniels, Dorothy
KAY, George
Lambert, Eric
KAY, Helen
Goldfrank, *Mrs* Herbert
KAY, Wallace
Arter, Wallace E
KAYE, Barbara
Muir, Marie
KAYE, Evelyn
Evans, Kathleen
KAYE, Harold B
Kampf, Harold Bertram
KAYE, Mary Margaret
Hamilton, Mary Margaret Kaye
KAYE, Tom
Kaye, Barrington
KEANE, Molly
Keane, Mary Nesta
KEATING, Walter S
Rosenberg, Henrietta
KEENE, Carolyn
Adams, Harriet S (*after*
Edward Stratemeyer)
KEENE, Carolyn
Stratemeyer, Edward
KEENE, Faraday
Jarrett, Cora
KEENE, Frances W
Casman, Frances White
KEENE, James
Cook, William Everett
KEESING, Nancy
Hertzberg, Nancy
KEIR, Christine
Pullein-Thompson, Christine
KEITH, Carlton
Robertson, Keith

KEITH, David
Steegmuller, Francis
KEITH, Donald
Monroe, Donald *and*
Monroe, Keith
KEITH, James
Hetherington, Keith James
KEITH, Marian
MacGregor, Mary Ester
KELL, Joseph
Wilson, John Anthony Burgess
KELLER, Dan
Kaufman, Louis
KELLEY, Ray
Paine, Lauran Bosworth
KELLIER, Elizabeth
Kelly, Elizabeth
KELLOW, Kathleen
Hibbert, Eleanor Alice Burford
KELLY, Patrick
Allbeury, Theo Edward le
Bouthillier
KELLY, Ralph
Geis, Darlene Stern
KELLWAY, Mary D
Hillyard, Mary Dorothy
KELSEY, Janice
King, Albert
KELWAY, Christine
Gwinn, Christine M
KEMP, Sarah
Butterworth, Michael
KENDAL, Robert
Forster, Reginald Kenneth
KENDALL, Jane
Martens, Anne Louise
KENDALL, Lace
Stoutenberg, Adrien
KENDRAKE, Carleton
Gardner, Erle Stanley
KENDRICKS, James
Fox, Gardner F
KENEU
Hazlewood, Rex

KENNEDY, Diana
Duggleby, Jean Colbeck
KENNEDY, Elliott
Godfrey, Lionel Robert
Holcombe
KENNEDY, Howard
Woolfolk, Josiah Pitts
KENNEDY, James
Kenafick, Joseph
KENNEDY, Milward
Burge, Milward Rodon Kennedy
KENNEDY, R C
Cortez-Columbus, Robert
Cimabue
KENNEDY, X J
Kennedy, Joseph Charles
KENNEGGY, Richard
Nettell, Richard
KENNIE, Jessie
Macpherson, Jessie
KENNINGTON, Alan
Kennington, Gilbert Alan
KENNY, Charles J
Gardner, Erle Stanley
KENSINGER, George
Fichter, George S
KENT, Alexander
Reeman, Douglas
KENT, David
Birney, Hoffman
KENT, Helen
Polley, Judith Anne
KENT, Kelvin
Kuttner, Henry *and*
Barnes, Arthur
KENT, Pamela
Barrie, Susan
KENT, Pete
Richardson, Gladwell
KENT, Philip
Bulmer, Henry Kenneth
KENT, Simon
Catto, Maxwell Jeffrey

KENTIGERN, John
Veitch, Thomas
KENTON, Maxwell
Southern, Terry *and*
Hoffenberg, Mason
KENWARD, Jean
Chesterman, Jean
KENWORTHY, Hugh
Walker, Rowland
KENYON, Larry
Engel, Lyle Kenyon
KENYON, Paul
Engel, Lyle Kenyon
KENYON, Robert O
Kuttner, Henry
KEPPEL, Charlotte
Torday, Ursula
KEPPS, Gerald E
Speck, Gerald Eugene
KERBY, Susan Alice
Burton, Alice Elizabeth
KERN, Gregory
Tubb, E C
KERR, Ben
Ard, William
KERR, Carole
Carr, Margaret
KERR, Frederick
Kerner, Fred
KERR, John O'Connell
Whittet, George Sorley
KERR, Lennox
Kerr, James Lennox
KERR, M E
Meaker, Marijane
KERR, Michael
Hoskins, Robert
KERR, Orpheus C
Newell, Robert Henry
KERRY, Lois
Cardozo, Lois S
KERSEY, John
Warriner, Thurman

KERSHAW, Peter
Lucie-Smith, Edward
KESTEVEN, G R
Crosher, Geoffrey Robins
KETCHUM, Jack
Paine, Lauran Bosworth
KETTLE, Pamela
Kettle, Jocelyn
KEVERNE, Richard
Hosken, Clifford James
Wheeler
KEW, Andrew
Morton, A Q
KEYES, Gordon
Bedford-Jones, Henry
KEYSTONE, Oliver
Mantiband, James
KHAN, Khaled
Crowley, Edward Alexander
KIDD, Russell
Donson, Cyril
KIEFER, Middleton
Middleton, Harry *and*
Kiefer, Warren
KILBOURN, Matt
Barrett, Geoffrey John
KILDARE, John
King, John
KILDARE, Maurice
Richardson, Gladwell
KILGORE, John
Paine, Lauran Bosworth
KILPATRICK, Sarah
Underwood, Mavis Eileen
KIM
Sweet, John
KIMBER, Lee
King, Albert
KIMBRO, Jean
Kimbro, John
KIMBROUGH, Katheryn
Kimbro, John
KINDLER, Asta
Hicken, Una

KINEJI, Maborushi
Gibson, Walter Brown
KING, Ames
King, Albert
KING, Arthur
Cain, Arthur Homer
KING, Arthur
Lake, Kenneth Robert
KING, Berta
King, Albert
KING, Charles
Avenell, Donne
KING, Christopher
King, Albert
KING, Clifford
King, James Clifford
KING, Evan
Ward, Robert Spencer
KING, Kennedy
Brown, George Douglas
KING, Norman A
Tralins, S Robert
KING, Oliver
Mount, Thomas Ernest
KING, Paul
Drackett, Phil
KING, Reefe
Barker, Albert H
KING, Richard
Huskinson, Richard King
KING, Robin
Raleigh-King, Robin Victor
Lethbridge
KING, Sampson
Bennett, Arnold
KING, Stella
Glenton, Stella Lennox
KING, Stephanie
Russell, Shirley
KING, Vincent
Vinson, Rex Thomas
KING, W Scott
Greenland, W K

KINGSLEY, Laura
Bennett, Dorothy
KINGSMILL, Hugh
Lunn, Hugh Kingsmill
KINGSTON, Charles
O'Mahony, Charles Kingston
KINGSTON, Syd
Bingley, David Ernest
KINKAID, Matt
Adams, Clifton
KINNOCH, R G B
Barclay, George
KINSEY, Elizabeth
Clymer, Eleanor
KINSEY-JONES, Brian
Ball, Brian N
KIPPAX, John
Hynam, John
KIRBY, Kate
Elgin, Betty
KIRK, Laurence
Simson, Eric Andrew
KIRK, Michael
Knox, William
KIRKE, Edmund
Gilmore, James Robert
KIRTLAND, G B
Joslin, Sesyle
KISH
Le Riche, P J
KITT, Tamara
De Regniers, Beatrice Schenk
KLAXON
Bower, John Graham
KLOSE, Norma Cline
Cline, Norma
KNAUFF, Ellen Raphael
Hartley, Ellen Raphael
KNICKERBOCKER, Cholly
Paul, Maury
KNIGHT, Adam
Lariar, Lawrence
KNIGHT, Brigid
Sinclair, Kathleen Henrietta

KNIGHT, David
Prather, Richard
KNIGHT, Frank
Knight, Francis Edgar
KNIGHT, Gareth
Wilby, Basil Leslie
KNIGHT, Isobel
Lockie, Isobel
KNIGHT, Mallory
Hurwood, Bernhardt J
KNIGHT-PATTERSON, W M
Kulski, W W
KNOTT, Bill
Knott, William Cecil
KNOTT, Bill
Knott, William Kilborn
KNOTT, Hermann
Smith, Walter Chalmers
KNOTT, Will C
Knott, William Cecil
KNOTTS, Raymond
Volk, Gordon
KNOWALL, George
O'Nolan, Brian
KNOX, Bill
Knox, William
KNOX, Bill
Macleod, Robert
KNOX, Calvin
Silverberg, Robert
KNOX, Gilbert
Macbeth, Madge Hamilton
KNUDSEN, Greta
Knudsen, Margrethe
KNYE, Cassandra
Disch, Thomas *and*
Sladek, John
KODAK
O'Ferrall, Ernest
KONING, Hans
Koningsberger, Hans
KRAMER, George
Heuman, William

KRAPP, Robert Martin
Adams, Robert Martin
KRAUSS, Bruno
Bulmer, Henry Kenneth
KREMLINOLOGIST
Zorza, Victor
KREUZENAU, Michael
Law, Michael
KRIN, Sylvie
Fantoni, Barry
KRISLOV, Alexander
Lee Howard, L A
KROLL, Burt
Rowland, Donald Sydney
KRUGER, Paul
Sebenthall, Roberta
KRULL, Felix
White, Stanley
KURZ, Arthur
Scortia, Thomas Nicholas
KUTHUMI
Fleishmann, Helle
KYD, Thomas
Harbage, Alfred
KYLE, Elisabeth
Dunlop, Agnes M R
KYLE, Sefton
Vickers, Roy

§ §

*What good can it do an ass to be
called a lion?*
— Thomas Fuller. Gnomologia

§ §

L L
Barry, John Arthur
LA FAYETTE, Rene
Hubbard, Lafayette Ronald
LA SPINA, Greye
La Spina, Fanny Greye (Bragg)

225

LACY, Ed
Zinberg, Len
LADNEK, Odlaw
Kendall, Carlton Waldo
LADWICK, Marty
Kirby, Derek Amos
LADY OF MANITOBA, A
Frank, *Mrs* M J
LADY OF QUALITY
Jones, *Lady* Roderick
LAFARGUE, Philip
Philpot, Joseph H
LAING, Kenneth
Langmaid, Kenneth Joseph
Robb
LAING, Patrick
Long, Amelia R
LAIRD
Lowther, Armstrong John
LAKE, Sarah
Weiner, Margery
LAKER, Rosalind
Øvstedal, Barbara
LAKLAN, Carli
Laughlin, Virginia Carli
LAMB, Charlotte
Holland, Sheila
LAMB, William
Jameson, Storm
LAMBERT, Christine
Loewengard, Heidi H F
LAMONT, Frances
Jourdain, Eleanor F
LAMONT, Marianne
Rundle, Anne
LAMONT, N B
Barnitt, Nedda Lemmon
LAMONT, Wood C
Sewall, Robert
LAMPLAUGH, Lois
Davis, Lois Carlile
LAMPREY, A C
Fish, Robert Lloyd

LAMPTON, Austen
Dent, Anthony
LAN
Landon, Melville de Lancey
LANARK, David
Marten, J Chisholm
LANCASTER, A F
Fleur, Anne Elizabeth
LANCASTER, David
Heald, Tim
LANCASTER, G B
Lyttleton, Edith Joan
LANCASTER, Sheila
Holland, Sheila
LANCASTER, Vicky
Ansle, Dorothy Phoebe
LANCE, Leslie
Swatridge, Irene M M
LANCE CORPORAL COBBER
Adcock, A St John
LANCER, Jack
Lawrence, James Duncan
LAND, Jane *and* Ross
Borland, Kathryn K *and*
Speicher, Helen Ross
LAND, Rosina
Hastings, Phyllis
LANDELS, D H
Henderson, Donald Landels
LANDELS, Stephanie
Henderson, Donald Landels
LANDER, Dane
Clarke, Percy A
LANDERS, Ann
Lederer, Esther Pauline
LANDESMAN, Jay
Landesman, Irving Ned
LANDGRAVE OF HESSE
Rosen, Michael
LANDIS, John
Bell, Gerard
LANDON, Louise
Hauck, Louise Platt

LANE, Carla
Barrett, Romana
LANE, Edward
Dick, Kay
LANE, Elizabeth
Farmers, Eileen Elizabeth
LANE, Grant
Fisher, Stephen Gould
LANE, Jane
Dakers, Elaine
LANE, Marvyn
Price, Jeremie
LANE, Mary D
Delaney, Mary Murray
LANG, Anthony
Vahey, John George Haslette
LANG, Frances
Mantle, Winifred Langford
LANG, Grace
Floren, Lee
LANG, Gregor
Birren, Faber
LANG, King
Tubb, E C
LANG, Martin
Birren, Faber
LANG, Theo
Langbehn, Theo
LANGART, Darrel T
Garrett, Randall
LANGDALE, Stanley
Moorhouse, Sydney
LANGDON, Mary
Pike, Mary Hayden
LANGE, John
Crichton, Michael
LANGFORD, Jane
Mantle, Winifred Langford
LANGHOLM, Neil
Bulmer, Henry Kenneth
LANGLAND, William
Muntz, Isabelle Hope
LANGLEY, Helen
Rowland, Donald Sydney

LANGLEY, John
Mason, Sydney Charles
LANGLEY, Lee
Langley, Sarah
LANGLEY, Peter
Fleming, Ronald
LANGSTAFF, Tristram
Lord, William Wilberforce
LANGWORTHY, Yolande
Reade, *Mrs* Frances Lawson
LANIN, E B
Dillon, E J
LANSBURY, Angela
Sharot, Angela
LANSING, Henry
Rowland, Donald Sydney
LANT, Harvey
Rowland, Donald Sydney
LANTRY, Mike
Tubb, E C
LANZOL, Cesare
Landells, Richard
LAREDO, Johnny
Cesar, Gene
LARRIMORE, Lida
Turner, Lida Larrimore
LARRY
Parkes, Terence
LARSEN, Egon
Lehrburger, Egon
LARSON, Eve
St John, Wylly Folk
LASCELLES, Alison
Parris, John
LATHAM, Mavis
Thorpe-Clark, Mavis
LATHAM, Murray
Latham, Alison *and*
Latham, Esther
LATHAM, O'Neill
O'Neill, Rose Cecil
LATHAM, Philip
Richardson, Robert S

LATHEN, Emma
Latsis, Mary J *and*
Henissart, Martha
LATHROP, Francis
Leiber, Fritz
LATIMER, Rupert
Mills, Algernon Victor
LAUDER, Afferbeck
Morrison, Alistair
LAUDER, George
Dick-Lauder, George Andrew
LAUGHLIN, P S
Shea, Patrick
LAUNAY, André
De Launay, André Joseph
LAUNAY, Droo
De Launay, André Joseph
LAURA
Hunter, Eileen
LAURENCE, Robert
Fischer, Matthias Joseph
LAURIER, Don
Sizer, Laurence
LAVINGTON, Hubert
Carrington, Hereward
LAW, Marjorie J
Liddelow, Marjorie Joan
LAWLESS, Anthony
MacDonald, Philip
LAWRENCE, Bertram
Bloxham, John Francis
LAWRENCE, Hilda
Kronmiller, Hildegarde
LAWRENCE, Irene
Marsh, John
LAWRENCE, Jack
Fitzgerald, Lawrence P
LAWRENCE, James
Tames, Richard Lawrence
LAWRENCE, Lesley
Lewis, Lesley
LAWRENCE, P
Tubb, E C

LAWRENCE, Steven C
Murphy, Lawrence D
LAWSON, Chet
Tubb, E C
LAWSON, Christine
Walker, Emily Kathleen
LAWSON, Michael
Ryder, M L
LAWSON, *Dr* Philip
Trimmer, Eric
LAWSON, W B
Jenks, George Charles
LAWTON, Charles
Heckelmann, Charles N
LAWTON, Dennis
Faust, Frederick
LAZLO, Kate
Angus, Sylvia
LE BRETON, Thomas
Ford, T Murray
LE CARRÉ, John
Cornwell, David John Moore
LE GRAND
Henderson, Le Grand
LE GRYS, Walter
Norgate, Walter
LEA, Timothy
Wood, Christopher
LEACROFT, Eric
Young, Eric Brett
LEADER, Charles
Smith, Robert Charles
LEADERMAN, George
Robinson, Richard Blundell
LEAR, Peter
Lovesey, Peter
LEATHER, George
Swallow, Norman
LEAVER, Ruth
Tomalin, Ruth
LEDGARD, Jake
Mason, Sydney Charles
LEE, Andrew
Auchincloss, Louis

LEE, Babs
Lee, Marion Van Der Veer
LEE, Carolina
Dern, Erolie Pearl
LEE, Charles H
Story, Rosamond Mary
LEE, David
Rush, Noel
LEE, Edward
Fouts, Edward Lee
LEE, Elsie
Sheridan, Elsie Lee
LEE, Gypsy Rose
Hovick, Rose Louise
LEE, Howard
Goulart, Ronald Joseph
LEE, Jae Gardiner
Lee, Polly Jae
LEE, Jesse
Mason, Sydney Charles
LEE, Julian
Latham, Jean Lee
LEE, Ranger
Snow, Charles Horace
LEE, Rowena
Bartlett, Marie
LEE, Steve
Parry, Michel
LEE, Vernon
Paget, Violet
LEE, Veronica
Woodford, Irene-Cecile
LEE, William
Burroughs, William
LEES, Hannah
Fetter, Elizabeth
LEES, Marguerite
Baumann, Margaret
LEGMAN, G
Legman, George Alexander
LEGRIS, Jean-Luc
Donaldson, William
LEIGH, Johanna
Sayers, Dorothy L

LEIGH, Olivia
Clamp, Helen M E
LEIGH, Roberta
Lindsay, Rachel
LEIGH, Ursula
Gwynn, Ursula Grace
LEIGHTON, Lee
Overholser, Wayne D
LEINSTER, Murray
Jenkins, William Fitzgerald
LEJEUNE, Anthony
Thompson, Edward Anthony
LEMON, Grey
Gray, Lindsay Russell Nixon
LENANTON, C
Lenanton, *Lady*
LENGEL, Frances
Trocchi, Alexander
LENTON, Anthony
Nuttall, Anthony
LEO, Alan
Allan, Frederick William
LEODHAS, Sorche Nic
Alger, Leclaire Gowans
LEONA
Button, Margaret
LEONARD, Charles L
Heberden, Mary Violet
LEONARD, Hugh
Byrne, John Keyes
LEONG, Gor Yun
Ellison, Virginia Howell
LEONID
Bosworth, Willan George
LESBIA
Lewis, Lydia T
LESIEG, Theo
Geisel, Theodor Seuss
LESLEY, J P
Lesley, Peter
LESLIE, A
Scott, Leslie
LESLIE, A Scott
Scott, Leslie

LESLIE, Colin
Roome, Gerald Antony
LESLIE, Doris
Fergusson Hannay, *Lady*
LESLIE, Henrietta
Schütze, Gladys Henrietta
LESLIE, O H
Slesar, Henry
LESLIE, Val
Knights, Leslie
LESLIE, Ward S
Ward, Elizabeth Honor
LESS, Milton
Marlowe, Stephen
LESSER, Anthony
Whitby, Anthony Charles
LESTER, Frank
Usher, Frank Hugh
LESTER, Jane
Walker, Emily Kathleen
LESTER-RANDS, A
Judd, Frederick
L'ESTRANGE, Anna
Ellerbeck, Rosemary
LETHBRIDGE, Olive
Banbury, Olive Lethbridge
LETHBRIDGE, Rex
Meyers, Roy
LEVINREW, Will
Levine, William
LEWIN, C L
Brister, Richard
LEWIS, Charles
Dixon, Roger
LEWIS, Ernest
Vesey, Ernest Blakeman
LEWIS, Francine
Wells, Helen
LEWIS, Lange
Beynon, Jane
LEWIS, Mervyn
Frewer, Glyn
LEWIS, Paul
Gerson, Noel Bertram

LEWIS, Roger
Zarchy, Harry
LEWIS, Roy
Lewis, J R
LEWIS, Voltaire
Ritchie, L Edwin
LEYTON, Sophie
Walsh, Sheila
LIDDELL, C H
Kuttner, Henry
LIGGETT, Hunter
Paine, Lauran Bosworth
LIMNELIUS, George
Robinson, Lewis George
LINCOLN, Geoffrey
Mortimer, John
LINCOLN, John
Cardif, Maurice
LIND, Jakov
Landwirth, Heinz
LINDALL, Edward
Smith, Edward Ernest
LINDARS, Barnabas
Lindars, Frederick C
LINDLEY, Erica
Quigley, Aileen
LINDLEY, Gerard
Pilley, Phil
LINDSAY, H
Hudson, H Lindsay
LINDSAY, Josephine
Story, Rosamond Mary
LINDSAY, Lee
Barre, Jean
LINDSAY, Perry
Dern, Erolie Pearl
LINDSEY, John
Muriel, John
LINESMAN
Grant, M H
LINKLATER, Lane
Watkins, Alex
LINSON
Tomlinson, Joshua Leonard

LINTER, Lavender
Alexander, John McKnight
LIPSTICK
Long, Lois
LISLE, Mary
Cornish, Doris Mary
LISTER, Richard
Worsley, T C
LISTON, Jack
Maloney, Ralph Liston
LITTLE, Conyth
Little, Gwenyth *and*
Little, Constance
LITTLE, Frances
Macauley, Fannie Caldwell
LITTLE, Sylvia
Leyland, Eric
LITTLEJOHN, Jon R
Kleinhaus, Theodore John
LIVINGSTON, Kenneth
Stewart, Kenneth Livingston
LIVINGSTONE, Margaret
Flynn, Mary
LLEWELLYN
Lucas, Beryl Llewellyn
LLEWELLYN, Richard
Lloyd, Richard Dafydd Vivian
Llewellyn
LLEWMYS, Weston
Pound, Ezra
LLOYD, Charles
Birkin, Charles
LLOYD, John
Cooper, John
LLOYD, Joseph M
Purves, Frederick
LLOYD, Levanah
Peters, Maureen
LLOYD, Wallace
Algie, James
LLOYD, Willson
Dennison, Enid
LOCHIONS, Colin
Jackson, Caary Paul

LOCKE, Martin
Duncan, William Murdoch
LODER, Vernon
Vahey, John George Haslette
LODGE, John
Leyland, Eric
LOEWENTHAL, Karen
Tripp, Kathleen
LOGAN, Agnes
Adams, Agnes
LOGAN, Ford
Newton, Dwight Bennett
LOGAN, Jake
Rifkin, Shepard
LOGAN, Mark
Nicole, Christopher
LOGROLLER
Le Gallienne, Richard
LOM, Josephine
Lomnicka, Josephine
LOMAX, Bliss
Drago, Harry Sinclair
LOMAX, Jeff
Mason, Sydney Charles
LOMBARD, Nap
Johnson, Pamela Hansford
and Stewart, Neil
LONDON, Anne
Gordon, Robert I
LONDON, Jane
Geis, Darlene Stern
LONDON, Laura
Curtis, Sharon *and*
Curtis, Thomas Dale
LONDON, Robert
Gordon, Robert I
LONG, Gerry
Larkins, William
LONG, Myles
Flanagan, James
LONG, Peter
Fowler, Gene
LONG, Shirley
Long, Leonard

LONG, William Stuart
Stuart, Vivian Alex
LONGBAUGH, Harry
Goldman, William
LONGCLOTHES, Ninon de
Haig, Emily Alice
LONGDON, George
Rayer, Francis G
LONGFIELD, Jo
Howard, Felicity
LONGLEY, John
Denton, John
LONSDALE, Frederick
Leonard, Lionel Frederick
LOONIE, Janice Hays
Hays, Janice Nicholson
LORAC, E C R
Rivett, Edith Caroline
LORAINE, Philip
Estridge, Robin
LORAN, Martin
Baxter, John
LORD, Douglas
Lord, Doreen Mildred Douglas
LORD, Jeffrey
Nelson, Radell Faraday
LORD, Jeremy
Redman, Ben Ray
LORD, Nancy
Titus, Eve
LORENZ, Sarah E
Winston, Sarah
LORINER
Williams, Dorian (Joseph
George)
LORING, Peter
Shellabarger, Samuel
LORNA
Stoddart, Jane T
LORNE, Charles
Brand, Charles Neville
LORRAINE, Anne
Chisholm, Lilian

LORRIMER, Claire
Clark, Patricia D R
LOTHROP, Amy
Warner, Anna Bartlett
LOUIS, Pat
Francis, Dorothy Brenner
LOVE, Arthur
Liebers, Arthur
LOVE, David
Lasky, Jesse L
LOVECRAFT, Linda
Parry, Michel
LOVEGOOD, John
Watson, Elliot Grant
LOVEHILL, C B
Nutt, Charles
LOVELACE, Linda
Boreman, Linda
LOVELL, Ingraham
Bacon, Josephine Dodge
LOVELL, Marc
McShane, Mark
LOW, Dorothy Mackie
Low, Lois
LOW, Rachel
Whear, Rachel
LOWE, Edith
Kovar, Edith May
LOWE, Kenneth
Lobaugh, Elma K
LOWELL, Elaine
Covert, Alice Lent
LOWELL, J R
Lowell, Jan *and*
Lowell, Robert
LOWING, Anne
Geach, Christine
LOWNDES, George
Dawson, William Henry
LOWNDES, Susan
Marques, Susan Lowndes
LOXMITH, John
Brunner, John

LUARD, L
Luard, William Blaine
LUCAS, J K
Paine, Lauran Bosworth
LUCAS, Victoria
Plath, Sylvia
LUCIO
Phillips, Gordon
LUCKLESS, John
Irving, Clifford
LUDLOW, George
Kay, Ernest
LUDLOW, Geoffrey
Meynell, Laurence Walter
LUDLOW, John
Palmer, Cecil
LUDWELL, Bernice
Stokes, Manning Lee
LUELLEN, Valentina
Polley, Judith Anne
LUIMARDEL
Martinez-Delgado, Luis
LUK, Charles
Lu Kuan Yu
LUKE, Thomas
Masterton, Graham
LUM, Peter
Crowe, *Lady* (Bettina)
LUMMINS
Melling, Leonard
LUNCHBASKET, Roger
Reeve-Jones, Alan
LUSKA, Sidney
Harland, Henry
LYALL, David
Swan, Annie S
LYALL, Edna
Bayly, Ada Ellen
LYDECKER, J J
Coltman-Allen, Ernest Vivian
LYMINGTON, John
Chance, John Newton
LYNCH, Brian
Liddy, James

LYNCH, Eric
Bingley, David Ernest
LYNCH, Frances
Compton, D G
LYNCH, Lawrence L
Van Deventer, Emma M
LYNDALE, Sydney M
Moorhouse, Sydney
LYNDE, H H
Huntington, Helen
LYNDON, Barrie
Edgar, Alfred
LYNN, Carol
Goetcheus, Carolyn
LYNN, Frank
Leisy, James Franklin
LYNN, Irene
Rowland, Donald Sydney
LYNN, Margaret
Battye, Gladys
LYNN, Patricia
Watts, Mabel Pizzey
LYNN, Stephen
Bradbury, Parnell
LYNTON, Ann
Rayner, Claire
LYON, Buck
Paine, Lauran Bosworth
LYON, Elinor
Wright, Elinor
LYON, Jessica
De Leeuw, Cateau W
LYON, Lyman R
De Camp, L Sprague
LYONS, Delphine C
Smith, Evelyn E
LYONS, Elena
Fairburn, Eleanor
LYRE, Pinchbeck
Sassoon, Siegfried
LYTE, Richard
Whelpton, Eric
LYTTON, Jane
Clarke, Percy A

§ §

'But still it would be a confusion',
Berenice insisted. 'Suppose we
all suddenly change to entirely
different names. Nobody would
ever know who anybody was
talking about.'
– Carson McCullers. The member
of the wedding

§ §

M
Milner, Alfred, *Viscount Milner*
M B
Faust, Frederick
M B OXON
Wallace, Lewis Alexander
M E S
Searle, M E
M R J
James, Montague Rhodes
MAARTENS, Marten
Poorten-Schwartz, J M
van der
MABLE, Peter
Wiedenbeck, Emilie Agnes
MACADAM, Eve
Leslie, Cecilie
McALPIN, Grant
McCulley, Johnston
MACALPIN, Rory
Mackinnon, Charles Roy
MACANDREW, Rennie
Elliot, Andrew George
McARTHUR, John
Wise, Arthur
McBAIN, Ed
Lombino, Salvatore A
MACBRIDE, Aeneas
MacKay, Fulton
McCABE, Cameron
Borneman, Ernest

McCABE, Rory
Greenwood, T E
McCALL, Anthony
Kane, Henry
McCALL, Isabel
Boyd, Elizabeth Orr
McCALL, Vincent
Morland, Nigel
McCANN, Edson
Del Rey, Lester
McCANN, Edson
Del Rey, Lester *and*
Pohl, Frederik
McCARY, Reed
Rydberg, Ernie
McCLEAN, Kathleen
Hale, Kathleen
MACCOLLA, Fionn
Macdonald, Thomas Douglas
McCONNELL, Will
Snodgrass, W D
McCORD, Whip
Norwood, Victor George
Charles
McCORMACK, Charlotte
Ross, William Edward Daniel
McCORMICK, Theodora
Du Bois, Theodora
McCOY, Hank
Martin, Reginald Alec
McCOY, Malachy
Caulfield, Max
McCOY, Marshall
Meares, Leonard F
McCREADY, Jack
Powell, Talmage
MACCREIGH, James
Pohl, Frederik
MACDIARMID, Hugh
Grieve, Christopher Murray
MACDONALD, Anson
Heinlein, Robert A
MACDONALD, Jo
Macdonald, Margaret Josephine

MACDONALD, John
Millar, Kenneth
MACDONALD, John Ross
Millar, Kenneth
MACDONALD, Malcolm
Ross-Macdonald, Malcolm
MACDONALD, Marcia
Hill, Grace
MACDONALD, Ross
Millar, Kenneth
MACDOUALL, Robertson
Mair, George Brown
McDOW, Gerald
Scortia, Thomas Nicholas
McDOWELL, Crosby
Freeman, John Crosby
MACDOWELL, Frederics
Frede, Richard
MACDUFF, Ilka
List, Ilka Katherine
MACE, Margaret
Lawrence, Dulcie
McELROY, Lee
Kelton, Elmer
MACEY, Carn
Barrett, Geoffrey John
MACFARLAND, Anne
MacDonald, Susanne
MACFARLANE, Kenneth
Walker, Kenneth Macfarlane
MACFARLANE, Stephen
Cross, John Keir
McGAVIN, Moyra
Crichton, Eleanor
McGAW, J M
Morris, John
McGILL, Ian
Allegro, John Marco
McGRATH, Mary
Murranka, Mary
McGRATH, Morgan
Rae, Hugh Crauford

McGREW, Fenn
McGrew, Julia *and*
Fenn, Caroline K
McGUINNESS, Brian
McGuinness, Bernard
MACGUIRE, Nicolas
Melides, Nicholas
McGURK, Slater
Roth, Arthur
MACHLIS, Joseph
Selcamm, George
McHUGH, Stuart
Rowland, Donald Sydney
McINTOSH, Ann T
Higginbotham, Anne D
McINTOSH, J T
Macgregor, James Murdoch
MACK, Evalina
McNamara, Lena
McKENZIE, Paige
Blood, Marje
McKENNA, Evelyn
Joscelyn, Archie Lynn
McKERN, Pat
Willett, Franciscus
MACKIE, Alice
Cummins, Mary Warmington
MACKIN, Anita
Donson, Cyril
McKINLEY, Karen
Runbeck, Margaret Lee
MACKINLOCH, Duncan
Watts, Peter Christopher
McLAGLEN, John J
Harvey, John
MACLAREN, Ian
Watson, John
MACLEAN, Art
Shirreffs, Gordon D
MACLEAN, Arthur
Tubb, E C
MACLEAN, Barry
Chosack, Cyril

MACLEAN, Christina
Casement, Christina
McLEAN, J Sloan
Wunsch, Josephine M
McLEISH, Dougal
Goodspeed, D J
MACLEOD, Finlay
Wood, James
MACLEOD, Fiona
Sharp, William
MACLEOD, Robert
Knox, William
MACLEODHAS, Sorche
Alger, Leclaire Gowans
McLOWERY, Frank
Keevill, Henry John
McMASTER, Alison
Baker, Marjorie
McMEEKIN, Clark
Clark, Dorothy *and*
McMeekin, Isabel
McMUD, Dok
McLachlan, Dan
MACNAMARA, Brinsley
Weldon, A E
MACNEIL, Duncan
McCutchan, Philip D
MACNEIL, Neil
Ballard, Willis Todhunter
McNEILL, Janet
Alexander, Janet
MACNELL, James
MacDonnell, James Edmond
MACNIB
Mackie, Albert David
McNUTT, Charles
Nutt, Charles
MACOMBER, Daria
Stevenson, Ferdinan *and*
Robinson, Patricia
MACQUEEN, Jay
Minto, Mary
MACRAE, Hawk
Barker, Albert H

MACRAE, Mason
Rubel, James Lyon
MACRAE, Travis
Feagles, Anita MacRae
MACTHOMAIS, Ruaraidh
Thomson, Derick S
MACTYRE, Paul
Adam, Robin
MACUMBER, Mari
Sandoz, Mari
MADDERN, Stan
Mason, Sydney Charles
MADDOX, Carl
Tubb, E C
MADEOC
Robinson, H
MADGETT, Naomi Long
Andrews, Naomi Cornelia
MADHAVIKUTTY
Das, Kamala
MADISON, Dolly
Paul, Maury
MADISON, Frank
Hutchins, Francis Gilman
MADISON, Hank
Rowland, Donald Sydney
MAGENHEIMER, Kay
Magenheimer, Cathryn Cecile
MAGILL, Marcus
Hill, Brian
MAGNUS, Gerald
Bowman, Gerald
MAGRISKA, Hélène *Countess*
Brockies, Enid Florence
MAINE, Charles Eric
McIlwain, David
MAINE, Stirling
Mason, Sydney Charles
MAINSAIL
Duff, Douglas Valder
MAIR, H Allen
Murray, Francis Edwin
MAIR, Margaret
Crompton, Margaret Norah

MAIZEL, Leah
Maizel, Clarice Louise
MAIZIE
Rose, Mary H
MAJORS, Simon
Fox, Gardner F
MAKANOWITZKY, Barbara
Norman, Barbara
MALCOLM, Charles
Hincks, Cyril Malcolm
MALCOLM, John
Batt, Malcolm John
MALCOLM, John
Uren, Malcolm
MALCOLM, Ronald
Hincks, Cyril Malcolm
MALCOLM X
Little, Malcolm
MALET, Lucas
Kingsley, Mary
MALET, Oriel
Vaughan, *Lady* Auriel
MALIN, Peter
Conner, Reardon
MALLERY, Amos
Gelb, Norman
MALLOCH, Peter
Duncan, William Murdoch
MALLORY, Drew
Garfield, Brian
MALLORY, Jay
Carey, Joyce
MALLOWEN, Agatha Christie
Christie, *Dame* Agatha
MALONE, Louis
MacNeice, Louis
MANAGER, Mo
Cassity, June
MANDEVILLE, D E
Coates, Anthony
MANN, Abel
Creasey, John
MANN, Avery
Breetveld, James Patrick

MANN, Deborah
Bloom, Ursula
MANN, Jack
Vivian, Evelyn Charles H
MANN, James
Harvey, John
MANN, John
Stevens, Henry Charles
MANN, Josephine
Pullein-Thompson, Josephine
Mary
MANN, Patricia
Earnshaw, Patricia
MANN, Patrick
Waller, Leslie
MANN, Stanley
Mason, Sydney Charles
MANNERING, Julia
Bingham, Madeleine
MANNERS, Alexandra
Rundle, Anne
MANNERS, Julia
Greenaway, Gladys
MANNERS, Miss
Martin, Judith
MANNGIAN, Peter
Monger, Ifor
MANNING, David
Faust, Frederick
MANNING, Lee
Stokes, Manning Lee
MANNING, Marsha
Grimstead, Hettie
MANNING, Roy
Reach, James
MANNINGHAM, Basil
Homersham, Basil Henry
MANNOCK, Jennifer
Mannock, Laura
MANNON, M M
Mannon, Martha *and*
Mannon, Mary Ellen
MANNON, Warwick
Hopkins, Kenneth

MANOR, Jason
Hall, Oakley Maxwell
MANSBRIDGE, Pamela
Course, Pamela
MANSELL, C R
Payne, Eileen Mary
MANSFIELD, Katherine
Beauchamp, Kathleen Mansfield
MANSFIELD, N
Gladden, Edgar Norman
MANTON, Jo
Gittings, Jo
MANTON, Paul
Walker, Peter Norman
MANTON, Peter
Creasey, John
MANVILLE, George
Fenn, George Manville
MAO
Addis, Hazel Iris
MAPES, Mary A
Ellison, Virginia Howell
MAPLESDEN, Ray
Pearce, Raymond
MARA, Thalia
Mahoney, Elizabeth
MARAS, Karl
Bulmer, Henry Kenneth
MARCH, Emma
Stubbs, Jean
MARCH, Hilary
Green, Lalage Isobel
MARCH, Jermyn
Webb, Dorothy Anna
MARCH, Stella
Marshall, Marjorie
MARCH, William
Campbell, William Edward
March
MARCHANT, Catherine
Cookson, Catherine
MARCHBANKS, Samuel
Davies, Robertson

MARCO
Mountbatten, *Lord* Louis
MARCUS AURELIUS
Padley, Walter
MARCUS, Joanna
Andrews, Lucilla
MARDLE, Jonathan
Fowler, Eric
MARGARET
Kent, Ellen Louisa Margaret
MARGERISON, David
Davies, David Margerison
**MARIA, Hermann Karl Georg
Jesus**
Pound, Ezra
MARIANA
Foster, Marian Curtis
MARICHAUD, Alphonse
Wilson, Florence Roma Muir
MARIN, A C
Coppel, Alfred
MARIN, Alfred
Coppel, Alfred
MARINER, David
Macleod-Smith, D
MARION, S T
Lakritz, Esther
MARJORAM, J
Mottram, Ralph Hale
MARK, David
Buitenkant, Nathan
MARK, Edwina
Fadiman, Edwin J
MARK, Matthew
Babcock, Frederic
MARKANDAYA, Kamala
Taylor, Kamala
MARKER, Clare
Witcombe, Rick
MARKET MAN
Lake, Kenneth Robert
MARKHAM, Robert
Amis, Kingsley

MARKOVA, Alicia
Marks, Lilian Alicia
MARKWELL, Mary
Hayes, Catherine E Simpson
MARLE, T B
Lambert, Hubert Steel
MARLIN, Roy
Ashmore, Basil
MARLOW, Joyce
Connor, Joyce Mary
MARLOW, Louis
Wilkinson, Louis Umfreville
MARLOW, Phyllis
Mason, Sydney Charles
MARLOWE, Hugh
Patterson, Harry
MARLOWE, Piers
Gribble, Leonard Reginald
MARLOWE, Stephen
Lesser, Milton
MARNEY, Suzanne
Johnston, Mabel Annesley
MARO, Judith
Jones, Judith Anastasia
MARQUIS, Don
Perry, Robert
MARR, Nancy J
Johnson, Nancy Marr
MARRECO, Anne
Acland, Alice
MARRIC, J J
Butler, William Vivian
('writing as')
MARRIC, J J
Creasey, John
MARRIOT, John
Elliot, Christopher
MARS, E C
Mazani, Eric C F N
MARSDEN, Anthony
Sutton, Graham
MARSDEN, James
Creasey, John

MARSDEN, June
Ingram-Moore, Erica
MARSH, Henry
Saklatvala, Beram
MARSH, J E
Marshall, Evelyn
MARSH, Jean
Marshall, Evelyn
MARSH, Joan
Marsh, John
MARSH, Patrick
Hiscock, Leslie
MARSH, Paul
Hopkins, Kenneth
MARSH, Rebecca
Neubauer, William Arthur
MARSHAL, James
Bounds, Sydney J
MARSHALL, Archibald
Marshall, Arthur Hammond
MARSHALL, Beverley
Holroyd, Ethel Mary
MARSHALL, Douglas
McClintock, Marshall
MARSHALL, E P
Montgomery, Rutherford
George
MARSHALL, Edmund
Hopkins, Kenneth
MARSHALL, Emily
Hall, Bennie Caroline
MARSHALL, Gary
Snow, Charles Horace
MARSHALL, James Vance
Payne, Donald Gordon
MARSHALL, Joanne
Rundle, Anne
MARSHALL, Joseph
Krechniak, Joseph Marshall
MARSHALL, Lloyd
Wilding, Philip
MARSHALL, Lovat
Duncan, William Murdoch

MARSHALL, Raymond
Raymond, Rene
MARSTEN, Richard
Lombino, Salvatore A
MARTELL, James
Bingley, David Ernest
MARTENS, Paul
Southwold, Stephen
MARTIN, Abe
Hubbard, Frank McKinney
MARTIN, Ann
Best, Carol Anne
MARTIN, Anthony
Zehnder, Meinrad
MARTIN, Bruce
Paine, Lauran Bosworth
MARTIN, Christopher
Hoyt, Edwin Palmer *Jr*
MARTIN, Chuck
Martin, Charles Morris
MARTIN, Dorothea
Hewitt, Kathleen Douglas
MARTIN, Frederick
Stern, Frederick Martin
MARTIN, Fredric
Christopher, Matt F
MARTIN, Gil
Overy, Jillian P J
MARTIN, John
Tatham, Laura
MARTIN, Nancy
Salmon, Annie Elizabeth
MARTIN, Peter
Chaundler, Christine
MARTIN, R J
Mehta, Rustam
MARTIN, Rex
Martin, Reginald Alec
MARTIN, Richard
Creasey, John
MARTIN, Richard
Harman, Richard
MARTIN, Robert
Martin, Reginald Alec

MARTIN, Ruth
Rayner, Claire
MARTIN, Scott
Martin, Reginald Alec
MARTIN, Shane
Johnston, George Henry
MARTIN, Stella
Heyer, Georgette
MARTIN, Tom
Paine, Lauran Bosworth
MARTINDALE, Spencer
Wolff, William
MARTINEZ, J D
Parkhill, Forbes
MARTON, Francesca
Bellasis, Margaret Rosa
MARTYN, Don
Borbolla, Barbara
MARTYN, Henry
Perry, Martin
MARTYN, Miles
Elliott-Cannon, Arthur Elliott
MARTYN, Oliver
White, Herbert Oliver
MARVEL, Holt
Maschwitz, Eric
MARVEL, Ik
Mitchell, Donald Grant
MARVIN, W R
Cameron, Lou
MARX, Magdeleine
Paz, Magdeleine
MARY THEODORE, *Sister*
Hegeman, Mary Theodore
MASON, Carl
King, Albert
MASON, Chuck
Rowland, Donald Sydney
MASON, Frank W
Mason, F Van Wyck
MASON, Howard
Ramage, Jennifer
MASON, Lee W
Malzberg, Barry Norman

MASON, Michael
Smith, Edgar
MASON, Stuart
Millard, Christopher S
MASON, Tally
Derleth, August William
MASON, Tyler
Mason, Madeline
MASS, William
Gibson, William
MASSARY, Isabel
Ramsay-Laye, Elizabeth P
MASSEY, Charlotte
Capriani, Vincent
MASSON, Georgina
Johnson, Marion
MASTERS, Robert V
Boehm, David Alfred
MASTERS, Steve
Mason, Sydney Charles
MASTERS, William
Cousins, Margaret
MASTERSON, Whit
Wade, Robert *and*
Miller, William
MATELOT
Uren, Malcolm
MATHER, Anne
Grieveson, Mildred
MATHER, Berkely
Davies, John Evan Weston
MATHER, Virginia
Leibler, Jean Mayer
MATHESON, Hugh
Mackay, Lewis
MATHESON, Sylvia A
Schofield, Sylvia Anne
MATT
Sandford, Matthew
MATTHESON, Rodney
Creasey, John
MATTHEWS, Anthony
Barker, Dudley

MATTHEWS, Brander
Matthews, James Brander
MATTHEWS, Kevin
Fox, Gardner F
MATUSOW, Marshall
Matusow, Harvey Marshall
MAUGHAM, Robin
Maugham, Robert Cecil Romer
Viscount
MAULE, Tex
Maule, Hamilton Bee
MAURICE, Furnley
Wilmot, Frank Leslie Thomson
MAURICE, Michael
Skinner, Conrad Arthur
MAXINE
Fortier, Cora B
MAXTON, Anne
Best, Allena
MAXWELL, Ann
Pattinson, Lee
MAXWELL, C Bede
Maxwell, Violet S
MAXWELL, Clifford
Leon, Henry Cecil
MAXWELL, Erica
Pyke, Lillian Maxwell
MAXWELL, John
Freemantle, Brian
MAXWELL, Peter
Cave, Peter
MAXWELL, Vicky
Worboys, Annette Isobel
MAXWELL, William
Allan, Ted
MAY, Jonathan
Wood, Christopher
MAY, Roberta E
Davidson, Edith May
MAY, Sophie
Clarke, Rebecca Sophia
MAYBURY, Anne
Buxton, Anne

MAYFIELD, Julia
Hastings, Phyllis
MAYHEW, Elizabeth
Bear, Joan E
MAYNE, Cora
Walker, Emily Kathleen
MAYNE, Rutherford
Waddell, Samuel
MAYNE, Xavier
Stevenson, Edward I P
MAYO, Arnold
Meredith, Kenneth Lincoln
MAYO, James
Coulter, Stephen
MAYO, Mark
Lane, Yoti
MAYRANT, Drayton
Simons, Katherine Drayton
Mayrant
MAYSON, Marina
Rogers, Rosemary
MAZ
Mazure, Alfred Leonardus
MAZE, Edward
Mazzocco, Edward
MEADE, L T
Smith, Elizabeth Thomasina
Meade
MEADOWS, Peter
Lindsay, Jack
MEDHURST, Joan
Liverton, Joan
MEDICA
Malleson, Joan Graeme
MEDICUS
MacLaren, James Paterson
MEDILL, Robert
McBride, Robert Medill
MEDLEY, Anne
Borchard, Ruth
MEE
Schube, Purcell G
MEE, Mary
Dean, Mary

MEIKLE, Clive
Brooks, Jeremy
MEINIKOFF, Pamela
Harris, Pamela
MELBOURNE, Ida
Ransome, L E
MELDRUM, James
Kyle, Duncan
MELLOR, Michael
Spooner, Peter Alan
MELMOTH
Tullett, Denis John
MELONEY, Franken
Franken, Rose *and*
Meloney, W B
MELVILLE, Alan
Caverhill, William Melville
MELVILLE, Anne
Potter, Margaret
MELVILLE, Jean
Cummins, Mary Warmington
MELVILLE, Jennie
Butler, Gwendolyn
MELVILLE, Lewis
Benjamin, Lewis S
MENANDER
Morgan, Charles
MENDEL, Jo
Bond, Gladys Baker
MENDEL, Jo
Gilbertson, Mildred
MENDL, Gladys
Schütze, Gladys Henrietta
MENTOR
Jones, Frank H
MENTOR
Lake, Kenneth Robert
MERCER, Frances
Hills, Frances Elizabeth
MERCURY
Eames, Helen Mary
MEREDITH, Anne
Malleson, Lucy

MEREDITH, Arnold
Hopkins, Kenneth
MEREDITH, David William
Miers, Earl Schenk
MEREDITH, Hal
Blyth, Harry
MEREDITH, Peter
Worthington-Stuart, Brian
Arthur
MERIVALE, Margaret
Frost, Kathleen Margaret
MERLIN, Christina
Keegan, Mary Constance
MERLIN, David
Moreau, David
MERLINI, The Great
Rawson, Clayton
MERRICK, Hugh
Meyer, Harold Albert
MERRICK, Spencer
Mason, Sydney Charles
MERRIL, Judith
Grossman, Judith
MERRILL, Lynne
Gibbs, Norah
MERRILL, P J
Roth, Holly
MERRIMAN, Chad
Cheshire, Gifford Paul
MERRIMAN, Henry Seton
Scott, Hugh Stowell
MERRIMAN, Pat
Atkey, Philip
MERRITT, E B
Waddington, Miriam
MERRIWELL, Frank
Whitson, John Harvey
MERWIN, Sam
Merwin, Samuel Kimball *Jr*
METCALF, Suzanne
Baum, Lyman Frank
METHUEN, John
Bell, John Keble

MEURON, Skip
Sands, Leo G
MEWBURN, Martin
Hitchin, Martin
MEYER, H A
Merrick, Hugh
MEYER, Henry J
Hird, Neville
MEYER, June
Jordan, June
MIALL, Robert
Burke, John Frederick
MICHAEL, Manfred
Winterfield, Henry
MICHAEL X
De Freitas, Michael
MICHAELHOUSE, John
McCulloch, Joseph
MICHAELS, Barbara
Mertz, Barbara
MICHAELS, Dale
Rifkin, Shepard
MICHAELS, Kristin
Williams, Jeanne
MICHAELS, Steve
Avallone, Michael Angelo *Jr*
MICHELMORE, Susan
Harvey, Margaret Susan Janet
MICKLEMANN, Henry
Cather, Willa
MIDLING, Perspicacity
Millward, Pamela
MIKAN, Baron
Barba, Harry
MILBURN, Cynthia
Brooks, Ann
MILECETE, Helen
Jones, Susan Carleton
MILES
Southwold, Stephen
MILES, David
Cronin, Brendan Leo
MILES, John
Bickham, Jack Miles

MILES, Keith
Tralins, S Robert
MILES, Miska
Martin, Patricia Miles
MILES, Susan
Roberts, Ursula
MILKY WHITE
Emerson, Ernest
MILLBURN, Cynthia
Brooks, Ann
MILLER, Benj
Loomis, Noel Miller
MILLER, Ellen
Pattinson, Lee
MILLER, Frank
Loomis, Noel Miller
MILLER, Joaquin
Miller, Cincinnatus H
MILLER, John
Samachson, Joseph
MILLER, Jon
Miller, John Gordon
MILLER, Marc
Baker, Marcell Genée
MILLER, Margaret J
Dale, Margaret
MILLER, Mary
Northcott, Cecil
MILLER, Olive Thorne
Miller, Harriet
MILLER, Patrick
Macfarlane, George Gordon
MILLER, Wade
Miller, William *and*
Wade, Robert
MILLS, Alan
Miller, Albert
MILLS, Martin
Boyd, Martin à Beckett
MILLS, Osmington
Brooks, Vivian Collin
MILNA, Bruno
Painting, Norman

MILNE, Ewart
Milne, Charles
MILNER, George
Hardinge, George
MILSEN, Oscar
Mendelssohn, Oscar Adolf
MINGSTON, R Gresham
Stamp, Roger
MINICAM
Russell, Henry George
MINIER, Nelson
Baker, Laura
MIRYAM
Yardumian, Miryam
MISS MANNERS
Martin, Judith
MISS READ
Saint, Dora Jessie
MITCHAM, Gilroy
Newton, William Simpson
MITCHEL, Jackson
Matcha, Jack
MITCHELL, Ewan
Janner, Greville
MITCHELL, K L
Lamb, Elizabeth Searle
MITCHELL, Kerry
Wilkes-Hunter, Richard
MITCHELL, Scott
Godfrey, Lionel Robert
Holcombe
MITCHUM, Hank
Newton, Dwight Bennett
MO, Manager
Cassity, June
MODELL, Merriam
Piper, Evelyn
MODERN JOB
Taber, Clarence Wilbur
MOKO
Mead, Sidney
MOLE, Oscar
Seaver, Richard

MOLE, William
Younger, William Anthony
MONAHAN, John
Burnett, W R
MONETT, Lireve
Worrell, Everill
MONIG, Christopher
Crossen, Kendell Foster
MONKLAND, George
Whittet, George Sorley
MONMOUTH, Jack
Pember, William Leonard
MONNOW, Peter
Croudace, Glyn
MONRO, Gavin
Monro-Higgs, Gertrude
MONROE, Lyle
Heinlein, Robert A
MONTAGU, Robert
Hampden, John
MONTAUBON, G DE
Greenough, William Parker
MONTGOMERY, Derek
Simmons, J S A
MONTROSE
Adams, Charles William Dunlop
MONTROSE, David
Graham, Charles
MONTROSE, Graham
Mackinnon, Charles Roy
MONTROSE, James St David
Appleman, John Alan
MONTROSS, David
Backus, Jean L
MOODIE, Edwin
De Caire, Edwin
MOOLSON, Melusa
Solomon, Samuel
MOOR, Emily
Deming, Richard
MOORE, Arthur
Matthews, Clayton
MOORE, Austin
Muir, Augustus

MOORE, Edward
Muir, Edwin
MOORE, Elizabeth
Atkins, Meg Elizabeth
MOORE, Frances Sarah
Mack, Elise Frances
MOORE, Nicholas
Nicolaeff, Ariadne
MOORE, Rosalie
Brown, Rosalie
MOORHOUSE, E Hallam
Meynell, Esther H
MOORHOUSE, Hopkins
Moorhouse, Herbert Joseph
MORDAUNT, Elinor
Mordaunt, Evelyn May
MORE, Caroline
Cone, Molly
MORE, Euston
Bloomer, Arnold
MORE, J J
Moffatt, James
MORECAMBE, Eric
Bartholomew, John Eric
MORENO, Nick
Deming, Richard
MORESBY, Louis
Beck, Lily Adams
MORETON, John
Cohen, Morton N
MORGAN, Angela
Paine, Lauran Bosworth
MORGAN, Arlene
Paine, Lauran Bosworth
MORGAN, Bryan
Morgan, Brian Stanford
MORGAN, Carol McAfee
Appleby, Carol McAfee
MORGAN, Claire
Highsmith, (Mary) Patricia
MORGAN, De Wolfe
Williamson, Thames Ross
MORGAN, Emanuel
Bynner, Witter

MORGAN, Frank
Paine, Lauran Bosworth
MORGAN, John
Paine, Lauran Bosworth
MORGAN, Marjorie
Chibnall, Marjorie McCallum
MORGAN, Mark
Overholser, Wayne D
MORGAN, Michael
Carle, C E *and*
Dorn, Dean M
MORGAN, Phyllis
Thompson, Phyllis
MORGAN, Scott
Kuttner, Henry
MORGAN, Ted
Gramont, Sanche de
MORGAN, Valerie
Paine, Lauran Bosworth
MORICE, Anne
Shaw, Felicity
MORISON, Elizabeth
Moberly, Charlotte Anne
Elizabeth
MORLAND, Dick
Hill, Reginald
MORLAND, Peter Henry
Faust, Frederick
MORNING, Alice
Haig, Emily Alice
MORPHY, *Countess*
Forbes, Marcelle Azra
MORRIS, Ira J
Jefferies, Ira
MORRIS, John
Hearne, John *and*
Cargill, Morris
MORRIS, Julian
West, Morris
MORRIS, Ruth
Webb, Ruth Enid
MORRIS, Sara
Burke, John Frederick

MORRISON, J Strang
Thom, William Albert Strang
MORRISON, Peggy
Morrison, Margaret Mackie
MORRISON, Roberta
Webb, Jean Frances
MORRISON, William
Samachson, Joseph
MORROW, Betty
Bacon, Elizabeth
MORROW, Charlotte
Kirwan, Molly
MORSE, Carol
Yeakley, Marjory Hall
MORTIMER, Chapman
Chapman-Mortimer, William
Charles
MORTIMER, Charles
Chapman-Mortimer, William
Charles
MORTIMER, June
Ryder, Vera
MORTIMER, Peter
Roberts, Dorothy James
MORTON, Anthony
Creasey, John
MORTON, Leah
Stern, Elisabeth Gertrude
MORTON, William
Ferguson, William Blair
Morton
MOSES, Ruben
Wurmbrand, Richard
MOSS, Nancy
Moss, Robert Alfred
MOSS, Roberta
Moss, Robert Alfred
MOSSMAN, Burt
Keevill, Henry John
MOSSOP, Irene
Swatridge, Irene M M
MOSTYN-OWEN, Gaia
Servadio, Gaia

MOTLEY, Mary
Reneville, Mary Margaret
Motley de
MOTTE, Nel
Harrison, *Mrs* E E
MOTTE, Peter
Harrison, Richard Motte
MOUNTFIELD, David
Grant, Neil
MOUTHPIECE
Porter, Maurice
MOWBRAY, John
Vahey, John George Haslette
MOWERY, Dorothy
Dunsing, Dee
MOYES, Robin
Bateman, Robert Moyes
MUIR, Alan
Morrison, Thomas
MUIR, Dexter
Gribble, Leonard Reginald
MUIR, Jane
Petrone, Jane Gertrude
MUIR, John
Morgan, Thomas Christopher
MUIR, Willa
Muir, Wilhelmina Johnstone
MULDOON, Omar
Matusow, Harvey Marshall
MULDOR, Carl De
Miller, Charles Henry
MULLER, Paul
King, Albert
MULLINS, Ann
Dally, Ann
MUN
Leaf, Munro
MUNDY, Max
Schofield, Sylvia Anne
MUNDY, V M
Cunningham, Virginia Myra
Mundy

MUNRO, C K
Macmullan, Charles W
Kirkpatrick
MUNRO, James
Mitchell, James
MUNRO, Mary
Howe, Doris Kathleen
MUNRO, Ronald Eadie
Glen, Duncan Munro
MUNROE, R
Cheyne, *Sir* Joseph
MUNTHE, Frances
Minto, Frances
MURPHY, C L
Murphy, Charlotte *and*
Murphy, Lawrence
MURPHY, Louis J
Hicks, Tyler Gregory
MURRAY, Beatrice
Posner, Richard
MURRAY, Cromwell
Morgan, Murray C
MURRAY, Edna
Rowland, Donald Sydney
MURRAY, Frances
Booth, Rosemary
MURRAY, Geraldine
Murray, Blanche
MURRAY, Jill
Walker, Emily Kathleen
MURRAY, Michael
McLaren, Moray David Shaw
MURRAY, Sinclair
Sullivan, Edward Alan
MURRAY, William
Graydon, William Murray
MURRELL, Shirley
Scott-Hansen, Olive
MURRY, Colin
Murry, Colin Middleton
MUSSEY, Virginia T H
Ellison, Virginia Howell
MYATT, Nellie
Kirkham, Nellie

247

MYDDLETON, Robert
Hebblethwaite, Peter
MYERS, Harriet Kathryn
Whittington, Harry

N D H
Dick-Hunter, Noel
N I
Camm, Frederick James
N O B
Bettany, F G
NA gCOPALEEN
O'Nolan, Brian
NADA, John
Langdon-Davies, John
NAMLEREP, Sidney
Perelman, S J
NAPIER, Geraldine
Glemser, Bernard
NAPIER, Mark
Laffin, John
NAPIER, Mary
Wright, Patricia
NASH, Chandler
Hunt, Katherine Chandler
NASH, Daniel
Loader, William
NASH, Newlyn
Smithies, Muriel
NASH, Simon
Chapman, Raymond
NAST, Elsa Ruth
Werner, Elsa Jane
NATALE, Francine de
Malzberg, Barry Norman
NATHAN, Daniel
Dannay, Frederic
NATIONS, Opal L
Humm, Martin J
NAUTICUS
Seaman, *Sir* Owen
NAYLOR, Eliot
Frankau, Pamela

NEAL, Hilary
Norton, Olive Marion
NEANISKOS
Smithers, Leonard
NEBY, Al
Johns, Walter T
NEIL, Frances
Geach, Christine
NEILSON, Marguerite
Tompkins, Julia
NELSON, Chris
Huff, Darrell
NELSON, Gertrude
Bobin, John W
NELSON, Lois
Northam, Lois Edgell
NELSON, Marguerite
Floren, Lee
NELSON, Ray
Nelson, Radell Faraday
NEMO
Douglas, Archibald C
NEON
Acworth, Marion W
NESBIT, E
Bland, *Mrs* Edith (Nesbit)
NESBIT, Troy
Folsom, Franklin Brewster
NESS, K T
Grant, Donald *and*
Wilson, William
NETTLETON, Arthur
Gaunt, Arthur N
NEVILLE, C J
Franklin, Cynthia
NEVILLE, Margot
Goyder, Margot *and*
Joske, Neville
NEVILLE, Mary
Woodrich, Mary Neville
NEVIN, Evelyn C
Ferguson, Evelyn
NEWCOMB, Norma
Neubauer, William Arthur

NEWELL, Crosby
Bonsall, Crosby Newell
NEWMAN, Barbara
Newman, Mona A J
NEWMAN, Ernest
Roberts, E N
NEWMAN, Margaret
Potter, Margaret
NEWTON, David C
Chance, John Newton
NEWTON, Francis
Hobsbawm, E J
NEWTON, Macdonald
Newton, William Simpson
NGUGI WA THIONGIO
Ngugi, J T
NIALL, Ian
McNeillie, John
NIALL, Michael
Breslin, Howard
NICHOLLS, Anthony
Parsons, Anthony
NICHOLS, Fan
Hanna, Frances
NICHOLS, Peter
Youd, Samuel
NICHOLS, Scott
Scortia, Thomas Nicholas
NICHOLSON, Christina
Nicole, Christopher
NICHOLSON, John
Parcell, Norman Howe
NICHOLSON, Kate
Fay, Judith
NICKLEMANN, Henry
Cather, Willa
NICODEMUS
Pearce, Melville Chaning
NICOLAI, C L R
Clair, Colin
NICOLAS, F R E
Freeling, Nicholas
NIELSEN, Koef
Koefed-Nielsen, Carl

NIELSON, Vernon
Clarke, Percy A
NIELSON, Virginia
McCall, Virginia
NIGHTINGALE, Charles
Duddington, Charles Lionel
NILE, Dorothea
Avallone, Michael Angelo *Jr*
NILSON, Bee
Nilson, Annabel
NINA
Nelson, Ethel
NITSUA, Benjamin
Austin, Benjamin Fish
NINESPOT
Phillips, Hubert
NIXON, Kathleen
Blundell, V R
NOBLE, Charles
Pawley, Martin Edward
NOBLE, Emily
Gifford, James Noble
NODSET, Joan L
Lexau, Joan M
NOEL, John
Bird, Dennis Leslie
NOEL, L
Barker, Leonard Noel
NONG
Lobley, Robert
NOON, Ed
Avallone, Michael Angelo *Jr*
NOON, T R ·
Norton, Olive Marion
NOONE, Carl
Chester, Charlie
NOONE, Edwina
Avallone, Michael Angelo *Jr*
NORAH
McDougall, Margaret
NORBURN, Martha
Mead, Martha Norburn
NORDEN, Charles
Durrell, Lawrence R

NORDICUS
Snyder, Louis Leo
NORHAM, Gerald
James, J W G
NORMAN, James
Schmidt, James Norman
NORMAN, John
Lange, John Frederick
NORMAN, Louis
Carman, Bliss
NORMYX
Douglas, Norman *and*
Fitzgibbon, Elsa
NORRIS, P E
Cleary, C V H
NORTH, Andrew
Norton, Alice Mary
NORTH, Colin
Bingley, David Ernest
NORTH, Eric
Cronin, Bernard
NORTH, Gil
Horne, Geoffrey
NORTH, Howard
Dudley-Smith, Trevor
NORTH, Mark
Miller, Wright
NORTH, Sara
Bonham, Barbara
NORTHE, Maggie
Lee, Maureen
NORTHERNER
Hughes, William
NORTHROP, *Capt* B A
Hubbard, Lafayette Ronald
NORTHUMBRIAN GENTLE-MAN
Tegner, Henry
NORTON, André
Norton, Alice Mary
NORTON, Bess
Norton, Olive Marion
NORTON, Jed
Lazenby, Norman

NORTON, S H
Richardson, Mary Kathleen
NORTON, Sybil
Cournos, Helen
NORTON, Victor
Dalton, Gilbert
NORVELL, Anthony
Trupo, Anthony
NORWAY, Kate
Norton, Olive Marion
NORWOOD, Elliott
Kensdale, W E N
NORWOOD, John
Stark, Raymond
NOSTALGIA
Bentley, James W B
NOTT, Barry
Hurren, Bernard
NOVAK, Joseph
Kosinski, Jerzy
NOVELLO, Ivor
Davies, Ivor Novello
NOX, Owen
Cory, Charles Barney
NUDLEMAN, Nordyk
Glassco, John
NUDNICK
Nerney, Patrick W
NUNQUAM
Blatchford, Robert
NURAINI
Sim, Katharine Phyllis
NYE, Harold G
Harding, Lee

§ §

Cases of a man writing under a woman's name are rare.
— Cassell's Encyclopaedia of literature

§ §

O K
Novikov, Olga
O P
Eccleshare, Colin
O S
Seaman, *Sir* Owen
OATES, Titus
Bell, Martin
OBOLENSKY, Ilka
List, Ilka Katherine
O'BRIAN, Frank
Garfield, Bryan
O'BRIEN, Bernadette
Higgins, Margaret
O'BRIEN, Dean D
Binder, Otto
O'BRIEN, Deirdre
McNally, Mary Elizabeth
O'BRIEN, Flann
O'Nolan, Brian
O'BRIEN, John
Hartigan, Patrick Joseph
O'BRIEN, Richard C
Conly, Robert Carroll
O'BYRNE, Dermot
Bax, *Sir* Arnold
O'CATHASAIGH, P
O'Casey, Sean
O'CONNELL, Peg
Ahern, Margaret McCrohan
O'CONNELL, Robert Frank
Gohm, Douglas Charles
O'CONNER, Clint
Paine, Lauran Bosworth
O'CONNER, Elizabeth
McNamara, Barbara Willard
O'CONNOR, Dermot
Newman, Terence
O'CONNOR, Frank
O'Donovan, Michael Francis
O'CONNOR, Liam
Liddy, James

O'CONNOR, Patrick
Wibberley, Leonard Patrick
O'Connor
O'CONNOR, Philip
Bancroft, Marie Constant
OCTAVIA
Barltrop, Mabel
ODDIE, E M
O'Donoghue, Elinor Mary
ODELL, Carol
Foote, Carol
ODELL, Gill
Foote, Carol *and* Gill, Travis
O'DONNELL, Donat
O'Brien, Conor Cruise
O'DONNELL, K M
Malzberg, Barry Norman
O'DONNELL, Laurence
Kuttner, Henry *and/or*
Moore, C L
O'DONNEVAN, Finn
Sheckley, Robert
O'FAOLAIN, Sean
Whelan, John
O'FINN, Thaddeus
McGloin, Joseph Thaddeus
OGDEN, Clint
King, Albert
O'GRADA, Sean
O'Grady, John
O'GRADY, Rohan
Skinner, June O'Grady
O'GRADY, Tony
Clemens, Brian
OHAN
Barba, Harry
O'HARA, Dale
Gillesse, John Patrick
O'HARA, Kenneth
Morris, Jean
O'HARA, Kevin
Cumberland, Marten
O'HARA, Mary
Sture-Vasa, Mary

O'HARRIS, Pixie
Harris, Rona Olive
OKADA, Hideki
Glassco, John
OKE, Richard
Millett, Nigel
OKE, Simon
Vann, Gerald
O'LAOGHAIRE, Liam
O'Leary, Liam
OLD COYOTE, Sally
Old Coyote, Elnora A
OLDCASTLE, John
Meynell, Wilfred
OLDFIELD, Peter
Bartlett, Vernon
OLDHAM, Hugh R
Whitford, Joan
O'LE LUK-OIE
Swinton, *Sir* Ernest Dunlop
OLGA
Phillips, Olga
OLIVER, Frances
Schneider, Monica Maria
OLIVER, Gail
Scott, Marian Gallagher
OLIVER, Jane
Rees, Helen
OLIVER, Laurence
Brown, Laurence Oliver
OLIVER, Mark
Tyler-Whittle, Michael
OLIVER, Owen
Flynn, *Sir* J A
OLIVER, Robert
Carrier, Robert *and*
Dick, Oliver Lawson
OLIVER, Roy
Walker, Roy
OLIVIA
Bussy, Dorothy
OLSEN, D B
Hitchens, Dolores

OLSEN, Herb
Olson, Herbert Vincent
OLYMPIC
Hutton, Andrew Nielson
O'MALLEY, Frank
O'Rourke, Frank
O'MALLEY, Patrick
O'Rourke, Frank
OMAN, Carola
Lenanton, *Lady*
O'MARA, Jim
Fluharty, Vernon L
O'NAIR, Mairi
Evans, Constance May
O'NEIL, Kerry
MacIntyre, John Thomas
O'NEILL, Egan
Linington, Elizabeth
O'NEILL, Moira
Skrine, Agnes Higginson
ONIONS, Berta
Oliver, Amy Roberta
ONIONS, Oliver
Oliver, George
ONLOOKER
Grant, William
ONOTO WATANNA
Reeve, Winifred Babcock
ONSLOW, Katherine
Dennys, Elisabeth
OPHIEL
Peach, Edward C
ORAGE, A R
Orage, Alfred James
ORAM, John
Thomas, John Oram
ORBISON, Keck
Orbison, Roy *and*
Keck, Maud
ORCHARD, Evelyn
Swan, Annie S
ORDERLY SERGEANT, THE
Murray, William Waldie

ORDON, A Lang
Gordon, Alan Bacchus
ORIEL
Sandes, John
O'RILEY, Warren
Richardson, Gladwell
ORION
Brooks, Ern
ORME, Alexandra
Barcza, Alicja
ORME, Eve
Williamson, Leila Isobel
ORMSBEE, David
Longstreet, Stephen
ORR, Mary
Denham, Mary Orr
ORTON, Joe
Orton, John Kingsley
ORVIS, Kenneth
Lemieux, Kenneth
ORWELL
Smith, Walter Chalmers
ORWELL, George
Blair, Eric
OSBORN, Reuben
Osbert, Reuben
OSBORNE, David
Silverberg, Robert
O'SHEA, Sean
Tralins, S Robert
O'SULLIVAN, Seumas
Starkey, James Sullivan
OSWALD, Sydney
Lomer, Sydney Frederick
McIllree
O'TOOLE, Rex
Tralins, S Robert
OUIDA
Ramé, Maria Louise
OUTLAW, THE
L'Hotellier, Alf
OVERY, Claire May
Bass, Clara May

OVERY, Martin
Overy, Jillian P J
OWEN, Dean
McGaughy, Dudley Dean
OWEN, Edmund
Teller, Neville
OWEN, Hugh
Faust, Frederick
OWEN, John Pickard
Butler, Samuel
OWEN, Ray
King, Albert
OWEN, Roderic
Fenwick-Owen, Roderic
OWEN, Tom
Watts, Peter Christopher
OXENHAM, Elsie Jeanette
Dunkerley, Elsie Jeanette
OXENHAM, John
Dunkerley, William Arthur
OYSTER, AN
Boyes, W Watson
OYVED, Moysheh
Good, Edward

P B
Braybrooke, Patrick
P C
Chalmers, Patrick
P C
Jackson, Charles Philip Castle
Kains
P O'D
Donovan, Peter
PACKER, Vin
Meaker, Marijane
PADESON, Mary
Magraw, Beatrice
PADGETT, Lewis
Kuttner, Henry *and/or*
Moore, C L
PADMORE, George
Nurse, Malcolm Ivan Meredith

PAGAN, Roberts
Plomer, William
PAGE, Eileen
Heal, Edith
PAGE, Eleanor
Coerr, Eleanor Beatrice
PAGE, Emma
Tirbutt, Honoria
PAGE, Lorna
Rowland, Donald Sydney
PAGE, Marco
Kurnitz, Harry
PAGE, Stanton
Fuller, Henry Blake
PAGE, Vicki
Avey, Ruby D
PAGET, John
Aiken, John
PAIN, Barry
Guthrie, P R
PALINURUS
Connolly, Cyril
PALMER, Edgar A
Posselt, Eric
PALMER, John
Watts, Edgar John Palmer
PALMER, Lilli
Peiser, Lilli
PAN
Beresford, Leslie
PANAVISION KID, The
Bowering, George
PANBOURNE, Oliver
Rockey, Howard
PANDORA
Moore, Mary McLeod
PANLAKE, Richard
Salmon, P R
PANSY
Alden, Isabella Macdonald
PANTOPUCK
Philpott, Alexis Robert
PAOLOTTI, John
Wilson, Guthrie E M

PARADISE, Mary
Eden, Dorothy
PARIOS
Lee, Henry David Cook
PARK, Jordan
Kornbluth, Cyril M
PARKER, James
Newby, Eric
PARKER, Leslie
Thirkell, Angela
PARKER, Seth
Lord, Phillips H
PARKES, Lucas
Harris, John Wyndham Parkes
Lucas Beynon
PARKES, Wyndham
Harris, John Wyndham Parkes
Lucas Beynon
PARKS, Ron
Guariento, Ronald
PARR, *Dr* John Anthony
Anthony, E
PARR, Robert
Gardner, Erle Stanley
PARRISH, Jean J
Church, Elsie
PARRISH, Mary
Cousins, Margaret
PARSONS, Bridget
Cox, Euphrasia Emeline
PARSONS, Paul
Haslam, Nicky
PARSONS, Tom
MacPherson, Thomas George
PARTRIDGE, Anthony
Oppenheim, E Phillips
PARTRIDGE, Sydney
Partridge, Kate Margaret
PASCHAL, Nancy
Trotter, Grace Violet
PASSMORE, Aileen E
Griffiths, Aileen Esther
PASTOR FELIX
Lockhart, Arthur John

PASTON, George
Symonds, E M
PATER, Elias
Friedman, Jacob Horace
PATER, Roger
Hudleston, Gilbert Roger
PATIENT OBSERVER, The
Strunsky, Simeon
PATRICK, Diana
Wilson, Desemea
PATRICK, John
Avallone, Michael Angelo *Jr*
PATRICK, John
Goggan, John Patrick
PATRICK, Keats
Karig, Walter
PATRICK, Maxine
Maxwell, Patricia Anne
PATRICK, Q
Wheeler, Hugh Callingham *and*
Webb, Richard Wilson
PATROCLUS
Lyall, James Robert
PATTEN, J
Cobb, Clayton W
PATTERSON, Duke
Leyland, Eric
PATTERSON, Henry
Patterson, Harry
PATTERSON, Innis
Patterson, Isabella Innis
PATTERSON, Olive
Rowland, Donald Sydney
PATTERSON, Shott
Renfrew, A
PAUL, Adrian
McGeogh, Andrew
PAUL, Barbara
Øvstedal, Barbara
PAUL, James
Warburg, James Paul
PAUL, John
Webb, Charles Henry

PAULSON, Jack
Jackson, Caary Paul
PAVITRA
Saint-Hilaire, P B
PAWNEE BILL
Lillie, Gordon W
PAXTON, Lois
Low, Lois
PAYE, Robert
Campbell, Gabrielle Margaret
Vere
PAYNE, Alan
Jakes, John
PAYNE, Robert
Payne, Pierre Stephen Robert
PEACE, Frank
Cook, William Everett
PEACHUM, Thomas
Oxman, Philip
PEARCE, A H
Quibell, Agatha
PEARL, Irene
Guyonvarch, Irene
PECKHAM, Richard
Holden, Raymond
PEDRICK, Gale
Pedrick-Harvey, Gale
PEEK, Bill
Peed, William Bartlett
PEEKNER, Ray
Puechner, Ray
PEEL, Wallis
Peel, Hazel
PEGDEN, Helen
Macregor, Miriam
PELHAM, Anthony
Hope, Charles Evelyn Graham
PELHAM, Randolph
Landells, Richard
PEMBROOKE, Kenneth
Page, Gerald W
PEMBURY, Bill
Groom, Arthur William

PENDER, Marilyn
Jacobs, Thomas Curtis Hicks
PENDLETON, Conrad
Kidd, Walter E
PENDLETON, Ford
Cheshire, Gifford Paul
PENDOWER, Jacques
Jacobs, Thomas Curtis Hicks
PENDRAGON, Eric
Parry, Michel
PENGREEP, William
Pearson, W T
PENMARE, William
Nisot, Mavis Elizabeth
PENN, Ann
Jacobs, Thomas Curtis Hicks
PENN, Arthur
Matthews, James Brander
PENN, Christopher
Lawlor, Patrick
PENN, John
Harcourt, Palma
PENN, Richard
Sproat, Iain Macdonald
PENN, Ruth Bonn
Rosenberg, Ethel
PENNAGE, E M
Finkel, George
PENNY, Rupert
Thornett, Ernest Basil Charles
PENT, Katherine
Shann, Renée
PENTECOST, Hugh
Philips, Judson Pentecost
PEPPER, Joan
Alexander, Joan
PEPPERWOOD, Pip
Stoddard, Charles Warren
PERCY, Edward
Smith, Edward Percy
PERCY, Florence
Allen, Elizabeth Chase
PEREZ, Faustino
Hoffenberg, Mason

PERKINS, Eli
Landon, Melville de Lancy
PERKINS, Virginia Chase
Chase, Virginia
PEROWNE, Barry
Atkey, Philip
PERRY, Clay
Perry, Clair Willard
PETERS, Alan
Spooner, Peter Alan
PETERS, Bill
McGivern, William Peter
PETERS, Bryan
George, Peter
PETERS, Elizabeth
Mertz, Barbara G
PETERS, Ellis
Pargeter, Edith Mary
PETERS, Fritz
Peters, Arthur A
PETERS, Geoffrey
Palmer, Madelyn
PETERS, Geoffrey
Trippe, Peter
PETERS, Jocelyn
Oakeshott, Edna
PETERS, Lawrence
Davies, Leslie Purnell
PETERS, Ludovic
Brent, Peter Ludwig
PETERS, Noel
Harvey, Peter Noel
PETERS, Roy
Nickson, Arthur
PETERSON, James
Zeiger, Henry Anthony
PETRIE, John
Hewison, Robert John Petrie
PETRIE, Rhona
Buchanan, Marie
PEYTON, K M
Peyton, Kathleen Wendy *and*
Peyton, Michael

PHEE, Hugh
McPhee, Hugh
PHELIX
Burnett, Hugh
PHILATICUS
Finlay, Ian
PHILEBUS
Barford, John Leslie
PHILIPPI, Mark
Bender, Arnold
PHILIPS, Steve
Whittington, Harry
PHILIPS, Thomas
Davies, Leslie Purnell
PHILLIP, Alban M
Allan, Philip Bertram Murray
PHILLIPS, John
Marquand, John Phillips
PHILLIPS, King
Perkins, Kenneth
PHILLIPS, Leon
Gerson, Noel Bertram
PHILLIPS, Mark
Garrett, Randall *and*
Janifer, Laurence M
PHILLIPS, Michael
Nolan, William F
PHILLIPS, Michael
Nutt, Charles
PHILMORE, R
Howard, Herbert Edmund
PHIPPS, Margaret
Tatham, Laura
PHIPSON, Joan
Fitzhardinge, Joan Margaret
PHOENICE, J
Hutchinson, Juliet Mary Fox
PICKARD, John Q
Borg, Philip Anthony John
PICKLE, Peregrine
Upton, George Putnam
PICTON, Bernard
Knight, Bernard

PIED PIPER, THE
Mallalieu, J P W
PIERCE, Katherine
St John, Wylly Folk
PIERCE, Matthew
Lucey, James D
PIKE, Charles R
Bulmer, Henry Kenneth
PIKE, Robert
Fish, Robert Lloyd
PIKE, Robert L
Fish, Robert Lloyd
PILE
Moreno, Virginia
PILGRIM
Wright, Marjory Beatrice
PILGRIM, Adam
Webster, Owen
PILGRIM, Anne
Allan, Mabel Esther
PILGRIM, David
Palmer, John Leslie *and*
Saunders, Hilary Aidan
St George
PILGRIM, Derral
Zachary, Hugh
PILIO, Gerone
Whitfield, John
PINDELL, Jon
Paine, Lauran Bosworth
PINDER, Chuck
Donson, Cyril
PINE, M S
Finn, *Sister* Mary Paulina
PINE, Theodore
Petaja, Emil
PINE, William
Harknett, Terry
PIPER, Evelyn
Modell, Merriam
PIPER, Peter
Langbehn, Theo
PIPER, Roger
Fisher, John

PITCAIRN, Frank
Cockburn, Claud
PITCHFORD, Harry Ronald
Ebbs, Robert
PLAIDY, Jean
Hibbert, Eleanor Alice Burford
PLAIN, Josephine
Mitchell, Isabel
PLAUT, Martin
Marttin, Paul
PLAYER, Robert
Jordan, Robert Furneaux
PLEDGER, P J
Tonkin, C B
PLOWMAN, Stephanie
Dee, Stephanie
PLUM, Jennifer
Kurland, Michael
PLUMMER, Ben
Bingley, David Ernest
POCRATES, *Dr* Hip
Schoenfeld, Eugene L
POE, Bernard
Hausman, Leon Augustus
POE, Edgar
Levine, Philip
POLLOCK, Mary
Blyton, Enid
POLWARTH, G Marchant
Polwarth, Gwendoline Mary
POMFRET, Joan
Townsend, Joan
PONDER, Patricia
Maxwell, Patricia Anne
PONSONBY, Doris Almon
Tempest, Sarah
PONT
Laidler, Graham
POOK, Peter
Miller, J A
POOLE, Michael
Poole, Reginald Heber
POOLE, Richard
Wells, Lee Edwin

POOLE, Vivian
Jaffe, Gabriel
POOTER
Hamilton, Alex
POPULUS
Cole, G(eorge) D(ouglas)
H(oward)
PORLOCK, Martin
MacDonald, Philip
PORTAL, Ellis
Powe, Bruce
PORTER, Alvin
Rowland, Donald Sydney
PORTOBELLO, Petronella
Anderson, *Lady* Flavia
PORTRAB
Bartrop, Edgar James
PORTSEA
MacKenzie, *Sir* Edward
POST, Mortimer
Blair, Walter
POTTER, Beatrix
Heelis, Beatrix
POWELL, Fern
Samman, Fern
POWER, Cecil
Allen, Grant
POWERS, M L
Tubb, E C
POWERS, Margaret
Heal, Edith
POWYS, Stephen
Wodehouse, Pelham Graham
POY
Fearon, Percy
PRAIZE, Ann
Blewitt, Dorothy
PREEDY, George
Campbell, Gabrielle Margaret
Vere
PREEDY, George R
Campbell, Gabrielle Margaret
Vere

PRENDER, Bart
King, Albert
PRENTIS, Richard
Agate, James
PRENTISS, Karl
Purdy, Ken
PRESCOT, Julian
Budd, John
PRESCOTT, Caleb
Bingley, David Ernest
PRESCOTT, John
Lucchetti, Anthony
PRESLAND, John
Bendit, Gladys
PRESTON, Jack
Buschlen, John Preston
PRESTON, James
Unett, John
PRESTON, Jane
Thomas, Reg
PRESTON, Richard
Lindsay, Jack
PREVOST, Francis
Prevost-Battersby, H F
PRICE, Evadne
Smith, Helen Zenna
PRICE, Jennifer
Hoover, Helen
PRICE-BROWN
Price-Brown, John
PRIESTLEY, Robert
Wiggins, David
PRIESTLY, Mark
Albert, Harold A
PRIMROSE, Jane
Curry, Winifred J P
PRIVATE 19022
Manning, Frederic
PROBERT, Lowri
Jones, Robert Maynard
PROBYN, Elise
McKibbon, John
PROCTER, Ida
Harris, Ida Fraser

PROCTOR, Everitt
Montgomery, Rutherford
George
PROFESSOR X
Boorstin, Daniel Joseph
PROLE, Lozania
Bloom, Ursula
PROTEUS
Whitaker, Peter
PROUDFOOT, Walter
Vahey, John George Haslette
PRUITT, Alan
Rose, Alvin Emmanuel
PRUTKOV, Kozma
Snodgrass, W D
PRYDE, Anthony
Weekes, Agnes Russell
PRYOR, Vanessa
Yarbro, Chelsea Quinn
PSEUDOMAN, Akkad
Northrup, E F
PULLING, Pierre
Pulling, Albert Van Siclen
PULVERTAFT, Lalage
Green, Lalage Isobel
PUNDIT, Ephraim
Looker, Samuel Joseph
PURE, Simon
Swinnerton, Frank
PUTNAM, Isra
La Spina, Fanny Greye (Bragg)
PUTNAM, John
Beckwith, Burnham Putnam
PUTNEY, Gail J
Fullerton, Gail
PUTRA, Kerala
Panikkar, Kavalam

Q
Quiller-Couch, *Sir* Arthur
Thomas
QUAD, M
Lewis, Charles Bertrand

QUAESTOR
Byford-Jones, Wilfred
QUARRY, Nick
Albert, Marvin H
QUARTERMAIN, James
Lynne, James Broom
QUARTUS
Hicks, E L *Bishop of Lincoln*
QUEEN, Ellery
Dannay, Frederic *and*
Lee, Manfred B
QUEEN, Ellery
Waldo, Edward Hamilton
QUENTIN, Patrick
Webb, Richard Wilson *and*
Wheeler, Hugh Callingham
QUEST, Erica
Sawyer, John *and*
Sawyer, Nancy
QUEX
Nichols, *Captain* G H F
QUILIBET
Fowler, Henry Watson
QUILL
Puddepha, Derek
QUILLER, Andrew
Bulmer, Henry Kenneth
QUILLET
Fowler, Henry Watson
QUIN, Dan
Lewis, Alfred Henry
QUIN, Shirland
Guest, Enid
QUINCE, Peter
Day, George Harold
QUINCE, Peter
Thompson, J W M
QUINLAN, William
Lash, William Quinlan
QUIRK
Squibbs, H W Q
QUIROULE, Pierre
Sayer, Walter William

QUOD, John
Irving, John Treat

§ §

No names, no pack-drill.
– British Army saying

§ §

R
Colfer, Rebecca B
R D A
Herbert, Robert Dudley
Sidney Powys
R H C
Orage, Alfred James
R H F
Fairburn, R H
R H S
Spring, Howard
R S
Zinsser, Hans
R T L
Vining, Charles A M
RACHEL
Ferguson, Rachel
RACHEN, Kurt von
Hubbard, Lafayette Ronald
RADCLIFFE, Janette
Roberts, Janet Louise
RADIO PADRE
Wright, Ronald Selby
RADLEY, Sheila
Robinson, Sheila
RADYR, Tomos
Stevenson, James Patrick
RAE, Doris
Rae, Margaret Doris
RAE, Scott
Hamilton, Cecily
RAESIDE, Jules
Reside, W J

RAFFERTY, S S
  Hurley, John J
RAG MAN
  Burrows, Hermann
RAGGED STAFF
  Coley, Rex
RAIKES, Robert
  Hayden, Eric William
RAILE, Arthur Lyon
  Warren, Edward Perry
RAIMOND, C E
  Robins, Elizabeth
RAINE, Richard
  Sawkins, Raymond Harold
RAKOSI, Carl
  Rawley, Callman
RALPH, Nathan
  Goldberg, Nathan Ralph
RALSTON, Jan
  Dunlop, Agnes M R
RAMAL, Walter
  De la Mare, Walter
RAME, David
  Divine, Arthur Durham
RAMEAUT, Maurice
  Marteau, F A
RAMPA, T Lobsang
  Hoskin, Cyril Henry
RAMSAY, Fay
  Eastwood, Helen
RAMSEY, Michael
  Green, T
RAN, Kip
  Randolph, Lowell King
RANA, J
  Bhatia, Jamunadevi
RAND, Brett
  Norwood, Victor George
  Charles
RAND, James S
  Attenborough, Bernard George
RAND, R H
  Holland, James R

RAND, William
  Roos, William
RANDALL, Clay
  Adams, Clifton
RANDALL, Janet
  Young, Janet Randall
RANDALL, Robert
  Garrett, Randall *and*
  Silverberg, Robert
RANDALL, Robert
  Silverberg, Robert
RANDALL, Rona
  Shambrook, Rona
RANDALL, William
  Gwinn, William R
RANDELL, Beverly
  Price, Beverly Joan
RANDELL, Janet
  Young, Robert William *and*
  Young, Janet Randell
RANDOLPH, Ellen
  Ross, William Edward Daniel
RANDOLPH, Jane
  Ross, William Edward Daniel
RANDOM, Alan
  Kay, Ernest
RANDOM, Alex
  Rowland, Donald Sydney
RANGELY, E R
  Zachary, Hugh
RANGELY, Olivia
  Zachary, Hugh
RANGER, Ken
  Creasey, John
RANKINE, John
  Mason, Douglas Rankine
RANSOME, Barbara
  Ransome, L E
RANSOME, Stephen
  Davis, Frederick Clyde
RAPHAEL, Ellen
  Hartley, Ellen R
RASKIN, Ellen
  Flanagan, Ellen

RATH, E J
Brainerd, Edith *and*
Brainerd, J Chauncey
RATTRAY, Simon
Dudley-Smith, Trevor
RAVENSCROFT, Rosanne
Ravenscroft, John R
RAY, Irene
Sutton, Rachel Irene Beebe
RAY, Nicholas
Kienzle, Raymond N
RAY, Wesley
Gaulden, Ray
RAYMOND, Mary
Keegan, Mary Constance
RAYNER, Olive Pratt
Allen, Grant
RAYNER, Richard
McIlwain, David
RAYTER, Joe
McChesney, Mary F
READ, Miss
Saint, Dora Jessie
READE, Hamish
Davidson, Simon
READE, Rolf S
Rose, Alfred
REDMAN, Joseph
Pearce, Brian
REDMAYNE, Barbara
Smithies, Muriel
REDWAY, Ralph
Hamilton, Charles Harold
St John
REDWOOD, Alec
Milkomane, George Alexis
Milkomanovich
REED, Cynthia
Nolan, Cynthia
REED, Eliot
Ambler, Eric *and*
Rodda, Charles
REED, Simon
Danby, Mary

REEDER, *Colonel* Red
Reeder, Russell P
REES, Dilwyn
Daniel, Glyn Edmund
REES, J Larcombe
Larcombe, Jennifer Geraldine
REEVE, Joel
Cox, William Robert
REEVES, Daniel
Liddy, James
REEVES, James
Reeves, John Morris
REEVES, Joyce
Gard, Joyce
REFUGITTA
Harrison, Constance Cary
REGAN, Brad
Norwood, Victor George
Charles
REGESTER, Seeley
Victor, Metta Victoria Fuller
REGNAL, F
d'Erlanger, *Baron* Frederic A
REID, Desmond
Baker, William Howard
REID, Frank
Vennard, Alexander Vindex
REID, Marshall
McBride, Robert Medill
REID, Philip
Ingrams, Richard *and*
Osmond, Andrew
REID, Wallace Q
Goodchild, George
REILLY, William K
Creasey, John
REINER, Max
Caldwell, Janet Taylor *and*
Reback, Marcus
REJJE, E
Hyde, Edmund Errol Claude
REMENHAM, John
Vlasto, John Alexander

REMINGTON, Jemima
Bevans, Florence Edith
REMINGTON, Mark
Bingley, David Ernest
RENAR, Frank
Fox, Frank
RENAULT, Mary
Challans, Mary
RENIER, Elizabeth
Baker, Betty
RENNIE, Jack
Spooner, Peter Alan
RENO, Mark
Keevill, Henry John
RENTON, Cam
Armstrong, Richard
RENTON, Julia
Cole, Margaret A
RENZELMAN, Marilyn
Ferguson, Marilyn
REVAL, Jacques
Laver, James
REYNOLDS, Adrian
Long, Amelia R
REYNOLDS, Dickson
Reynolds, Helen Mary
Greenwood Dickson
REYNOLDS, Jack
Jones, Jack
REYNOLDS, John
Fear, William H
REYNOLDS, John
Whitlock, Ralph
REYNOLDS, Mack
Reynolds, Dallas McCord
REYNOLDS, Madge
Whitlock, Ralph
REYNOLDS, Maxine
Reynolds, Dallas McCord
REYNOLDS, Peter
Long, Amelia R
RHODE, John
Street, Cecil John Charles

RHOSCOMYL, Owen
Vaughan, Owen
RICE, Craig
Randolph, Georgiana Ann
RICH, Barbara
Riding, Laura
RICH, Robert
Trumbo, Dalton
RICHARDS, Allen
Rosenthal, Richard Allen
RICHARDS, Clay
Crossen, Kendell Foster
RICHARDS, Duane
Hurley, Vic
RICHARDS, Francis
Lockridge, Frances Louise
and Lockridge, Richard
RICHARDS, Frank
Hamilton, Charles Harold
St John
RICHARDS, Henry
Morrissey, Joseph Lawrence
RICHARDS, Hilda
Hamilton, Charles Harold
St John
RICHARDS, Paul
Buddee, Paul
RICHARDS, Peter
Monger, Ifor
RICHARDS, Stella
Starr, Richard
RICHARDSON, Henry Handel
Richardson, Ethel Henrietta
RICHARDSON, Humphrey
Gall, Michel
RICHES, Phyllis
Sutton, Phyllis Mary
RICHMOND, Fiona
Harrison, Julia
RICHMOND, George
Brister, Richard
RICHMOND, Grace
Marsh, John

RICHMOND, Mary
Lindsay, Kathleen
RICHMOND, William
Fell, William Richmond
RICKARD, Cole
Barrett, Geoffrey John
RIDDELL, John
Ford, Corey
RIDGWAY, Jason
Lesser, Milton
RIDING, Laura
Gottschalk, Laura Riding
RIEFE, Barbara
Riefe, Alan
RIFT, Valerie
Bartlett, Marie
RIGHT CROSS
Armstrong, Paul
RILEY, Tex
Creasey, John
RIMMER, W J
Rowland, Donald Sydney
RING, Adam
Reed, Blair
RING, Basil
Braun, Wilbur
RING, Douglas
Prather, Richard S
RINGO, Johnny
Keevill, Henry John
RINGOLD, Clay
Hogan, Ray
RIORDAN, Dan
Cooke, William Everett
RIPLEY, Alvin
King, Albert
RIPLEY, Jack
Wainwright, John
RIPOSTE, A
Mordaunt, Evelyn May
RITA
Humphreys, Eliza M J
RITCHIE, Claire
Gibbs, Norah

RITSON, John
Baber, Douglas
RIVERINA
Winter, C H
RIVERS, Gayle
Brooks, Raymond
RIVERS, Georgia
Clark, Marjorie
RIVERS, Ronda
Sveinsson, Solveig
RIVERSIDE, John
Heinlein, Robert A
RIVES, Amelia
Troubetzkoi, *Princess*
RIX, Donna
Rowland, Donald Sydney
RIXON, Annie
Studdert, Annie
RIZA, Ali
Orga, Irfan
ROADSTER
Bays, J W
ROBB, John
Robson, Norman
ROBBINS, Harold
Rubins, Harold
ROBBINS, Tod
Robbins, Clarence Aaron
ROBERTS, Dan
Ross, William Edward Daniel
ROBERTS, David
Cox, John
ROBERTS, Desmond
Best, Rayleigh Breton Amis
ROBERTS, I M
Roberts, Irene
ROBERTS, Ivor
Roberts, Irene
ROBERTS, James Hall
Duncan, Robert Lipscomb
ROBERTS, John
Bingley, David Ernest
ROBERTS, Ken
Lake, Kenneth Robert

ROBERTS, Lee
Martin, Robert Lee
ROBERTS, Lionel
Fanthorpe, Robert Lionel
ROBERTS, McLean
Machlin, Milton
ROBERTS, Wayne
Overholser, Wayne D
ROBERTSON, E Arnot
Robertson, Eileen Arbuthnot
ROBERTSON, Elspeth
Ellison, Joan
ROBERTSON, Helen
Edmiston, Helen J M
ROBERTSON, Muirhead
Johnson, H
ROBESON, Kenneth
Goulart, Ronald Joseph
ROBIN
Roberts, Eric
ROBINS, Patricia
Clark, Patricia D R
ROBSON, Dirk
Robinson, Derek
ROCHARD, Henry
Charlier, Roger Henri
ROCHE, John
Le Roi, David de Roche
ROCK, Richard
Mainprize, Don
ROCKWELL, Matt
Rowland, Donald Sydney
ROCKWOOD, Harry
Young, Ernest A
RODD, Ralph
North, William
ROE, M S
Thomson, Daisy
ROE, Richard
Cowper, Francis
ROE, Tig
Roe, Eric
ROFFMAN, Jan
Summerton, Margaret

ROGERS, Anne
Seraillier, Anne
ROGERS, Floyd
Spence, William Duncan
ROGERS, Keith
Harris, Marion Rose
ROGERS, Kerk
Knowlton, Edward Rogers
ROGERS, Mick
Glut, Don F
ROGERS, Phillips
Idell, Albert Edward
ROGERS, Rachel
Redmon, Lois
ROHMER, Sax
Ward, Arthur Sarsfield
ROLAND, John
Oliver, John Rathbone
ROLAND, Mary
Lewis, Mary Christianna
ROLAND, Nicholas
Walmsley, Arnold
ROLLS, Anthony
Vulliamy, Colwyn Edward
ROLPH, C H
Hewitt, Cecil Rolph
ROLYAT, Jane
McDougall, E Jean Taylor
ROMANY
Evens, George Bramwell
ROMLEY, Derek
Romley, Frederick J
ROMNEY, Brent
Larralde, Romulo
ROMNEY, Steve
Bingley, David Ernest
ROME, Anthony
Albert, Marvin H
ROME, Tony
Albert, Marvin H
RONALD, E B
Barker, Ronald Ernest
RONNS, Edward
Aarons, Edward Sidney

ROOKE, Dennis
Rotheray, Geoffrey Neville
ROOME, Holdar
Moore, Harold William
ROOS, Kelley
Roos, William *and*
Kelley, Audrey
ROOT, Henry
Donaldson, William
ROSCOE, Charles
Rowland, Donald Sydney
ROSCOE, Janet
Prior, Mollie
ROSCOE, Mike
Roscoe, John *and*
Ruso, Michael
ROSE, Hilary
Mackinnon, Charles Roy
ROSE, Jennifer
Weber, Nancy
ROSE, Phyllis
Thompson, Phyllis
ROSE, Robert
Rose, Ian
ROSENTHAL, Richard A
Richards, Allen
ROSNA
Rosman, Alice Grant
ROSS
Martin, Violet Florence
ROSS, Adrian
Ropes, Arthur
ROSS, Albert
Goldstein, Arthur
ROSS, Angus
Giggal, Kenneth
ROSS, Barnaby
Dannay, Frederic *and*
Lee, Manfred B
ROSS, Catherine
Beaty, Betty
ROSS, Clarissa
Ross, William Edward Daniel

ROSS, Dan
Ross, William Edward Daniel
ROSS, Dana
Ross, William Edward Daniel
ROSS, Deborah
Stoffer, Edith G
ROSS, Diana
Denney, Diana
ROSS, Gene
Newton, William
ROSS, George
Ross, Isaac
ROSS, Helaine
Daniels, Dorothy
ROSS, Ivan T
Rossner, Robert
ROSS, J H
Lawrence, T E
ROSS, Jean
Hewson, Irene Dale
ROSS, John
Winnington, Richard
ROSS, Jonathan
Rossiter, John
ROSS, Katherine
Walter, Dorothy Blake
ROSS, Laurence
Hyland, Ann
ROSS, Leonard Q
Rosten, Leo C
ROSS, Maggie
Bermange, Maurine J L
ROSS, Malcolm
Ross-Macdonald, Malcolm
ROSS, Marilyn
Ross, William Edward Daniel
ROSS, Martin
Martin, Violet Florence
ROSS, Michael D H
Rosenthal, Michael D H
ROSS, Patricia
Wood, Patricia E W
ROSS, Sutherland
Callard, Thomas H

ROSS, W E D
Ross, William Edward Daniel
ROSS, Z H
Ross, Zola Helen
ROSSE, Ian
Straker, J F
ROSSETTI, Minerva
Rowland, Donald Sydney
ROSSITER, Jane
Ross, William Edward Daniel
ROSTANT, Robert
Hopkins, Robert Sydney
ROSTREVOR, George
Hamilton, *Sir* George Rostrevor
ROSTRON, Primrose
Hulbert, Joan
ROTHBERG, Winterset
Roethke, Theodore
ROTHMAN, Judith
Peters, Maureen
ROTHWELL, Annie
Christie, Annie Rothwell
ROUSSEAU, Victor
Emanuel, Victor Rousseau
ROWAN, Deidre
Williams, Jeanne
ROWAN, Hester
Robinson, Sheila
ROWANS, Virginia
Tanner, Edward Everett
ROWE, Alice E
Rowe, John Gabriel
ROWLAND, Iris
Roberts, Irene
ROWLANDS, Effie Adelaide
Albanesi, Effie Maria
ROWLANDS, Lesley
Zuber, Mary E I
ROYAL, Dan
Barrett, Geoffrey John
ROYCE, Kenneth
Gandley, Kenneth Royce
RUBICON
Lunn, *Sir* Arnold

RUCK, Berta
Oliver, Amy Roberta
RUDD, Margaret
Newlin, Margaret
RUDD, Steele
Davis, Arthur Hoey
RUDOMIN, Esther
Hantzig, Esther
RUELL, Patrick
Hill, Reginald
RUFFLES
Tegner, Henry
RUNYON, Damon
Runyan, Alfred Damon
RURIC, Peter
Cain, Paul
RUSHOLM, Peter
Powell, Eric
RUSHTON, Charles
Shortt, Charles Rushton
RUSSELL, Arthur
Goode, Arthur Russell
RUSSELL, Erle
Wilding, Philip
RUSSELL, James
Harknett, Terry
RUSSELL, Lindsay
Stonehouse, Patricia Ethel
RUSSELL, Raymond
Balfour, William
RUSSELL, Sarah
Laski, Marghanita
RUSSELL, Shane
Norwood, Victor George
Charles
RUTHERFORD, Douglas
McConnell, James Douglas
Rutherford
RUTHERFORD, Mark
White, William Hale
RUTLEDGE, Brett
Paul, Elliot Harold
RUYERSON, James Paul
Rothweiler, Paul R

RYAN, J M
McDermott, John Richard
RYBOT, Doris
Pensonby, Doris Almon
RYDELL, Forbes
Forbes, Deloris Stanton *and*
Rydell, Helen
RYDELL, Wendell
Rydell, Wendy
RYDER, James
Pattinson, James
RYDER, Jonathan
Ludlum, Robert
RYDER, Thom
Harvey, John
RYE, Anthony
Youd, Samuel
RYERSON, Lowell
Van Atta, Winfred Lowell
RYLAND, Clive
Priestley, Clive Ryland

§ §

I got an insurance card here.
Under the name of Jenkins.
See? Bernard Jenkins. Look.
It's got four stamps on it.
Four of them. But I can't
go along with these. That's
not my real name, they'd
find out, they'd have me in
the nick. I been going around
under an assumed name.
— Harold Pinter. The caretaker

§ §

S, Elizabeth von
Freeman, Gillian
S H S
Spender, Stephen
S S
Sassoon, Siegfried

S V F G
Fitzgerald, Seymour Vesey
SABATTIS
Gill, T M
SABBAH, Hassan i
Butler, Bill
SABER, Robert O
Ozaki, Milton K
SABIAD
White, Stanhope
SABIN, Mark
Fox, Norman Arnold
SABRE, Dirk
Laffin, John
SABRETACHE
Barrow, Albert Stewart
SACKERMAN, Henry
Kahn, H S
SADBALLS, John
Matusow, Harvey Marshall
SADDLER, K Allen
Richards, Ronald C W
SADLER, Mark
Lynds, Dennis
SAGITTARIUS
Katzin, Olga
ST ANBECK, Roland
Beck, Roland Stanley
ST CLAIR, Dester
Winchell, Prentice
ST CLAIR, Everett
Mansell, *Mrs* C B
ST CLAIR, Philip
Howard, Munroe
ST CLAIRE, Yvonne
Hall, Emma L
ST CRISPIAN, Crispin de
Waugh, Auberon
SAINT-EDEN, Dennis
Foster, Don
ST E A OF M AND S
Crowley, Edward Alexander
ST EBBAR
Rabbets, Thomas G

ST GEORGE, Arthur
Paine, Lauran Bosworth
ST GEORGE, David
Markov, Georgi *and*
Phillips, David
ST GIRAUD
Knott, William Cecil
ST HERETICUS
Brown, Robert McAfee
ST JAMES, Andrew
Stern, James
ST JOHN, Christopher
Marshall, Christabel
ST JOHN, David
Hunt, E Howard
ST JOHN, Leonie
Bayer, William
ST JOHN, Nicole
Johnston, Norma
ST JOHN, Philip
Del Rey, Lester
SAINT-LUC, Jean de
Glassco, John
ST MARS, F
Atkins, Frank A
SAKI
Munro, Hector Hugh
SALISBURY, Carola
Butterworth, Michael
SALISBURY, John
Caute, David
SALT, Jonathan
Neville, Derek
SALTAR THE MONGOL
Williamson, Thames Ross
SALTEN, Felix
Saltzmann, Sigmund
SALTER, Cedric
Knight, Francis Edgar
SALTER, Mary D
Ainsworth, Mary Dinsmore
SALTER AINSWORTH, Mary D
Ainsworth, Mary Dinsmore

SAMPSON, Richard Henry
Hull, Richard
SANBORN, B X
Ballinger, William Sanborn
SANDERS, Brett
Barrett, Geoffrey John
SANDERS, Bruce
Gribble, Leonard Reginald
SANDERS, Daphne
Randolph, Georgiana Ann
SANDERS, Dorothy Lucy
Walker, Lucy
SANDERS, Jeanne
Rundle, Anne
SANDERS, Winston P
Anderson, Poul
SANDHURST, B G
Green, Charles Henry
SANDON, J D
Harvey, John
SANDS, Martin
Burke, John Frederick
SANDYS, Oliver
Evans, Marguerite Florence
SANTA MARIA
Powell-Smith, Vincent
SANTEE, Walt
King, Albert
SAPPER
Fairlie, Gerard
SAPPER
McNeile, H C
SARA
Blake, Sally Mirliss
SARAC, Roger
Caras, Roger
SARASIN, J G
Salmon, Geraldine Gordon
SARBAN
Wall, John W
SARGENT, Joan
Jenkins, Sara Lucile
SARI
Fleur, Anne Elizabeth

269

SARNE, Michael
Plummer, Thomas Arthur
SARNIAN
Falla, Frank
SASHUN, Sigma
Sassoon, Sigfried
SAUER, Muriel S
Stafford, Muriel
SAUNDERS, Abel
Pound, Ezra
SAUNDERS, Anne
Aldred, Margaret
SAUNDERS, Caleb
Heinlein, Robert A
SAUNDERS, Carl McK
Ketchum, Philip
SAUNDERS, David
Sontup, Daniel
SAUNDERS, Ione
Cole, Margaret A
SAUNDERS, John
Nickson, Arthur
SAUNDERS, Lawrence
Davis, Burton *and*
Davis, Clare Ogden
SAUNDERS, Marshall
Saunders, Margaret Marshall
SAUNDERS, Wes
Bounds, Sydney J
SAVA, George
Milkomane, George Alexis
Milkomanovich
SAVAGE, Blake
Goodwin, Harold Leland
SAVAGE, David
Hossent, Harry
SAVAGE, Leslie
Duff, Douglas Valder
SAVAGE, Richard
Roe, Ivan
SAVAGE, Steve
Goodavage, Joseph F
SAWLEY, Petra
Marsh, John

SAWYER, Mark
Greenhood, David
SAXON
Matthews, Edith J
SAXON, Alec
Pronzini, Bill
SAXON, John
Gifford, James Noble
SAXON, John
Rumbold-Gibbs, Henry St
John C
SAXON, Peter
Baker, William Howard
SAXON, Richard
Morrissey, Joseph Lawrence
SAXTON, Judith
Turner, Judy
SAYRE, Gordon
Woolfolk, Josiah Pitts
SCARLETT, Roger
Blair, Dorothy *and*
Page, Evelyn
SCARLETT, Susan
Streatfeild, Noel
SCARLETT, Will
Redman, William Xavier
SCARROTT, Michael
Fisher, A Stanley T
SCHAW, Ruth
Drummond, Alison
SCHOFIELD, Paul
Tubb, E C
SCHOLEFIELD, Edmund O
Butterworth, William Edmund
SCHWARTZ, Bruno
Mann, George
SCIENCE INVESTIGATOR
Speck, Gerald Eugene
SCIPIO
Watson, Adam
SCOBEY, Marion
Coombs, Joyce
SCOFIELD, Jonathan
Rothweiler, Paul R

SCOLLAN, E A
O'Grady, Elizabeth Anne
SCOLOPAX
Grant, Maurice Harold
SCORPIO
Tucker, William Joseph
SCOT, Neil
Grant, *Lady* Sybil
SCOTLAND, Jay
Jakes, John
SCOTT, A
Bloor, W A
SCOTT, Agnes Neill
Muir, Wilhelmina Johnstone
SCOTT, Alastair
Allen, Kenneth Sydney
SCOTT, Bradford
Scott, Leslie
SCOTT, Bruce
McCartney, R J
SCOTT, Casey
Kubis, Patricia Lou
SCOTT, Catherine
Ehrenberg, Golda
SCOTT, Dana
Robertson, Constance Noyes
SCOTT, Denis
Means, Mary *and*
Saunders, Theodore
SCOTT, Douglas
Thorpe, John
SCOTT, Elizabeth
Capstick, Elizabeth
SCOTT, Grover
King, Albert
SCOTT, Jack S
Escott, Jack Leonard
SCOTT, Jane
McElfresh, Adeline
SCOTT, Janey
Lindsay, Rachel
SCOTT, John-Paul
Farquhar, Jesse Carlton *Jr*

SCOTT, Martin
Gehman, Richard Boyd
SCOTT, Milward
Rayer, Francis G
SCOTT, Norford
Rowland, Donald Sydney
SCOTT, O R
Gottliebsen, Ralph Joseph
SCOTT, Thurston
Leite, George Thurston *and*
Scott, Jody
SCOTT, Valerie
Rowland, Donald Sydney
SCOTT, Warwick
Dudley-Smith, Trevor
SCOTT, Will
Scott, William Matthew
SCOTT-MORLEY, A
Oakley, Eric Gilbert
SCROPE, Mason
Mason, Arthur Charles
SCRUTATOR
Sidebotham, Herbert
SEAFARER
Barker, Clarence Hedley
SEAFORD, Caroline
Cook, Marjorie Grant
SEAFORTH
Foster, George Cecil
SEAFORTH
Skues, George Edward
Mackenzie
SEAGRAVE, Barbara Ann
Garvey
Jackson, Barbara Ann
Garvey Seagrave
SEA-LION
Bennett, Geoffrey Martin
SEAL, Basil
Barnes, Julian
SEALE, Sara
MacPherson, A D L
SEAMARK
Small, Austin J

SEARCH-LIGHT
Frank, Waldo David
SEARE, Nicholas
Whitaker, Rod
SEARS, Deane
Rywell, Martin
SEA-WRACK
Crebbin, Edward Horace
SEBASTIAN, Lee
Silverberg, Robert
SEC
Manner, Marya
SECRIST, Kelliher
Kelliher, Dan T *and*
Secrist, W G
SEDGES, John
Buck, Pearl S
SEDGWICK, Modwena
Glover, Modwena
SEEBLE
Beresford, Claude R De La
Poer
SEEKER, A
Eagan, Frances W
SEFTON, Catherine
Waddell, Martin
SEGUNDO, Bart
Rowland, Donald Sydney
SEIFERT, Elizabeth
Gasparotti, Elizabeth
SELDEN, George
Thompson, George Selden
SELKIRK, Jane
Chapman, Mary I *and*
Chapman, John Stanton
SELL, Joseph
Haley, W J
SELMARK, George
Seldon Truss, Leslie
SENCOURT, Robert
George, Robert Esmonde
Gordon
SERAFIAN, Michael
Martin, Malachi

SERANNE, Ann
Smith, Margaret Ruth
SERANUS
Harrison, Susie Frances
SERJEANT, Richard
Van Essen, W
SERNICOLI, Davide
Trent, Ann
SETH, Andrew
Pattison, Andrew Seth P
SETON, Graham
Hutchison, Graham Seton
SETOUN, Gabriel
Hepburn, Thomas Nicoll
SEUFFERT, Muir
Seuffert, Muriel
SEVERN, David
Unwin, David Storr
SEVERN, Forepoint
Bethell, Leonard Arthur
SEVERN, Richard
Ebbs, Robert
SEWELL, Arthur
Whitson, John Harvey
SEYMOUR, Henry
Hartmann, Helmut Henry
SHALIMAR
Hendry, Frank Coutts
SHALLOW, Robert
Atkinson, Frank
SHAN
McMordie, John Andrew
SHANE
Richardson, Eileen
SHANE, John
Durst, Paul
SHANE, Mark
Norwood, Victor George
Charles
SHANE, Martin
Johnston, George Henry
SHANE, Rhondo
Norwood, Victor George
Charles

SHANE, Susannah
Ashbrook, Harriette Cora
SHANE, Victor
Norwood, Victor George
Charles
SHANNON, Carl
Hogue, Wilbur Owings
SHANNON, Dell
Linington, Elizabeth
SHANNON, Monica
Katchamakoff, Atanas
SHANNON, Steve
Bouma, J L
SHANNON, Terry
Mercer, Jessie
SHANWA
Haarer, Alec Ernest
SHARMAN, Miriam
Bolton, Miriam
SHARON, Rose
Grossman, Judith
SHARP, Helen
Paine, Lauran Bosworth
SHARP, Luke
Barr, Robert
SHAUL, Frank
Rowland, Donald Sydney
SHAW, Adelaide
O'Shaughnessy, Marjorie
SHAW, Artie
Arshavsky, Abraham Isaac
SHAW, Brian
Tubb, E C
SHAW, Irene
Roberts, Irene
SHAW, Jane
Evans, Jean
SHAW, Jill A
Keeling, Jill Annette
SHAW, Josephine
Clarke, Dorothy Josephine
SHAW, T E
Lawrence, T E

SHAWN, Frank S
Goulart, Ronald Joseph
SHAYNE, Gordon
Winter, Bevis
SHAYNE, Nina
Gibbs, Norah
SHEAFFER, Louis
Slung, Louis Sheaffer
SHEARING, Joseph
Campbell, Gabrielle Margaret
Vere
SHELBOURNE, Cecily
Ebel, Suzanne
SHELBY, Cole
King, Albert
SHELDON, John
Bloch, Robert
SHELDON, Lee
Lee, Wayne C
SHELDON, Raccoona
Sheldon, Alice B
SHELDON, Roy
Tubb, E C
SHELLEY, Frances
Wees, Frances Shelley
SHELLEY, Peter
Dresser, Davis
SHELTON, Michael
Stacey, P M de Cosqueville
SHEPARD, Fern
Stonebraker, Florence
SHEPARD, Sam
Rogers, Samuel Shepard
SHEPARD, Stratton
Van Deurs, George
SHEPHERD, Joan
Buchanan, B J
SHEPHERD, John
Ballard, Willis Todhunter
SHEPHERD, Michael
Ludlum, Robert
SHEPHERD, Neal
Morland, Nigel

273

SHERASHEVSKI, Boris
Brown, John J
SHERATON, Neil
Smith, Norman Edward Mace
SHERMAN, George
Moretti, Ugo
SHERMAN, Joan
Dern, Erolie Pearl
SHERRY, Gordon
Sheridan, H B
SHIEL-MARTIN
Old, Phyllis Muriel Elizabeth
SHIVAJI, Mahatma Guru Sri Paramahansa
Crowley, Edward Alexander
SHONE, Patric
Hanley, James
SHORE, Norman
Smith, Norman Edward Mace
SHORE, Philippa
Holbeche, Philippa
SHORT, Francis
Harris, *Mrs* Herbert
SHORT, Luke
Glidden, Frederick Dilley
SHOTT, Abel
Ford, T W
SHROPSHIRE LAD
Barber-Starkey, Roger
SHURA, Mary Francis
Craig, Mary
SHUTE, Nevil
Norway, Nevil Shute
SHY, Timothy
Wyndham Lewis, D B
SIBLEY, Lee
Landells, Anne
SIDNEY, Margaret
Lothrop, Harriet Mulford
SIDNEY, Neilma
Gantner, Neilma B
SIGMA SASHUN
Sassoon, Siegfried

SILLER, Van
Siller, Hilda van
SILURIENSIS, Leolinus
Machen, Arthur
SILVER, Nicholas
Faust, Frederick
SILVER, Richard
Bulmer, Henry Kenneth
SILVESTER, Frank
Bingley, David Ernest
SIMA, Caris
Mountcastle, Clara H
SIMMONDS, Mike
Simmonds, Michael Charles
SIMMONS, Catherine
Duncan, Kathleen
SIMMONS, Kim
Duncan, Kathleen
SIMON
Blakeston, Oswell *and*
Burford, Roger d'Este
SIMON, Robert
Musto, Barry
SIMON, S J
Skidelsky, Simon Jasha
SIMONS, Peter
Punnett, Margaret *and*
Punnett, Ivor
SIMPLE, Peter
Herbert, John; Hogg, Michael;
Welch, Colin *and*
Wharton, Michael
SIMPLEX, Simon
Middleton, Henry Clement
SIMPSON, Warwick
Ridge, William Pett
SIMS, John
Hopson, William L
SIMS, *Lieut* A K
Whitson, John Harvey
SINBAD
Dingle, Aylward Edward
SINCLAIR, Alasdair
Clyne, Douglas

SINCLAIR, James
Staples, Reginald Thomas
SINCLAIR, Jo
Seid, Ruth
SINCLAIR, Michael
Shea, Michael
SINDERBY, Donald
Stephens, Donald Ryder
SINGER, Adam
Karp, David
SINGER, Bant
Shaw, Charles
SINGER, Burns
Singer, James Hyman
SINJOHN, John
Galsworthy, John
SIOGVOLK, Paul
Mathews, Albert
SION, Mari
Jones, Robert Maynard
SIR TOPAZ
Agate, James
SISE, Annie
Reid, Phillipa
SISTER MARY AQUINAS
Weinrich, Anna Katharina
SISTER MARY THEODORE
Hegeman, Mary Theodore
SKALDASPILLIR, Sigfriour
Broxon, Mildred Downey
SKEEVER, Jim
Hill, John Alexander
SKOOKUM CHUCK
Cumming, Robert Dalziel
SKY, Kathleen
Goldin, Kathleen McKinney
SLADE, Gurney
Bartlett, Stephen
SLAGG, Glenda
Fantoni, Barry
SLATER, Patrick
Mitchell, John
SLAUGHTER, Jim
Paine, Lauran Bosworth

SLINGSBY, Rufus
Siddle, Charles *and*
Peel, Frederick
SLOANE, Sara
Bloom, Ursula
SLOLUCK, J Milton
Bierce, Ambrose
SLY, Christopher
Neild, James Edward
SMALACOMBE, John
MacKay, Louis Alexander
SMALL, Ernest
Lent, Blair
SMALL, William
Eversley, David E C
SMEE, Wentworth
Burgin, G B
SMEED
Taylor, Deems
SMEED, Frances
Lasky, Jesse L
SMITH, Adam
Goodman, George Jerome W
SMITH, Bryan
Knott, William Cecil
SMITH, C Busby
Smith, John
SMITH, Caesar
Dudley-Smith, Trevor
SMITH, Clyde
Smith, George
SMITH, Cordwainer
Linebarger, Paul
SMITH, Dodie
Smith, Dorothy Gladys
SMITH, Elvet
Marshall, Margaret
SMITH, Essex
Hope, Essex
SMITH, Harriet
Scott, Hilda R
SMITH, Jean
Smith, Frances C

SMITH, Jessica
Penwarden, Helen
SMITH, John
Herrick, Marvin Theodore
and Hudson, Hoyt
SMITH, Lew
Floren, Lee
SMITH, Naomi
Vinter, Helen
SMITH, S S
Williamson, Thames Ross
SMITH, Shelley
Bodington, Nancy Hermione
SMITH, Spartacus
Johnston, Alexander
SMITH, Stevie
Smith, Florence Margaret
SMITH, Surrey
Dinner, William *and*
Morum, William
SMITH, Wade
Snow, Charles Horace
SMITH, Z Z
Westheimer, David
SMYTHE, James P
McGarry, William Rutledge
SNAFFLES
Payne, Charles J
SNOW, Lyndon
Ansle, Dorothy Phoebe
SOHL, Jerry
Sohl, Gerald Allen
SOMERS, Bart
Fox, Gardner F
SOMERS, J L
Stickland, Louise Annie Beatrice
SOMERS, Jane
Lessing, Doris
SOMERS, Paul
Winterton, Paul
SOMERS, Suzanne
Daniels, Dorothy
SOMERSET, Percy
Hollis, Christopher

SOMERVILLE
Somerville, Edith Oenone
SON OF THE SOIL
Fletcher, J S
SORACE, Richard
Williamson, Lydia Buckland
SOREL, Julia
Drexler, Rosalyn
SOSKIN, V H
Ellison, Virginia Howell
SOSTHENES
Coad, Frederick R
SOUTHCOTE, George
Aston, *Sir* George
SOUTHERN CROSS
Hill, *Mrs* E E
SOUTHWORTH, Louis
Grealey, Tom
SOUTTER, Fred
Lake, Kenneth Robert
SOUZA, Ernest
Scott, Evelyn
SPADE, Mark
Balchin, Nigel
SPADE, Rupert
Pawley, Martin Edward
SPAIN, John
Adams, Cleve Franklin
SPALDING, Lucille
Jay, Marion
SPALT, Karl Heinz G
Spalding, Keith
SPANNER, Valerie
Grayland, Valerie M
SPARLIN, W
Spratling, Walter Norman
SPAULDING, Leonard
Bradbury, Ray
SPELLMAN, Roger G
Cox, William Robert
SPENCE, Betty E
Tettmar, Betty Eileen
SPENCE, Duncan
Spence, William

SPENCER, Cornelia
Yaukey, Grace
SPENCER, Edward
Mott, Edward Spencer
SPENCER, John
Vickers, Roy
SPENSER, James
Guest, Francis Harold
SPERLING, Maria Sandra
Floren, Lee
SPERRY, J E
Eisenstat, Jane Sperry
SPIEL, Hilde
De Mendelssohn, Hilde
SPILLANE, Mickey
Spillane, Frank Morrison
SPINELLI, Marcos
Spinelli, Grace
SPOONHILL
Reaney, James
SPRINGFIELD, David
Lewis, J R
SPROSTON, John
Scott, Peter Dale
SPROULE, Wesley
Sproule, Howard
SPURR, Clinton
Rowland, Donald Sydney
SQUARE, Charlotte
Haldane, Robert Aylmer
SQUIRES, Phil
Barker, S Omar
STACY, O'Connor
Rollins, William
STAFFORD, Ann
Pedlar, Ann
STAFFORD, Peter
Tabori, Paul
STAGG, Delano
Sabre, Mel R *and*
Eiden, Paul
STAGGE, Jonathan
Webb, Richard Wilson *and*
Wheeler, Hugh Callingham

STAINES, Trevor
Brunner, John
STAMPER, Alex
Kent, Arthur
STAN, Roland
Rowland, Donald Sydney
STAND, Marguerite
Stickland, M E
STANDISH, Buck
Paine, Lauran Bosworth
STANDISH, Burt L
Patten, Gilbert
STANDISH, J O
Horler, Sydney
STANDISH, Robert
Gerahty, Digby George
STANFIELD, Anne
Coffman, Virginia
STANGE, Nora K
Stanley, Nora Kathleen Begbie
STANHOPE, Douglas
Duff, Douglas Valder
STANHOPE, John
Langdon-Davies, John
STANHOPE OF CHESTER
Norman, C H
STANLEY, Arthur
Megaw, Arthur Stanley
STANLEY, Bennett
Hough, Stanley Bennett
STANLEY, Chuck
Strong, Charles Stanley
STANLEY, Dave
Dachs, David
STANLEY, F
Crocchiola, Stanley Francis
Louis
STANLEY, Margaret
Mason, Sydney Charles
STANLEY, Marge
Weinbaum, Stanley Grauman
STANLEY, Michael
Hosie, Stanley William

STANLEY, Warwick
Hilton, John Buxton
STANSBURY, Alec
Higgs, Alec S
STANSTEAD, John
Groom, Arthur William
STANTON, Borden
Wilding, Philip
STANTON, Coralie
Hosken, Alice Cecil Seymour
STANTON, Marjorie
Phillips, Horace
STANTON, Paul
Beaty, David
STANTON, Schuyler
Baum, Lyman Frank
STANTON, Vance
Avallone, Michael Angelo *Jr*
STAR, Elison
Comber, Rose
STARK, Joshua
Olsen, Theodore Victor
STARK, Michael
Lariar, Lawrence
STARK, Richard
Westlake, Donald Edwin
STARR, Henry
Bingley, David Ernest
STARR, John A
Gillesse, John Patrick
STARR, Leonora
Mackesy, Leonora Dorothy
Rivers
STARRET, William
McClintock, Marshall
STATTEN, Vargo
Fearn, John Russell
STAVELEY, Robert
Campbell, R O
STEEL, Byron
Steegmuller, Francis
STEEL, Kurt
Kagey, Rudolf

STEEL, Robert
Whitson, John Harvey
STEELE, Addison
Whitson, John Harvey
STEELE, Erskine
Henderson, Archibald
STEELE, Howard
Steele, Harwood Elmes Robert
STEELE, Tex
Ross, William Edward Daniel
STEEN, Frank
Felstein, Ivor
STEER, Charlotte
Hunter, Christine
STEFFAN, Jack
Steffan, Alice Jacqueline
STEFFANSON, Con
Goulart, Ronald Joseph
STEPHENS, Casey
Wagner, Sharon Blythe
STEPHENS, Frances
Bentley, Margaret
STEPHENS, Reed
Donaldson, Stephen R
STERLING, Anthony
Caesar, Gene
STERLING, Helen
Hoke, Helen L
STERLING, Maria Sandra
Floren, Lee
STERLING, Peter
Stern, David
STERLING, Stewart
Winchell, Prentice
STERN, Elizabeth
Uhr, Elizabeth
STERN, John
Stearn, John Theodore
STERN, Paul F
Ernst, Paul F
STERN, Stuart
Rae, Hugh Crauford
STEVENS, Andy
Danby, Mary

STEVENS, Blaise
Whittington, Harry
STEVENS, Christopher
Tabori, Paul
STEVENS, Dan J
Overholser, Wayne D
STEVENS, J D
Rowland, Donald Sydney
STEVENS, Jill
Mogridge, Stephen
STEVENS, John
Tubb, E C
STEVENS, Maurice
Whitson, John Harvey
STEVENS, Peter
Geis, Bernard *and*
Geis, Darlene Stern
STEVENS, Robert Tyler
Staples, Reginald Thomas
STEVENS, S P
Palestrant, Simon
STEVENS, William Christopher
Allen, Stephen Valentine
STEVENSON, Christine
Kelly, Elizabeth
STEVENSON, J P
Haldane-Stevenson, James
Patrick
STEVENSON, John P
Grierson, Edward
STEVENSON, Robert
Naismith, Robert Stevenson
STEWART, C R
Adam, C G M
STEWART, David
Politella, Dario
STEWART, Eleanor
Porter, Eleanor
STEWART, Jay
Palmer, Stuart
STEWART, Jean
Newman, Mona A J
STEWART, Kaye
Howe, Doris Kathleen

STEWART, Logan
Savage, Lee
STEWART, Logan
Wilding, Philip
STEWART, Marjorie
Huxtable, Marjorie
STEWART, Scott
Zaffo, George J
STEWART, Will
Williamson, Jack
STEWART-HARGREAVES, E H I
White, Frank James
STEWER, Jan
Coles, Albert John
STIRLING, Jessica
Rae, Hugh Crauford
STIRLING, Stella
Ransome, L E
STIRLING, Veda
Drummond, Edith Victoria
STITCH, Wilhelmina
Collie, Ruth
STOCKBRIDGE, Grant
Page, Norvell W
STODDARD, Charles
Kuttner, Henry
STOKES, Cedric
Beardmore, George
STONE, Eugene
Speck, Gerald Eugene
STONE, Hampton
Stein, Aaron Marc
STONE, Simon
Barrington, Howard
STONE, Thomas H
Harknett, Terry
STONER, Oliver
Bishop, Morchard
STONG, Pat
Hough, Richard Alexander
STORM, Christopher
Olsen, Theodore Victor

STORM, Lesley
Clark, Mabel Margaret
STORM, Virginia
Swatridge, Irene M M
STORME, Peter
Stern, Philip Van Doren
STORY, Josephine
Loring, Emilie
STORY, Sydney A J
Pike, Mary Hayden
STRAND, Paul E
Palestrant, Simon
STRANG, Herbert
L'Estrange, C James *and*
Ely, George Herbert
STRANGE, John Stephen
Tillett, Dorothy Stockbridge
STRANGER, Joyce
Wilson, Joyce Muriel
STRANGEWAY, Mark
Leyland, Eric
STRATEGICUS
O'Neill, Herbert Charles
STRATHEARN-HAY
Robertson, William
STRATTON, John
Alldridge, John Stratten
STRATTON, Thomas
Coulson, Robert Stratton *and*
De Weese, T Eugene
STRAVOLGI, Bartolomeo
Tucci, Niccolo
STREAMER, *Col* D
Graham, Harry
STREET, Emmett
Behan, Brendan
STRETTON, Hesba
Smith, Sarah
STRIPPER
Wilson, John
STRODE, Mary
Saunders, Cicely
STRONG, Susan
Rees, Joan

STRONG, Zachary
Mann, E B
STROVER, Dorothea
Tinne, Dorothea
STRUTHER, Jan
Maxtone-Graham, Joyce
STRYDOM, Len
Rousseau, Leon
STRYFE, Paul
Newman, James Roy
STUART, Alan
Weightman, Archibald John
STUART, Alex
Stuart, Vivian Alex
STUART, Alex R
Gordon, Richard
STUART, Anthony
Hale, Julian Anthony Stuart
STUART, Brian
Worthington-Stuart, Brian
Arthur
STUART, Charles
Mackinnon, Charles Roy
STUART, Clay
Whittington, Harry
STUART, Don A
Campbell, John Wood *Jr*
STUART, Florence
Stonebraker, Florence
STUART, Frederick
Tomlin, Eric
STUART, Gordon
Wood, James
STUART, Ian
Maclean, Alistair
STUART, John Roy
McMillan, Donald
STUART, Logan
Wilding, Philip
STUART, Margaret
Paine, Lauran Bosworth
STUART, Matt
Holmes, Llewellyn Perry

STUART, Sheila
Baker, Mary Gladys Steel
STUART, Sidney
Avallone, Michael Angelo *Jr*
STUART, V A
Stuart, Vivian Alex
STUART, Vivian
Stuart, Vivian Alex
STUDENT OF POLITICS, A
Sidebotham, Herbert
STUDENT OF WAR, A
Sidebotham, Herbert
STURGEON, Theodore
Waldo, Edward Hamilton
STURGUS, J B
Bastin, John
STURROCK, Jeremy
Healey, Benjamin James
STUYVESANT, Polly
Paul, Maury
STYLITES, Simeon
Luccock, Halford Edward
SUAREZ LYNCH, B
Borges, Jorge Luis *and*
Bioy-Casares, Adolfo
SUBHADRA-NANDAN
Prafulla, Das
SUBOND, Valerie
Grayland, Valerie M
SUDORF, Fingal von
Rosenquist, Fingal
SULLIVAN, Eric Harrison
Hickey, Madelyn E
SULLIVAN, Reese
Lutz, Giles A
SULLIVAN, Sean Mei
Sohl, Gerald Allen
SUMMERFOREST, Ivy B
Kirkup, James
SUMMERS, D B
Barrett, Geoffrey John
SUMMERS, Diana
Smith, George H

SUMMERS, Gordon
Hornby, John Wilkinson
SUMMERS, Rowena
Saunders, Jean
SUMMERSCALES, Rowland
Gaines, Robert
SUNDOWNER
Tichborne, Henry
SURFACEMAN
Anderson, Alexander
SURREY, Kathryn
Matthewman, Phyllis
SUTHERLAND, Elizabeth
Marshall, Elizabeth Margaret
SUTHERLAND, Joan
Collings, Joan
SUTHERLAND, William
Cooper, John Murray
SUTTLING, Mark
Rowland, Donald Sydney
SUTTON, Henry
Slavitt, David
SUTTON, I M
Coad, Frederick R
SUTTON, John
Tullett, Denis John
SUTTON, Penny
Cartwright, Justin
SUTTON, Rachel B
Sutton, Rachel Irene Beebe
SVAREFF, *Count* Vladimir
Crowley, Edward Alexander
SWAN, Annie S
Burnett-Smith, Annie S
SWAYNE, Geoffrey
Campion, Sidney
SWEETLAND, Nancy Rose
Rose, Nancy A
SWIFT, Anthony
Farjeon, Joseph Jefferson
SWIFT, Benjamin
Paterson, W R
SWIFT, Julian
Applin, Arthur

SWIFT, Rachelle
Lumsden, Jean
SWIFT, Stella
Whish, Violet E
SYDNEY, Cynthia
Tralins, S Robert
SYLVESTER, Philip
Worner, Philip A I
SYLVIA
Ashton-Warner, Sylvia
SYLVESTER, Anthony
Laurencic, Karl
SYLVIN, Francis
Seaman, Sylvia Sybil *and*
Schwartz, F
SYNGE, Don
Edelstein, Hyman

T
Thorp, Joseph
T J V
Pound, Ezra
T P
O'Connor, T P
T S
Seccombe, Thomas
TAAFFE, Robert
Maguire, Robert A J
TABARD, Peter
Blake, Leslie James
TAD
Dorgan, Thomas Aloysius
TAFFRAIL
Dorling, Henry Taprell
TAGGART, Dean
King, Albert
TAINE, John
Bell, Eric Temple
TAKI
Theodoracopulos, Peter
TALBOT, Hake
Nelms, Henning
TALBOT, Henry
Rothwell, Henry Talbot

TALBOT, Hugh
Alington, Argentine Francis
TALBOT, Kathrine
Barker, Ilse Eva L
TALBOT, Kay
Rowland, Donald Sydney
TALBOT, Lawrence
Bryant, Edward
TALL, Stephen
Crook, Compton Newby
TANIS
Davies, Hilda A
TANNER, John
Matcha, Jack
TAPER
Levin, Bernard
TARRANT, Elizabeth
Leyland, Eric
TARRANT, John
Egleton, Clive
TATE, Ellalice
Hibbert, Eleanor Alice Burford
TATE, Mary Anne
Hale, Arlene
TATE, Richard
Masters, Anthony
TATHAM, Campbell
Elting, Mary
TAVEREL, John
Howard, Robert E
TAYLOR, Ann
Brodey, Jim
TAYLOR, Daniel
Schneider, Daniel Edward
TAYLOR, H Baldwin
Waugh, Hillary Baldwin
TAYLOR, John
Magee, James
TAYLOR, Sam
Goodyear, Stephen Frederick
TAYLOR, Toso
Taylor, Thomas Hilhouse
TEARLE, Christian
Jacques, Edward Tyrrell

TEG, Twm
Vulliamy, Colwyn Edward
TELLAR, Mark
Collins, Vere Henry
TELSTAR
Goodwin, Geoffrey
TEMPEST, Jan
Swatridge, Irene M M
TEMPEST, Sarah
Ponsonby, Doris Almon
TEMPEST, Theresa
Kent, Louise Andrews
TEMPEST, Victor
Philipp, Elliot Elias
TEMPLAR, Maurice
Groom, Arthur William
TEMPLE, Ann
Mortimer, Penelope
TEMPLE, Dan
Newton, Dwight Bennett
TEMPLE, Paul
Durbridge, Francis *and*
McConnell, James Douglas
Rutherford
TEMPLE, Ralph
Alexander, Robert William
TEMPLE, Robin
Wood, Samuel Andrew
TEMPLE-ELLIS, N A
Holdaway, Neville Aldridge
TEMPLETON, Jesse
Goodchild, George
TENN, William
Klass, Philip
TENNANT, Carrie
Kelly, *Mrs* T
TENNANT, Catherine
Eyles, Kathleen Muriel
TENNENBAUM, Irving
Stone, Irving
TENNESHAW, S M
Nutt, Charles
TERAHATA, Jun
Kirkup, James

TERKEL, Studs
Terkel, Louis
TERRY, C V
Slaughter, Frank Gill
TERRY, William
Harknett, Terry
TERSON, Peter
Patterson, Peter
TEW, Mary
Douglas, Mary
TEXAS RANGER
Wallace, John
TEY, Josephine
Mackintosh, Elizabeth
THALER, M N
Kerner, Fred
THAMES, C H
Lesser, Milton
THANE, Elswyth
Beebe, Elswyth Thane
THANET, Neil
Fanthorpe, Robert Lionel
THANET, Octave
French, Alice
THAYER, Geraldine
Daniels, Dorothy
THAYER, Jane
Woolley, Catherine
THAYER, Lee
Thayer, Emma Redington
THAYER, Peter
Wyler, Rose
THEOPHANY
Tofani, Louise E
THERION, The Master
Crowley, Edward Alexander
THERSITES
Whibley, Charles
THETA, Eric Mark
Higginson, Henry Clive
THIRLMERE, Rowland
Walker, John
THISTLETON, *Hon* Francis
Fleet, William Henry

283

THOMAS, Andrea
Hill, Margaret
THOMAS, Carl H
Doerffler, Alfred
THOMAS, Caroline
Dorr, Julia Caroline
THOMAS, Carolyn
Duncan, Actea
THOMAS, Dorothy
Thomashower, Dorothy
THOMAS, G K
Davies, Leslie Purnell
THOMAS, Gerrard
Kempinski, Tom
THOMAS, Gough
Garwood, Godfrey Thomas
THOMAS, H C
Keating, Lawrence Alfred
THOMAS, Ivor
Bulmer-Thomas, Ivor
THOMAS, J Bissell
Stephen, Joyce Alice
THOMAS, Jim
Reagan, Thomas B
THOMAS, Joan Gale
Robinson, Joan Gale
THOMAS, Lately
Steele, Robert V P
THOMAS, Lee
Floren, Lee
THOMAS, Michael
Benson, Michael
THOMAS, Murray
Ragg, Thomas Murray
THOMAS, Tay
Thomas, Mary
THOMPSON, Buck
Paine, Lauran Bosworth
THOMPSON, China
Lewis, Mary Christianna
THOMPSON, Eileen
Panowski, Eileen Janet
THOMPSON, Gene
Lutz, Giles A

THOMPSON, James H
Freeman, Graydon La Verne
THOMPSON, Madeleine
Greig, Maysie
THOMPSON, Russ
Paine, Lauran Bosworth
THOMSON, Audrey
Gwynn, Audrey
THOMSON, Edward
Tubb, E C
THOMSON, Joan
Charnock, Joan
THOMSON, Jon H
Thomson, Daisy
THOMSON, Neil
Johnson, Henry T
THORN, Barbara
Paine, Lauran Bosworth
THORN, Ismay
Pollock, Edith Caroline
THORN, Whyte
Whiteing, Richard
THORNE, Nicola
Ellerbeck, Rosemary
THORNTON, Maimee
Jeffrey-Smith, May
THORNTON, W B
Burgess, Thornton W
THORP, Ellen
Robertson, Margery Ellen
THORP, Morwenna
Robertson, Margery Ellen
THORPE, Dobbin
Disch, Thomas
THORPE, Sylvia
Thimblethorpe, June
THORPE, Trebor
Fanthorpe, Robert Lionel
THORSTEIN, Eric
Grossman, Judith
THRIBB, E J
Fantoni, Barry *and*
Ingrams, Richard

THURLEY, Norgrove
Stoneham, Charles Thurley
THURLOW, Robert
Griffin, Robert John Thurlow
THURMAN, Steve
Castle, Frank
TIBBER, Robert
Friedman, Eve Rosemary
TIBBER, Rosemary
Friedman, Eve Rosemary
TIGAR, Chad
Levi, Peter
TILBURY, Quenna
Walker, Emily Kathleen
TILLEY, Gene
Tilley, E D
TILLRAY, Les
Gardner, Erle Stanley
TILTON, Alice
Taylor, Phoebe Atwood
TIM
Martin, Timothy
TIMON, John
Mitchell, Donald Grant
TINA, Beatrice
Haig, Emily Alice
TINNE, E D
Tinne, Dorothea
TIPTREE, James *Jr*
Sheldon, Alice B
TIVEYCHOC, A
Lording, Rowland Edward
TODD, Paul
Posner, Richard
TODHUNTER, Philippa
Bond, Grace
TOIL, Cunnin
Lehmann, R C
TOKLAS, Alice B
Stein, Gertrude
TOLER, Buck
Kelly, Harold Ernest

TOLLER
Lyburn, *Dr* Eric Frederic
St John
TOMKINSON, Constance
Weeks, *Lady* Constance Avard
TOMLINE, F Latour
Gilbert, William Schwenck
TONKONGY, Gertrude
Friedberg, Gertrude
TONSON, Jacob
Bennett, Arnold
TOONDER, Martin
Groom, Arthur William
TOPICUS
Goodwin, Geoffrey
TORQUEMADA
Mathers, Edward Powys
TORR, Iain
Mackinnon, Charles Roy
TORRANCE, Lee
Sudgrove, Sidney Henry
TORREY, Marjorie
Hodd, Torrey
TORRIE, Malcolm
Mitchell, Gladys
TORRO, Pel
Fanthorpe, Robert Lionel
TORROLL, G D
Lawson, Alfred
TOULMIN, David
Reid, John
TOWERS, Tricia
Ivison, Elizabeth
TOWNE, Stuart
Rawson, Clayton
TOWNSEND, Timothy
Robey, Timothy Lester
Townsend
TOWRY, Peter
Piper, David Towry
TRACEY, Grant
Nuttall, Anthony

TRACEY, Hugh
Evans, Kay *and*
Evans, Stuart
TRACY, Catherine
Story, Rosamond Mary
TRACY, Leland
Tralins, S Robert
TRAFFORD, F G
Riddell, *Mrs* J H
TRAFFORD, Jean
Walker, Edith
TRAILL, Peter
Morton, Guy Mainwaring
TRAILRIDER
Hyland, Ann
TRAINOR, Richard
Tralins, S Robert
TRALINS, Bob
Tralins, S Robert
TRALINS, Robert S
Tralins, S Robert
TRAPROCK, Walter E
Chappell, George S
TRASK, Katrina
Trask, Kate Nichols
TRASK, Merrill
Braham, Hal
TRAUBE, Ruy
Tralins, S Robert
TRAVEN, B
Torsvan, Traven
TRAVEN, Robert
Voelker, John Donaldson
TRAVERS, Hugh
Mills, Hugh Travers
TRAVERS, Kenneth
Hutchin, Kenneth Charles
TRAVERS, Stephen
Radcliffe, Garnett
TRAVERS, Will
Rowland, Donald Sydney
TRAVIS, Gerry
Trimble, Louis

TRAVIS, Gretchen
Mockler, Gretchen
TRAWLE, Mary Elizabeth
Elwart, Joan Frances
TREDGOLD, Nye
Tranter, Nigel
TREE, Gregory
Bardin, John Franklin
TREHEARNE, Elizabeth
Maxwell, Patricia Anne
TREMAYNE, Sydney
Taylor, Sybil
TRENT, Gregory
Williamson, Thames Ross
TRENT, Lee
Nuttall, Anthony
TRENT, Paul
Platt, Edward
TRENT, Peter
Nelson, Lawrence
TRESILIAN, Liz
Green, Elizabeth Sara
TRESSALL, Robert
Noonan, Robert
TRESSELL, Robert
Noonan, Robert
TRESSIDY, Jim
Norwood, Victor George
Charles
TREVANIAN
Whitaker, Rod
TREVARTHEN, Hal P
Heydon, J K
TREVELYAN, Percy
Thomas, Charles
TREVENA, John
Henham, Ernest George
TREVES, Kathleen
Walker, Emily Kathleen
TREVOR, Elleston
Dudley-Smith, Trevor
TREVOR, Glen
Hilton, James

TREVOR, Ralph
Wilmot, James Reginald
TREVOR, William
Cox, William Trevor
TREW, Cecil G
Ehrenborg, *Mrs* C G
TRIFORMIS, D
Haig, Emily Alice
TRING, A Stephen
Meynell, Laurence Walter
TRIPP, Karen
Gershon, Karen
TRITON, A N
Barclay, Oliver Rainsford
TRIX, Mo
Hayman, Sheila
TROLLOPE, Joanna
Potter, Joanna
TROOPER GERARDY
Gerard, Edwin
TROTTER, Sallie
Crawford, Sallie
TROTWOOD, John
Moore, John
TROUT, Kilgore
Farmer, Philip José
TROY, Alan
Hoke, Helen L
TROY, Katherine
Buxton, Anne
TROY, Simon
Warriner, Thurman
TRUAX, Rhoda
Aldrich, Rhoda Truax
TRUSCOT, Bruce
Peers, Edgar Allison
TRY-DAVIS, J
Hensley, Sophia Margaret
TSUYUKI SHIGERU
Kirkup, James
TUCKER, Lael
Wertenbaker, Lael Tucker
TUCKER, Link
Bingley, David Ernest

TUGENDHAT, Julia
Dobson, Julia Lissant
TURK, Midge
Richardson, Midge Turk
TURNER, Bill
Turner, W Price
TURNER, C John
Whiteman, William Meredith
TURNER, Josie
Crawford, Phyllis
TURNER, Len
Floren, Lee
TURNER, Mary
Lambot, Isobel Mary
TURNER, Peter Paul
Jeffery, Grant
TURVEY, Winsome
Rusterholtz, Winsome Lucy
TUSTIN, Elizabeth
White, Celia
TWAIN, Mark
Clemens, Samuel Langhorne
TWEEDALE, J
Bickle, Judith
TWIGGY
Hornby, Lesley
TWIST, Ananias
Nunn, William Curtis
TWO EAST LONDONERS
Nash, Vaughan *and*
Smith, Llewellyn
TYLER, Clarke
Brookes, Ewart Stanley
TYLER, Ellis
King, Albert
TYSON, Teilo
McFarlane, David

§ §

I am become a name.
— Alfred, Lord Tennyson. Ulysses

§ §

UBIQUE
Guggisberg, *Sir* F G
ULSTER IMPERIALIST
Wilson, Alec
UNADA
Gliewe, Unada G
UNCLE GORDON
Roe, F Gordon
UNCLE GUS
Rey, Hans Augusto
UNCLE HENRY
Wallace, Henry
UNCLE MAC
McCulloch, Derek
UNCLE MONTY
Hamilton-Wilkes, Edwin
UNCLE REG
Woodcock, E Page
UNCLE REMUS
Harris, Joel Chandler
UNCUT CAVENDISH
Meares, John Willoughby
UNDERCLIFFE, Errol
Campbell, Ramsay
UNDERHILL, Charles
Hill, Reginald
UNDERWOOD, Keith
Spooner, Peter Alan
UNDERWOOD, Michael
Evelyn, John Michael
UNDERWOOD, Miles
Glassco, John
UNDINE, P F
Paine, Lauran Bosworth
UNOFFICIAL OBSERVER
Carter, John Franklin
UPDYKE, James
Burnett, W R
URIEL, Henry
Faust, Frederick
URQUHART, Guy
McAlmon, Robert
URQUHART, Paul
Black, Ladbroke Lionel Day

USHER, Margo Scegge
McHargue, Georgess
UTTLEY, Alison
Uttley, Alice Jane

V V V
Lucas, E V
VACE, Geoffrey
Cave, Hugh Barnett
VAGABOND
Blake, George
VAIL, Amanda
Miller, Warren
VAIL, Philip
Gerson, Noel Bertram
VALE, Keith
Clegg, Paul
VALENTINE
Pechey, Archibald Thomas
VALENTINE, Alec
Isaacs, Alan
VALENTINE, Jo
Armstrong, Charlotte
VALLEE, Rudy
Vallee, Hubert Prior
VAN BUREN, Abigail
Phillips, Pauline
VAN DINE, S S
Wright, Willard Huntington
VAN DYKE, J
Edwards, Frederick Anthony
VAN DYNE, Edith
Baum, Lyman Frank
VAN HELLER, Marcus
Zachary, Hugh
VAN LHIN, Erik
Del Rey, Lester
VAN SOMEREN, Liesje
Putland van Someren, Elisabeth
VANCE, Ethel
Stone, Grace Zaring
VANCE, Jack
Vance, John Holbrook

VANDEGRIFT, Margaret
Janvier, Margaret Thomson
VANE, Brett
Kent, Arthur
VANE, Michael
Humphries, Sydney
VANE, Phillipa
Hambledon, Phyllis MacVean
VANSITTART, Jane
Moorhouse, Hilda
VARANGE, Ulick
Yockey, Francis Parker
VARDON, Roger
Delafosse, Frederick Montague
VARDRE, Leslie
Davies, Leslie Purnell
VARLEY, John Philip
Mitchell, Langdon Elwyn
VAUGHAN, Carter A
Gerson, Noel Bertram
VAUGHAN, Gary
Boggis, David
VAUGHAN, Julian
Almond, Brian
VAUGHAN, Richard
Thomas, Ernest Lewys
VEDDER, John K
Gruber, Frank
VEDETTE
Fitchett, W H
VEDEY, Julien
Robinson, Julien Louis
VEE, Roger
Voss, Vivian
VEHEYNE, Cherry
Williamson, Ethel
VEITCH, Tom
Padgett, Ron
VENISON, Alfred
Pound, Ezra
VENNING, Hugh
Van Zeller, Claud H
VENNING, Michael
Randolph, Georgiana Ann

VERA
Bottomley, Kate Madeline
VERDAD, S
Kennedy, John McFarland
VERDON, Dorothy
Tralins, S Robert
VERNON, Claire
Breton-Smith, Clare
VERNON, Kay
Vernon, Kathleen Rose
VERNON, Marjorie
Russell, Shirley
VERONIQUE
Fisher, Veronica Suzanne
VERVAL, Alain
Laude, Lawrence Montague
and Greenwood, Thomas
VERWER, Hans
Verwer, Johanne
VERYAN, Patricia
Bannister, Patricia V
VESEY, Paul
Allen, Samuel Washington
VESTAL, Stanley
Campbell, Walter Stanley
VET, T V
Straiton, Edward Cornock
VICARION, *Count* Palmiro
Logue, Christopher
VICARY, Dorothy
Rice, Dorothy
VICESIMUS
Oakley, John, *Dean of Manchester*
VICKER, Angus
Felsen, Henry Gregor
VICTOR, Charles B
Puechner, Ray
VIDENS
Mumford, A H
VIGILANS
Partridge, Eric
VIGILANS
Rice, Brian Keith

VIGILANTES
Zilliacus, Konni
VILLIERS, Elizabeth
Thorne, Isabel Mary
VINCENT, Heather
Walker, Emily Kathleen
VINCENT, Honor
Walker, Kathleen
VINCENT, Jim
Foxall, P A
VINCENT, John
Farrow, R
VINCENT, Mary Keith
St John, Wylly Folk
VINSON, Elaine
Rowland, Donald Sydney
VINSON, Kathryn
Williams, Kathryn
VINTON, V V
Dale, R J
VIOLA
Worthley, R G
VIPONT, Charles
Foulds, Elfrida Vipont
VIPONT, Elfrida
Foulds, Elfrida Vipont
VIRAKAM, Soror
Sturges, Mary d'Este
VISIAK, E H
Physick, Edward Harold
VIVA
Wilson, Viva
VIVIAN
Moynihan, Cornelius
VIVIAN, E Charles
Vivian, Evelyn Charles H
VIVIAN, Francis
Ashley, Arthur Ernest
VLOTO, Otto
Parkhill, Forbes
VON MUELLER, Karl
Miller, Charles Dean
VOX, Agnes Mary
Duffy, Agnes Mary

VOYLE, Mary
Manning, Rosemary
VUL'INDLELA
Becker, Peter

§ §

Bingo had told him that I was the author of a lot of mushy novels by Rosie M Banks, you know. Said that I had written them, and that Rosie's name on the title-page was my what d'you call it.
— P G Wodehouse. Bingo and the little woman

§ §

W M
Jennings, Richard
WACE, W E
Nicoll, *Sir* William Robertson
WADE, Alan
Vance, John Holbrook
WADE, Bill
Barrett, Geoffrey John
WADE, Henry
Aubrey-Fletcher, *Sir* Henry Lancelot
WADE, Jennifer
Wehen, Joy De Weese
WADE, Robert
McIlwain, David
WADE, Thomas
Looker, Samuel Joseph
WAGNER, Peggy
Wagner, Margaret Dale
WAINER, Cord
Dewey, Thomas Blanchard
WAKE, G B
Haynes, John Harold
WAKEMAN, Evans
Wakeman, Frederic Evans

WALDO, Dave
Clarke, David
WALDO, E Hunter
Waldo, Edward Hamilton
WALDRON, Simon
King, Albert
WALES, Hubert
Piggott, William
WALES, Nym
Snow, Helen Foster
WALFORD, Christian
Dilcock, Noreen
WALKER, Barbara
Middleton, Maud Barbara
WALKER, Harry
Waugh, Hillary Baldwin
WALKER, Holly Beth
Bond, Gladys Baker
WALKER, Ira
Walker, Irma Ruth
WALKER, J
Crawford, John Richard
WALKER, Jean Brown
Walker, Edith
WALKER, Lucy
Sanders, Dorothy Lucie
WALL, Max
Lorimer, Maxwell
WALLACE, Agnes
King, Albert
WALLACE, Betty
Wallace, Elizabeth Virginia
WALLACE, Doreen
Rash, Dora
WALLACE, Ian
Pritchard, John Wallace
WALLACE, John
Davis, Will R
WALSER, Sam
Howard, Robert E
WALTER, Katherine
Walter, Dorothy Blake
WALTER, Kay
Walter, Dorothy Blake

WALTERS, Hugh
Hughes, Walter Llewellyn
WALTERS, Rick
Rowland, Donald Sydney
WALTERS, T B
Rowe, John Gabriel
WALTON, Francis
Hodder, Alfred
WAND, Elizabeth
Tattersall, Muriel Joyce
WANDERER
Smith, Lily
WARD, Artemus
Browne, Charles Farrar
WARD, Brad
Peeples, Samuel Anthony
WARD, Herbert B S
Molloy, Edward
WARD, Jonas
Cox, William Robert
WARD, Jonas
Garfield, Brian
WARD, Kate
Cust, Barbara Kate
WARD, Kirwan
Kirwan-Ward, Bernard
WARD, R Patrick
Holzapfel, Rudolf Patrick
WARD, Robert
Howard, Robert E
WARDEN, Florence
James, Florence Alice Price
WARE, Monica
Marsh, John
WARE, Wallace
Karp, David
WARLOCK, Peter
Heseltine, Philip Arnold
WARNER, Frank
Richardson, Gladwell
WARNER, Jack
Waters, John
WARNER, Leigh
Smith, Lillian M

WARNER, Matt
Fichter, George S
WARREGO, Paul
Wenz, Paul
WARREN, Andrew
Tute, Warren
WARREN, Mary D
Greig, Maysie
WARREN, Tony
Simpson, Anthony McVay
WARREN, Wayne
Braun, Wilbur
WARRINGTON, George
Agate, James
WARSHOFSKY, Isaac
Singer, Isaac Bashevis
WARWICK, Jarvis
Garner, Hugh
WARWICK, Pauline
Davies, Betty Evelyn
WASH, R
Cowlishaw, Ranson
WATANNA, Onoto
Reeve, Winifred Babcock
WATER, Silas
Loomis, Noel Miller
WATKINS, Gerrold
Malzberg, Barry Norman
WATSON, Andrew
Watson, Albert Ernest
WATSON, C P
Agelasto, Charlotte Priestley
WATSON, Frank
Ames, Francis
WATSON, Will
Floren, Lee
WATT, William
Scott, William Matthew
WAVERLEY, John
Scobie, Stephen Arthur Cross
WAY, Wayne
Humphries, Adelaide
WAYFARER
Cosens, Abner

WAYLAN, Mildred
Harrell, Irene Burk
WAYLAND, Patrick
O'Connor, Richard
WAYNE, Anderson
Davis, Dresser
WAYNE, Donald
Dodd, Wayne D
WAYNE, Heather
Gibbs, Norah
WAYNE, Joseph
Overholser, Wayne D
WAYNE, Marcia
Best, Carol Anne
WAYSIDER
Camm, Frederick James
WEALE, B Putnam
Simpson, Bertram L
WEARY, Ogdred
Gorey, Edward
WEAVER, Ward
Mason, F Van Wyck
WEBB, Christopher
Wibberley, Leonard Patrick
  O'Connor
WEBB, Neil
Rowland, Donald Sydney
WEBSTER, Gary
Garrison, Webb Black
WEBSTER, Jean
Webster, Alice Jane Chandler
WEBSTER, Jesse
Cassill, Ronald Verlin
WEBSTER, Noah
Knox, William
WEETWOOD, E M
Tetley, Edith Madeline
WEI WU WEI
Gray, Terence J S
WEINER, Henri
Longstreet, Stephen
WEIR, Jonnet
Nicholson, Joan

WEIR, Logan
Perry, James Black
WELBURN, Vivienne
Furlong, Vivienne
WELCH, Ronald
Felton, Ronald Oliver
WELCH, Rowland
Davies, Leslie Purnell
WELCOME, John
Brennan, John
WELLES, Elizabeth
Roby, Mary Linn
WELLINGTON, Anne
Hewett, Anita
WELLINGTON, John
Farnill, Barrie
WELLS, Hondo
Whittington, Harry
WELLS, J Wellington
De Camp, L Sprague
WELLS, Jane Warren
Picken, Mary
WELLS, John J
Coulson, Juanita *and*
Bradley, Marion Z
WELLS, Susan
Siegel, Doris
WELLS, Tobias
Forbes, Deloris Stanton
WELLS, Tracey
Nuttall, Anthony
WELTHORPE, Edna
Orton, John Kingsley
WENTWORTH, John
Child, Philip A G
WENTWORTH, Patricia
Turnbull, Dora Amy
WERNER, Jane
Werner, Elsa Jane
WERNER, Peter
Booth, Philip Arthur
WERRERSON, Talbot
Robertson, Walter George

WESLEY, Elizabeth
McElfresh, Adeline
WESLEY, James
Rigoni, Orlando Joseph
WESLEY, Mary
Siepmann, Mary
WESSEX, Martyn
Little, D F
WESSEX REDIVIVUS
Dewar, Hubert Stephen Lowry
WEST, Anna
Edward, Ann Elizabeth
WEST, Dorothy
Wirt, Mildred
WEST, Douglas
Tubb, E C
WEST, Keith
Lane, Kenneth Westmacott
WEST, Laura M
Hymers, Laura M
WEST, Lindsay
Weber, Nancy
WEST, Mark
Huff, Darrell
WEST, Michael
Derleth, August W
WEST, Nathanael
Weinstein, Nathan Wallenstein
WEST, Nigel
Allason, Rupert
WEST, Rebecca
Fairfield, Cecily Isabel
WEST, Token
Humphries, Adelaide
WEST, Tom
Reach, James
WEST, Trudy
West, Gertrude
WEST, Ward
Borland, Harold Glen
WESTALL, Lorna
Houseman, Lorna
WESTERHAM, S C
Alington, Cyril Argentine

WESTERN, Barry
Evans, Gwynfil Arthur
WESTERN, Mark
Crisp, Anthony Thomas
WESTERN-HOLT, J C
Heming, Jack C W
WESTGATE, John
Bloomfield, Anthony John
Westgate
WESTLAND, Lynn
Joscelyn, Archie Lynn
WESTLAW, Steven
Pyke, John
WESTMACOTT, Mary
Christie, *Dame* Agatha
WESTON, Allen
Norton, Alice Mary *and*
Hogarth, Grace Allen
WESTON, Helen Gray
Daniels, Dorothy
WESTON, Patrick
Hamilton, Gerald
WESTON, William
Milsom, Charles Henry
WESTRIDGE, Harold
Avery, Harold
WESTWOOD, Perry
Holmes, Llewellyn Perry
WETHERELL, Elizabeth
Warner, Susan Bogert
WETZEL, Lewis
King, Albert
WEYMOUTH, Anthony
Cobb, Ivo Geikie
WHARTON, Anthony
Macallister, Alister
WHEEZY
Hounsfield, Joan
WHETTER, Laura
Mannock, Laura
WHIM WHAM
Curnow, Allen
WHITAKER, Ray
Davies, John

WHITBY, Sharon
Peters, Maureen
WHITE, Dale
Place, Marian Templeton
WHITE, Harry
Whittington, Harry
WHITE, Heather
Foster, Jess Mary Mardon
WHITE, James Dillon
White, Stanley
WHITE, Jane
Brady, Jane Frances
WHITE, Jonathan
Harvey, John
WHITE, Milky
Emerson, Ernest
WHITE, Ted
White, Theodore Edwin
WHITEBAIT, William
Stonier, George
WHITEFRIAR
Hiscock, Eric
WHITEHAND, Satherley
Satherley, David *and*
Whitehand, James
WHITEHOUSE, Arch
Whitehouse, Arthur George
Joseph
WHITEHOUSE, Peggy
Castle, Frances Mundy
WHITINGER, R D
Place, Marian Templeton
WHITLEY, George
Chandler, Arthur
WHITNEY, Hallam
Whittington, Harry
WHITNEY, Spencer
Burks, Arthur J
WHITTINGHAM, Sara
Gibbs, Norah
WHITTINGTON, Peter
Mackay, James Alexander
WHITTLE, Tyler
Tyler-Whittle, Michael Sidney

WHITTLEBOT, Hernia
Coward, Noël
WHITTON, Barbara
Chitty, Margaret Hazel
WHYE, Felix
Dixon, Arthur
WICK, Carter
Wilcox, Collin
WICK, Stuart Mary
Freeman, Kathleen
WICKHAM, Anna
Hepburn, Edith Alice Mary
WICKLOE, Peter
Duff, Douglas Valder
WIDGERY, Jan
Widgery, Jeanne-Ann
WIEST, Grace L
Deloughery, Grace L
WIGAN, Christopher
Bingley, David Ernest
WIGG, T I G
McCutchan, Philip D
WIGGEN, Henry H
Harris, Mark
WILDE, Hilary
Breton-Smith, Clare
WILDE, Leslie
Best, Rayleigh Breton Amis
WILDER, Cherry
Grimm, Barbara Lockett
WILDING, Eric
Tubb, E C
WILEY, Gerald
Barker, Ronnie
WILEY, Margaret L
Marshall, Margaret Lenore
WILKINSON, Tim
Wilkinson, Percy F H
WILL
Lipkind, William
WILLEY, Robert
Ley, Willy
WILLIAM, Arnold
Meadowcroft, Ernest

WILLIAMS, Beryl
Epstein, Beryl
WILLIAMS, F Harald
Orde-Ward, F W
WILLIAMS, J R
Williams, Jeanne
WILLIAMS, Joel
Jennings, John Edward
WILLIAMS, Michael
St John, Wylly Folk
WILLIAMS, Patry
Williams, D F *and* Patry, M
WILLIAMS, Rex
Wei, Rex
WILLIAMS, Richard
Francis, Stephen D
WILLIAMS, Robert
Hoskins, Bob
WILLIAMS, Rose
Ross, William Edward Daniel
WILLIAMS, Roth
Zilliacus, Konni
WILLIAMS, Russell
Whitson, John Harvey
WILLIAMS, Tennessee
Williams, Thomas Lanier
WILLIAMS, Violet M
Boon, Violet Mary
WILLIAMS, Wetherby
Williams, Margaret Wetherby
WILLIAMSON, Paul
Butters, Paul
WILLOUGHBY, Cass
Olsen, Theodore Victor
WILLOUGHBY, Hugh
Harvey, Nigel
WILLOUGHBY, Lee Davis
Webb, Jean Frances
WILLOUGHBY-HIGSON, Philip
Higson, Philip John Willoughby
WILLS, Chester
Snow, Charles Horace
WILLS, Ronald
Thomas, Ronald Wills

WILLS, Thomas
Ard, William
WILMER, Dale
Miller, William *and*
Wade, Robert
WILSON, Ann
Bailey, Francis Evans
WILSON, Barbara
Harris, Laurence Mark
WILSON, Christine
Geach, Christine
WILSON, D M
Bentley, Frederick Horace
WILSON, Dave
Floren, Lee
WILSON, David
MacArthur, David Wilson
WILSON, Edwina H
Brookman, Laura L
WILSON, Elizabeth
Ivison, Elizabeth
WILSON, Gwendoline
Ewens, Gwendoline Wilson
WILSON, Holly
Wilson, Helen
WILSON, John Burgess
Wilson, John Anthony Burgess
WILSON, June
Badeni, June
WILSON, Lee
Lemmon, Laura Lee
WILSON, Martha
Morse, Martha
WILSON, Mary
Roby, Mary Linn
WILSON, Romer
Wilson, Florence Roma Muir
WILSON, Snoo
Wilson, Andrew James
WILSON, Yates
Wilson, Albert
WINCH, John
Campbell, Gabrielle Margaret
Vere

WINCHESTER, Jack
Freemantle, Brian
WINCHESTER, Kay
Walker, Emily Kathleen
WINDER, Mavis
Winder, Mavis Areta
WINDSOR, Rex
Armstrong, Douglas
WINE, Dick
Posner, Richard
WINFIELD, Allen
Stratemeyer, Edward
WINFIELD, Arthur M
Stratemeyer, Edward
WING ADJUTANT
Blake, Wilfred Theodore
WINGFIELD, Susan
Reece, Alys
WINIKI, Ephraim
Fearn, John Russell
WINN, Alison
Wharmby, Margot
WINN, Patrick
Padley, Arthur
WINSLOW, Donald
Zoll, Donald Atwell
WINSLOWE, John R
Richardson, Gladwell
WINSTAN, Matt
Nickson, Arthur
WINTER, John Strange
Stannard, Eliza Vaughan
WINTERS, Bernice
Winters, Bayla
WINTERS, Mary K
Hart, Caroline Horowitz
WINTON, John
Pratt, John
WINWAR, Francis
Vinciguerra, Francesca
WITHERBY, Diana
Cooke, Diana
WITHERS, E L
Potter, George William

WODEN, George
Slaney, George Wilson
WODGE, Dreary
Gorey, Edward St John
WOLF, Frederick
Dempewolff, Richard F
WOLFENDEN, George
Beardmore, George
WOOD, J Claverdon
Carter, Thomas
WOOD, Jerry
Freeman, Graydon La Verne
WOOD, Kerry
Wood, Edgar Allardyce
WOOD, Laura Newbold
Roper, Laura Wood
WOOD, Mary
Bamfield, Veronica
WOOD, Quality
Wood, Violet
WOOD, Ursula
Vaughan Williams, Ursula
WOODCOTT, Keith
Brunner, John
WOODFORD, Cecile
Woodford, Irene-Cecile
WOODFORD, Jack
Woolfolk, Josiah Pitts
WOODROOK, R A
Cowlishaw, Ranson
WOODRUFF, Philip
Mason, Philip
WOODS, Jonah
Woods, Olwen
WOODS, P F
Bayley, Barrington John
WOODS, Ross
Story, Rosamond Mary
WOODS, Sara
Bowen-Judd, Sara Hutton
WOODWARD, Lillian
Marsh, John
WOOLLAND, Henry
Williams, Guy Richard Owen

WOOLRICH, Cornell
Hopley-Woolrich, Cornell
George
WORBOYS, Anne Eyre
Worboys, Annette Isobel
WORCESTER, Roland
Rayer, Francis G
WORTH, Martin
Wigglesworth, Martin
WORTH, Maurice
Bosworth, Willan George
WORTH, Nicholas
Page, Walter Hines
WRAITH, John
Devaney, Pauline *and*
Apps, Edwin
WREFORD, James
Watson, James Wreford
WREN, Jenny
Cruttenden, Nellie
WRIGHT, Elnora A
Old Coyote, Elnora A
WRIGHT, Francesca
Robins, Denise
WRIGHT, Josephine
Weaver, Harriet Shaw
WRIGHT, Kenneth
Del Rey, Lester
WRIGHT, Rowland
Wells, Carolyn
WRIGHT, Sally
Old Coyote, Elnora A
WRIGHT, Ted
Wright, George T
WRIGHT, Wade
Wright, John
WU WU MENG
Beiles, Sinclair
WYANDOTTE, Steve
Thomas, Stanley A C
WYATT, Escott
Leyland, Eric
WYCLIFFE, John
Bedford-Jones, Henry

297

WYLCOTES, John
Ransford, Oliver
WYLIE, Laura
Matthews, Patricia
WYNDER, Mavis Areta
Winder, Mavis Areta
WYNDHAM, Esther
Lutyens, Mary
WYNDHAM, John
Harris, John Wyndham Parkes
Lucas Beynon
WYNDHAM, Lee
Hyndman, Jane Andrews
WYNDHAM, Robert
Hyndman, Robert Utley
WYNGARD, Rhoda
Truax, Rhoda
WYNMAN, Margaret
Dixon, Ella Hepworth
WYNNE, Anthony
Wilson, Robert McNair
WYNNE, Brian
Garfield, Brian
WYNNE, Frank
Garfield, Brian
WYNNE, May
Knowles, Mabel Winifred
WYNNE, Pamela
Scott, Winifred Mary
WYNYARD, John
Harrison, J H

X
Bloxam, John Francis
X Y Z
Tilsley, Frank
XARIFFA
Townsend, Mary Ashley
XENO
Lake, Kenneth Robert

Y Y
Lynd, Robert

YARBO, Steve
King, Albert
YATES, Dornford
Mercer, Cecil William
YERUSHALMI, Chaim
Lipschitz, *Rabbi* Chaim
YES TOR
Roche, Thomas
YLLA
Koffler, Camilla
YORICK, A P
Tindall, William York
YORK, Andrew
Nicole, Christopher
YORK, Georgia
Hoffman, Lee
YORK, Jeremy
Creasey, John
YORK, Peter
Wallis, Peter
YORKE, Katherine
Ellerbeck, Rosemary
YORKE, Margaret
Nicholson, Margaret Beda
YORKE, Roger
Bingley, David Ernest
YORKE, Susan
Telenga, Suzette
YOUNG, Agatha
Young, Agnes
YOUNG, Bob
Young, Robert William *and*
Young, Janet Randall
YOUNG, Carter Travis
Charbonneau, Louis
YOUNG, Edward
Reinfeld, Fred
YOUNG, Filson
Bell, Alexander
YOUNG, Jan
Young, Janet Randall
YOUNG, Kendal
Young, Phyllis Brett

YOUNG, Robert
Payne, Pierre Stephen Robert
YOUNG, Rose
Harris, Marion Rose
YOUNG, Thomas
Yoseloff, Thomas
YUILL, P B
Williams, Gordon Maclean *and*
Venables, Terry
YUKON BILL
Hayes, Catherine E Simpson
YULYA
Whitney, Julie

ZACHARIA, Dan
Novak, Cornelius Dan Zacharia
ZED
Dienes, Zoltan
ZERO
Ramsay, Allan

ZETA
Cope, *Sir* Zachary
ZETFORD, Tully
Bulmer, Henry Kenneth
ZEV BEN SHIMON HALEVI
Kenton, Warren
ZILIOX, Marc
Fichter, George S
ZINKEN
Hopp, Signe
ZONIK, Eleanor Dorothy
Glaser, Eleanor Dorothy

§   §

*Wherefore is it that thou dost
ask after my name?*
− *Bible. Genesis 32, 29*

§   §